MEMOIRS

of

ELDER JESSE MERCER.

JESSE MERCER, D.D.
1769-1841

MEMOIRS

of

ELDER JESSE MERCER.

BY CHARLES D. MALLARY.

NEW-YORK:
PRINTED BY JOHN GRAY.
1844.

he Baptist Standard Bearer, Inc.
NUMBER ONE IRON OAKS DRIVE • PARIS, ARKANSAS 72855

Thou hast given a *standard* to them that fear thee;
that it may be displayed because of the truth.
-- Psalm 60:4

*Reprinted
by*

THE BAPTIST STANDARD BEARER, INC.
No. 1 Iron Oaks Drive
Paris, Arkansas 72855
(501) 963-3831

THE WALDENSIAN EMBLEM
lux lucet in tenebris
"The Light Shineth in the Darkness"

ISBN #1-57978-024-5

Advertisement

The following work was undertaken in accordance with the request and appointment of the Baptist State Convention, at its annual session at Lagrange, Georgia, in 1842. Its preparation for the press has been retarded by some difficulty and delay in collecting the necessary materials, by other numerous and pressing duties, but more especially by that feeble state of health, which for many years past has imposed upon the writer the necessity of taking much time to accomplish even an inconsiderable task. The volume is not altogether what the Author could have wished, and what perhaps the public have expected, nor what, under different circumstances, the writer could have made it; yet with all its defects, it is hoped that it will be found entertaining to the surviving friends and acquaintances of Mr. Mercer, and not altogether useless to the religious community in general. The work contains some reflections and historical details not absolutely necessary to illustrate the life and character of Mr. Mercer; yet they generally relate to affairs with which he was more or less connected, and may be in some degree interesting and useful to Southern Baptists, and particularly to the Baptists of Georgia. And it is proper here to state, that the Author in preparing the work has had particular reference to its usefulness upon that field where it was natural to suppose it would find its principal patronage and circulation. On this account, it is to be hoped, that the more distant reader will look with forbearance on what might seem to him to be the redundancies and defects of the publication.

Numerous quotations from the writings of Mr. Mercer are interspersed through the volume - more than what many might deem judicious, though fewer than what others no doubt would desire. In the selections, reference has been had, in some cases, to their practical excellence, in others, to their adaptedness to give a clear and impartial view of Mr. Mercer's various religious opinions. After all, these quotations constitute but a very small portion of his writings, and would not therefore supersede the desirableness of publishing his most important productions in a separate volume. The Biographer has in his possession most of these productions, having collected them at considerable pains, and could now very readily arrange them for publication, did he know that the general wish and anxiety of his brethren were such as to justify the undertaking.

The likeness which accompanies this volume is not as accurate as could be desired. There is no complete likeness of Mr. Mercer extant, from which an artist could copy; but still his surviving acquaintances cannot fail to recognize in the one which is here presented, the most striking peculiarities of his interesting features, and to regard it as a valuable appendage to the book. The engraved facsimile of his hand writing, which is inserted in the volume, will no doubt be also highly valued.

In the conclusion of this prefatory notice, the Biographer would tender his most sincere thanks to all the brethren and friends who have generously assisted him in various ways during the prosecution of his labor; and especially would he offer up a tribute of thankfulness to the Great Head of the Church, who has enabled him, through manifold infirmities, to press on to the conclusion of his toil, so that he can now present to the Christian public a volume which, notwithstanding all its deficiencies, may tend somewhat, with the Divine blessing, to perpetuate the usefulness of ONE, whose name will ever hold an honored place upon the catalogue of the WISE, the GREAT, and the GOOD.

Twiggs Co., February 9, 1844.

Foreword

Few books merit wider dissemination that this. In 1848 Joseph Baker, editor of the *Christian Index*, urged that the "Memoirs of Jesse Mercer should be in the hands of every minister." The urgency is greater today. Mercer modeled Christlike devotion and leadership. He practiced a piety that was characterized by humility and selfless labor. He preached in the simple trust that God blessed the plain exposition and application of the truths of Scripture. He insisted that sound theology was the pillar of godliness and ought to understand the full range of systematic theology. He zealously urged sinners to faith in Christ and organized missionary activity. He led his denomination to promote and organize schools, missionary boards, and religious publishing. He gave generously of his own wealth to the noble causes he promoted. He pastored his churches with a wisdom that combined gentle tenderness with unflinching obedience to New Testament church discipline. He defended Baptist distinctives, yet without the parochial prejudices and petty animosity that often characterize Christian polemics. Few Christians have left such monuments to the grace of God. Few are as remarkably emulated.

Mercer's influence was remarkably wide. Adiel Sherwood, who was professor and president of Baptists colleges in Georgia, Illinois, Missouri and Washington, D.C., judged that Mercer "wielded an influence in the denomination second to that of no other." The source of his influence was the great esteem in which Baptists held him for his spirituality. Sherwood summarized it: "sincere and ardent piety, great intellectual strength, large liberality, unbounded zeal and great pulpit power." He possessed a "kind and courteous demeanor" and "great meekness and humility." Mercer purchased the *Christian Index* in 1833 and moved it from Philadelphia to Washington, Georgia. As editor, Mercer hoped to extend his usefulness as a minister of the gospel. His clear expositions of Scripture truth and his firm defense of Baptist Ecclesiology gained him many admirers. A number of leaders in the Central Baptist Association honored him in 1835 with an "elegant silver medal; on one side was engraved, 'Jesse Mercer, the able expounder of gospel discipline;' on the other, 'Government is in the Church - the Christian Index, the scourge of ecclesiastical tyranny.'"

Others praised him too. The Baptist church in Mobile, Alabama commissioned and sold engravings of Mercer's likeness in order to raise money to erect a church building. Individuals turned to him for his advice, especially in matters of church discipline. Georgia Baptists called him, "Father Mercer." One Primitive Baptist preacher told his congregation that many Baptists were tempted by idols, among them the image of Mercer.

Mercer concerned himself primarily with the salvation of sinners and the godliness of the saints. He proclaimed justification by faith in Christ. He conducted preaching tours and protracted meetings (though he never approved of inviting persons to the "anxious bench" or the the "altar"). He helped establish many new churches. He urged the saints in his congregations to worship Christ and honor him with their conduct. He encouraged worship in the family and in the church and published a hymnal to foster worship in song. He insisted on purity in the churches. As pastor he moderated the monthly church meetings in which he guided the church's administration of rebukes, excommunications and restorations. He gained a reputation for wisely managing the moral discipline of the churches.

In his sermons he often engaged in extensive discussions of some part of systematic theology. For Mercer and his congregations, the theology was not a burden that preaching must bear, it was rather the power of it. Mercer was satisfied when the doctrines of Christ's person and work sounded forth clearly. He wept when young Basil Manly, long before he became a denominational leader, proclaimed these. Richard Furman, the prominent Charleston, South Carolina preacher, became excited and engrossed when Mercer dwelt upon them.

His theology was Baptist Calvinism: "We have from our youth up, been taught the predestination, free grace plan of doctrine, and the independent plan of church government, as the characteristic doctrine and discipline of the Baptists; and these we now most freely and fully believe and advocate." He was assured that the great itinerant evangelists of the former generations believed the same: "The fathers and founders of the Baptist denomination in Georgia were strictly predestinarian." Mercer called upon Baptists to hold fast to this doctrine, for it was "full of comfort and calculated to promote humility and gratitude."

He identified his Calvinism more with that of John Gill than with that of Andrew Fuller. He announced that he was "rather of the old, than of the new school." He explained that he "inclined to the doctrine of such men as Gill, Owen, Brown, Toplady, Hervey, etc. That the atonement is special, both in its provisions and applications; but the men (and the doctrine) who teach that, the atonement is general in its provisions, but special in its application form the new school. To this representation, though taught by the excellent Fuller, we do not incline."

Mercer saw no conflict between the doctrines of limited atonement and predestination on the one hand, and missionary activity on the other. He encouraged and organized "benevolent societies," as they were called, especially missionary societies. He rejected the notion that Calvinism contradicted these: "By far the majority of those engaged in benevolent efforts are strictly Calvinistic." In 1801 he organized the first of the influential Powelton Conferences, which promoted itinerant preaching and mission activity among the Creek Indians. In 1815 he was elected the president of the Powelton Baptist Society for Foreign Missions. He helped persuade Georgia Baptists to establish a state convention in 1822 - it functioned deliberately as a missionary society. He served as president of the national Baptist Board of Foreign Missions from 1830 to 1841. He also gave leadership and financial support to temperance societies (he published a temperance newspaper for six years), Bible and tract societies, Sunday School societies, Baptist colleges, and theological schools (Mercer University was named in his honor for his organizational and financial support).

Mercer contended that Christians were obligated to establish churches according to the pattern found in the New Testament. This meant that all church power was congregational - each church had full ecclesiastical authority to accomplish all church affairs. There was no higher spiritual authority on earth. It meant also that all members of each local church held ecclesiastical authority jointly. The churches were democracies, not monarchies, aristocracies, or oligarchies. Each church ruled itself as a democracy, without enjoyment of bishops, presbyteries, presiding elders, or popes.

Mercer was nevertheless a strong advocate of the associational organization of Baptist churches. Mercer argued the traditional Baptist view that associations had no church power. They helped the churches by giving wise counsel and promoting unanimity of doctrine and practice. Mercer summarized: "The Baptists are democrats in relation to their church government in the strictest sense of that term. The little communities which they call churches, are their highest tribunals. Their associations and conventions are only advisory councils. They are designed to promote union by the interchange of views, but nothing comes from these bodies in the form of law. The association may advise the churches, but cannot control them."

New Testament democracy did not mean individual freedom in the modern sense. Mercer asserted churches had no authority over large areas of moral action and theological belief. Where church membership is concerned, Mercer taught, "equal rights must cease where iniquity begins." When converts joined Baptist churches they pledged to submit themselves to the church's control in these areas. Mercer reminded Baptists frequently that they could not afford to slacken their zeal for church purity - they must keep up church discipline. God would bless pure churches with spiritual vigor and revival. Mercer held, "A well executed discipline is the ecclesiastical life of a Gospel Church."

Mercer's teaching, piety and service should inspire all Christians who long for deeper love of God, greater knowledge of truth, and warmer zeal to serve both church and community. When Jesse Mercer died, the Sarepta Baptist Association noted the loss of their "esteemed Father in the Gospel." They remembered his "wise counsels" and his testimony to the "great truths of the gospel." They hoped his example would continue to be a blessing to God's people. "May the truths which he has published among us, live in our midst, and may we all profit by his virtuous example, and the recollection of his effusive benevolence." May the republication of this volume grant their wish anew.

Gregory A. Wills
Archivist - Boyce Centennial Library
Professor of Church History
Southern Baptist Theological Seminary
Louisville, Kentucky
June 13, 1997

CONTENTS.

CHAPTER I.

Introductory remarks—Brief notice of Mr. Mercer's paternal Grandfather—Sketches of the life of Silas Mercer—Early life of Jesse Mercer—His conversion.   9

CHAPTER II.

Mr. Mercer's first public exercises—His marriage—Brief notice of his first wife—His ordination—Personal appearance—Call to Hutton's Fork Church—Attends to his mental improvement—call to another Church and removal to Oglethorpe—His doubts as to his call to the ministry—Distressing temptation—Death of his Father and his return to Wilkes—Succeeds his Father in the charge of his churches.   26

CHAPTER III.

Mr. Mercer's ministerial labors—Sardis Church—Phillips' Mill—Bethesda—Powelton—Gov. Rabun—Extracts from Mr. Mercer's funeral Sermon on the occasion of Gov. R.'s death—Eatonton Church—Thomas Cooper   41

CHAPTER IV.

Number of immediate conversions not a certain test of a minister's usefulness—Mr. Mercer set for the defence of the gospel—His care to establish his churches in the truth—Skilful to aid the tempted—Anecdotes—His caution in receiving members—Able disciplinarian—His manner of presiding at church

CONTENTS.

meetings—His punctuality—No respecter of persons—His churches benevolent—Defects in the prevailing system of pastoral labor—Mr. Mercer in revivals—His views on Revivals—Ministerial support—Estimation in which he was held. 58

CHAPTER V.

Mr. Mercer's labors on his journeys from home, at Associations, &c.—Circulates useful books—his Cluster—Extracts from his correspondence—His relation to political affairs. 81

CHAPTER VI.

Death of Mrs. Mercer—Mr. Mercer removes to Washington—A church constituted there—His second marriage—Editorial labors—The degree of D. D. conferred on him—Letters to various individuals. 102

CHAPTER VII.

Mr. Mercer's connexion with the Georgia Association—Extracts from his Circular Letters—Connexion with the General Committee—Baptist State Convention. 137

CHAPTER VIII.

Mr. Mercer's efforts in behalf of Education—Mt. Enon—Columbian College—Attempts at co-operation with South Carolina—Mr. Mercer's views on the subject—His aid to Mercer University—Brief History of the Institution—Project of College at Washington—Sermon on Education—Extracts from the same, and from Christian Index 160

CHAPTER IX.

Mr. Mercer's efforts in the Missionary cause—Formation of Powelton Mission Society—Mission Board of the Ga. Association—Mission to the Creeks—His favorite argument for Missions—Letters in defence of benevolent plans from the Index—Letter to Mr.

Shuck—To Mr. Bolles on the abolition excitement—
Remarks from the Index on the same subject—His
kind feelings towards his northern brethren—Skeleton of a missionary Sermon—Letter on the "Imprisonment of the Missionaries to the Cherokees." 188

CHAPTER X.

Mr. Mercer and the Temperance Cause—At first
stands aloof—His reasons for this in a letter to Mr.
Brantly—Mr. B.'s editorial comments—Finally
takes the pledge—Establishes a Temperance paper—
Opposes the use of wine—His opinion on the traffic
in spirits—Remarks from the Index—Sketch of a
Temperance Discourse—Short notes on the wine
question. 223

CHAPTER XI.

Mr. Mercer's pecuniary contributions to benevolent
objects. 236

CHAPTER XII.

Unhappy divisions in the churches—Mr. Mercer's
opinion as to the causes—His Circular Letter published in the Convention Minutes of 1831—Usefulness at ministers' meetings—Extracts from his sermon on Ministerial Union—Letters to Mr. B. and
Mr. L. 245

CHAPTER XIII.

Mr. Mercer as a writer—Speaking the truth in love—
His Ten Letters on the Atonement—Extracts—Sermon on the Excellency of the Knowledge of Christ,
and Extracts from the same—Essay on Lord's Supper—History of Ga. Association—Review of a certain Report—Essay on forgiveness of sins—Extracts
from his Editorial pieces. 281

CHAPTER XIV.

Narrative of Mr. Mercer's Life resumed—Letter to
Mrs. R.—Severe indisposition—Address to patrons

of Index—Letter to the Ga. Association—Letter to Mrs. R.—To Heman Lincoln—Death of Mrs. Mercer—Letter to Mr. M.—Letter of Mr. Curtis to Mr. Mercer—Mr. Mercer's reply—" Hear what the Spirit saith to the churches," 3 nos.—His feelings in view of his approaching end. 332

CHAPTER XV.

Mr. Mercer's decline regarded with sorrow—His last Sermon—Sketch of the Sermon—Visits Penfield—Letter to Mr. Sturgis—Visits Indian Springs—Letter to Mr. Sturgis—His death—Mr. Carter's Letter in relation to his death—Resolutions of the Washington Baptist Church—Of the Presbyterian Church—Notice of Mr. Sturgis' Funeral Sermon. 373

CHAPTER XVI.

Mr. Mercer's personal appearance—Various traits of character described—Mr. Mercer in his social relations—Character of his mind and attainments—His character as a preacher—His gift in Prayer—His piety—His faults—His great influence. 395

APPENDIX.

A

Memoranda of occasional remarks made by Mr. Mercer, in his sermons, private conversation, &c. 431

B

Recollections of one of Mr. Mercer's sermons, furnished by Rev. W. H. Stokes. 434

C

Obituary Notice of Mrs. Nancy Mercer. 436

D

Mr. Mercer's Opinions upon various subjects connected with Church Discipline, &c. 441

MEMOIRS

of

ELDER JESSE MERCER.

MEMOIRS

OF

ELDER JESSE MERCER.

CHAPTER I.

Introductory Remarks.—Brief Notice of Mr. Mercer's paternal Grandfather.—Sketch of the Life of Silas Mercer.—Early Life of Jesse Mercer.—His Conversion.

UPON the map of an extended country, we do not expect to see a distinct exhibition of every hill and rivulet and valley. An attempt at such minuteness would defeat the design of geographical delineation, exhibiting nothing to the eye but a confused and blotted chart. The most interesting and prominent objects only can be sketched, and if this is performed with judgment and accuracy, every reasonable expectation is satisfied. So upon the map of Zion, which is to be held up to public view and handed down to future ages, we do not expect to find a distinct and prominent exhibition of the life and labors of every saint who may have contributed a share by his work of faith and labor of love, and patience of hope, to enrich and beautify the spiritual landscape. If it were possible for mortals on earth to construct and exhibit such a chart, how vast would be its dimensions, how complicated its parts, how wearisome its details. It would take a long life to scan one little province; and even in this limited and partial field, the eye would wander over a thousand objects which would fail to make any deep and salutary impression on the mind. For the present, it is enough for us to know that such an extended and perfect memorial is in the course of preparation in a brighter and better world. The record of all the saints is on high. On that record, the life and services of the most obscure believer, as well as of the most eminent, are traced in clear immortal lines. At length the glorious chart will be unfolded to our view in all its minute and mighty delineations. The little rill will then be as distinctly seen as the majestic river; the flowery hillock as the cloud-capt mountain; and then shall we learn, as we gaze with strong and admiring eyes upon the heavenly portraiture, in what manner the beauty and influence of all the redeemed had been combined to complete the glory of Zion, and show forth the manifold wisdom and matchless grace of the Triune God.

But if, at present, it would be as useless as it is impossible, to render distinct and prominent in the annals of the church, the life and death of every good man, yet there has ever prevailed a just and general expectation that those who have been blessed with distinguished gifts and graces, and selected by heaven as the instruments of extensive and lasting good, should be honored after death with some enduring memorial in which they may still live for the glory of God and the benefit of mankind. Upon the map of Zion, which is to give faithful instruction to future ages, the Baptist denomination in the United States will be laid down as an extensive and important province; and in that province our children will expect to see some traces of the life and services of JESSE MERCER.

The patriarchal head of the Mercer family was a native of Scotland, who emigrated to this country about the close of the seventeenth century. The paternal grandfather of Jesse Mercer was one of his children, and was born in Virginia, in 1713. He married his first wife in that state, by whom he had three children, Lydia, Silas and Rhoda. His second wife was Sarah Simmons, of Currituck county, North Carolina, by whom he had nine children; viz. Jacob, Thomas, Sarah, Chloe, Mary, Vashti, James, Caleb and John. Two only of this numerous family are now living, Mr. James Mercer of Coweta county, and Col. John Mercer of Lee county. The father removed from Virginia to North Carolina, (at what time it is not certainly known,) and resided in Currituck county and elsewhere in the state until about 1767, when he emigrated to Georgia and settled in what is now Wilkes county. He and his family suffered many hardships during the revolutionary struggle. He was upwards of sixty years of age at the commencement of the war, and although from age and infirmity he performed no actual service, yet he embraced in feeling the cause of his country, with patriotic zeal. Two of his sons, Jacob and Thomas, notwithstanding they had families, were engaged in active service during nearly the whole war, the care of their families in the mean time devolving mainly upon their aged parent. He died at the residence of his son Silas, in Wilkes county, in the seventy-seventh year of his age. Through youth and middle age he was a High Churchman, and for a long time officiated in North Carolina as clerk of the parish, and perhaps as curate. In his old age he and his wife professed conversion, embraced the peculiar sentiments of the Baptists, and were baptized, probably by Daniel Marshall.

Silas Mercer, the father of Jesse, whose name will ever occupy an honored place in the records of American Baptists, was born near Currituck bay, North Carolina, February, 1745. As his mother died when he was but an infant, his early training devolved more exclusively upon the hands of the father, who being a zealous member of the Church of England, very carefully instructed him in the doctrines and ceremonies of that religious denomination. From early childhood, young Silas was the subject of serious impressions, but it was not till after he arrived at manhood, that he experienced a saving change. Previous to this happy event, he had been most devotedly attached to the rites of the Episcopal church, and as violently opposed to other religious denominations, and especially the Baptists. These were the people that above all others, he had been taught to dread; and he carefully and conscientiously shunned them as a company of deceivers, and a people infected with absurd and dangerous heresies. But possessing an independent spirit, and endowed with a vigorous and discriminating mind, when he came under the decided influence of correct religious principles, he was very naturally led into that course of investigation which gradually carried him beyond the control of educational prejudice and traditionary systems, and established him at last in a faith and practice more in harmony with the simplicity of the gospel. He very soon began to question the validity of sprinkling as scripture baptism, and in accordance with the rubric of the Episcopal church, which enjoined *immersion* except when the health of the child might seem to require a milder mode, he had two of his children dipped. The first was Jesse, the subject of this memoir, who was immersed in a barrel of water at the clergyman's house; the other was a daughter who was subjected to the same ceremony in a tub prepared for the purpose in the Episcopal meeting-house.

In his progress towards more just and scriptural views, he was compelled to encounter the most formidable opposition. His father, under the influence of mistaken zeal and affection, cast every possible obstruction in his way; and to this were superadded the strenuous efforts of the clergyman, in connexion with all his Episcopal brethren around him. They spared no pains to keep alive his prejudices against the heretical Baptists, and to prevent all intercourse with that blind and infatuated sect. But in spite of his own long cherished antipathies, and the untiring opposition of beloved and honored friends, he gained his consent at length to attend a meeting of Baptists, and listen to a discourse from one of their ministers. This presumptuous and daring act provoked his father's resentment; and as the tears of grief and anger gushed from his eyes, he exclaimed, "*Silas, you are ruined!*" But neither the tears nor the rebukes of the disappointed father proved availing. The unreasonable prejudices of the son soon began to yield, and he was inclined to cherish more kind and charitable feelings towards the people he had so long despised. Not long after this he removed with his family to Georgia, and settled in Wilkes county. Having at length become thoroughly convinced of the propriety of believers' baptism, he was immersed about the year 1775, by Mr. Alexander Scott, and became a member of the Kiokee church. He rose from the water as it were, a minister of the gospel; for before he left the stream where he was immersed, he ascended a log and exhorted the surrounding multitude. Having been formally licensed by the church, he at once entered upon a course of ministerial labor, which was characterized by much zeal, ability and usefulness. During the revolutionary struggle, he fled for safety to Halifax county in his native state, where he remained six years, during which time he was incessantly engaged in the work of the ministry. It appears from his journal, that he preached, upon an average, oftener than once a day; so that during his six years' residence in North Carolina, he delivered more than two thousand discourses.

About the close of the war, he returned with his family to his former residence in Georgia, some seven miles south of Washington, where he remained to the end of his days. He was justly regarded as one of the most exemplary, useful and pious ministers in the Southern states. Several interesting churches were reared up under his faithful labors. Though not distinguished for his literary attainments, he was nevertheless the devoted friend of education, especially in the ministry; and to promote this noble object, he established a school near his own house, and procured an able teacher to superintend its interests. In the midst of his active and useful labors, he was arrested by disease, and after a short illness, he entered into his heavenly rest, in the fifty-second year of his age.

He devoted considerable time to study, wrote several pieces on important subjects, one of which, entitled "Tyranny Exposed, and True Liberty Discovered," was published in a pamphlet of sixty-eight pages. He was, however, more distinguished as a preacher than a writer.

JESSE MERCER was born in Halifax county, North Carolina, December 16, 1769. He was the eldest of a family of eight children, consisting of five sons and three daughters.*

---

* The following are their names: Jesse, Ann, Mary, Daniel, Mourning, Hermon, Mount Moriah, and Joshua. The third and fifth died in infancy. ANN was born in 1774, joined the church at Phillips' Mill in her fifteenth year, and married Mr. Robertson, of Wilkes county, in her seventeenth. She removed with her husband to West Tennessee in 1822, where she is still living, in widowhood, Mr Robertson having died the second year after their removal

DANIEL was born in 1780. His father gave him a good education, and he made teaching his profession, in which he was highly distinguished. A large portion of the eminent men in the state received their education, in whole or in part, under his care. He was a distinguished Latin scholar, and was also able to give instruction in the Greek. He was a man of considerable research, and spoke the English language with great purity and precision. He was quite facetious, and quick at repartee; a person of pleasing address, and fine colloquial powers. At the same time he is said to have been a person of sound judgment, great energy and decision of character, and possessing talents of a higher order, in the estimation of many good judges, than those of his brother Jesse. He married Miss Sarah Tuggle, of Greene county, about 1812, removed to Henry county in 1826, and died without issue in 1827.

Mount Moriah was born in 1787, joined the church at Williams' Creek in 1809, married Miss Ann Edge, of Wilkes, in 1816, and died in Oglethorpe, in the thirty-fifth year of his age, leaving a widow and three children, who are still living. He also was a school master by profession; but not having received a classical education, his labors as a teacher were confined to common schools. In this sphere he is said to have been distinguished. He was remarkable for his peaceable, humane, kind-hearted, and affectionate disposition.

HERMON and JOSHUA are still living. The former was born in 1784, the latter about 1790; they have both been for a long time

The youthful character of Jesse is described by surviving friends as almost without a stain. In very early life there was seen the budding of many of those amiable and virtuous traits, which so much distinguished him in after life. Under the influence of his strong, native good sense, a remarkably tender conscience, and great self-control, he was enabled to avoid, not only the more gross excesses of youth, which are often witnessed with the deepest regret and sorrow; but those more slight deviations from uprightness and propriety, which, in subsequent years, are frequently called to remembrance with mortification and self-reproach. A venerable uncle,* at the particular request of the writer, has generously furnished him with a sketch of the youthful days of his nephew, as well as of some interesting incidents connected with his more advanced life. Several extracts from this sketch, (with a few unimportant corrections,) will be introduced into the following narrative; as they will furnish very suitable materials for illustrating some important portions of Mr. Mercer's history, which must have remained an entire blank, but for this kind and seasonable contribution.

Shortly after the return of Silas Mercer to Georgia, he visited his aged father, who had previously removed from North Carolina, and settled on Brier Creek, in

members of the Baptist church, and are also ministers of the gospel.

The descendants of the original Mercer family are now scattered through the whole of the middle, southern and western states, and Texas. Tradition says that the gallant General Mercer, who fell during the Revolution, was one of the family relatives. Many of them are yet in Virginia, amongst whom is the distinguished Charles Fenton Mercer.

* Col. John Mercer, of Lee county.

Burke county. Whilst there, he gained his father's consent to remove with his family to his own farm in Wilkes, that he might be more comfortably provided for in his declining years. "He came down, (says the writer of the sketch above referred to,) for my father and his family the ensuing fall, and brought with him his son Jesse, a very spare lad about thirteen years of age. This was the first time I had ever seen him. He was my senior by nearly seven years.* I soon became much attached to him, because he was free-hearted, sociable and kind, and called me his *little uncle*. From this time, we were brought up on the same farm, about seven miles south of Washington. From the intimacy of our association, I of course knew him well, and it gives me great pleasure to bear testimony to the rectitude of his juvenile deportment. Although a mere boy, he acted the part of the prudent man, that foreseeth the evil and hideth himself. Perhaps I may as well say here, that I not only never knew him use a profane word, or an impious expression myself, but that I heard him say, in his latter years, he had never used an oath in his life, not even one of those petty oaths that too often fall from the lips of persons considered moral, or that indeed sometimes deform the conversation of professors of religion. Nor did he ever pronounce in vain the Deity's name, as in those common exclamations, My God! Good Lord! &c. So far did he carry the principle all through his life, that in relating an incident, or an anecdote, he scrupulously refrained from repeating such oaths as might be connected with it.

* The writer of this sketch was only a half brother of Silas Mercer, being the son of a second wife: this will account for his being so much younger than his nephew Jesse.

"There was another remarkable trait in the character of his boyhood, that I must not omit. He had no taste for the common plays and pastimes of other boys, such as marbles, fives, town-ball, and the like; and seldom, or never, took part in any of them, nor in the athletic exercises of jumping, wrestling, and boxing. Once only did I ever see him engaged in wrestling, and that was with his uncle James, who was about his own age. They were ploughing in a field, when I suppose they agreed to make trial of their skill in wrestling, of which, by the by, it was manifest that neither had any, from their awkward, main-strength efforts to bring each other down. Down they came at length, and rolled and tumbled in the dirt until they were both fairly exhausted; when they arose in good humor, brushed each other's clothes, and resumed their ploughing.

"Although he had no relish for games of chance, nor those athletic sports that would have brought him into direct collision with others, it was not from a solitary and morose disposition; for he was ever ready to join his associates, when opportunity offered, in hunting and fishing. Indeed, these were recreations in which he always, even down to a late period, took great delight. At that early day, game was plentiful, and when he had leisure, no weather was so inclement as to prevent him from ranging the woods for deer and turkeys, or coursing the river and mill-ponds in search of wild ducks. At a later day, when the large game had disappeared, he often amused himself in hunting squirrels, rabbits, and other small game. He was a good shot, and I have known him spend half a day at a time, in firing at a mark.

"He took no less delight in fishing, and would angle

with great patience, or join a party to draw the seine, or to muddy or drain a pond. After we were nearly grown up, I was with him often in his hunting and fishing excursions, and remember well his zeal in those amusements. We would lash a bundle of split pine upon our backs, like a knapsack, and with a torch in one hand, and a gig in the other, sally forth to the river, a distance of two or three miles, where we would fish with great zeal, often till midnight, and perhaps for all this toil be rewarded with not more than half a dozen *molly-crawl-bottoms*, as he used to call them. No way discouraged, however, it would not be long before we would try it again in the hope of better luck. He and myself alone put a fall-trap in Little River, in which we were very successful in taking fish, whenever we would take the precaution to lie by it all night, so as to keep the rogues off.

"Swimming, a useful acquirement, and an exercise so highly recommended by the great Franklin, was an art that he practised much, and of which he was very fond. This leads me to speak of an act of heroism and magnanimity, (and I record it with the most grateful feelings,) by which I was rescued from a watery grave. To him, indeed, I owe the extension of my natural life for the last fifty-eight years, and to his instrumentality, under the providence of God, I also owe the hope I have of eternal life. The incident alluded to occurred when he was about seventeen years of age, and was as follows: He and my brother James agreed to go one afternoon to practise swimming, and I accompanied them. They seemed greatly to enjoy the pastime, while I was only a spectator, for I was only ten years old and could not swim. Withal the place was deep, and the bank on the side we approached precipitous. But on the opposite side, there was a nice sandy beach and shoal water; and if I could only reach it, I too might enjoy the diversion. My nephew, seeing my anxiety, said that if I would undress myself, he would take me across on his back. He was particular in directing me how to hold on, and not to climb on him, as that would put him under. To all this I promised compliance, but we had no sooner set out, than sinking deeper in the water than I had anticipated, I became frightened, and notwithstanding his remonstrances, kept climbing on him as he sank down, until we both went to the bottom. His only resource was to disengage himself from me, which he did, and rising, he reached the shore in almost a lifeless state. He nevertheless kept an anxious lookout for me, expecting me to rise. I shortly did so at some distance down the stream, when, notwithstanding his exhaustion, he fearlessly plunged after me, and reaching the spot where I was going down, succeeded, by diving, in laying hold of me, and brought my apparently lifeless body ashore with one hand, whilst he swam with the other. By rolling me in the sand, and using such means as they had heard recommended in such cases, he and my brother succeeded in restoring me to life.

"He was a staid, discreet and sober youth, and never visited the haunts of dissipation, unless imperiously called there by business. He was very even-tempered and uniform in his conduct; was never dejected, morose and sulky, nor, on the other hand, did he give way to uproarious mirth, which was very common in those days, at log-rollings, house-raisings, corn-shuckings, &c. He would, however, in relating little stories and anecdotes, indulge freely in a kind of quiet humor that was peculiar to him, and would set off his narrative with a variety of posture and gesticulation wholly original, and somewhat awkward and rustic, such as tossing his head in a peculiar manner; shrugging up his shoulders; or if on his feet, walking to and fro with a peculiar swing of the body, using now a short step, and then a longer one, placing one arm behind him and resting it across his back, advancing and then receding, &c. Much of this peculiarity of manner he retained through his life, as you and thousands of others will remember. These peculiarities, aided perhaps by his natural gravity, occasioned some to say that he was proud; and by being privately informed of it by a friend, he took no other notice of it than in a sermon shortly after, when he had occasion to speak of pride and to define it. Said he, 'some say that *I* am proud; true, so I am, as proud as Beelzebub can make me, but I pray for more grace.' He was benefited by the improvement of manners consequent upon the increase of wealth and learning in the country, yet he never attained, either to a very polite carriage in his private intercourse with society, or to a graceful manner in the pulpit.

"He had great command of his passions, as I have before intimated. I never knew him to have a fit of anger on account of any accident that was either providential, or the result of carelessness, nor on account of any personal wrong or insult. Indeed, I do not think he ever had a personal quarrel with either man or woman through his whole life. He was also a man of great fortitude and firmness; and met with calm determination every untoward event of his life, both temporal and religious.

"He was a pattern of filial obedience, submitting

cheerfully to every command of his parents. During the frequent absence of his father, who was from home at least one half of his time, he was never disobedient to his mother, but on the contrary, treated her with the utmost respect and deference, and obeyed her with alacrity. Death alone parted him and his mother, between whom there was a reciprocal warmth of affection that I have scarcely ever seen equalled, certainly never surpassed. He was the favorite child of his father also, and the tenderness and indulgence which he showed towards him, would, if a boy of ordinary parts and disposition, have made a spoiled child."

Mr. Mercer enjoyed in his early youth but limited advantages for mental improvement. It is not certain that he had ever been sent to school previous to the return of his father from North Carolina. Owing to the scattered state of the population, it was some little time before a school could be established; but after some delay one was opened about four miles from his father's residence, which he attended for a time, walking the whole distance night and morning. The year following, a school was organized about a mile and a half nearer, in which he was a pupil for the space of two years.

Some of the circumstances related in the foregoing narrative may seem to many quite unimportant; yet there is often a peculiar satisfaction in contemplating even trifling incidents in the lives of great men, and especially those connected with their youthful history, which shadow forth those noble qualities that afterwards distinguish them. Those who have been intimately acquainted with the life and character of that great and good man whose history we are now recording, cannot fail of discerning in some of the little incidents just rehearsed, at least a few glimmering types of that stable and unaffected kindness, that marked decorum and prudence, that striking originality, that manlike firmness and independent rectitude, that quiet, yet unwavering zeal in the prosecution of approved objects, which were so conspicuous in subsequent life.

But it is time to notice a more important portion of his youthful history; that which refers to his early religious exercises, and which cannot fail to interest the pious reader. A brief outline of these exercises were many years after imbodied by himself in a hymn which he published in his Cluster;* but his uncle has furnished a more full and satisfactory account of his experience, which he relates in substance, as he often heard it from the lips of his honored relative in private conversation, and in fragments from the pulpit. It is as follows:

"'Having been raised,' said he, 'by pious parents, I was taught to believe that the scriptures were the word of God, and that I must conform my life to them, that it might be well with me in this world, and that which is to come. When I was no more than five or six years old, I felt conscious that I was a sinner, and was concerned about my future state, so much so, that I frequently prayed; and so I continued alternately praying and sinning until I was about fifteen years old. At this age, I was more seriously impressed with a sense of the wickedness of my heart, and its alienation from God. I believed he was too holy to conform himself to my pleasure, and allow me to live in sin, and not bring me into judgment for it.

* No. 233.

I feared the judgment, because I had done only evil and that continually; and now to do good and please God was the important work before me. This I believed was to be accomplished by praying, reading the scriptures, and going to meeting to hear the gospel preached. To all this I gave attention, with sometimes more and sometimes less anxiety and diligence for nearly three years, when I found myself nothing better, but rather worse than when I first began to seek the Lord. My heart became hard and unfeeling, and I wondered that God, who was angry with the wicked every day, had not long since cut me off and sent me to destruction,—a condemnation which my conscience could not but have approved. I now felt a deeper and more abiding concern, but what to do I knew not, for it was now suggested that there was no hope for me, but that the time once was, when I first sought the Lord, when my conscience was tender, when I was young and had committed but little sin, that the Saviour would have taken me in the arms of his love and blessed me; but, inasmuch as I had cast off those early impressions, and desired that God would connive at my love of sin, and still take me to heaven when I died, and thus rejected the Lord in my childhood, the promise "suffer little children to come unto me and forbid them not, for of such is the kingdom of heaven," was to me lost, for ever lost. I now thought I was given over to unbelief and hardness of heart, to spend the remainder of my days in hopeless despair. Whatever my end might be, it was, however, my heart's desire that I might sin no more.

"'I now thought I had a clear view of the plan of salvation through Jesus Christ, and saw plainly how sinners might be saved who would come unto him aright, confessing their sins and believing on his name. Seeing it thus, I tried with all the faculties of my soul to believe, but could not; and so I concluded I had not come aright, and was rejected. I was glad, and in my greatest distress rejoiced that others could believe in Christ, and by believing, flee the wrath to come. My heart's desire was to be holy, and I loved God because he was holy. I trembled at the thoughts of the great day of final retribution, when I must be driven out from the presence of the great God who made me, and whom I adored. My secret desire then was, that others might be saved, for I wanted none to accompany me in my banishment from Heaven to the regions of misery and despair to which I believed I was doomed. I had been some three years earnestly seeking the forgiveness of my sins, and had seen the time when I could weep over them, but now my heart was hardened, and my tears all dried up, save only to weep because I could not weep. While on the verge of despair, I was walking alone along a narrow, solitary path in the woods, poring over my helpless case, and saying to myself wo is me! wo, wo is me! for I am undone for ever! I would I were a beast of the field!—At length, I found myself standing with my eyes steadfastly fixed on a small oak that grew by the path-side, and earnestly wishing that I could be like the little oak when it died and crumbled to dust. At that moment light broke into my soul, and I believed in Christ for myself and not another, and went on my way rejoicing.'"

It appears from the records of the Phillips' Mill church, that he made a relation of his Christian experience to that church, July 7th, 1787, and was received as a candidate for baptism. He was baptized by his father, (probably on the following day,) being then in the eighteenth year of his age.

CHAPTER II.

Mr. Mercer's first public exercises.—His marriage.—Brief notice of his first wife.—His ordination.—Personal appearance.—Call to Hutton's Fork church.—Attends to his mental improvement — Call to another church and removal to Oglethorpe.—His doubts as to his call to the ministry.—Distressing temptation.—Death of his father and his return to Wilkes.—Succeeds his father in the charge of his churches.

SHORTLY after Mr. Mercer connected himself with the church, an intense anxiety was awakened in his bosom for the salvation of his fellow men. He was strongly impelled to address them on the way of life through a crucified Redeemer, and an opportunity soon presenting itself for the gratification of his desires, he commenced his public exercises in a manner which afforded pleasing evidence of his strong natural powers, and of the purity and warmth of his Christian zeal; and which excited amongst his pious friends high expectations of future usefulness and distinction. "His first public efforts," says the venerable relative from whose narrative we have already quoted so freely, "was made in his grandmother Mercer's house, an humble log cabin, within a hundred yards from his father's dwelling, on the occasion of a Sabbath-day prayer meeting. The subject of his exhortation was the general judgment. He became deeply excited in warning his neighbors, and more particularly his associates, to flee from the wrath to come, and to prepare for that tremendous day. I was much astonished at his gestures, his ardor and his expressions, many of which I remember to this very hour. His grandmother seemed to be overwhelmed with joy at this first attempt, spoke much of it in the family, and in some degree predicted his subsequent usefulness. There was preaching occasionally in my mother's house, and a few pious persons kept up a prayer-meeting there and at other places in the neighborhood. This gave him frequent opportunities for exercising in prayer and exhortation, which he took advantage of with manifest improvement. Witnessing his zeal, piety, and doctrinal ability, he was encouraged by his father, by his uncle Thomas Mercer, who was a minister of the gospel, his uncle Jacob Mercer, and some others of the leading members of the church, so that he soon began to preach, and to hold forth Christ publicly as the way of life and salvation to a perishing world." It does not appear from the records of the church at what time he received a formal license, but there is every reason to justify the belief that from the first commencement of his public efforts, he had the entire approbation of his brethren generally.

On the 31st of January, 1788, being then in his nineteenth year, he was united in marriage to Miss Sabrina Chivers, daughter of Mr. Joel Chivers, and at the time of their marriage, step-daughter of Mr. Oftnial Weaver, of Wilkes county. She was a pious and orderly member of the Phillips' Mill church, having been baptized about the same time that Mr. Mercer became a member. This union seemed to have been peculiarly suitable, and was the source, in after years, of much domestic enjoyment. Miss Chivers was a poor orphan girl, bringing to her husband upon their marriage, a no larger portion of worldly goods, than a feather bed; yet she possessed what was far more essential than mere earthly treasures, piety, prudence, industrious habits, and a heart devoted to the comfort and usefulness of her companion. The writer cannot forbear, in this connexion, presenting in her favor, the testimony of one that knew her well. "She was indeed a *help-meet* for her husband; for, beside her ordinary domestic duties, she spun and wove with her own hands, all the cloth he wore, and gained not a little renown through the country, for the neatness and beauty of her manufacture. Notwithstanding she was a most affectionate wife, and delighted in the company of her husband, she was very careful to throw no obstacle in the way of his fulfilling his appointments punctually, and was always mindful to have his clothes put up, and every thing ready. She submitted with great fortitude to the lonely life that she led in his absence, which was relieved only by the company of one of her maiden sisters, (of whom she had several,) who usually staid with her. It was from a proper estimate of the importance of the work in which he was engaged, and not from any indifference towards him, that she so cheerfully gave up his company. If there was a probability of his detention by high waters and inclement weather, she could hardly be drawn off to talk of any thing else; and accustomed to his punctuality, she would be constantly peering through a little chink, (she had one opening towards each end of the road,) looking with the liveliest interest for his return. As soon as he appeared, she would cry out 'yonder he comes! poor thing!' and dropping every thing, would run out to meet him with the greatest joy.

"For the first ten or twelve years after their marriage, she was, in the strictest sense, a keeper at home, and proved herself a most frugal and industrious wife; in which respect, indeed, few females ever excelled her. She was extravagantly fond of infants and children, (it mattered little whose they were,) caressed them much, and treated them with the uttermost tenderness and affection. In the absence of these objects her passion seemed to be transferred, in a measure, to the young of the inferior animals, such as lambs, pigs, and even poultry, which she would feed and nurse with great care. After this, when the family had become more affluent, she travelled much with her husband, and eventually died in the upper part of South Carolina, in the month of September, 1826."

But to return to the history of Mr. Mercer, "I do not remember distinctly," says his uncle, "how he employed himself for the first year after his marriage, but am under the impression that he went to school. He lived in his father's house. His father gave him a hundred acres of land about a mile distant, and in the Fall or Winter of that year, he erected upon it a neat log-cabin, and opened a small farm to which he removed, and where he resided for two years." In the mean time he zealously prosecuted his ministerial labors, expounding the scriptures in an orthodox and able manner, and affording gratifying evidence to those who heard him, of his rapid advancement in the knowledge of divine things. A short time before the completion of his twentieth year, he was called by the church to ordination, and was solemnly set apart to the work of the gospel ministry. From his credentials, of which the following is a copy, it appears that his father, Silas Mercer, and Sanders Walker were the officiating ministers.*

* It is probable that a Mr. Hutson also assisted on this occasion. In the minutes of the church conference held November 7th, 1789,

"GEORGIA,
Wilkes County, } These are to certify, that we, being duly called as a Presbytery, have examined into the character, call and qualifications of our beloved brother, Jesse Mercer, and with the consent of the church of Christ at Phillips' Mill, to which he belongs, have, by fasting and prayer, and imposition of hands, set him apart to the great work of the ministry.

"And he is hereby authorized to exercise himself in the several parts of the ministerial functions, where he may be called, whether occasionally or stated[ly]. Given under our hands, this seventh day of November, one thousand seven hundred and eighty-nine.

SANDERS WALKER,
SILAS MERCER."

From the above it appears that *fasting* was connected with the ordination services; a practice which the subject of this memoir uniformly recommended as important on such solemn occasions, being in his view enforced by the scripture example recorded in Acts xiii. 3.

It might not be unsuitable in this place, to say something of Mr. Mercer's personal appearance in the pulpit at the commencement of his public ministry. It is said to have been any thing but prepossessing. He was slender, and awkward in the extreme. Old Mr. Whatley, who was a very good but eccentric

there is the following item: "Brethren Sanders Walker and James Hutson met according to appointment, and proceeded to examine into the call and qualifications of Brother Jesse Mercer, and being satisfied with him, he was set apart by imposition of hands to the great work of the ministry." If Mr. Hutson was one of the ordaining presbytery, his name should have been to the certificate of ordination. Its absence the writer is not able to account for.

brother, and of whom some of our aged brethren retain many pleasant and amusing recollections, was once heard to say, " when Jesse was young, he was one of the ugliest, most unpromising creatures I ever saw; but *we* have made him a pretty boy." In after life, when his mind began to develope itself, and the roughness of his manners was somewhat softened down, this same old brother remarked, that he thought Jesse was one of the prettiest men he ever saw in his life. But the slender frame and awkward manners of his youthful days could not conceal his worth; as veins of gold glitter through the sides of an unpolished mountain crag, so his vigorous mind and ardent zeal darted their brilliant fires through the rough exterior, engaging the notice and exciting the admiration of all around.

After his ordination, he seemed to feel that, in a peculiar sense, he belonged to Christ and to his blessed cause, and it was the habitual and absorbing desire of his heart, that he might be a useful minister of the gospel. An increased interest was felt by his brethren in his ministrations, and though so very young, he received a call to the pastoral care of the church called Hutton's Fork, (now Sardis,) in Wilkes county. He accepted the call, and continued his useful and faithful labors amongst that people, for more than twenty years.

His improvement was perceptible, and yet he needed and desired more. His father, who, as we have seen, was a liberal patron of education, encouraged him to engage in the study of the learned languages. His consent was easily gained, and selling out his little farm, he removed with his wife to a small dwelling on Fishing Creek, near a respectable school.

The institution was under the charge of the Rev. Mr. Springer, a Presbyterian clergyman of considerable learning and talent; and withal, an able minister of the gospel. At this school he continued for two years, not neglecting, however, in the mean time, his duties at Hutton's Fork, nor allowing his other Sabbaths to pass by unoccupied. He would occasionally accompany Mr. Springer to his meetings, who, it seems had become strongly attached to Mr. Mercer, for his Christian zeal and promising talents, and who readily embraced every convenient opportunity to give him instruction in theology. The parental care and faithful counsels and instructions of this good man were of great advantage to Mr. Mercer. Of this he was fully sensible, and he never ceased to cherish towards this worthy benefactor, feelings of the greatest respect and veneration. At his death, which occurred about the year 1800, he composed an appropriate and affecting eulogy on his character. The friendship which existed between these individuals at that day, when sectarianism and religious bigotry held a more powerful sway than at present, reflects great honor upon them both.

About the time that Mr. Mercer removed to Fishing Creek, his father, assisted by some of his wealthy and intelligent neighbors, established his school, (known by the name of Salem,) under the rectorship of Mr. Rodolphus Brown; who dying in the course of the year, was succeeded by Mr. James Armor. Under the care of the last named gentleman, who continued in charge of the institution for several years, it acquired considerable celebrity. Its advantages being sufficiently inviting, Mr. Mercer, after an absence of about two years, returned to his father's, put up a cabin within a few yards of the academy, and continued for another year the study of the languages, and such other branches of learning as were deemed of the most importance. He still prosecuted his ministerial labors, visiting regularly the church of which he had taken the oversight, preaching in the school house of nights, and improving his vacant Saturdays and Sundays in such openings around as were providentially presented. But he did not escape the animadversions and complaints of the prejudiced and the ignorant. "It is not Latin and Greek, and mathematics," said they, "that make a preacher, but grace in the heart, and a call to the work." They thought it a needless waste of time for Mr. Mercer to pore over his musty school books, when the field was open before him for the preaching of the gospel.

His academic course was, however, rather limited and imperfect; he did not attain to a very intimate acquaintance with the learned languages, though it was sufficient to assist him much in after life, to make out criticisms on difficult passages of Scripture. His knowledge of the principles of English grammar was not entirely thorough; his orthography was incomplete, and indeed continued defective through life; and in other respects he came short even of an accurate elementary education. Still his limited course of literary and theological training was of inestimable advantage. It taught him the use of books, improved his language, gave him a more exact and comprehensive view of the gospel scheme, and enabled him to give to his thoughts a more clear and logical arrangement. It also served to awaken in his bosom the needful consciousness of his own mental capabilities, and brought into wholesome and well directed action those acute and vigorous powers which, in their more full and ample development, enabled him to grapple with a master hand, the most difficult and sublime subjects in the system of revealed truth.

In the acquisition of his education, he derived but little assistance from his father, whose circumstances were limited, hardly allowing him the means for the education of his rising family, much less for the assistance of his married son. His own industry and frugal management, with perhaps some occasional donations from his brethren, constituted the resources upon which he had mainly to depend. It is proper, however, that it should here be stated that in 1792, "the General Committee for the Charleston Baptist Education Fund," assisted him with £10, and afterwards, with a small supply of books. That very respectable and efficient body could hardly have made a more judicious and fortunate appropriation.

The field of Mr. Mercer's labors was soon enlarged. In the course of 1793, he accepted of the pastorship of the church at Indian Creek, (or Bethany,) in Oglethorpe county, and removed the ensuing winter to its vicinity. He there was enabled, principally by the assistance of hired labor, to support his family, whilst he devoted himself with great diligence to the duties of his sacred calling. Occasionally, however, he would labor diligently with his own hands, (for from childhood he was industrious and inured to hardship;) but he did not allow the cares of his farm to interfere with his ministerial duties, the proper and faithful discharge of which he ever kept before him, as the great object and aim of his life.

Mr. Mercer, like most other ministers, was occasionally harassed with fears that he was not called of God, to the work of preaching the Gospel. About the time to which our narrative has now brought us, (possibly a little earlier,) he accompanied his father to North Carolina, where a trifling incident occurred which gave him great uneasiness. For a time, it caused him to doubt whether he was even a Christian, much more whether he was a Christian minister. "I was travelling," said he, "with my father in North Carolina: we had preached at —— Meeting-House, and gone home with an old friend of my father's to spend the night. Having preached that day, and travelled a considerable distance, and, withal, through a drizzling rain, I was a good deal fatigued when we arrived, and I complained of my weariness. After supper, the kind-hearted old brother had a fine armed chai brought out for my accommodation, which I occupied with great comfort during the *tete a tete* betwixt him and my father. Bed time at length arriving, the family assembled for evening worship, in which my father officiated. During the service, I fell fast asleep in my comfortable arm-chair, and slept so soundly that I lost the whole of the prayer, and awoke only upon the rattling of the chairs in the rising up of the company. Instantly I was awake, and wide awake, for I was filled with remorse, shame and confusion. We soon retired to bed, but there was no rest for me that night. As soon as I was alone, I said within myself—what shall I do now? O, that I was at home! for how shall I look my father and this genteel family (for they were people of wealth and distinction) in the face, after this! and the report of my shameful conduct will, no doubt, soon go abroad. It will be said that the Rev. Silas Mercer and his son Jesse, who is also commencing minister, are travelling and preaching in North Carolina. The old gentleman, it is true, is a preacher of some distinction, but as for his son, we think he had better give up preaching: why, he preached the other day at ——, and upon going home with Mr. ——, fell fast asleep in an arm-chair during solemn family devotion, conducted by his father —did not know, nor even say *amen!* Surely, although he seems to be zealous in the pulpit, and exhorts others to watch and pray, his heart cannot be in it, or he would not fall asleep in an *arm-chair* in a strange country, in a strange family, in the very midst of the solemnities of family worship. In truth, said I within myself, it is a very bad sign, and I must talk with my father about it in the morning, and tell him I cannot preach to-morrow. Upon introducing the subject to him, he gravely smiled at what had occurred, and said he feared the adversary had gotten the advantage over me, and that he thought I was troubled over much. ' Do you expect to be more watchful and circumspect,' said he, ' and heavenly-minded than the immediate followers of our Lord, who fell asleep on a much more solemn and trying occasion? And do you not remember the kind manner in which he reproved them—*the spirit, indeed, is willing, but the flesh is weak?* I am sure here is ground for comfort and encouragement, and you should not lay it so much to heart. Trust in God, and apply yourself to the work before you.' My father saw proper to mention the subject at the breakfast table, where it excited nothing but laughter at first, which my bad looks soon turned to pity. The family treated it as a venial matter, and said the same thing might befall the most pious man living. I was surprised myself that the case of the sleeping disciples had not occurred to me; so that, upon the whole I was persuaded to preach that day, though it was a long time before I got entirely over it. But I have always found more peace of mind and Christian comfort in the discharge of my ministerial duties than in the omission of them."

A few years subsequent to the little incident above related, probably in 1795, he was, on a certain occasion, assaulted by a most distressing and awful temptation, of which the following is a brief account. I still quote from his uncle's narrative, in which the circumstance is recorded, as nearly as can be recollected, in Mr. Mercer's own words:

"'I was,' said he, 'on a preaching tour, and having filled one of my appointments on a certain day, was proceeding on my way towards the next, when I heard the muttering of distant thunder, and, upon looking up, saw the outline of a rising cloud in the west. Borne onward by the wind, it arose with unprecedented haste, while the lightning flashed, and the thunder roared louder and nearer. I was convinced that I was about to be overtaken by a storm in the wild woods, for there was no covert at hand. The sky was soon overcast, and the air darkened. The loud, hoarse hum of the approaching tempest now fell upon my ear, the flashes of lightning were swallowed up in a continual glare; peal on peal of thunder fell around me, and the sturdy trees of the forest were trembling in the blast. My horse, startled by the lightning, the thunder and the crash of falling trees, from becoming restive, began to plunge from side to side, so that it was with great difficulty I could hold on. In the midst of this fearful commotion of the elements, and drenched with rain, it was suggested to me to curse the wind, and the thunder, and the lightning, and the God who ruled them. The storm gathered strength, and so did the temptation. I feared I should commit the awful sin, notwithstanding all the powers of my soul were arrayed against it. I clenched my teeth, grasped my bridle convulsively, and my whole system was in a state of the utmost tension. In my agony I cried, continually, Lord, help me! Lord, help me! Preserve thy poor servant that trusteth in thee, from this most heinous—this blackest sin! Such was the anguish of my soul that I forgot the storm. The temptation may have lasted some five or six minutes, when all on a sudden it left me. My nerves relaxed, and I felt as weak as a child; but my mouth was filled with praises to God for my deliverance. It was, however, quickly suggested to me, if you did not curse God aloud, yet you thought it. I replied, with increased joy, if I did, blessed be God, my heart was not in it. So the temptation proved a blessing in the end, for by it my faith was strengthened.'"

In the month of August, 1796, Mr. Mercer was called to mourn the death of his honored father. The removal of such a wise counsellor and faithful friend, to a person possessing a heart so kind and tender, and in which resided so much filial love and devotion, must have been a most painful bereavement. The following winter, yielding to the call of duty, he returned to his father's residence, (at the same time, probably, resigning the pastoral charge of his church in Oglethorpe county,) for the purpose of administering upon his deceased parent's estate, and otherwise assisting the bereaved family. At the same time, Mr. Armor gave up the rectorship of the Salem Academy, of which he immediately took the superintendence, being assisted in his labors by his brother Daniel.

The churches, which had been so faithfully served

by his father, and which had grown up to respectability under his care, now called for the services of the son. These were Phillips' Mill, Powelton, and Whatley's Mill (now Bethesda) : he accepted of these several calls, and entered at once upon the cultivation of this new and extended field. It seems that the mantle of the ascended Elijah rested upon the young Elisha. Those who knew him best esteemed and loved him most; he was a prophet truly honored in his own country, and amongst his own kindred. His profiting had appeared to all; his ministerial gifts had become much improved; and he had taken a high stand as an able expounder of the doctrines of the gospel.

He continued at his father's place for several years, until he had settled the business of the estate; after which he removed to the Fork of Little River, in Green county, some five or six miles below Whatley's Mill. Here he settled again on a small farm, supporting himself and family as before, chiefly by hired help, although he still continued to labor occasionally himself. Nothing, however, was allowed to disturb his uniform zeal and punctuality in the discharge of his ministerial duties.

About this time, he had a few young ministers under his instruction, amongst whom were Thomas Rhodes and Malachi Reeves. At certain appointed times, these young brethren would meet him at his own house, when he would hear their recitations, and give the necessary directions as to their course of reading and study. These services were rendered gratuitously. How much good might be done by our wise and experienced ministers, were they more frequently to imitate this praiseworthy example, and encourage their younger brethren, especially those whose peculiar circumstances deny them the advantages of good theological schools, to come to their own houses, and receive such instructions as would tend to advance their piety and usefulness.

From what has already been stated, it would seem, that during the early years of his ministry, Mr. Mercer received but little pecuniary assistance from his churches. Individual members would occasionally assist him with small donations of corn, pork, and other articles of provision, " but as to a compensation in gold and silver, such a thing," says his uncle, " was scarcely thought of."

"After about 1800, he received more on funeral and marriage occasions, than from any other quarter. He had acquired great fame in the performance of the marriage ceremony, and I have very often heard young ladies say, when we marry we shall send for Mr. Mercer, for we do not think we should be frightened; he goes through the ceremony so quickly and genteelly. The rich and fashionable used to call him for this purpose, the distance of from thirty to fifty miles, and would frequently, for his services, present him with from twenty to fifty dollars. In like manner, he would be called equal distances to preach funeral sermons; and when any thing was given, which was not uncommon, he would be presented with similar sums of money. In his tours of preaching, beyond the bounds of his churches, wealthy brethren, knowing his poverty, would sometimes give him a few dollars, especially when he visited their families; and pious ladies would give him some articles of clothing of their own manufacture, besides many little presents that were made through him to his wife. By an economical use of all these little means, he contrived, not only to live in comfort, but to increase constantly, though slowly, his property. He was prudent, industrious, and economical, and cautiously regulated his expenditures by his income; so that he always met, with the utmost punctuality, his pecuniary engagements."

CHAPTER III.

Mr. Mercer's ministerial labors.—Sardis Church.—Phillips' Mill.—Bethesda.—Powelton.—Gov. Rabun.—Extracts from Mr. Mercer's funeral sermon on the occasion of Gov. R.'s death.—Eatonton Church.—Thomas Cooper.

THE last chapter brought up the history of Mr. Mercer to the time when he became well established in his ministerial character, and had entered, in a formal manner, upon an interesting and extensive field of labor. In this chapter, and the one or two chapters which immediately follow, it is proposed to take a brief and cursory view of his ministerial labors during the most active portion of his life. This view will confine us mainly to the period extending from 1796, to 1827. There will be found some occasional reference to events already noticed in the preceding chapter, and to some of a later date than 1827, as well as some statements and reflections of a general character, which will apply to most of his ministerial course from first to last. The other various departments of useful and pious labor in which he was employed, and in which, as well as in the more immediate discharge of his duties as a minister, he gained for himself a pre-

3*

cious and venerated name, will be noticed by themselves in their appropriate places.

The sketch now proposed must necessarily be very imperfect, and, in all probability, will fall far short of the expectations of surviving acquaintances, as well as of those who had only heard of him by the hearing of the ear. The writer had no personal acquaintance with Mr. Mercer till towards the close of the period above referred to, and then the acquaintance was formed at some distance from the field of his active labors. Mr. Mercer kept no regular journal of his labors, nor of the various religious exercises through which he passed in the prosecution of his ministerial duties. But little, referring to this period, can be gathered from his correspondence; the traces of many incidents are entombed with the venerable cotemporaries, who entered into their rest before him; and many things, which might interest, have glided from the memory of those who still survive. In addition to all this, it must be remembered, that the course of most ministers, even of such as are greatly distinguished, is generally monotonous and unimposing, being marked with but few incidents to excite admiration and wonder.

The field occupied by Mr. Mercer was one of the most important in the state; and there was a mutual adaptedness of minister and people, which very naturally suggests to our minds the wisdom of that providence, which assigned him the bounds of his habitation. How greatly the influence and usefulness of a minister depend upon such a coincidence, must be obvious to all. The churches which he served, were in the midst of a dense population, embracing a large proportion of individuals in comfortable circumstances, of solid, practical sense, with a respectable number beside of considerable intelligence and refinement. In the main, they were a people that could well appreciate the plain, rich, sound instructions of their gifted minister; whilst at the same time they felt the most entire complacency in his unadorned and simple manners.

Our sketch will commence with some account of Mr. Mercer's services in immediate connexion with the several churches which he supplied during the period just specified.

SARDIS CHURCH.

This church, (first called Hutton's Fork,) was gathered by the labors of Silas Mercer, in 1788. It is situated in Wilkes county, about twelve miles northwest from Washington. As the reader has already noticed, this was the first church which Jesse Mercer was called to preside over, as pastor. It prospered under his ministry, and was favored with some seasons of special refreshing from the presence of the Lord. At the Association of 1802, thirty-three were reported as having been added by baptism, during the preceding year. In the years 1808 and 1809, there was a precious revival, and something like one hundred were baptized as the fruit of God's merciful visitation at that time, The whole number received into the membership of the church, during Mr. Mercer's connexion with it, the author has not the means of ascertaining, though it must have been quite respectable. In 1817, he gave up the charge of this interesting church, much to the regret of the members that composed it. They were greatly attached to their pastor, and accepted of his resignation with extreme reluctance.

PHILLIPS' MILL.

This is one of the oldest churches in the State, and owes its birth to the instrumentality of the elder Mercer. It was constituted in 1785. Its location is in Wilkes county, some nine miles in a southwest direction from Washington, on the road leading from that place to Crawfordville. As the pious and intelligent Baptist passes by the antique meeting-house, now occupied by this venerable mother-church, the most thrilling reflections are awakened in his bosom. Not far distant from this very place, resided for many years, and finally died, the holy, zealous and indefatigable Silas Mercer; here his distinguished son was baptized, and ushered into the gospel ministry; and here, for more than fifty years, was his voice often heard, warning the ungodly, pointing the weary and heavy-laden to the Saviour of sinners, and reproving, instructing and comforting the children of God. Shortly after the death of his father, Mr. Mercer, as has already been recorded, was called to the pastoral charge of this church. The date of this transaction was September 10th, 1796. On the same day, he and his wife united again with the church, having been dismissed in March, 1795. He served the church regularly, as pastor, thirty-nine years, with the exception of a few short periods when he obtained permission to be absent, for the purpose of travelling. In the latter part of 1798, he visited the north, and Rev. B. Mosely supplied his pulpit during his absence. During his absence, in 1817, to attend the Triennial Convention at Philadelphia, his pulpit was supplied by a Rev. Mr. Robinson; and when absent for a similar purpose, in 1826, the Rev. B. M. Sanders officiated in his place. In 1802, this church, in common with all the other churches which Mr. Mercer supplied, was favored with a pleasant revival. Thirty-eight were reported to the Association that year as added by baptism. In successive years, the numbers 7, 12, 14, 19 and 25 are occasionally found reported, though not unfrequently much smaller numbers. During Mr. Mercer's pastoral connexion with the church, something like 230 were added by baptism.

In the earlier part of Mr. Mercer's labors at Phillips' Mill, as well as at the other places which he supplied, his congregations were generally large; in later years, the population of the country around having been much diminished by death and emigration, and other churches, also, having sprung up in contiguous regions, the attendance upon his ministry, except on special occasions, was less crowded. In 1835, Mr. Mercer resigned the charge of this church, and was succeeded by Rev. W. H. Stokes.

BETHESDA, *formerly* WHATLEY'S MILL.

This church is in Green county, about twelve miles east of Greensboro. In its origin, it was another monument of the untiring zeal and successful labor of Silas Mercer. There are some still living who remember the time when his voice was lifted up in the forest, to instruct the gathering multitudes in the way of life, before the church was formed, or a house of worship erected. The church was constituted in 1785, and enjoyed the labors of Silas Mercer as its first pastor. Abraham Marshall and James Heflin were also pastors. Jesse Mercer commenced his pastoral labors in this church in 1796, and continued them until 1827. From the year 1807, till 1817 his membership was also here. The population around, in former years, was dense, and an unusually large congregation attended on the ministry of Mr. Mercer. In 1818, a brick meeting-house, sixty feet by forty, and two stories high, was erected, to which the pastor himself was a liberal subscriber. At this time, the name was changed from Whatley's Mill to Bethesda.

This has been an active, useful and prosperous church. It has been the mother of several valuable ministers, has aided much in the cause of benevolence, and enjoyed some delightful revivals of religion. In the memorable year of 1802, forty-nine were added by baptism. Other respectable accessions are noted on its records.

The uncle of Mr. Mercer gives the following interesting account of the commencement of a revival in this church: "At a certain time, he had been on a preaching tour for a fortnight, and had spent most of the time in a revival, and upon his return, attended his church at Whatley's Mill, at their regular meeting. He was aware that the church was in a very languid state, and his sermon was on the deceitfulness of the heart, in crying *peace, peace, when there is no peace*. At the close of his discourse he became deeply affected, and addressed the congregation about as follows: 'Dear brethren and friends, I have been, for a great part of the last two weeks, addressing a people that I believe are truly awakened to a sense of their lost, helpless, and ruined state, and are crying out in their agony, *what shall we do to be saved?* Amongst them my tongue seemed to be loosed, and I could point them with great freedom to the way of salvation through a crucified Saviour. On my way hither, I have felt the deepest concern in contrasting your lifeless situation with theirs, until I even bedewed the pommel of my saddle with tears;' and here lifting up his hands, he exclaimed, ' O, my congregation, I fear you are too good to be saved!' and again burst into an irrepressible flood of tears. Descending from the pulpit, and recovering himself a little, he poured forth a most solemn and empassioned exhortation, during which many came forward and asked that prayer might be made in their behalf; and thus commenced one of the most interesting revivals which has ever blessed that favored church."

Much of the fruit of Mr. Mercer's valuable labors at Bethesda appeared after he had resigned his pastoral charge. In 1828 the church was permitted to enjoy one of the most powerful revivals of religion that has ever been witnessed in the State of Georgia. From March to October, not less than 270 were added to the church by baptism. Fifty and sixty were sometimes added in a day. Amongst this number were some who had been converted many years before, under the preaching of Mr. Mercer; and there were others, whose conversions were recent, that still referred to his faithful instructions as the means of their first awakening. The seed which he had long been sowing in tears ripened at length into a joyful harvest.

Before dismissing this item of his narrative, the writer thinks it proper to state, that, in 1820, a meeting of the Mission Board of the Georgia Association was held at Bethesda, at which time the several ministers present united in the ordination of *Rev. Adiel Sherwood*, a brother whose name has long been identified with the history and successful progress of the Baptists of Georgia.

POWELTON.

This church, (at first known by the name of Powel's Creek,) is another monument to the pious labors of the father Silas, who planted, of the son Jesse, who watered, and to the grace of God which gave the happy increase. It is located at the little village of Powelton, Hancock county, about fourteen miles northeast from Sparta, the county town, near Powel's creek and the Ogechee river. It was constituted on the 1st of July, 1786, with twenty-six members, by Silas Mercer, John Harvey, and John Thomas. On the 4th of February, 1797, Mr. Jesse Mercer assumed the pastoral charge of this interesting church, and remained its minister till the latter part of 1825. It appears from the records of the church, that he was received into its fellowship by a letter from Whatley's Mill, (Bethesda,) Feb. 28th, 1818, about which time, or perhaps a little before, he removed with his family from Green county to Powelton, where he resided for the next nine or ten years. Under the wise and faithful training of their much beloved and venerated pastor, the Powelton church became one of the most active, efficient, and benevolent bodies in the state. It was for a long time one of the important rallying points of the denomination. The benevolent and hospitable spirit of its members drew to the place many of those sacred convocations of ministers and lay brethren, which were appointed from time to time, to deliberate upon the interests of Zion. The Georgia Association held several of its annual sessions with this church. Here was organized in 1803, " *The General Committee of the Georgia Baptists;*" here was formed, in 1822, the *Baptist State Convention*, and its sessions for 1823, and 1832, were held with this church. An efficient missionary society was also organized at Powelton, as early as the 5th of May, 1815. In 1814 or 1815, by the efforts of this intelligent and enlightened church *mainly*, an academy was established, which has ever since been maintained upon a respectable footing, and has been greatly serviceable to the denomination, and to the country generally. Though the academy has been surrounded by a Baptist community, and has been principally sustained from its commencement by Baptists and their adherents, yet the trustees have ever been guided by the most liberal policy, and without respect to denominational considerations, have endeavored to secure the most competent teachers. It has so happened, that most of the instructers have been pædobaptists. The liberality of the patrons, however, in cheerfully sustaining them, has not been altogether unrewarded, for some of these individuals have come useful and prominent members of the Baptist denomination. The Rev. Otis Smith, long known as one of the most successful teachers in the state, and for some years president of the Mercer University, is one of the individuals to whom reference is here made.

The accessions to the Powelton church under the ministry of Mr. Mercer, were not remarkably large. In 1802, twenty-nine were reported to the Association as added by baptism. Occasionally, a considerable length of time would transpire without any increase; at other times, several would be received at each successive monthly meeting. About two hundred were baptized during Mr. Mercer's connexion with this church. If the accessions were not large, they nevertheless embraced a highly respectable number of individuals, distinguished for their intelligence, piety and usefulness.

Gov. Rabun was, for many years, a distinguished member and ornament of the Powelton church.

In the following extract from a communication from President Sherwood, there is honorable mention made of this good man, as well as some reference to Mr. Mercer, which may not be uninteresting to the reader. "In June, (1819,) I attended his (Mr. Mercer's,) Powelton meeting, and by previous invitation spent two or three days at his house. *Governor Rabun* was then clerk and chorister of the church. I was struck with the simplicity of his character. Some men, if they had been elevated by office as was he, would have supposed themselves too high to record the doings or lead the devotions of a country church; but here was exhibited the spectacle of the highest officer in the state mingling with his brethren as one of them, far removed from that *hauteur* which little folks sometimes assume, as if he were the most insignificant of their number. In the fall of this year, Mr. Mercer was sick of a bilious attack, and seemed to have escaped very narrowly from the grave. I can never forget the grief portrayed in *Judge Cobb's* countenance when it was announced that he was actually dead; but it was a mere rumor. At the meeting of the Georgia Association that fall, he was pale and feeble; Governor Rabun was the picture of health; but before the month had expired, e had bowed to the summons of death. So uncertain are all appearances on which to place our hopes." Shortly after the death of this excellent man, Mr. Mercer, at the request of the legislature, preached a funeral discourse on the melancholy occasion, which was afterwards published, and passed through two editions.

A few extracts from this discourse may be gratifying to the reader.

"Called as I am, by the General Assembly of a State in mourning for the sudden and unexpected death of her beloved Chief Magistrate, to express the high consideration in which he was so justly held, and to afford a tribute of respect due his departed worth, I tremble as I advance; and feeling as I do, a particular and melancholy interest in this afflictive dispensation while I make the effort, the tenderest sensibilities of my heart mourn, and an unutterable grief thrills through my soul.

"Your late excellent Governor was the pleasant and lovely companion of my youth; my constant friend and endeared Christian brother in advancing years, and, till death, my unremitted fellow-laborer and able support in all the efforts of benevolence and philanthropy in which I had the honor and happiness to be engaged, calculated either to amend or meliorate the condition of man."

After this short introduction, the author proceeds to quote the passage of Scripture upon which he founds his discourse: this is 2 Sam. iii. 38—"*Know ye not that there is a prince and a great man fallen in Israel?*" From this text he takes occasion to consider the *importance* and *character* of a *great man* in a nation, and the light in which his *fall* is to be regarded.

"A man is great," says Mr. Mercer, "according to his strength of thought, the information he possesses, and the manner in which he employs his time and talents for the public good and the divine glory. He should be estimated from his mind rather than his attainments; or, as Dr. Watts beautifully expresses it—

> "'Were I so tall to reach the pole,
> Or grasp the ocean with my span,
> I should be measured by my soul—
> The soul's the standard of the man.'

* * * * * * * *

"Next to a noble mind, wisdom constitutes and is the great man's ornament. It consists not in any degree of knowledge, but in the right use of what is possessed, and differs from it as pleasures differ from the means which afford them. It is to folly what knowledge is to ignorance. It originates in the fear of God, flourishes in patriotic philanthropy and terminates in glory and renown. A wise man is attentive to the experience and examples of individuals and nations, * * * and increases in wisdom. In his intercourse with men he is directed by the good old golden rule, and in politics it is his joy to associate individual happiness with the public good. He is generous in feeling, open in candor and firm in complaisance; in pleasures prudent, in trials patient, and sterling in worth. He thinks modestly, speaks cautiously, and acts humbly. His whole deportment is regulated by the fear of God, and directed by the public good and the divine honor; *and such was* GOVERNOR RABUN.

* * * * * * * *

"But to crown the character of the great man, piety is indispensable. This is that gracious temper of heart which fulfils the whole law; it originates in renovation, and is perfected in love to God and man. 'Tis that temper of heart towards God, without which all religion is vain, devotion is solemn mockery, and righteousness becomes sin. 'Tis this that consecrates both the persons and works of great men to wise and holy purposes, and constitutes them the seed of the land, so that for their sakes a nation may be preserved. But in those who are great in impiety, there is no pledge for the public safety. God indeed may use them as he did Pharaoh, Nebuchadnezzar, and Cyrus, as instruments for the accomplishment of *his* designs, by overruling *theirs;* but it shall be with them as it was with the king of Assyria, who, when he had done the work assigned him as an instrument in the hand of the Almighty, was punished for the haughtiness of his high looks. But 'tis on account of the persons and the prayers of pious men, that God is graciously pleased to stay his wrath, and hush the threatened storm of vengeance to rest. Of what vital worth then are men of piety to a sinful nation? pious men, who, like the friend of God, suing for guilty Sodom, constantly bend the knee of devotion before the throne of God, and give him no rest till he establish and settle the state in peace :—especially men of early piety, whose hearts have been long right with God, and whose morals are all fixed by the most firm and rigid habit. These are the strong pillars of the state, the pledges of the public safety, and the blessed of God. And such was GOVERNOR RABUN.

* * * * * * * *

"It was his felicity to have many friends, few enemies, rare equals, and no superiors. He is gone, and has left an awful chasm behind him.—A widow bereft of a tender and kind husband; children of an affectionate and loving father; servants of a humane and indulgent master; neighbors of a constant friend and pleasant companion; the Baptist church of her bright ornament, member and scribe; two mission societies of their secretary; the Georgia Association of her clerk, and the state of a firm politician and her honored chief. O, what an eventful death was Governor Rabun's! *The beauty of Georgia is fallen!*

* * * * * * * *

"He is gone, but in glorious hope :—a hope which he obtained in Christ 'as the end of the law for righteousness to every one that believeth,' after a severe conflict of soul under that conviction which the divine Spirit affords of sin, of righteousness, and judgment; and which sustained him from seventeen years of age till death, as 'an anchor to the soul, sure and steadfast.'

* * * * * * * *

"In death [he was] resigned in the arms of Jesus, and cried, 'now lettest thou thy servant depart in peace, for mine eyes have seen thy salvation.' Yes, fellow citizens of the General Assembly, and other auditors, there is a power in the gospel of Christ that 'makes a dying bed feel soft as downy pillows are;' and the consistent, dying Christian, leaning his head on the breast of redemption, 'breathes his life out sweetly there.' *And thus died* Goveror Rabun. His remains are deposited in the gloomy mansions of the dead, where clustering sorrows grow with luxuriance, and the silence of death flourishes in vernal bloom, but his departed spirit is gone to that unknown region where 'the clock strikes *one*, and the pendulum vibrates *ever always, ever always, ever always*, and the clock strikes no more.'"*

---

* The following condensed sketch of the life of Gov. Rabun is from Mr. Sherwood's Gazetteer of the State of Georgia : "Hon. Wm. Rabun was born in Halifax County, North Carolina, April, 1771. His

EATONTON.

In 1818, a commodious house of worship was erected in Eatonton, Putnam county, by the community at large, for the accommodation of several religious denominations, and the Baptists amongst the rest. On November 17th of the same year, a Baptist church was constituted with *ten* members, Elijah Moseley and Frederick Crowder, acting as the Presbytery on the occasion. From this beginning, respectable for its worth, though small in numbers, has risen up a most liberal, pious, efficient and well disciplined church. Much of its early prosperity is no doubt to be attributed to the valuable labors of Mr. Mercer. Yielding to the urgent solicitations of the little band, he took charge of the church on the 25th of January, 1820, and continued as its pastor till the close of 1826. Much of the last year, however, he was absent from the church. During his connexion with it, about sixty were added by baptism, and forty by letter. In the years 1827 and '8, under the ministry of Brother Sherwood, his esteemed successor in the pastoral office, the church was blessed with large and valuable accessions; to what extent the previous la-

father removed to Georgia while he was a young man. He was an able representative from Hancock a number of years, and long President of the Senate and Governor ex-officio, and also Governor from 1817 to 1819. Mr. Rabun was truly a religious man. He united with the Baptist church now worshipping at Powelton, in 1787 or '8. His house was the house of prayer. To all the benevolent institutions of the day he lent his influence and his purse. It was a pleasing sight to witness the Governor of the state taking the lead in singing at a country church. Office did not *bloat* him as it does some. He died while Governor, at his plantation, near Powelton, October, 1819."

bors of Mr. Mercer, may, under God, have contributed to this glorious result, the writer is not prepared to say, yet it can hardly be doubted that more or less of the fruit of his tears and prayers, and faithful instructions, was mingled with that copious harvest. The revival which commenced in Eatonton in 1827, was not long confined to the place; it seemed to be the beginning of a blessed and wide-spread religious excitement, which resulted in the addition of some twelve or fourteen thousand to the Baptist churches of Georgia.

It might not be improper to state, that in 1824 and '25, the Baptist State Convention (then denominated the General Association,) held its sessions at Eatonton. On one of these occasions, Mr. Mercer preached a missionary sermon, which was followed by a collection from the congregation of $220.

The session o' the first named year was one of peculiar interest. The memory of many Christian friends still living, clings to that occasion with strong and tender fondness, as one of the brightest spots in the range of their spiritual history. The presence and labors of the Rev. Basil Manly, then young in the ministry, who had spent some portion of 1819 with the church as a licentiate, added much to the interest of the occasion. He preached the word with unusual unction and power. Weeping congregations hung upon his lips for three successive days. During his discourse on the Sabbath, a large congregation were continually bathed in tears. In a letter to the writer, in which brother Manly refers with much emotion to some of the incidents of that memorable day, he says: "I dare say you will find many in Georgia who recollect the facts. Among others, one of the brother

Milners was present, whom I remember especially for this, that when we came down out of the pulpit to meet the rushing crowd for prayer, this brother Milner fell on his knees, and began a prayer more remarkably tender and melting than any I ever heard; in which he thanked God that he himself *had had a pious mother*. His prayer was a sort of *soliloquy*, a tissue of penitence and faith and rapture, of supplication and joy and triumph :—and the place was glorious."

Whilst connected with the Eatonton church, Mr. Mercer was favored with the co-operation of some brethren of much efficiency and rare Christian worth. Amongst these, stood forth in striking prominence, the late pious and excellent Thomas Cooper. He was baptized by Mr. Mercer in Powelton, in 1811, removed to Eatonton and connected himself with the Baptist church in that place in 1822, and in 1824 was ordained one of its deacons. Brother Cooper was scarcely less distinguished as a *lay member*, than Mr. Mercer was as a *minister*. In him were joined to a native intellect remarkably clear, discriminating and vigorous, the most excellent qualities of heart; and all was sanctified by fervent and exalted piety. Three times a day would he retire to commune with God. For the last twelve or fifteen years of his life, this wise and venerable man was an humble pupil in a bible class. His faithfulness, in encouraging, counselling, and if necessary, reproving his brethren, was worthy of all praise; and as a judicious, watchful, conscientious, punctual, pains-taking deacon, a brighter model has never appeared in our churches. His pecuniary bounties were scattered over a broad field with a liberal hand. For many years before he died, his entire income beyond his necessary expenses was consecrated to pious purposes; and towards the close of life, his benefactions would sometimes encroach upon his capital. For a long time, to the writer's knowledge, he contributed annually one hundred dollars to each of some half a dozen religious objects; whilst his extra contributions of from one hundred to one thousand dollars, (unknown indeed to many,) were not unfrequent. In his last will and testament, the claims of Zion were as sacredly remembered as the children of his own body. Long will it be before we shall see in our midst such a *minister* as Jesse Mercer, and perhaps as long before we shall see such a *deacon* as THOMAS COOPER. He entered into his rest, July, 1843, in the 73d year of his age.

CHAPTER IV.

Number of immediate conversions not a certain test of a minister's usefulness.—Mr. Mercer set for the defence of the gospel.—His care to establish his churches in the truth.—Skilful to aid the tempted.—Anecdotes.—His caution in receiving members.—Able disciplinarian.—His manner of presiding at church meetings.—His punctuality.—No respecter of persons.—His churches benevolent. —Defects in the prevailing system of pastoral labor.—Mr. Mercer in revivals.—His views on revivals.—Ministerial support.—Estimation in which he was held.

FEW ministers in our country have scattered more faithfully and copiously the unadulterated seed of divine truth than Mr. Mercer, though it would seem from the preceding sketch, that his labors did not result in the immediate and frequent ingathering of large crowds into his church. There are no doubt many now in heaven, and a goodly number now on their pilgrimage to the promised land, who recognise him as the honored instrument of their conversion; yet it is highly probable that there have been many ministers of inferior gifts, and of a lower grade of piety, who have been more directly successful in turning sinners from the error of their ways. Those indeed are highly favored instruments whose messages of love the Lord is pleased in an eminent degree, to clothe with effectual and convincing power, and whose personal labors he employs in gathering multitudes into the fold of Christ. Every minister should humbly covet this honor, should labor with holy and fervent intensity, for the speedy conversion of his people—of all his people; and if from year to year, his labors seem unfruitful, it should be with him a matter of solemn and honest inquiry, whether there may not be some radical deficiency in his faith and zeal, his preparation and his prayers; or in the manner and matter of his communications from the pulpit; or in his more private labors for the good of souls; or whether he may not have mistaken his particular and appropriate field of labor. But after all, it must be remembered, that the number of immediate conversions is to be regarded as a very imperfect standard of a minister's usefulness. In the ingathering of sinners, we see the result of the combined influence of a thousand instrumentalities, and for aught we can tell, of a thousand laborers; and who can determine the precise amount of usefulness that is to be put to the credit of each instrumentality, of each laborer? For the want of just and proper reflection on this point, many eminently pious and useful ministers are often undervalued, and it may be said dishonored by their brethren; whilst others, whose labors seem to be more directly and visibly successful, are caressed and praised as the only ones whose services are to be much esteemed, and by whom the cause of Christ can be well sustained. Who but Omniscience can properly decide the question of relative importance and usefulness? There are various departments of labor in the great field which is to be cultivated, and a great diversity of gifts are required that they may all be properly filled. It does not accord with the arrangements of infinite wisdom that all possible excellencies shall be concentrated in every individual whose duty it may be to preach the gospel; nor that the usefulness of all should be manifested in the same way. There are some to plant, and some to water; some to sow and some to reap; some to lay the foundation, and others to carry up the superstructure. Here is a brother who, the first year of his ministry, was the instrument in one small neighborhood of converting a hundred souls. He is highly honored; we bless the Lord for such a laborer. But who has been the most useful in God's account, he, as the highly favored instrument of their immediate conversion; or the venerable man of God, who for twenty or thirty years, poured the lessons of divine truth upon the minds and consciences of the people, and by the faithful training of their moral sensibilities, prepared them for the hearty and saving reception of the gospel message; or the man of capacious mind and exalted piety, who, a hundred years before, and a thousand miles distant, brought into operation a benevolent enterprise, by which the gospel was ultimately carried to that community, a church reared up, the regular and long continued administration of the ordinances secured, and many important auxiliary plans brought into healthful operation? These inquiries are propounded to show how difficult it must be to determine the relative usefulness of those whom the Lord employs as instruments in advancing his cause and kingdom on earth. They are well calculated to furnish those with motives to humility, who are permitted to reap large harvests of immortal souls, as well as to present the most cheering grounds of encouragement to those who sow the seed in darkness and tears; whilst all should be stimulated to faithful and unwearied efforts in their respective spheres, to promote the great common cause of righteousness and truth; since they are assured by the infallible word of God, that the toils and sacrifices of each and all are needful in their place; that their labors shall not be in vain in the Lord, and that the weeping sower, and the joyful reaper shall at last meet and triumph together.

If, in the manner already alluded to, the labors of Mr. Mercer were not as extensively blessed as those of some other servants of Christ, yet in other respects, not less important, when viewed in all their results, he stood upon an elevation which has seldom been reached, even by the most gifted and eminent ministers in our land.

It may be said of him, that, in a peculiar sense, he was set for the defence of the gospel. Its great leading truths he had studied intensely and profoundly; and if in the clear, well-defined, original, and masterly exhibition of these truths from the pulpit, he has had superiors, or even equals, amongst the Baptists of our country, they certainly have been rare.

Mr. Mercer took much pains to establish his churches

in the truth. He fed the lambs—he fed the sheep. He seemed at all times to entertain a deep and solemn sense of his ministerial responsibility, and kept back nothing which he considered would be profitable to his brethren. He labored under fewer temptations than most men to pass by, or soften down, an unpalatable doctrine, out of regard to the unreasonable prejudices of his hearers; with the true spirit of Christian boldness and intrepidity, he rose above the frowns of men, the complaints and cavilling of the carnal heart, and proclaimed fearlessly, though affectionately, the message which he had received from the Lord. He studied duty; consequences he left with the Master whom he served. By frequently presenting, in their scriptural connexions, those doctrines which have been most condemned by the unregenerate, and which sometimes are converted into stumbling blocks by weak believers, his people were generally convinced that they were doctrines that tended to godliness; and even those of his stated hearers whose hearts did not become reconciled to these soul-humbling themes, in view of his clear illustrations and overpowering arguments, were compelled to regard them as integral and inseparable parts of the system of revealed truth. Churches enjoying the stated ministrations of such ministers as Mr. Mercer, would not be easily driven about by every wind of doctrine; happily defended against the sly insinuations of artful deceivers, as well as the more direct assaults of men of corrupt minds.

Let it not be supposed, from what has been said, that Mr. Mercer failed to instruct his churches in the practical duties of christianity. These, in their place, were faithfully enforced, and often with great power. The readiness of his people to engage in works of benevolence, the enlarged views which they took of their relation to a world lying in wickedness and death, afford pleasing evidence that there was nothing in the tenor of Mr. Mercer's instructions, calculated to encourage, amongst his brethren, the spirit of antinomian slumber. Yet being well persuaded that a correct and godly practice must be based upon a sound scriptural faith, he was more painstaking than most ministers, to establish his hearers in right views of doctrinal truth. The influence of Mr. Mercer's preaching upon the community generally, where he statedly labored, was of a salutary character, tending to the suppression of vice, and the encouragement of quietness, order, and sound morality. It was once remarked by an intelligent and observing individual, that the standard of morality, amongst the youth connected with Mr. Mercer's congregations, was decidedly more elevated than amongst the same class in other congregations in the surrounding country.

In explaining to his people the character of a gospel church, its materials, its design, its ordinances and laws, he performed the part of a well-instructed scribe. There are multitudes, who well remember with what clearness and ability these various and important subjects were unfolded in his pulpit expositions. "Judge Cobb," says Mr. Sherwood, "who was many years in congress, was a great admirer of his talents and originality. He had incidentally, in a discourse which was listened to by many of the bar, discussed the subject of baptism. On retiring, Judge Cobb exclaimed to the lawyers in his loud, blunt manner, ' Who of your ministers can beat that ?' "

He was not ignorant of Satan's devices, and possessed great skill in disengaging the minds of his brethren from the temptations of the adversary. In cases of spiritual distress, his brethren valued the sympathy and counsel of Mr. Mercer above those of any other man, and almost innumerable were the cases in which, under such circumstances, application was made to him for instruction. We may be excused for referring to one or two instances. "I know an old brother," (the instances are presented in the language of his uncle,) "full fifty years of age, and who had been for twenty years a member of the church, that got into great darkness and distress about his spiritual state; so much so, that he mounted his horse and rode twenty-five miles to lay his case before him. He found him at home, and soon contrived to draw him aside, when, with great concern, he told his errand, and in conclusion, remarked, 'I would not, for a thousand worlds, say that *I am a Christian.*' 'Would you,' said he, 'for as many worlds, say you are not a Christian?' 'No, I would not.' 'Do you believe the devil suggests to one deceived, that he is deceived, and strives to convince him of it?' 'Certainly not.' 'Do you not believe he often worries the Christian by such suggestions, persuading him that he is deceived, and in proof of it, calls to his mind his daily departures from the path of rectitude and purity?' 'No doubt of it.' By this short category, and by narrating some of his own trials, the brother was greatly relieved, and went home with a light heart.

"Another brother, who had not been long in the church, while reading the scriptures regularly through, was greatly shocked at many of the heinous sins of the saints of old, particularly some of the acts of Lot and of David. He inquired within himself, how could holy men commit such deeds? Could the vilest of sinners do worse? He reasoned upon the matter, until he was almost persuaded that religion was a farce, and the scriptures an imposture. Whilst he was in great distress, he had an interview with my nephew, and communicated the whole to him. 'Why,' said he, 'if the scriptures had recorded none but virtuous and holy acts of the ancient saints, they would not have met *my* case; but they give an honest and impartial history of their lives; their bad and their good acts are alike recorded, and from their weakness I gather strength.' The brother received the explanation, and found its application in himself, and though living to this day, has not since been annoyed by such reflections."

In receiving members into the church, he exercised a prudent caution. Whilst he would not throw impediments in the way of the worthy and deserving, he was not favorable to that incautious haste with which some ministers hurry individuals forward to baptism. He desired to find, in every case, a sound scriptural experience. That comfort which is preceded by clear and profound views of the evil nature of sin, and the awful plague of the human heart, in connexion with a proper conception of the plan of salvation by a crucified Redeemer, afforded him great satisfaction. He once exposed and rebuked some mistaken notions of Christian experience in a rather singular manner, and yet in a way quite in character with himself. An individual came before the church for the purpose of giving some account of what he conceived to be the dealings of God with his soul. He had considerable to say about his own tenderness and feeling, and seemed to lay much stress on that fact, without being able to give a very satisfactory account of the reason why he felt so much. Mr. Mercer related an anecdote. "When I was a boy," said he, "my father sent me out into the woods to call up the stock. I took my wallet of corn and went out, and to amuse myself, called the swine in a very sad and melancholy tone. As I was proceeding in this way, the first I knew I found myself weeping at the mournful sound of my own voice." The application of the circumstance was not difficult. The individual concerned, and all present, were very forcibly reminded, that mere tenderness and animal excitement, form but a small part of Christian experience.

In expounding and carrying into practical effect the principles of gospel discipline, Mr. Mercer was truly a master in Israel. He had studied the regulations of the Saviour for the government of his church with the greatest attention, and though, upon every point, his decisions may not accord with the opinions of all his brethren, yet on the whole, he must be regarded as one of the most judicious, correct, and able expounders of discipline, that has ever been connected with the Baptist denomination. With just and sound views upon nearly every subject connected with the government of the church, he united an admirable talent for administering that government wisely and efficiently. He generally acted with great faithfulness, firmness, and decision, feeling that for the proper exercise of the ministerial authority, which he had received from the great head of the church, he was to be held accountable. "He used frequently to impress on his brethren," says a Christian friend, "in regard to discipline, the importance of *straight-forward* business, and not to delay when matters were ripe for settlement. He was opposed to '*dodging*,' and attempts at creeping out of responsibility. 'It does not become the gospel. If I go according to the scriptural path,' he would observe, 'I am safe, whether we exclude or retain.'"

He presided at his church conference meetings with much gravity and ministerial decorum; calling up business according to some just method, and not allowing questions under consideration to be entangled and swallowed up with extraneous matter. During the discussion of a subject, irregularity and disorder seldom went unreproved; "even the whispers of an old sister," says one, "could scarcely escape a reprimand." A listless and languid manner of attending to the business of the Lord, he greatly disapproved. Many years ago, the clerk of one of his churches was calling over the names of the male members preparatory to the adjournment of the conference. It was a cold day and a cold church. The members answered to their names in such a lifeless tone of voice, that they could scarcely be heard; and in some cases, the languid answer would not come until the name had been two or three times repeated. The clerk, however, patiently continued to call the names, and attentively to listen for the answers, until he had finished the list. Mr. Mercer, whose head all the while had been hanging very low, arose from his seat with much concern on his countenance, and gravely said, "*well, brethren, if your religion is as weak as your voices, it is weak indeed; let us pray.*" The reproof was deeply felt, and during the prayer, which was the concluding service, many heavy groans were heard, apparently acknowledging the justness of the minister's rebuke. " Its good effects," adds the narrator of the above circumstance, " were manifest for a great while, and I doubt if its influence is entirely lost to this day."

Mr. Mercer was remarkably punctual in meeting all his appointments. It would be difficult to find a brighter example in this respect, in the whole history of ministerial labor. Nothing but sickness, or some other unavoidable necessity was ever allowed to keep him from his meetings, or even to delay his arrival at the appointed place later than the usual hour. Small impediments he found no difficulty in surmounting. For instance, if he came to a creek swollen to a dangerous torrent, he could strip his horse, drive him across the stream, and with his saddle and saddle-bags on his back, search out for himself a crossing place on some log or fallen tree. This he once did on his way to a Saturday meeting at Bethesda. At the next monthly meeting, some of the brethren in making their excuses for absence at the previous conference, observed that they started for the meeting, but upon finding the creek impassable, they returned. "If you had waited a little longer," replied Mr. Mercer, "*I would have shown you the way.*" No man was better qualified than he, to show to others the WAY in regard to the prompt and exact discharge of duty. On another occasion, after he had been for a long time engaged in the ministry, he was travelling in his carriage, and was compelled, by high waters, to turn aside from his meeting, and spend the Sabbath at the house of a pious Baptist sister. He seemed very restless, and often walked the house in great apparent disquietude. The kind sister inquired into the cause of his uneasiness. "Ah," said he, "I feel like a fish out of water; this is the very first time, since the commencement of my ministry, that I have been absent from public worship on the Sabbath, when my health would allow my attendance."

He was equally punctual in his attendance on the business meetings of his brethren, where his presence was expected; and when present on such occasions, he was not like many, who hurry business through to a premature conclusion, or break abruptly away before it is finished; he could find time and patience for the due consideration of every important matter, and seldom left till the business of the meeting was all properly disposed of.

In his intercourse with his brethren, he was no respecter of persons; there was great uniformity in the manner in which he treated the rich and the poor, the ignorant and the more refined. When he visited his more distant churches, he would spend his nights, first with one, and then with another, without regard to the distinctions of rank and wealth; leaving none any ground to make the complaint, which is sometimes urged against ministers, that he was always careful to search out those places where he could get the best suppers and the most comfortable bedding.

It has already been intimated, that Mr. Mercer's churches were forward to acknowledge the claims of benevolence. In this respect, they stood in the front ranks. His own bright example, his frequent appeals from the pulpit, and his private, personal applications to persons in and out of the church, were generally successful in securing a respectable tribute for the treasury of the Lord. He accomplished less by the agency of societies, than many have done, thinking it best, in the general, for the churches, as such, to act as benevolent societies, without too many separate organizations. Where churches, however, were divided in sentiment as to benevolent operations, or were not disposed to act efficiently, he was ever forward to encourage these other auxiliary measures.

So many churches were resting upon his pastoral care, and so large was the territory to be occupied by his ministry, it would appear next to impossible for Mr. Mercer to perform all those labors, and carry into complete, practical operation, all those plans, which would seem to be important to meet all the spiritual wants of his people. The sick could not always be visited; intimate and frequent personal intercourse could not be kept up with the scattered members of his various flocks; and on this account, their spiritual wants being in some respects imperfectly understood, there could not have been as perfect an adaptation of ministerial instruction to all the varied necessities of his people as would have been desirable. And how could it be expected, that in the number of discourses which he delivered to his several churches, notwithstanding the rich and faithful instructions which they contained, there could be imbodied, without a miracle, that unbroken compass and full variety of scriptural truth, so important for the *perfecting* of the saints, and the *complete* edifying of the body of Christ.

Never can the churches be brought up to their matured strength and glory, until there is poured upon them a more complete and powerful concentration of pastoral labor and influence, than is allowed by that scattered, diluted system, which too generally prevails in our southern churches. In addition to the evils already hinted at, the system has a direct tendency to prevent the proper improvement and useful employment, of many of our ministerial gifts. The churches, being too well satisfied with their monthly supplies, an order of things which, in many instances, originated in the peculiar necessities of our denomination in the early settlement of the country, have very naturally been disposed to seek the services of the most popular preachers, though they might reside twenty, or fifty miles distant, and overlook the less improved and shining gifts springing up in their midst. Had these gifts been properly nurtured, the churches might have had an ample supply of useful pastors; and enjoying the constant ministrations of faithful men, though of but moderate abilities, how much more healthful would have been their condition, than with the occasional and desultory labors of more gifted ministers. But this system, which would have called at first for a little more patience and self-denial, and perhaps pecuniary aid, did not suit the taste of our brethren: " Give us at once the fruit from those choice vines, and if we can obtain but now and then a small supply, we shall be satisfied. We had rather have the monthly labors of Abram Marshall, or James Armstrong, or Jesse Mercer, than the constant attendance of brother such a one, and brother such a one." What was the consequence ? The branches of our noble vines were spread over such extended fields, that their rich fruit fell in scattered clusters; whilst many pious and precious brethren, that, with sufficient encouragement, might have risen to respectability, languished in the shade. The subject of this memoir has been heard to lament the evil; and it is more than probable, that this consideration was not overlooked, when, in subsequent years, he was induced to limit his labors to a narrower field. But notwithstanding what has just been said, it is with peculiar satisfaction the writer records the fact, that but few ministers in our country have more fully and faithfully occupied a field of the same extent. Before advancing years and bodily infirmities called for some relaxation, he was in labors abundant. A formal, monthly visit to his churches, was far from meeting his views of ministerial duty; he spent a large portion of his time in holding meetings in contiguous and intermediate neighborhoods, sometimes preaching day and night for weeks in succession. By these zealous and multiplied labors, some of the evils of the system complained of were greatly mitigated; much precious seed was scattered far and wide; multitudes were brought under the influence of Mr. Mercer's wise instructions, and not a few were aroused by his warnings to timely reflection, and induced to flee from the wrath to come.

"He always," says a friend who sat many years under his ministry, "wore an aspect of deep solemnity in times of revival, seemed to feel deeply his responsibility, and to take the sincerest interest in the salvation of his hearers, especially such as were mourning and weeping on account of their sins, and crying, what shall we do to be saved? On such occasions, he would hold on, and preach, exhort, and pray, night and day, warning the unfeeling and impenitent, and instructing and encouraging the humble and contrite. On the part of the latter, I have observed him when he would apparently pour forth his whole soul in prayer, at the same time calling to their minds the invitations and promises of the gospel; and so deeply would he feel, and so solemn and devout would be his exercises, that the whole congregation would be wrapped in the profoundest silence. Many were brought to the knowledge of the truth through his instrumentality, and such was his constant zeal, his serious deportment, and devout conversation, that he seemed to give tone and depth to the revivals in which he was engaged."

From the foregoing, it is evident that Mr. Mercer was a believer in the reality and desirableness of revivals of religion, and that he labored to encourage and promote them amongst his churches. How often and feelingly he repeated the quotation, "*Lord, revive us, Lord, revive us,*" in his letters to pious friends, many can well remember. He probably depended more upon the stated and uniform administration of the means of grace, and less upon special and extraordinary efforts, than many of his brethren; yet upon all suitable occasions, he was ready to assist at protracted meetings, and he generally brought to them a fervent, prayerful and anxious heart. On such occasions, he never lost sight of the absolute necessity of the Spirit's influence to give efficacy to the means of grace. This sentiment seemed to be interwoven, in the most complete, scriptural, and engaging manner, with his prayers, his exhortations and preaching. Every thing like glorying in men and measures, to the forgetfulness of human weakness, and the glory of God, his humble, holy spirit, deeply deplored and sincerely loathed. He had no fellowship for forced, unnatural, and mechanical efforts to move the sympathies, "*and get up a revival.*" Every thing boisterous, confusing and disorderly, in the progress of religious meetings, was abhorrent from his judgment and feelings. "Let every thing be done decently and in order," was the rule which he inculcated on others, and by which his own course was habitually governed.

Some of Mr. Mercer's views upon the subject of revivals may be learned from the following extracts from a communication published in the Christian Index, in 1832 : "I have little difficulty with C. S. A. in all he has said of '*Christian* obligation,' in regard to revivals. I would not take a jot or tittle from it, but still I do not admit that a revival is the result of this obligation, performed in its most pure degree, but rather that the highest state of practical godliness, which we ever witness, is produced by the revival itself. I think it probable your excellent correspondent and I do not understand each other. He seems to have his eye fixed on the *practical*, while mine is intensely directed to the *radical* cause. He is looking at the issue of living waters; I am examining for the reservoir of divine power and efficacious grace. * * *

"When men grasp the means, even of God's appointment, with a design of accomplishing the end, both shall be nothing, except it be to produce *Ishmaelites—sons of the flesh*. It is one thing for men to take hold of the means, *as agents*, and go to work like Jehu, to show their zeal for the Lord of Hosts; and quite another thing to go forth with equal zeal, but with *entire dependence* on the power that moves them, like the axe, or saw, *shaken* by the hand of a cunning workman. I have seen, (as it appears to me,) too much leaning to the efficiency of means, (or to the sufficiency of human ability to comply,) if they were faithfully plied. Thus the success of some ministers in the conversion of sinners, more than others, has been merged into the difference of mode used in addressing them. As if, [were] the means rightly used, and sinners properly addressed, the success would necessarily follow, which to me robs God of his glory.

"What we often hear of *getting up and continuing* revivals, seems to be too of the same sort. As if, whenever Christians will unite in, and faithfully use the means, a revival will of consequence follow; which renders the cause of the conversion of sinners, into the *faithful* use of the means, or holds God dependent on his people for the success of his gospel. Not but Christians ought to live always in the faithful discharge of every duty, looking to God for his reviving grace, to give effect to all their efforts. But I fear that revivals are too often gotten up *in appearance only*. That Satan, the better to effect his purposes, assumes *the angel of light*, and does wonders by the *slight of men*, I doubt not. When God works, Satan goes to work also. Thus it may be in revivals; a great wind, followed by earthquake and fire, may rend the mountains and break the rocks of human passions, while God may pass on *only* in *milder forms* of divine power, at which the prophets of the Lord wrap their blushing faces in the mantle of humble acknowledgment. My desire is, that in the use of the means, whether for the revival of grace, or the awakening of sinners, *he that glories, may glory in the Lord.*"

It has already been noticed, that in the early part of Mr. Mercer's ministry, he received but little pecuniary assistance from his churches; at a later period, as their resources improved, and they became better instructed in their duty, they afforded him a more ready and liberal compensation. Believing that it was a part of God's declared will, that he that preaches the gospel should live of the gospel, he was not afraid nor ashamed, on suitable occasions, to remind his brethren of their duty in this particular. The criminal backwardness of the churches in contributing of their carnal things to those who minister to them in spiritual things, he attributed, in a great measure, to the unfaithfulness of ministers in not expounding to their brethren this portion of the counsel of God.

But whilst he would have the churches discharge their duties to their pastors, he was very far from encouraging his ministering brethren in the neglect of their solemn obligations. He would have them devote themselves wholly to the work of the ministry, casting themselves with a generous confidence upon the liberality of their brethren, and exercising, at all times, unshaken faith in the promises of the Lord. "It was a custom with him," says President Sherwood, (to whom the writer of this memoir is indebted for much valuable assistance,) "to reason with his ministering brethren for their want of faith, especially if they engaged in secular pursuits, to the neglect of their sacred profession. 'There is no trust in God,' he would say, 'if a certain salary is secured you. Go out to labor in the Lord's vineyard constantly, and he will see to the support of your family.' If it were objected that some had tried it, and a sufficient support had not been furnished, he would answer, that it was a half-hearted kind of faith, by which such were actuated, and not unshaken confidence in God, else a failure would not have happened."

In this connexion, a short extract from a letter written to the Rev. B. Manly, Nov. 13, 1825, might not be inappropriate. "I am very much pleased," says he, "with the resolution you have formed, both as it respects your continuance where you are, and the making a fair trial 'whether a minister of Christ cannot be supported on gospel principles.' The views you take in regard to going to Philadelphia, (and I will add to Charleston,) are very *proper* and *forcible.* As it respects the '*fair trial,*' you must not be too soon discouraged. And you must lay it up in your heart, (and Mrs. M. too,) that many temptations and great tribulations will come to your lot, and you will suffer many things, which a *fashionable* world around you, and those *lusts* which war in your members, which are unsanctified *as yet*, will call *privations;* so that you must be willing to suffer, taking for your example, the Lord Jesus and his apostles."

At this point, might it not be well to pause a moment and solemnly inquire, if there has not been a great fault amongst ministers touching the important subject just brought to view. The churches, especially in the Baptist denomination, have no doubt involved themselves in great criminality, by neglecting to provide properly for the temporal support of their pastors; but does charity and truth forbid us to suppose, that this may often have been permitted by the Lord, as a just, though painful retribution to ministers for their worldly-mindedness and want of faith. They often complain of the churches, but in all cases are they certain that by faith, by enduring hardness as good soldiers, by a reasonable and patient continuance, by a prayerful, hearty, and entire devotion to their work, they have proved what the churches would do for their support, or rather, what the Lord, in his faithfulness and love, would do for them ? Can there be any doubt but what, if our young brethren would bring to their work more of that zeal, and energy, and "*martyr spirit*," which characterized the labors of apostolic days, and which Christ requires of all his ministers, and cast themselves upon the promises of God, and the Christian generosity of their brethren, a more ample and certain support might be expected ? The labors of such ministers would be valued and sought for; such devoted servants would be esteemed very highly in love for their work's sake; and the churches, being abundantly comforted and edified by their ministrations, might be reasonably expected, in return, to communicate more liberally of their temporal supplies. Are all those, who have made experiments and failed, certain that they have made "*a fair trial?*" Are they certain that they have not made it with "*a half-hearted kind of faith?*" When a minister is too soon discouraged, distrusts the Lord, and distrusts his brethren, and, to provide for his temporal wants, hastily, and incautiously encumbers himself with those wordly cares, which leave but a fragment of his time, and heart, and hands, for the duties of his calling, is it strange that his church, or churches, half-taught, half-disciplined, should fall into error on their part, and by their parsimonious policy, at last rivet permanently upon his hands, those fetters, which, in part at least, he had prepared for himself? There is no doubt a double fault: the ministers are in fault; the churches are in fault; and it becomes both churches and ministers to bemoan the evil which exists, and seriously inquire into the causes which have produced it, and the remedies by which it might be healed.

But to return to Mr. Mercer and his churches. It would be improper to close this chapter without saying something of the estimation in which he was held amongst the people where he labored. On this subject, facts would justify the use of the strongest expressions. Never was a minister more immoveably rooted in the respect, confidence, and affection of his people. There were many like the Galatians, who would have been ready, as it were, to have plucked out their eyes and given them to him; though, unlike the Galatians, their good will and devotion endured to the end. To all classes of the community he was an object of deep interest. Childhood and youth looked up to him with filial awe; manhood and old age were ever ready to do him honor. The wise regarded him with admiration; whilst the most illiterate could see enough in him to revere and love. Though he was a terror to evil doers, yet the profligate and profane, who would stand abashed in his presence, or even hide themselves from his view as he passed along the streets, would speak of him in terms of exalted commendation. Nor was it strange that all this should be so. Such an exhibition as he made, for a long series of years, of high intellectual power, sound, discriminating judgment, engaging and amiable virtues, strict and unbending integrity in all his dealings with men, and above all, of sincere, honest, and undeviating devotion to the cause of his Divine Master, would naturally secure to him the position which he occupied in the hearts of his brethren, and the estimation of his fellow-citizens at large. He had his faults, and he had his enemies; but the former were small in comparison with his virtues; and the latter could never dislodge him from the affection and confidence of the people. The following extracts from a letter written by one of his intimate friends, on hearing a report of Mr. Mercer's death, (which, however, soon proved to be erroneous) may serve as an illustration of the respect and attachment which were felt for him by those who knew him best.

"*New-York, 25th Aug.*, 1819.
"Reuben T. Battle, Esq.,

"*My Dear Friend :*—On Monday last * * * I received from my son G. the melancholy tidings of the death of Rev. Jesse Mercer. I have one, and only one method, by which I can communicate my feelings on this awfully solemn and melancholy occasion, which is by referring you to your own feelings on the memorable 7th August, 1819, when this great herald of his Master—the faithful pastor of the church of *Christ*—the sincere and unassuming Christian—the lovely, loving and beloved friend—the kind and manly husband—the friendly neighbor—the sound and punctual dealer—your and my particular friend, made his exit from this world of sorrow and misery, to inhabit that heavenly mansion which his blessed Saviour had prepared for him. * * We know not how to estimate a blessing but by its loss. Oh, my dear Reuben, how shall we sustain the stroke! New-York, and all the beauties of the north, are to me *now* worse than blanks: my Mercer is gone! Oh, how often did his expressive eyes, (now sealed in death,) swim in tears, giving evidence of the ardor of his soul, whilst his humble and plaintive voice, with indescribable pathos, strongly supplicated the throne of grace for my poor soul, and the souls of my dear family, that we might be partakers of those invaluable blessings, which he himself so richly enjoyed. * * *

"I am anxious to see Powelton and its inhabitants; but oh, what shall I do, Mercer is gone! The great Head of his church surely has a controversy with his people, or he would not so soon have called his servant home. Oh, my friend, what shall we do, our Mercer is gone! I shall leave this now dreary city

to-morrow. My respects to poor Mrs. Mercer and your family, Dr. Battle, and other friends.
"Yours, truly,
"Isaiah Tucker."

"*Philadelphia,* 28*th Aug.* 1819.
"Dear Sir :—

"After having written the preceding lines in New-York, I concluded to come on and put it in the P. O. here. Dr. Holcombe shows me a letter from Frances, three days after date of Germain's, and mentions a report contradicting that of Mercer's death, but that his physicians had given him over. Oh, my heart trembles in suspense; but my hope is small indeed. I have written on to Germain to strew the road before me with letters, that I may be in possession of facts as soon as possible.
"Yours, I. T."

CHAPTER V.

Mr. Mercer's labors on his journeys from home, at Associations, &c.—Circulates useful books.—His Cluster.—Extracts from his Correspondence.—His relation to political affairs.

In estimating the extent and value of Mr. Mercer's ministerial labors, we are by no means to confine our attention to those bestowed upon his churches, and regions immediately contiguous. The destitution of more distant communities called forth his benevolent and useful exertions, and often, either in company with other zealous preachers, or by himself, he would make lengthy excursions, proclaiming with great power the gospel of the kingdom. He not only travelled extensively in his own state, but often extended his routes into neighboring states. There has already been an allusion to his visit to North Carolina in company with his father. Most of the year 1799 he spent in travelling and preaching in the states of South Carolina, North Carolina and Virginia. On this tour he travelled upwards of three thousand miles. He also visited the city of Charleston once or twice, preached with much acceptance to the people, and was much gratified with the Christian intercourse he there enjoyed with his Baptist brethren.

Besides attending the annual meetings of the Georgia Association, and the State Convention, he was in the habit of visiting regularly, for several years, the Hephzibah, Sarepta, and Ocmulgee Associations, and occasionally several others in the state, and in South Carolina. On his way to these bodies, as well as on his return, he generally preached from place to place, always ready to embrace every opportunity to unfold the excellency of the glorious gospel of Jesus Christ. The great respect which was everywhere entertained for his Christian and ministerial character, generally secured large and attentive congregations; and there are multitudes still living, who cherish, with peculiar delight, the remembrance of these occasional visits.

At the annual meetings of these various religious bodies, he might be said truly to magnify his office, as a zealous and able minister of the New Testament. They were occasions well calculated to warm his affections, to arouse his intellectual powers, and unlock his rich store-house of Christian experience and scriptural knowledge. There would he often meet some of the aged veterans, with whom he had been associated in the trials, and toils, and sacrifices of his youthful ministry. There would he find himself surrounded by many, who, in times past, had been convicted under his preaching, or conducted by him to the Saviour's feet, or comforted by him in some season of peculiar affliction, or ushered by his kind and fatherly attentions into the ministry, or had received some other spiritual benefit from his stated or occasional ministrations. There also would be many, who had been familiar, from childhood, with the name of Jesse Mercer, but had never before been permitted to gaze upon his venerated form, and who were more anxious to hear something from his lips than from those of any other minister living. Though he sought not the highest seat, yet the respect and affection of his brethren, generally assigned it to him; he was almost invariably appointed to preach when he would have an opportunity of addressing the largest congregations. At such times, he would select some weighty doctrinal theme, or perhaps a subject that would lead him to discuss the merits of some of the leading benevolent operations of the age; and cheered by the countenances of his brethren, and roused by the presence of a vast and attentive assemblage, he would bring to his work the thoroughly awakened strength of his devout affections, and his original and powerful mind, and pour forth his instructions with such clearness and force of argument, and with such sweet and tender pathos, as seldom failed to make a deep and lasting impression upon the assembled multitude. These occasions were highly valued by his ministering brethren; and those preachers must have made great advancement in the knowledge of divine things, who were not the wiser at the conclusion of his discourses. They were often entertained with such a lucid illustration of deep and difficult subjects, such a masterly exposure of error, such a satisfactory solution of perplexing cases of conscience, such a rich and delightful exposition of Christian experience, as could hardly fail to increase their store of scriptural knowledge, give a fresh impulse to their investigations, suggest new and profitable trains of thought, and thus tend greatly to benefit them in their subsequent ministerial labors. Few preachers could be named, who, in this way, have exerted a more powerful influence upon the minds of other ministers; and it is through this channel that we are to search for much of the lasting and greatly extended usefulness of Mr. Mercer.

In 1817 he attended the General Convention in Philadelphia, travelling through the Atlantic states in his own carriage, and preaching very frequently both going and returning. He also attended the meetings of that body in 1820, 1826, and 1835.

By the appointment of the General Convention, he and Mr. Sherwood, in 1823, visited the Valley Towns Mission Station in North Carolina. His wife accompanied him, as she did on many of his journeys; and their carriage passed over hills and mountains, which had never before witnessed such a conveyance. Whilst at the Valley Towns, Mr. Mercer had an opportunity of preaching to the Indians, through an interpreter.

In making an estimate of the ministerial labors of Mr. Mercer, we must not omit the vast amount of service which he rendered at ministers' meetings, at the ordination of ministers, the constitution of churches, the anniversaries of various benevolent societies, and the almost numberless protracted and general meetings, which he attended during his long and luminous career of more than half a century. On all such occasions, his presence and aid were most highly valued, and the salutary influence of his prayers and instructions uniformly felt.

Auxiliary to these labors, he was in the habit, for many years, of keeping on hand a small assortment of useful religious works, such as Fuller's, Buck's, Life of Mrs. Judson, &c., which he carried with him on his numerous preaching tours, and sold to such as could be induced to purchase. In this way, he encouraged amongst his brethren a taste for useful reading, and brought into circulation a large number of valuable publications.

Finding a great want of hymn books for the use of the rapidly increasing churches, he compiled a small work called the "*Cluster*." This work was first published, unbound, in Augusta: subsequently two more editions were published in the same place, which were bound; amounting in all to two thousand five hundred copies. Whilst attending the General Convention, in 1817, in Philadelphia, he published a revised edition of two thousand five hundred copies, and had the copyright secured. Editions were also published in 1820, 1826, and 1835. In this hymn book are to be found many valuable hymns, with other pieces less interesting: with some imperfections, it has, nevertheless, had an extensive circulation in many parts of Georgia, Alabama, and Mississippi, and has comforted the hearts and animated the devotions of thousands of the saints of God. The work contains several hymns of his own composition, not, however, greatly distinguished for their poetical excellence; for neither nature nor art ever bestowed upon Mr. Mercer the attributes of a poet.

The following is inserted as a favorable specimen of the few hymns which Mr. Mercer composed. It appears in the Cluster as the second part of the 235th hymn:

"Resolving thus, I entered in,
    Though trembling and depressed;
I bowed before the gracious King,
    And all my sins confessed.

"Sweet majesty and awful grace,
    Sat smiling on his brow;
He turned to me his glorious face,
    And made my eyes o'erflow.

"He held the sceptre out to me,
    And bade me touch and live;
I touched, and (O, what mercy free!)
    He did my sins forgive.

"I touched and lived, and learned to love,
    And triumphed in my God;
I set my heart on things above,
    And sang redeeming blood.

"Come, sinners grieved, with sins distressed,
    And ready to despair,
Take courage, though with guilt oppressed,
    Jesus still answers prayer.

"Come enter in with cheerful haste;
    You may his glory see;
You may his richest mercy taste—
    He has forgiven ME."

Some extracts from Mr. Mercer's correspondence will now be introduced. They are selected from the letters which bear the earliest date of any that have fallen into the biographer's hands; and one or two of these will form a very natural connexion with the foregoing sketch of his ministerial labors, as they bring to view his sentiments on some of the leading doctrines of the gospel, and his method of meeting the inquiries and difficulties of individuals in a state of concern about their salvation. The writer would here beg leave to observe, once for all, that there is but little in the letters of Mr. Mercer to gratify the wishes of the critical and fastidious: they are generally written in the most unaffected style, not always with perfect grammatical correctness; in the main, presenting a just and fair reflection of the plain, simple, transparent character of their author. Most of those, which will appear in this volume, it is believed will be acceptable, at least to his numerous surviving friends and acquaintances; as these memorials will tend to revive, in a pleasing and impressive manner, their recollections of one whom they so much revered and loved.

The following letter was addressed to a distant friend, who, in a state of religious anxiety, had sought his counsel:

"*Grantsville, Green Co., Ga., May* 17, 1815.
" My dear Sir :—

"According to agreement, I received your very interesting introductory communication, when at Washington last, and have duly weighed its contents; and now sit down to make an effort to comply with my promise. May the Lord bless it to your instruction and comfort. You have shown that you have already an improved knowledge in the things which belong to the kingdom of God, and a fervid desire for the righteousness thereof. But still you desire me to direct you into a proper understanding of the gospel. In order to a proper view of the gospel way of salvation, 'tis necessary to entertain just and adequate notions of the state of sinful nature from which it delivers, and which makes it necessary. In sinning against God, we have violated his law and come short of his glory, Rom. 3 : 23 ;—are obnoxious to divine wrath, and abhorrent to holiness, Rom. 1 : 13, and on ;—and liable to everlasting banishment as our just desert, 2 Thes. 1 : 9. Ps. 28 : 4. Ezek. 7 : 27. This sentence of severe condemnation must be acknowledged just, not only as it is legal, but as it is an effort of divine justice to vindicate its own holiness against the total want of it in us. From this view of the case, the loss of the sinner seems inevitable. But God, who is rich in mercy, according to his great love towards us, when we were dead in sin, hath abounded towards us in all wisdom, and prudence, according to his eternal purpose in Christ, through whose blood we have redemption—the forgiveness of our sins.

"Such was the nature of our offence, that it required an infinite satisfaction, or the satisfaction of an infinite Being; therefore, it became him who should interpose, to be allied to us, and yet possess infinite capacities. God hath laid help on one that is mighty to save, in sending Christ Jesus into the world for this purpose; he being verily our kinsman, yet possessing the fulness of the Godhead bodily, was able to render the violated law such obedience and sufferings as it required, and to give them such vicarious merit as should be satisfactory to injured, infinite justice; and so to bring in an everlasting righteousness for the justification of the ungodly, which a just and holy God could not do without such a righteousness, to render him justified in the act. Compare Dan. 9 : 24. with Rom. 1 : 17. 3 : 26. and 10 : 4. God accounting us in Christ, makes him to us wisdom, righteousness, sanctification and redemption. *Wisdom*, whereby we know our danger and remedy:—*righteousness*, whereby we are acquitted from guilt according to law :—*sanctification*, whereby we are renewed, and saved from the damning nature of sin ;—*redemption*, whereby our sins are forgiven, and we receive the spirit of adoption in our hearts, crying *Abba, Father.* 1 Cor. 1 : 30. (Compare Rom. Rom. 3 : 19, 20, with John 17 : 3. Acts. 13 : 39. Ezek. 36 : 25, 26. 1 Cor. 6 : 11. Titus 3 : 5. Eph. 1 : 7. Titus 2 : 14.) All this Jesus Christ is to him that believeth; not to him that has any kind of faith, but to him whose faith is the *fruit of the Spirit—the gracious gift of God.* Gal. 5 : 22. Eph. 2 : 8.

"You desire me to explain to you your difficult situation, and to give you counsel therein. This I will endeavor to do. You seem to yourself to have the requisite *faith* in Christ, and to be *humble* and *sincere* in prayer, and yet to be without *grace*, which *staggers* you. You seem, notwithstanding your faith and other virtuous exercises, to be barred from the *mercy* by the *justice* of God, which has excited wonder. This too has produced the embarrassment from the doctrine of election, of which you speak. Now, my dear sir, all this arises from a misapplication of these *exercises* and *virtues.* 'Tis the common opinion of mankind, that when they become believers in

Christ, and make an humble, penitent, and sincere application for grace, *it will follow*. But it never was intended of God, that salvation should follow these as a *cause*, or *condition*. If it did as a *cause*, then these would supersede the necessity of the merits of Christ; if as a *condition*, then salvation would be uncertain, if not impossible, because men could really perform no such condition. Besides, such a plan would make the sinner a partner in his salvation, and share the honor of it with God, who is ever jealous of his glory, and will not give it to another.

"The light of God has, I hope, so shone into your heart, as to convince you that these are insufficient, and will lead you to know that they are not the *reason*, but the *evidence* of hope, when they exist in their proper degree, to which yours have not yet come. Your faith, '*good*' as it is, has not yet appropriated the Saviour whom it has apprehended, and therefore leaves you without comfort. The light of nature, or a legal spirit, will endeavor to set you down securely on your present faith and duties; but an enlightened conscience will never be satisfied without the sprinkling of the blood of Jesus, who only can take away sins. When you are enabled to come to God in your true, though humbling character as a sinner, *publican-like*, you will cease to inquire 'whether such prayers as yours can be heard,' or whether any of your exercises may be acceptable; for then your eyes, *your dying eyes* will be turned to Christ, from whose expiatory sacrifice all pleas for acceptance will be sought and found. Then election will open to your view in a new and striking light, a glorious door of hope. You will have been brought to see the utter inapplicability of the conditional plan to you, who can neither fulfil the law in works nor faith, and of course your thoughts on such a plan, can only go out to meet *despair*. But in God's eternal purpose you will see the *means* as well as the *ends* alike finished. Here God designs to show mercy to those who seem least to deserve it; and provides salvation for those who have neither money nor price to obtain it. Ps. 68 : 18. Isa. 55 : 1. Examine the beatitudes in Matt. 5th chapter. Notice to whom the promises apply the provisions of the gospel. The *dead, sick, poor, heavy-laden, ungodly,* and *lost*. To one brought into these characters by the quickening spirit, the sovereign and free grace of God opens the only sovereign remedy, and anchor of hope.

" *My counsel is* that you search the scriptures, (John 5 : 39. 2 Tim. 3 : 15, 16.) and attend on the word preached in order to obtain a spiritual understanding. Here you will have pointed out to you your true character, danger and remedy, with all their attendant qualities and consequences.

" *Be instant in prayer*. Not with any view to the virtue of the exercise, but with a due regard to the invaluable worth and indispensable demand of the blessing God may be pleased to afford in answer to it. The nature of the case will suggest the propriety of self-denial, or the forsaking all known sins. But the alarmed conscience, newly roused from its security and negligence, cries out *what shall I do?* The instruction afforded in the case of Saul is in point, Acts 9 : 6; compare 16 : 30, 31. Instruction is necessary to show our right in privileges and duties, lest we offend in the deeds we design should please. As to your baptism, the propriety of it depends on the nature and degree of your faith; whenever it removes from your conscience *the guilt of sin*, by appropriating the merits of Christ, by which the justice of God ceases to bar the mercy off, and gives you an evidence of interest in divine favor; then, and not till then, it will be proper for you to give the outward sign. An examination of the scriptures, (a list of which you request me to give,) on this subject will afford direction in the pathway of duty, and enable you by the blessing of God to act with propriety. Matt. 3 chap. Mark 16 : 16. Acts 8 : 12, 37. Rom. 6 : 3, 4. Col. 2 : 11, 12. Heb. 10 : 32, is thought to refer to baptism; if so, it shows the proper time of the duty. 1 Pet. 3 : 21. with many other texts to the same effect, spread over the New Testament.

"And now, my dear sir, the goodness of God in Christ Jesus is your only sovereign balm, and his spirit is the physician. And blessed be his adorable name! he is free, infinitely free in his applications. I hope and pray, if ere this reaches you, you have not obtained a sense of his favor, you will soon be brought into the liberty of the sons of God, when the justice of God will, instead of barring you off, lead you to the love, mercy, and goodness of God, and be the principle of your safety and confidence. And believe me, I am, as I have been and ever shall be,

" Yours in the gospel of Jesus Christ our Lord.
"JESSE MERCER."

The following letter without date, but probably written about the same time with the preceding, was addressed to a female friend who was somewhat concerned upon the subject of religion.

"Dear Madam—Some time since the few times I have seen you, I have suggested to myself that there was a seriousness on your countenance indicative of some inward anxiety, and it was most easy to me to suppose it to be about the state of your soul, and the concerns of eternity. I thought of writing to you, but this seemed rather bold. I therefore hesitated. I inquired of your friend Mrs. G., who said you were solicitous to know of religion and its attainment. On stepping in the other day on the very friendly invitation of Mr. S., and finding you somewhat indisposed, and of a solemn though inviting countenance, I determined, and have set down, to address a few thoughts to you on the subject of *the religion of Jesus.*

"Now, madam, of all the subjects in the world, this is doubtless the most important. *Be it false,* and we are without hope. *Be it true,* and it is the only hope. *It is serious any how.* This subject, as it is revealed in the scriptures, proceeds on the consideration of man's being totally lost and ruined in sin, i. e. that he is by nature under the law and curse of God, and so under the sentence of eternal destruction; which is the case of not this and that wicked man [only,] but even of us all indiscriminately. That such is our state under the moral government of God, universal death and the terrors we feel on the approaches of eternity, will fully testify; together with an almost endless variety of circumstances, the concomitants of living in this miserable world of sin, which will agree to no other state of things. But what shall we do to be saved? is the question.

"Why, madam, indeed if it were not for the gospel of Jesus Christ, we should be at so profound a loss, as for ever to be unable to answer this question in any way satisfactory to a troubled mind, which, enveloped in thick darkness, must have yielded to desperation under its guilt, without a gleam of hope. But in the gospel, life and immortality break forth, as from the blackest night, in all the effulgence of noon-day glory. Here we see the Son of God clothed in our nature, *the nature that sinned*, for the express purpose of doing what we ought to have done, and what was indispensably necessary to be done in order to salvation. And now, through him is preached to us the forgiveness of sins, and by him, all that *believe*, are justified from all things which they could not by the law, which by sin had become the administration of death only. To believe this to the saving of the soul, is the fruit of the spirit of grace, bringing us to know God in his *glorious justice;* and Christ in his satisfaction (arising from the works of his life, and the sufferings of his death) so as to deliver the burdened conscience from guilt and terror, restoring to us an inward peace with God, through our Lord Jesus Christ; and giving a comfortable hope of acceptance into glory. This will at first excite deep, inward, and heart-breaking views of our sinfulness, in relation to God, and unworthiness of his mercy; and bring us to acknowledge the justness of the divine conduct towards us in condemnation. It will next lead to desires or hungerings and thirstings for salvation, in some way which may be consistent with the law and justice of God. When it is made known that this is all done in Christ, the soul then looks to him as the only true way to eternal life, with ardent desire, and constant prayer to God for an interest in him, till it pleases God to afford the poor soul the power of believing, or trusting in, and receiving from Christ, a full discharge from his guilt and fears. Then he rejoices as a redeemed prisoner, loves God as his heavenly Father, blesses Christ as his Redeemer, friend, and brother, has a strong affection for the saints, or such as appear to be real Christians, and is desirous above all things, to live in the favor, and according to the pleasure of God, till death; and then hopes to be happy with him to all eternity.

"How far, dear madam, you have realized these things, is a tender point between God and your own soul. Believe me, your soul is the most precious jewel you have in all your store, and its salvation the most important of all your concernments. I think you have [made], do, and will make, these topics your study and prayer, and will never give over till God give, by his Spirit, an inward evidence of your forgiveness, and acceptance through Jesus Christ. And I do, and if God will give the Spirit, will pray that you may, with *your dear Mr. S.*, be successful, and obtain that salvation, which is made and provided of God in Christ for sinners lost and undone. Then you will be blessed here, and happy yonder for ever.

"Pardon, dear madam, the liberty I take in addressing this to you, and believe me, I am most cordially

"Yours, in the gospel of our Lord Jesus Christ,

"JESSE MERCER."

TO MRS. T., OF VIRGINIA.

"*Powelton, July* 6, 1819.

"MY DEAR SISTER:—

"I little thought, when I left you and dear Mr. T. in the road, that it would be almost two years before I should write to so interesting and distant friends; but so it is. I have thought from time to time I would set about it, and give a long letter to my beloved sister in the Lord; but still have delayed, partly for want of heart-cheering matter, and partly for want of time and resolution to begin a letter.

"Well, now I have begun; but O what a heart of barrenness I have! What shall I tell, what shall I write, to afford my sister any comfort, or to animate her afflicted and distressed soul? Why, let me lead her views to the *Rock* that is higher than she—the Rock of ages—the precious, tried, and of course, *sure* foundation for a sinking sinner—the only shelter for one exposed to the flood of divine vengeance. But in this cleft the sinner, the chief of sinners, may be safe and happy; yea, when 'deluges of *fiery* wrath shall drown the world, he may, with a serene soul and dauntless courage, stand and see the last catastrophe of the wicked. 'Tis a consolation to contemplate, when all outward good is perishing under the common pressure, when flesh and heart are failing, and even time and nature dying, that there is an undecaying substance, an unfailing fulness, and a treasure that fadeth not away, reserved in heaven for those who love, and look for, the coming of our Lord Jesus Christ. I hope my sister is training up for glory by the successive afflictions she wades through.

'For I reckon that the sufferings of the present time are not worthy to be compared with the glory which shall be revealed in us.' *Glory therefore in tribulations also.*

"Religion is in a low degree with us, but I trust there are a few names even amongst us, who shall be counted worthy to walk with the dear Emmanuel in *white.* I would indulge the hope of better times with you.

* * * * * * * *

"Give wife's sweetest affections with mine to Mr. T., and other friends with whom we formed any acquaintance in Orange. And be assured of our most affectionate and pious wishes for yourself."

The following extracts are from a letter to Rev. B. Manly, a short portion of which, on ministerial support, appears on a preceding page:

"*Powelton, Nov.* 13, 1825.

"MY VERY DEAR BROTHER:

"I was quite pleased with the obtrusion of your 'poor thoughts' on me, which I found waiting for me in the office on my return home last. The time anticipated between us, when last together, of passing through Edgefield, was rather, I think, on my way up to the Saluda Association, than to the Convention: however, this was mostly on my mind, and I held it in contemplation till I was taken ill on a journey below Augusta, in June, when I despaired of my anticipated pleasure, and, as soon as I conveniently could, went up into Pendleton, where I might invigorate my health, and be ready to meet the Saluda Association. But in this I was disappointed also. Since that, my health has been quite uneven, and lately, worse. I am at this moment the captive of affliction. At the Sarepta Association, I became feverish, and ever since I have been the subject of increasing fever till I came to this place, Friday was a week ago. On Saturday, at our monthly meeting, I could scarcely preach; on Sabbath, I only served at the table. Monday, took an emetic, and have been, till now, in a state of *poor* convalescence, unable to get on the way of my appointments; and am therefore the Sabbath at home, *not*, I trust, *committing the sin which is unto death*, in answering my dear brother's kind and much esteemed letter; the writing of which, I am satisfied, was so far from being 'the sin unto death,' that it was no sin at all. Through the continuance of disease, and the frequent returns of fever, I am admonished of being 'near the margin, and just ready to pass the flood.'

"As to the opinion you have formed of my talents, *I thank you for it;* but I assure you, it is to me, what you so much regret as 'a discouraging and very disastrous fact,' and therefore must be excused in yielding a very *sparing* promise to your 'strong solicitude and desire.' I have, however, come to the determination, should God lengthen the days of the years of my pilgrimage, to become stationary, and to devote my time to reading and study, perhaps some to writing. But my talent for composition is *so poor*, that I have all along been kept back, and have done very little in that way. On some of the points you mention, I have had a *desire* to write at times; but seeing the many volumes written on all, I have held a strong rein on it.

* * * * * * *

"Your Convention may rely on a little aid from

Georgia; and I fear it will be but little. The death of Mr. Gillison and Dr. Furman, I fear will have a very appalling effect on the designs of that body. But if you can feel truly that the Lord of Hosts is with you, you may go forward, for you will be 'well able.' I should be happy, could I say in truth some fine things about religion among us; but I have no such news to send you. Some of my brethren in the new counties are baptizing goodly numbers, as I hear. I hope the Lord is affording you some joyful harvests in your fields of labor. Wife sends her christian affection to you and lady, which, with my own, you will receive in the same spirit, and pass mine over to your second self, and any of the dear brethren about Edgefield.—I have tired myself several times writing this letter; I hope you will not faint in reading. Pray for a *poor, old and declining man.* Farewell."

It will be seen from what has passed under the reader's notice, with what care and conscientiousness Mr. Mercer ever kept in mind the duties of his vocation, and brought all his plans into proper subordination to what he considered the great business of his life. It is much to be regretted, that occasionally, some of our venerable fathers in the gospel would become entangled in political affairs, and thus sustained much loss in their religious zeal and ministerial influence. Fortunately, through his long life, Mr. Mercer generally kept himself aloof from the strifes of party politics; though he did not consider himself excluded by the obligations of his sacred office, from the right of forming his own opinions of men and measures, and of expressing these opinions on proper occasions.

In 1798, he was a member of the convention which was appointed to amend the state constitution. His attendance in that body could not be condemned, as important, fundamental principles of government were to be settled, which would not only deeply affect the civil and political interests of the commonwealth, but might have a direct bearing on ecclesiastical affairs. The best talent and influence of the state were needed to give a wise and happy direction to the deliberations of that important body. It was moved, during the session of the convention, by one of the members who, it seems was a lawyer, that *ministers* be ineligible to the office of legislator, and the motion was warmly urged by both *lawyers* and *doctors*. Mr. Mercer moved so to amend the resolution, as that *lawyers* and *doctors* should be included. During an adjournment which ensued before the matter was adjusted, Mr. Mercer was visited by some of the members of the body, and urged to drop his amendment, as the projectors of the original motion had agreed to yield their ground. To this he assented.

About 1816, he was a candidate for the office of senator in the state legislature, but very fortunately it may be concluded, he was unsuccessful. For this defeat he seemed ever afterwards grateful. " This defeat, or something else," remarks Mr. Sherwood, " convinced him that but few occasions should call down ministers from their elevated office to engage in legislation. He did not wish to see them deprived by enactments, of their rights; yet thought only the most important crises should induce them to serve their country as political men. For a number of years he observed he had taken no part even in exercising the right of suffrage, for he said all parties had aberrated so far from the constitution, that he could not conscientiously vote for the candidates."

"A report went abroad in 1819, that he had drunk for a toast the 9th verse of the 109th Psalm, 'Let his days be few; and let another take his office,' and applied it to the governor. This gained credence, and actually soured the minds of many of his brethren; * * * but he said he had never *drunk a toast on any occasion.*"

It was, perhaps, in 1833 that some of his friends entertained a serious intention of bringing him before the people as a candidate for governor; he was consulted on the subject, but would not listen to any such proposal. Some time subsequent to this, he was named in some of the public prints as a suitable person to be chosen as one of the presidential electors; he refused, however, to accept of the nomination, and his name was withdrawn.

In 1833, a convention which had been previously summoned by the legislature, agreed upon certain amendments to the state constitution, and submitted the same to the people for their approval or rejection. Mr. Mercer regarded the occasion as one of peculiar importance, and in the exercise of what he regarded a sacred right, he published his reasons condemnatory of the proposed amendments. For this he was censured with some degree of severity. This reproach he met with the following reply: "In reference to the constitutional question which was proposed to the people, (and to us as well as others,) for their approval or otherwise, we did assign our reasons for not ratifying the proposed amendments of the constitution, and permitted them to be circulated; and for this we have been held up to public contempt. As it regards our single self, we care little for it; but as an effort *to control* the elective franchise, or *to disturb* the freedom of speech, we denounce it as highly un-republican and proscriptive. We do not at all approve of ministers of the gospel tampering with the every-day politics of the country; yet on constitutional questions, we regard it not only their right, but their indispensable duty, as public sentinels, to be on their watchtower, and guard every article, section, and sentence of that great and only palladium of our civil and religious privileges."

CHAPTER VI.

Death of Mrs. Mercer.—Mr. Mercer removes to Washington.—A church constituted there.—His second marriage.—Editorial labors.—The degree of D. D. conferred on him.—Letters to various individuals.

Mr. Mercer delayed his return from the General Convention in 1826, till the month of September. As he was passing through the upper part of South Carolina, his estimable and devoted wife was brought low by disease, and on the 23d of the above named month, was called home to her heavenly rest, at Andersonville, Pendleton district, in the fifty-fifth year of her age.* For nearly forty years, she had been the sharer

* By his first wife, Mr. Mercer had two children. They were both daughters, and were both called Miriam. The first died in King and Queen county, Virginia, Sept. 21st, 1799, aged nine months and twenty-one days. The other died in Green county, Georgia, December 15th, 1814, aged nine years and eight months. "I was present," says his uncle, "several times during the illness of the second, and was also at the burial. He evidently felt deeply, but did not shed a tear."

of his joys and sorrows; and the stroke that terminated their long and happy union, was to the survivor, a most heavy affliction. But those abundant consolations and supports, to which he, as an affectionate and faithful minister, had so often pointed the sorrowful and bereaved, were present for his own relief in this the hour of his calamity—he calmly yielded, for the Lord, his best Friend, had done it.

Subjoined is an extract from a letter to Dr. Lucius Bolles, of Salem, Mass., dated Powelton, October 4th, 1826, in which there is an affecting allusion to the death of his wife, and other afflictions.

"I must close by informing you of the melancholy manner in which I returned home. I seemed to myself like a vessel which had been a long voyage, had met with rude winds and waves, but had rode them all till just coming into port, [when] a storm rose and carried her mainmast, ribboned her rigging, and caused her *precious* lading to be cast forth into the sea, and she comes to her moorings only with a *shattered* hull. Yes, brother, the influenza hung to me and rent me sore in the spring, and other things of a minor consideration made my journey unpleasant. But when I had gained the sight once more of the shore of Georgia, on the banks of the Tugulo river, the bilious fever set hard on Mrs. Mercer, and on the eighth day, say 23d of September, she fell in death. But joyful in hope, she never yielded to fear. I was taken on the day of her interment, and have returned home, contending with the fever; but I have gotten the victory. I am able to sit up and write through mercy. Sickness prevails to an alarming degree, even in the more healthy parts. I hope the Lord will be with you and bless you. Love to Sister B. and the brethren. Farewell in the Lord."

In the following letter to a Christian sister, there is also some reference to the death of Mrs. Mercer:

"*Sister L————'s, Jan.* 14, 1827.

"My very dear Sister in the Lord:—

"With much pleasure I received yours yesterday, by Brother Green. My feelings were grieved at our last meeting, because it was so slight. I was busy when you came up, and while I was talking to several about me, lo, you were gone! I looked for you, *but found you not.* I know not when I shall see you. I, with you, *would mourn* over the sad state of Zion. I think really we are generally in a sad state of decline. How all is *precisely* at Countyline, I know not, but fear all has not been right at any time since the times of trouble on account of Thomy.* Truly we may adopt the petition of the Syrophenician woman, for all our help is in the Lord—in the Lord alone. When I can come to Countyline I know not; and fear now to come, for I am of the impression, from what took place at Phillips', sundry would not be pleased in my company. This I say *in confidence.* But this may be a false impression. I fear the brethren are not of a good spirit; but the Lord can remove all evils, both outward and inward. Let us seek unto the Lord, and unto the Lord commit our cause.

"I am now poor and needy, the Lord having desolated me in a melancholy widowhood. I hope to share in the prayers of my brethren, that I may live the remnant of my days in a manner suited to promote the good of our Jerusalem, and His glory whom I hope I serve, and whose I trust I am. I would be glad to write you a full history of my dear departed

* Thomas Rhodes.

wife's last exercises. Truly the Lord had mercy on her, and not on her only, but on me also. I have great reason to be thankful that she was enabled to triumph over death with all his terrors. She sunk in calm repose without a struggle or a groan. Truly, she never yielded to fear. She was very much racked with pain in her affliction, and I feared she would have a hard struggle in death; but she had a *soothed passage*, and left a smoothed countenance, rather lovely in death than otherwise. She wished to be remembered to all her friends in Georgia, and though she was cut off from the expected pleasure of seeing them in this life, she [said that she] would soon meet them in a better world, where she would more enjoy them than she could here. She had the songs sung, "Jerusalem, my happy home," and "How happy's every child of grace;" and wished, when she knew herself dying, "The Consolation in Affliction" to be sung, but no one could sing it to her. I read it to her; she seemed to make it all her own. It is, "In the floods of Tribulation." You may see all these in the Cluster, and read them, and remember her that was dear unto you, and by whom your affection was reciprocated. Remember me to Mr. C. I long for his salvation. If any brethren in Countyline would be glad to hear from me, in your opinion, mention to them my poor name, and request their prayers to God for me. Let me ever share in your effusions before the throne in secret."

From a remark in his letter to Mr. Manly, which the reader has already noticed in the preceding chapter, it would seem that Mr. Mercer was beginning to reflect seriously upon the propriety of confining his labors to a more circumscribed sphere. Being now about fifty-seven years old, it was to be expected that he would begin to feel the approaching infirmities of age, especially as his natural force had much abated under the influence of disease. The arduous labors which he had so long encountered, and most of the time without injury, were now too much for his declining strength; and he found an additional motive for giving up his itinerant mode of living, in the desire he had to increase, by reading and study, his store of scriptural knowledge.

It was at the close of 1826, or very early in 1827, that Mr. Mercer took up his residence in Washington, Wilkes county. The circumstances under which he determined to settle at this place, were such as afforded a very striking illustration of his disinterestedness, and his conscientious adherence to his convictions of duty. When his purpose was fully matured to give up most of his churches, and provide for himself a more settled residence, the Powelton brethren, to whom he was most ardently attached, and by whom his affection was fully reciprocated, appointed a committee to wait on him for the purpose, if possible, to secure his permanent settlement with them. They were fully authorized to say to him, that if he would yield to their wishes in this respect, his temporal support should be provided for. It would seem that comfort, interest, and his strong personal attachments, would have dictated a ready compliance. In Washington, there was, as yet, no Baptist Church in existence; his ministerial services had been less appreciated in that community than in any place where he had ever labored, and no inducement was offered in relation to pecuniary support. And yet the impression was deeply riveted on his mind, that *there* the

Lord would have him take up his abode. The question of *duty* being settled in his mind, nothing remained for him but a ready and cheerful compliance. For nearly forty years previous to Mr. Mercer's settlement in Washington, he had been in the habit of preaching in that place, generally on week days, about once a month. The house usually occupied for divine service, was an old brick academy, which stood near the dwelling where Mr. Mercer resided after his second marriage. There were a few scattering Baptists in the village and the immediate vicinity, yet not enough to justify the organization of a church until 1827. In March of this year, a branch of the Phillips' Mill Church was established at Washington; a commodious house of worship was so far completed by April, as to accommodate the meeting of the Baptist State Convention; and on the 29th of December following, a church was constituted, consisting of ten members. James Armstrong, B. M. Sanders, J. L. Brooks, (with some other ministers,) were the officiating Presbytery. On the 20th of January, 1828, Mr. Mercer was called to the pastoral charge of this infant church. This call was accepted, and he continued its faithful and much beloved pastor until death.

Under the ministry of Mr. Mercer, this church gradually increased in numbers, zeal and efficiency. In 1832, it numbered forty-nine members; in 1835, sixty-three; in 1840, the year previous to Mr. Mercer's death, eighty-seven. In active benevolence, this little band, during the lifetime of Mr. Mercer, presented an example which has seldom been surpassed by any church in the denomination. In 1835, the church, (assisted by some of the liberal members of the congregation,) sent up to the Georgia Association, for various benevolent purposes, the sum of *six hundred* dollars; and for five successive years, their annual contributions were of the most liberal character. It must be remembered, that these amounts were principally gathered from a small number of contributors. A portion of the church were colored members, who had but little, if any thing, to give; and of the white members, there were not many whose circumstances would justify very ample donations.

Mr. Mercer's general method at Washington for raising money was this: he prepared a subscription paper and put it in his pocket. As he passed about amongst the members of his church and congregation, he presented it personally to such as he judged proper persons to be applied to, allowing each one that subscribed to designate the particular benevolent object to which he wished his money to be appropriated. At a suitable time the individuals were again called on for the payment of the amounts thus pledged. Some such plan as this, Mr. Mercer greatly preferred to the precarious method, mainly relied on by many of the churches, of having an occasional missionary discourse, and then two or three old hats passed rapidly through the congregation to receive the little, scanty change, which might happen accidentally to be in their pockets. Many persons, that might satisfy their consciences by throwing twenty-five, or fifty cents, into the deacon's hat, when personally approached with a subscription paper, would put down from five to twenty dollars.

On the 11th of December, 1827, Mr. Mercer was united in marriage to Mrs. Nancy Simons, widow of

Captain A. Simons, deceased, and then residing in Washington. His last marriage brought a considerable increase to his worldly possessions, and that he might not be needlessly encumbered by secular cares, most of this property was sold, and the proceeds thrown into such investments, as would yield him a reasonable income, with the least possible inconvenience and anxiety to himself.

Mr. Mercer considered himself truly fortunate in his last marriage. His second companion was no less devoted to his wishes and happiness than the first; possessing a spirit of unbounded liberality, she entered heartily into all his benevolent plans for the advancement of the Redeemer's kingdom, and was entirely willing that the avails of her large estate should be consecrated to pious purposes. How pleasant are such instances of conjugal unanimity in the blessed work of doing good. A more extended notice of Mrs. Mercer will be found in a subsequent part of this volume.

After Mr. Mercer's removal to Washington, he found himself placed in circumstances, in many respects, suited to his declining years; yet he did not feel at liberty to sit down in slothful inactivity, and be satisfied with any effort in behalf of the cause of Christ, less than what his health and strength would justify. Besides supplying the church at Phillips' Mill once a month, and the one at Washington the rest of the time, he continued to attend the anniversaries of the most important bodies of the denomination, and many occasional religious meetings in various regions; preaching as he had been wont to do on the way from place to place, and wherever he went, cheering his brethren by his sweet and heavenly deportment, and imparting to them in the pulpit, and in their public deliberations, and in the social circle, the fruits of his matured wisdom.

His pen was now employed in keeping up a more regular correspondence with his brethren on matters pertaining to the interests of Zion, and in the occasional preparation for the press of essays on important subjects.

In 1833, the Christian Index, which had been edited for several years by the Rev. W. T. Brantly, at Philadelphia, with the approval of the Baptist Board of Foreign Missions, under whose auspices the paper was first commenced at Washington City, and the desire of many brethren, was transferred to Mr. Mercer. This necessarily brought him into a new sphere of effort, and imposed on him much anxiety, labor, and responsibility. The purchase of an office, of a new press and suitable type, subjected him to the expense of between two and three thousand dollars; and from year to year the partial and tardy returns from his subscribers compelled him to sustain a considerable pecuniary loss.

The duties of an Editor were not very congenial with Mr. Mercer's taste and feelings: had he been more thoroughly drilled in the art of composing, and his previous habits been more decidedly literary, his task would have been less irksome; still, though laboring under some disadvantages, he was enabled to render his paper the vehicle of much useful, solid, religious instruction. The burden of his editorial cares was much lightened by the assistance of the Rev. W. H. Stokes, who for several years was associated with him as an assistant Editor.

His name and character gave much weight to his

editorial communications, and they generally contained much important thought, plainly, though often forcibly expressed. His reputation as a wise counsellor, able divine, and skilful expounder of the discipline of the church, brought to him from his numerous friends and correspondents, many queries upon a great variety of subjects pertaining to doctrine, duty, church, and associational affairs. These he generally answered in a sensible, judicious, and scriptural manner, and much to the satisfaction of candid, reflecting minds. Through the columns of his paper, the benevolent operations of the day were constantly urged and defended, and in meeting the various objections that have been urged from time to time against them, Mr. Mercer displayed a readiness, skill, and originality, that have seldom been surpassed.

For some time after the removal of the paper to Washington, its pages contained much controversial matter that was considered objectionable, particularly by the more distant subscribers; yet the peculiar condition of many of the churches and associations in the state rendered this almost unavoidable. Many important and vital questions arose, that it was important to have settled upon scriptural ground; discussion seemed absolutely necessary; and though there was often mingled with it a degree of severity and bitterness that could not be justified, yet in the result it was evident, that much light had been thrown upon subjects which had before been too imperfectly understood; and that many of the churches were settling down in a quiet, stable manner, upon more scriptural principles. In another chapter of this work, we shall have occasion to refer more particularly to this subject. .

The occasion for these unpleasant controversies

having in a good degree passed away, the pages of the paper assumed a more peaceful and inviting aspect, and yielded a larger space to important religious intelligence, and the discussion of such subjects as possessed more general interest.

In 1840, the Christian Index, with the press and all its appendages, was generously tendered by the proprietor to the Baptist State Convention: the liberal donation was accepted, and at the close of the year the paper was removed to Penfield, where it has since been published under the general supervision of the Executive Committee.

In 1835, the degree of D. D. was conferred on Mr. Mercer by the Board of Fellows of Brown University. The cordiality with which this honor was conferred, may be learned from a short extract from a letter from the Rev. Lucius Bolles to Mr. Mercer. "In relation to the *Degree*, I hope it may not be unpleasant. It has been in contemplation for two or three years as what *ought* to be done, provided the thing is proper in any case, and I assure you it was conferred with great cordiality; and for myself I can say, never with more pleasure." The sentiments of Mr. Mercer on the occasion, may be learned from an extract from a letter to Mr. Bolles, dated Sept. 24th, 1835; and from his letter to President Wayland, which immediately follows. "Another matter has turned up and given me some perplexity. The late act of the Fellows of Brown University, in conferring the degree of Doctor of Divinity *unanimously* on me, has *astounded* me. To receive the *meritless* [unmerited] honor, seems hardly just to myself and the cause; to refuse it is to hold in contempt the kind expression of the sense which my brethren of high standing entertain of my character and services. I am at a loss to determine. If I were in the vigor of life, I should surely refuse it; but as I am nearly worn out any how, it may be best to let it pass."

TO PRESIDENT WAYLAND.

"*Washington, Sept.* 25, 1835.

"REV. AND DEAR SIR

" I have the honor of acknowledging the receipt of yours of the 9th inst., informing me, 'that at the late meeting of the Board of Fellows of Brown University, the *Degree of Doctor of Divinity* was unanimously conferred upon me by that authority; and that the act was duly announced on Commencement day,' and that the same was addressed to me by you, ' in the hope that this testimonial of your (the Board's) respect for my character and services would be acceptable.'

" Now, my dear Sir, permit me, through you, to say to the Board of Fellows of Brown University, that, so far as it respects themselves, and all whose feelings, on this subject, may be in unison with theirs, for *this testimonial* of respect for my character and services, from so high an authority, I am grateful, and do accept it with all readiness of mind; but so far as it relates to myself, and the unknowing and unthinking multitude, I must beg leave to be excused the acceptance of a *meed* of praise so rich, of which I feel myself entirely undeserving, and altogether unable to sustain."

The title of Dr. was seldom given to Mr. Mercer, except by his brethren at a distance. His intimate brethren at home had a kind of instinctive feeling, that the title did not accord with the simplicity of his character; and they also felt, that the relation between Mr. Mercer and themselves was too sacred, tender, and endearing, to allow the use of such a formal and stately epithet. *Father*, and *Brother*, were the only terms which suited their *ears* and their *hearts*, when addressing this eminent servant of Christ.

Some extracts from Mr. Mercer's correspondence will conclude this chapter.

TO MRS. C.

"*Washington, Sept. 30th, 1829.*
" Dear Sister C.

" Your kind letter of the 27th came to us this morning; we were glad to hear from you, though the contents were melancholy. We sympathize with you and Mr. C. in the affliction occasioned by the deaths of dear friends and relations. Affliction and death have surrounded us also.

* * * *

"We hope you may be able to be at the Association, where we may meet once more. The hymn you mention is good. A similar one has often occurred to my mind in troubles; to wit:

'God is our refuge in distress,
A ready help when dangers press,' &c.

"It is, my dear sister, a comfortable thought that our refuge is God, and *everywhere*. May the Lord sustain you in all your afflictions, and prepare dear Mr. C. for whatever a gracious God has in view for him."

TO THE SAME.

"*Washington, Feb.* 21*st*, 1830.
"DEAR SISTER C.
" We have received your letters, recounting your and the protracted afflictions of Mr. C. The Lord does not afflict the sons of men nor grieve them in vain. Faith says, ' 'tis all for the best;' and scripture says, ' we know that all things work together for good to them that love God, to them who are the called according to his purpose.' If, however, you in *weakness* cannot see how all these trials and miseries can be for good, only be patient, and you shall in a little while know all about it. This is to you a time a little like that spoken of in Zechariah 14th chap. 6th and 7th verses: "And it shall come to pass in that day, that the light shall not be *clear*, nor *dark* ; but it shall be one day, which shall be known to the Lord, not *day*, nor *night*; but it shall come to pass that at evening time *it shall be light*.' Also read Isa. 50th chap. and 10th verse, which encourages to trust in the Lord at all times.

* * * *

" Tell dear Mr. C. that 'to all the living there is hope,' and to call on the Lord while he may be found, and possibly is near; that now is the accepted time *with him*, and only possible day of salvation."

TO THE SAME.

"*Washington, April* 26*th*, 1830.
"DEAR SISTER C.
" Your letter, bearing the melancholy intelligence of the departure of your dear husband, was duly

brought us by last mail. The departure of an immortal spirit is always an occurrence of deep concern; but when it happens in any of our dear intimates and close connexions, it is more so; especially when our happiness in life is intimately bound up in their life; but still more solemn and interesting and heart-rending, when we cast a longing anxious look on their everlasting flight, and can't see one ray of certain, heavenly light on their passage! O, how we would rejoice to hear some good word to settle our fears, and give us hope in their final and everlasting state!

"It seems that your unhappiness is to reflect on a life of many variations and serious changes:—a long and painful illness, at last to have ended without giving you *one* solid reason [on which] to rest your disconsolate spirit. Well then, sister Dorothy, there is yet one refuge for your weary soul—resignation to the will of your heavenly Father. He is in the hand of Him who is Judge of all the earth, and will do right with all his creatures. 'Tis yours, (and I hope you will have grace,) to say with David, 'I was dumb with silence and opened not my mouth, because thou (Lord) did'st it.' There are many comfortable scriptures for the *widow;* fly, my dear sister, to the rest which these promises give, and trust in the Lord, and you shall never be confounded, world without end."

TO THE SAME.

"*Washington, May 3d,* 1830.

"Dear Sister,

"Yours of first inst. was handed us yesterday as we returned from meeting. We truly condole with you in your solitary state, and would do you good if in our power. But all we can do, is to advise you as Eliphaz did Job, *to seek unto God, and unto him to commit your cause;* because he doeth great things and unsearchable ; marvellous things without number. You have suffered much, but not so much as many. You have many good and gracious friends, whilst many are friendless, as well as propertyless. You know the way, and you must walk in it, and you will find peace to your soul.

* * * *

"You say you have no bridle nor saddle—*all burnt!* well, you must have them, in order to go about to see your friends, and to meetings. I advise you to buy some, and trust for the means to pay. I hope and pray you may be guided into the right way by your heavenly Father, who is the widow's God."

TO THE SAME.

"*Jan'y 9, 1832.*

"As to religious feeling among us, I can give you but a bad account. It seems that the winter has frozen every thing like pious or zealous feeling in all parties. I am somewhat chagrined at the *seasonable* appearance which the late revivals have taken, to spring up in the hot weather and decline with it, and die in winter. I want a revival which will live all winter."

The following letter is addressed to the same individual as Sister S., her name having been previously changed by a second marriage :

"*December* 26, 1832

"DEAR SISTER S.

"Your letter of 9th inst. was duly received, and read with interest. After detailing your woes, you ask whether we have such feelings. 'Tis but too true a picture you give of our exercises. Read in the Cluster, page 338 Newton's, and also on the next page; and our own on page 340. But these should not discourage us. We are taught in the Bible, that we must walk by faith, and not by sight. It is God's design, that we shall *trust him for his grace.* Paul was taught this lesson by a severe discipline, and which God only remedied by a simple declaration, 'My grace is sufficient for thee.' We must learn to walk through darkness and not fear. It is God-honoring to trust and not be afraid. But yet how weak are we to trust even the 'oath and promise' of our heavenly Father, who is, and ever will be, faithfulness itself. We too often look for some good qualities in ourselves, instead of looking at his faithfulness and unchanging love. We sometimes are too much at ease in the possession of earthly blessings, and the Lord, *as a correction,* leaves us awhile to their enjoyment, to let us know their little worth, without better blessings, even his Spirit and grace to sanctify, and make them the means of our being more useful in the use of them."

TO THE REV. LUCIUS BOLLES, BOSTON.

"*Washington, Dec.* 26, 1832.

* * * * *

"I rejoice in the abundant success the Lord has given his servants, both to the east and west. There were in the Saluda Association, S. C., within the associational year (ending August) with only twenty churches, baptized about one thousand three hundred, and in six new churches added about two hundred; in all, one thousand five hundred. And you have seen in the Index, about one thousand seven hundred in the Edgefield. In our state there is not much excitement in religious affairs. I hope the hands of the Board of Foreign Missions are strengthened day by day. You have seen we too are trying to do something. Our manual labor school is rising, and will go into operation on the second Monday in next month. The prospect is fair—applications overflowing. But in the project and furtherance of this scheme, I have no great share of praise; for I have rather opposed and hung back, because I wished to see other and previous great objects further advanced and more firmly fixed on terra firma. But I could not hold back the zeal which has eaten up our brethren, to be doing something at home. It has had its effect. I am constrained to go with my brethren, and work with them, and have my hands full and a place for all my surplus funds. Of course, I cannot do abroad what might have been looked for. I cannot accept a project from Burmah in favor of a Palestine mission. I must, and will try, while God permits me life, to keep our Board of Foreign Missions, in their enlarged operations, on their feet. This, and the Columbian College, and our own school affairs, are too weighty for me.

"Our political matters are truly alarming. Interest, local interest, is likely to ruin us. True, I think the burdens of the government are unequally distributed by the tariff laws, but the south complains too much, perhaps. Will it be better for manufacturers to be thrown on their own capital and risk their individual success, rather than to dissolve the Union? But our true consolation is, *the Lord reigneth*.

"God has bereaved you indeed in the death of our valuable brother, E. Lincoln. But He who gave, and trained him for usefulness, can fill the place He has vacated.

"Give my most fervent love to all the dear brethren, and believe me to be, dear brother,
"Yours in Christ our Lord,
"JESSE MERCER."

The following was written to Mrs. S. shortly after the death of her second husband:

"*Washington, June* 22, 1833.
"MY DEAR SISTER S.

"Your letter intended for me at Crawfordville, the night I had an appointment there, but was hindered by high waters, was handed me at Phillips' by Brother Davant. I was on my way to our Convention, when I was first informed of the distressing termination of Mr. S.'s dangerous illness, of which you informed us about two weeks before. I had hoped better, but the will of our merciful and heavenly Father had determined otherwise. I hope and pray *the God of all grace*, in whom you trust, will grant you faith and patience to endure *as beholding him who is invisible*. 'All things work together for good to them who love God.' In this you are fully persuaded, and on this, and such-like promises, you will cast your whole burden. We are, dear sister, by these dispensations of bereavement, taught the vanity of all our best earthly enjoyments, and led to have our hearts set on a better, and a more enduring substance. The Lord's ways are not our ways; but it is our happiness to make his ways ours, and to be resigned to them. It should be our daily prayer, that he would lead us into the way which he has chosen we should go; and that we might walk willingly therein, and find rest to our souls: yea, and we should find peace and comfort to our souls, if we did but walk aright in his paths. Let your mind be stayed on Him: He who has provided hitherto will still provide."

The following letter was addressed to a female friend through the columns of the Index.

"MY DEAR SISTER IN THE LORD,

"Your interesting letter was duly received, and has laid by for some time, in order that I might be able to give you a more satisfactory answer; and I have taken this method of reply, that if I might be so happy as to afford you any relief, in the subjects of your inquiry, I might also help others, in the same perplexities. I regret that you should have had any hesitance in presenting your distress of mind to me, especially under ideas of *disparity between us.* None should be too humble to express their complaints, and none too great to listen to them with an attentive ear, in order to afford any possible relief. By communicating our perplexities freely to our friends, they may be readily obviated, and our minds relieved. Your present distress is, that your sentiment, in reference to the plan of salvation, is *so unlike* to those of some of your brethren, that you fear lest you may be in error. You, therefore, desire to make them known to me, that if, in my judgment, they are erroneous, or defective, I may correct them, and give you the instruction you need. You make the following statement of your sentiments: 'I believe that by the fall of Adam, his whole posterity became alienated from God; that they are totally depraved; that they are as destitute of spiritual life, as the body will be of temporal life, when consigned to the grave, until the Holy Spirit operates on the heart; that when this work is commenced, it will eventually be completed; that the salvation of every believer is the purchase of Christ's blood; that *He* is their Redeemer, and their atoning sacrifice; that in *Him* the justice of God is satisfied in their stead; and that this salvation is immutable.' These particulars are doubtless essentially true, according to the scriptures. That all men are dead in sins from Adam, is clearly sustained from Rom. 5 : 12. 'By one man sin entered into the world, and death by sin; and so death passed upon all men, *for that all have sinned.*' That all are totally depraved, is proven by the testimony of God himself. Gen. 6 : 5. 'And God saw that the wickedness of man was great in the earth, and that *every imagination of the thoughts* of his heart was *only evil continually.*' See also Ps. 14 : and Rom. 3 : 10–18. That men are entirely destitute of spiritual life, is evident from Eph. 2 : 1, 5. 'Dead in sins,' is the contrast of that life, by which believers are 'quickened;' or it is that state, in which they are before faith, as expressed in verse 12, 'Without God;' and so without any spiritual life. This connexion proves very clearly, that the *state of wrath* continues until the quickening influences of the spirit of life in Christ are felt on the heart. Regeneration is found in the *renewing of the Holy Ghost;* and Christ says *it is the spirit that quickeneth.* That when this work is commenced, it will eventually be completed, is as evident, as Paul's confidence is true. Phil. 1 : 6. 'Being confident of this very thing, that he who hath begun a good work in you, will perform it until the day of Jesus Christ.' That the salvation of every believer is the purchase of Christ's blood; or rather, that it is the free gift of God, through the redemption that is in Christ Jesus, as their Redeemer and atoning sacrifice, in whom God is well pleased, is, I presume, denied by none; and that their salvation is *immutable*, is certain, because it is *eternal*, Heb. 5 : 9, and results from an 'unchangeable Priesthood.' 7 : 24.

"The irrefragable certainty in the salvation of all God's people, which your mind holds, from this state of things, with a pleasing tenacity, seems to you, to be untenable with the sentiments of some, who suspend the salvation of sinners under the gospel, on their free volitions, or voluntary choice. In conversation with some of your brethren, you have been referred to Rev. Mr. Brantley's third Sermon. On reading of which you say, 'I must confess, I there find sentiments which, to me, appear as if the salvation of sinners depended on the use of means, placed within their power.' Taking parts of this discourse, separate and apart from the rest, such would seem to be their import; but taking it *as a whole*, I conceive from a careful reading, that the reverse is established. The main object of Brother B. is to do away from the minds of his readers, the notion that God save smen by *coercion;* and to establish the sentiment that sinners are saved with their own free consent or voluntary choice. The truth of this position must strike your mind at once, by considering the absurdity of the contrary opinion, carried out. Suppose a sinner *coerced* to be saved, as a culprit is *coerced* to court; and can he be happy, or glorify God for his salvation? Certainly not: so then he cannot be saved by *coercion*. Although Brother B. contends most strenuously against the opinion that God saves sinners by 'coercive necessity,' yet he does not hold that the salvation of God's chosen people, is at all the less certain. His words are: 'The power which grace exerts is the power of persuasion, of illumination, or of attraction. The energy which accompanies it, is far from the asperities of constraint; the efficiency which it possesses, though approaching towards compulsion, yet stops short of it.' And why? Because salvation by mere force would defeat God's gracious purpose and promise to the Redeemer, 'Thy people *shall be willing* in the day of thy power.' Our brother continues, 'It calls the soul *effectually*, moves it by rational inducement, rouses it from the sleepy torpor of unbelief, and informs it by the teachings of the Holy Spirit; but in all this there is nothing that impairs the freedom of choice, or of action.' But I will add, excites and improves it in both. Again, Brother B. states, 'The mind is perfectly free in believing, for though the evidence may be *so strong* as to make unbelief *impracticable*, yet belief itself is a spontaneous movement.' Brother B., in maintaining 'that salvation is so propounded to all men, as to make its acceptance or rejection a possible thing,' states that 'what I am now insisting upon is in full view of the fact, that some are converted and some are not; some regenerated and some not; some are true penitents and others never feel one genuine emotion of the sort; some love God and bear the impress of sanctity, while others remain under the dominion of unbelief and hardness of heart; and all this diversity is witnessed under the same administration of visible means.' And how does Brother B. account for all this? Why, says he, 'The Holy Spirit does exert a greater influence upon some minds than upon others within the pale of the same visible administrations of means; and that this greater influence must account for the conversion of some, while others remain unconverted, is what I fully believe. That salvation too is wholly of the grace of God, and that it is God that worketh in us both to will and to do, is a position to which my mind fully accords.' He also declares that 'God's free and sovereign grace in the redemption of sinners, and in all the influences by which that redemption is applied and rendered effectual, is most clear and undeniable.'

"These quotations sufficiently show that Brother B. holds the salvation of sinners to be the effect of the special and effectual operations of the Holy Spirit—by free grace alone; yet he does not think that any are put under 'a coercive necessity' to be saved. And you, yourself, admit that sinners, under the quickening and illuminating influences of God's Spirit, 'need no other *coercive necessity* to impel them to use the means; for the salvation of their souls has now become the all-conquering principle: Therefore, it cannot be said that they 'yield to the necessity of being saved, just as they yield to the necessity of dying.' Thus you agree with Brother B. when he says, that 'spiritual influences are carried on almost to compulsion, but stop short of it,' because a conquest is gained—the sinner yields, and is saved.

"It should always be kept in mind, that the dispensations of God embrace two departments; the one including things as they lie with himself, or between himself and Christ. To this department belong all the purposes and promises of mercy, which are all absolute and infrustrable; and rest for their accomplishment on the free and sovereign grace of a faithful and covenant God. The other embraces things as they lie between God and his rational creatures, and is founded on the rights and authority of God over them, and their duties and obligations to him as their Creator. Here God has an indisputed authority to command, and (if he graciously please) to invite, beseech and entreat; and doubtless it is their duty to obey and yield a cordial compliance with the divine and all gracious proposals; and it must be their condemnation if they refuse. But let it be remembered that *this done* saves no man; for God saves men only *through faith in Christ's blood*. But if God has been pleased to place the evidences of his grace in a righteous obedience to his commands, is it safe to seek them elsewhere? I think not. It is true all men resist the claims and refuse the grace of the dispensation of *calls and means*, and will not comply. It is, therefore, that God puts forth a *mightier* energy of divine influence into these *means and invitations*, by which they are rendered effectual, by 'the persuasion, illumination or attractions of the Holy Spirit,' to salvation. So, then, it comes to pass that all who are saved, are saved by the free and unmerited grace of God; while they that perish, sink under the weight of their own unbelieving refusals of the just claims of God over them.

"According to the covenant stipulation, 'all things were finished from the foundation of the world;' and all given to the Son, as the reward of his sufferings, were *complete in him*—were fully justified and pardoned in the sight of God, while as yet *there was none of them*. But according to the dispensation of his grace, there are times and seasons, which the Father has reserved under his own power. In these we sin, repent, and are forgiven. And again, sin, repent, and are forgiven, &c.—Thus we must be careful, not to confound the things which belong to the times and seasons of God's dispensation to men, with the purposes and things which were ordered and sure in his everlasting covenant.

"You hear it said, 'The atonement was made for all mankind; but the application definite, or how could the offer of salvation be held forth in the gospel to all, if the atonement was not made for all.' This you think inconsistent with the value of the precious blood of Christ, and the nature of the relation it holds in the covenant of redemption. They who hold this language, confound the atonement with the rights and authority of God over mankind, and which are given to Christ, as Mediator, and which he exercises, as his right by inheritance, and not from his death. Moreover, the word *for* must be used very loosely; for if the atonement is made *as a price*, which benefits no one until *applied*, then it is properly made *for* no one. The word *offer*, too, so often and so sweetly used, is not used in scripture in that sense. Christ has commanded his gospel to be preached to every creature; and all men are called on, nay, commanded, to repent and believe the gospel; and assurance is given that they that do so cordially, shall be saved.

"The views you have given of the relation there

was between the shedding of the blood of Christ, and those who are profited by it, are certainly correct. If there were no persons in the view of the Father and the Son, for whom Christ shed his blood, I see not how it could be applied to any. For an illustration, suppose the executive of the state to make out a number of reprieves without any names in them, can any criminal be discharged by one of them? Certainly not. The reprieve must be made out in the name of the person to be benefited. So the precious blood of Christ must have been spilled, in the design of the Father and the Son, for those who will be finally saved. This the Bible fully sustains.

"Dear Sister, if these reflections shall give you or any of the readers of the Index, any satisfaction of mind, or comfort in the love of Christ, or confirmation in the truth of the gospel, I shall rejoice with you and them, for the mercy of our Lord and Saviour Jesus Christ, unto eternal life.

"I am your servant, for Jesus' sake,

"JESSE MERCER."

TO DR. WM. H. TURPIN.

"*Washington, Feb.* 10, 1834.

* * * *

"It would give me joy to be able to give you some *good* news, but it is a scarce commodity with us. Brother Allen passed along like a summer breeze, and effected little; he is a pleasant brother. Brother Welch has also passed on without doing any thing. Mr. Shepherd had made such a heavy draw on the people that W. thought it best to attempt nothing. Mr. S. had obtained a subscription of about $150.

We had a Mr. Woodbridge, Agent for the A. G. T. S, for foreign distribution, but I think he got but little. I was not present, and did not see him. I think we are somewhat like a cow owned by several families, and subject to be milked at pleasure. These families might send out their milk-maids *so frequent* as to be unable to draw any milk from the poor creature. I think our benevolent societies had better have a meeting, and so arrange their visits as not to defeat their object. Indeed sir, I am, I *think*, friendly to the benevolent objects of our day; but agents are become like musketoes, one can hardly be beaten off but another is here. But enough of this. The revival above in Franklin and Elbert is still going on I learn, but I fear not likely to spread much.

"Our school is quite full. Brother and sister Sanders are quite at home, chin deep in business. I fear when they quit, we shall be at a great loss to find another yoke of the same mind. Our beneficiaries are increasing also. A young man passed me last week from the Tugulo, *S. C. side*, from a region of much opposition, and equal amount of ignorance.

" We have been graciously preserved this inclement season in common health. The spring-like weather now promises to compensate us for all our winter's sufferings. I hope and trust you are all in good health. Tell brother M.* his 'meal and grits' are out. The last, though not so fine as he might have wished, has been used up without much (if any) complaint. I hope his 'head of water' is now full, and his stones pecked and sharp, and that he will soon send us a good supply."

---

* A brother who occasionally contributed to the columns of the Index.

TO MRS. S.

"*Washington, Feb* 23*d*, 1836.
" DEAR SISTER D.

"I have received several kind letters from you, and always am pleased with them, though I do not answer them, owing to my engagement in the business of the paper. I hope you will not be led to think that I am indifferent towards you or your letters; far from this. I read with interest yours of 21st inst. last night, and have concluded, as I am confined to the house by rain to-day, I would spend a little of it in writing a few lines to my sister Dolly.

"I am glad to learn that you are likely to get on in your temporal affairs without any sacrifice, or particular injury to yourself. You have great right to trust in the Lord who has proclaimed himself specially to be the widow's *refuge and defence*. If you could come up to the picture given by Paul to Timothy in his first Epistle 5 : 5, it would be all you need to request, for then all the rest would be sure.

"Truly, that piece you mention, 'hints to young converts,' is well calculated to bring times past into present view; to make us go back to those days when the Lord brought our souls *from darkness into light*, and by his grace *created us new creatures in Christ;* or made us 'young converts.' O, how have things changed since then! I am sometimes ready to say of myself, '*if thou art he: but ah, how altered!*' This is, however, our joy that though *we* change, the *Rock of our salvation* remains the same. We may truly rejoice in the Lord, and make our boast of him all the day long.

"You speak of sermons which I have preached in days gone by, as precious seasons to you, still held in tenacious recollection. Well then, I rejoice I was able ever to preach so as to leave a sweet or savory memory behind for the consolation of any believer in Christ. O, it was not I, but the Lord that spoke through me, as a *certain* sound is given by a skilful blower of a trumpet. To him be all the praise. I hope you find many things in the Index to comfort and edify you. Though there are, and of necessity will be, many articles of controversy till we learn to be of a more meek and quiet disposition like Christ our pattern; yet it is the most ardent desire of my heart to afford the readers of that paper some solid food to strengthen their faith, and improve their spiritual health: and I hope I do not altogether miss my aim. Every christian soldier cannot fail to be anxious to know how the kingdom of Christ advances in the nations of the earth, and therefore, I should think, would read missionary news with rapture.

"Nancy joins in best wishes for your happiness, and be assured, I am as ever, yours, &c."

TO THE REV. MR. BOLLES.

"*Washington, May* 14*th*, 1836.
"DEAR BROTHER BOLLES,

"I wrote to you, directed to the care of Rev. G. F. Davis, Hartford, Connecticut, intended for the Board at its last meeting in that city; but I suppose it did not come to hand, as I see no notice of it in the proceedings.

"I am gratified to find you had so full a meeting; but regret to see so great a deficit in the receipts into the mission funds. The resolve to raise $100,000 will fail by a considerable amount. Alas!

"The bible question is an important one. I presume it will be advisable to form a Baptist American Bible Society or some plan equivalent. Perhaps societies formed for the purpose, to send up their funds to the treasurer of the Board, would answer, without incurring the expense of a national society. I hope the brethren while together, came to some conclusion what would be ultimately best for the denomination to do. I am inclined to think it would be best (if it could be so) for the A. B. Society to be restricted to the distribution of the English bible, and then let every Foreign Mission Society provide for their own translations. * * *

"Our late state Convention was a very pleasant meeting. We feel much encouraged. The interest taken in that section in our operations, was far greater than we anticipated. I think the dagon of opposition is crumbling before the ark of benevolent effort. Our funds have been enlarged. The resolution of the A. B. S. has brought us in a considerable amount for the publication of the Burman bible. At our last year's Convention, it was resolved that we would make an effort to raise $3000, to aid the raising of the $100,000 resolved on at Richmond. This resolve has been redeemed, including the sums sent up for the Bible cause, almost doubled! Our treasurer reports since last Convention, between 5 and 6000 dollars.

"A project to build a college (in our town) has been in agitation for some time. This project was presented to the Convention for their patronage, &c. and it was received with peculiar pleasure, and the necessary measures taken for carrying it forward to completion. Something like $60,000 are pledged, at least proposed to be raised for it, already. Two agents are appointed to raise the funds for its accomplishment. I hope it will go on now, well. Sunday Schools begin to be more patronized in our state, and measures were taken at our late meeting to further them. I think a Baptist Sunday School Union would be of great usefulness to our churches. I am not opposed to unite on common ground with the Pedoes; but I feel opposed to the inference which must be made by every child of common sense, from the restriction not to publish any thing but what *all agree in*, which will be, *that those things not published and taught are of no importance.*

"We greatly need a Sunday school library, from which a supply could be had everywhere, and at any time.

"I hope the brethren are in health, and that the work of the Lord abounds and prospers in their hands.

"With sentiments of brotherly love, I am, dear brother, yours and theirs in the Lord.

JESSE MERCER."

TO THE SAME.

"*Washington, Oct. 19th,* 1838.

"DEAR BROTHER BOLLES,

"The circular of Brother Malcom did not reach me timely for the session of our Association; but we had just published it in the paper, and we anticipated it in our proceedings. I had hoped the churches would, notwithstanding the pecuniary embarrassments of the country, have sent up an increased amount for foreign missions. This they did; at least the amount sent up for the several objects before the body, was greater *somewhat* than in previous years; near $3000. I offered a resolution, stating the duty of the churches to increase their efforts to sustain the Foreign Mission Board in its operations. In the argument, the embarrassments of the Board were stated, when a motion was made to test the feelings of the members in reference to the resolution; and which would be a specimen of what might be looked for from the churches next year. In carrying out this motion, the members present subscribed to be paid next session, $1200. The pastors of churches promised to endeavor to provoke the brethren to imitation in this work. It was hoped $5000 might be brought up to the next meeting. But I would not have the Board rely on it.

"When Brother Maclay, agent for the A. & F. B. Society was with us, the church and friends at this place subscribed over $700 to be paid in three annual instalments: one third of that sum we sent up to the Association, and $366 for foreign missions. Not to praise ourselves, but if all the churches would thus show their faith by their works, the cause would not be hindered or retarded. I can but hope from another cause. The Lord has in many places poured out his Holy Spirit in a copious manner on the churches, and an increase of between six and seven hundred has been added to the churches in our associational bounds. From these we may look for some fruit, which, as the apostle says, may abound to their account. But there is a cause which will for some years hinder, or render small the amount which otherwise might be afforded to the foreign cause. That is the raising and endowing our university. This is a great work, and will absorb the means of many of our liberal brethren; and many *will think* they cannot do any thing more than what they have promised to do for that institution, for years; as the subscriptions are taken for three or five years. Anti-ism, too, prevails much in the western part of our state. Churches and Associations rent and torn to pieces, as you have seen in the Index. I hope, however, it has reached its acme, and is now ready to take its downward aim, and may tumble much faster than it arose. I may be deceived in this, as some think pride and covetousness are its foundations; if so, they are strong pillars, and will be hard to break. We have met, in the providence of God, with a severe trial. One of our Professors elect, a young and promising man, son of our brother Col. A. Janes, has been taken to a world unknown. He had been converted hopefully to God while at Franklin College, and united with the Baptist church in Athens, some three or four years ago. He, by divine help, was enabled to withstand all the buffetings of a college life, and came out with the *first* degree. But the Lord did it, and we must be 'dumb with silence.' This, though not to be placed *side* with your *trial* in the death of the *lamented* Knowles, yet is of the same cast, and gives us a similar shock. I should like to be informed what is the prospect of the Christian Review. Is it likely to be sustained? It would be of service to it, if it could be known as early as possible. The present suspense holds some back, who would subscribe if they could be assured it would be continued. The eleventh number is just received. I have not had time to look it over. Such a work will commend itself to the thinking mind.

"I have reflected on the operations of the American and Foreign Bible Society, and have thought it might do the foreign mission cause an unintentional injury. The causes which gave that institution birth are very exciting to Baptist minds, and will lead many to do under the excitement of the moment, more than they ought to do, all things considered. I pressed this consideration on the mind of brother Maclay when here. From this view, I am of opinion that the A. & F. B. S. should bring all their energies to bear on the Burman bible cause for years to come. This should be the all absorbing cause with us in the bible cause. As the Board last spring were pleased to continue me in the President's chair, I feel guilty as it regards communicating with them. I have this apology; the paper informs the Board of all the important matters of this country, and leaves little for private correspondence; but this does not excuse my own mind. You will present this to the Board, and give them the kindest affections of my heart, as brethren in the cause of Christ our Lord and master. In the execution of the work of universal benevolence, faith and patience must have their perfect work. I hope and pray the Lord may sustain us all in our united labors of love; but in particular, those who are at the windlass, 'holding the rope.'

"My health has been feeble this summer, much interrupted by diarrhœa, and sometimes rather severe. At present, through mercy, in better health. May health and blessings attend the members of the Board and all friends.

"I am, dear Brother, yours and theirs,
"for Jesus Christ's sake,
"JESSE MERCER."

CHAPTER VII.

Mr. Mercer's connexion with the Georgia Association.—Extracts from his Circular Letters.—Connexion with the General Committee.—Baptist State Convention.

The preceding pages exhibit a record (imperfect indeed in many respects) of Mr. Mercer's labors as a preacher and pastor: it is now proposed to give a more particular and systematic view of his services as connected with the operations of several important religious bodies of the Baptist denomination, and as contribute to the support of some of the most prominent benevolent plans of the age. These services were varied, efficient, and useful, and established for him a strong claim upon the affectionate and grateful remembrance of the friends of Zion.

For a long series of years, his name and influence were identified with most of the prominent operations of the Georgia Association. This body was organized in 1784, according to Mr. Mercer's History of the Association; though Mr. Sherwood, in his manuscript History of Georgia Baptists, dates its formation a year later. At its organization, it embraced some five or six churches; but so rapidly did it increase, that as early as 1792, it numbered fifty-six churches. From its first origin, it has been much distinguished for the piety and ability of its members, the wisdom of its counsels, and the readiness and efficiency with which it has sustained liberal and useful measures for the advancement of the kingdom of Christ. It has been referred to as a kind of model at the organization of most of the other Associations in the state; its opinions have been widely circulated and generally respected; it has dismissed a multitude of churches from time to time, to aid in the formation of other similar bodies; reared up in its bounds many able and successful ministers, who have gone forth to labor in other regions in our southern country; and secured for itself (through God's favor) the reputation of being, on the whole, one of the most respectable and useful Associations in the United States. But it is most evident, to all acquainted with its history, that much of its respectability and usefulness is to be attributed to the commanding influence of Mr. Mercer. He was present at its formation, (though then but a lad;) not long after his connexion with the church, he appeared as a delegate; and from that time till 1839, when he was prevented by sickness, he regularly attended its annual meetings. From 1795, till the session of 1816, he generally officiated as the Clerk of the body; at the session of the last named year, he was chosen Moderator, an office to which he was uniformly re-elected till 1839. His name was generally attached to the most important committees, and many of the ablest reports presented from time to time to the body, were from his pen. The Circular Letters of 1801, 1806, 1811, 1816, and 1821, were prepared by him. They imbody much valuable instruction, particularly on matters connected with the discipline and order of the church of Christ, and the practical duties of christians; and some of them are written with great force and ability.

In the discussion of all weighty and difficult subjects, he generally took a prominent part, and it is believed that neither in the Georgia Association, nor in scarcely any other important religious body of our denomination, with which he has been connected, would the members present be willing to decide upon any prominent question or measure, without ascertaining the opinion of Mr. Mercer. Hardly any question could arise, upon which he had not reflected deeply, and upon which he was not prepared to pour forth the light of sound instruction and cogent argument. Occasionally, he displayed in discussion uncommon, and even surprising strength. Some difficult and unexpected subject would perhaps be brought up during the progress of business, which would call forth in protracted debate, the resources of the ablest brethren. At a suitable time, the venerable Moderator would call some brother to the chair, and with a meek and childlike air, step forth to give his opinion. All would be attention and silence, for every one felt that a wise man was about to speak. On such occasions, he was seldom less than interesting and instructive; and sometimes he would rise to a height and power of argument and illustration, that would enchain the mind of every listener, and bear down all opposition. The intricacies of the subject would give way to his close and lucid expositions; each prominent point would be brought out to view in the light of plain and convincing demonstration; leaving all to admire, at the same time that they would generally yield to his opinions, the strength of his mind, the clearness of his views, the richness of his resources; and in doubt upon what field to consider him the greatest, whether in the pulpit at his favored times, expounding the deep mysteries of the gospel, or on the floor of discussion, clearing away the intricacies and unfolding the merits of difficult and important subjects.

A circumstance is now present to the writer's mind, which may serve as a pleasant illustration of the estimation in which Mr. Mercer's views and instruction were generally held at important meetings for religious deliberation and counsel. It occurred at a ministers' meeting. Some weighty subject had been before the body for a considerable time, and many of the brethren had presented their views. At length a pious and worthy brother rose up, and in his honest and simple-hearted way, observed, "Well, I now move that Brother Mercer give us his views on the subject, and that the question then be put without any further debate," seeming to intimate that it would be improper for the question to be taken until the Gamaliel of the meeting had expressed his opinion, and that after he should speak, little more of importance could well be said.

As the Moderator of the Georgia Association, and it might be also said, as the presiding officer of every body where he was called to act in that character, he performed his duties with much correctness and dignified propriety. He was familiar with the ordinary rules of debate and business; he seldom lost sight of the proper point amidst protracted discussion, and the intricacies of substitutes and amendments; and without urging business forward in undue haste, he seldom allowed it to drag along to the useless consumption of time. In the various bodies where he presided, particularly in his more advanced years, a careful observer would more naturally think of him as an affectionate, grave, and venerable patriarch, seated in the midst of kind and respectful children, securing attention and order by the strong hold which he had upon their love and veneration, than as a person invested by ballot with official dignity, squaring the proceedings of the members by the nice and rigid formalities of parliamentary rules.

His circular letters have been referred to: a more particular notice of them may be proper, and a few extracts would, no doubt, be highly acceptable to the pious reader. The first complains of a worldly-minded spirit amongst the churches, the want of a tender, uniting, brotherly affection, and urges the brethren to a practical improvement of a few weighty and engaging thoughts. The letter is short, and the greater portion of it is here subjoined.

"Dear brethren, we fear you have drunk deeply into the intoxicating spirit of the world, by which you have conceived an *eager* lust for the flesh-pots in Egypt, or an *anxious* solicitude after the *flattering* fooleries, *vain* fashions and *carnal* pleasures of this wicked world, *which children and fools admire*, and by which you have greatly lost that meek, quiet and harmless spirit which abode in Christ, and which should designate you as the children of God in the midst of this adulterous and sinful generation.

"Brotherly love too, we fear, abounds too much in *word* and *tongue;* while you foster in your hearts that *ungodly*, nay, that *unchristian* disposition of *be ye clothed and be ye filled*, and at the same time close all the bowels of mercy towards those objects of compassion which are placed in your way as proofs of your love to God.

"Amongst many of you, a friendly, uniting and endearing spirit is too little cultivated; you often meet each other with an air of as cold indifference, as you do a wicked neighbor. It has become extremely difficult to distinguish you as a body, or as individuals, from a surrounding wicked world, except in a few formalities. The phrase *brother* and *sister* is kept up in some sort; but that too has lost its savor, having become formal, it communicates little or no christian affection. We fear you are too great strangers to the spirit of prayer and earnest travail for the outpouring of the Spirit of God from on high, and the coming of the kingdom of Christ with power.

"And in this time of Jacob's trouble, instead of being helpers one of another, bearing each other's burdens, and grieved for the affliction of Joseph, every one pulleth away his shoulder from the burden of his brother, and careth almost, if not altogether, alone for his own *individual*, and perhaps *carnal* concerns, while the things of the blessed Jesus and his people are out of sight, or looked on with indifference.

" Brethren, *these things ought not to be so*. And that they may not be so, we call upon you in the most pressing manner, to seriously consider, and make a pious and practical improvement on the following engaging thoughts.

" 1. View your high calling, with which nothing on earth can vie. That calling which separates a man from the mass of his equals, and seats him on a throne of *elated* glory, and puts the royal ensign in his hand, falls infinitely below that calling of which you are gracious partakers; and by which you have been taken from the mass of sinners, *your guilty equals*, and translated into the kingdom of God's dear Son, made heirs with Christ, and happy expectants of a blessed immortality. O delightful thought! O glorious expectation! Never, O never lose sight of it, but keep your eye intent on it while you run for the prize of the high calling of God in Christ Jesus.

"2. Be mindful of the designs of grace through you. Remember that God has purposed by you to make known to principalities and powers the exceeding riches of his wisdom; and therefore, you are called to be instruments of his glory; to appear on the same theatre; to engage in the same exercises, and to act on the same exalted plan of action with himself, in the accomplishment of those things in which very intimately consist the glory and perfection of saints, the glory and joy of angels, the glory and honor of God, and, in short, the glory and excellency of all heaven. *O, amazing, stupendous,* and *ineffable grace!* That will delight to take such *futile* creatures as sinful men, deformed with wickedness, absorbed in darkness, emaciated with wo; brands of the burning, all vile with pollution, and fit only to be engines of perfidy for the devil; and make them the very means by which he will accomplish such all important events. *O the depths of the riches both of the wisdom and knowledge of God! How unsearchable are his judgments, and his ways past finding out!* Let a sense of these things at once humble and exalt you, fill you with pious grief and ineffable joy, and with unfeigned delight, not only to know, but to do the will of God unreservedly.

"3. Earnestly anticipate that weight of glory which God has prepared for you, and for which he is keeping you through faith unto salvation. Know ye, that here you have no continuing city; but are as sojourners turned in for a night; your promised land, your everlasting portion, your final rest, your heavenly home, are all before; let your hearts be also there; and with steadiness pursue the happy road till you in person arrive at the mount of God. Let nought below the sun beguile your cautious feet. Let nothing court your stay on this side Jordan, save to do the will of God, which you cannot do in heaven. And be ready, like laboring children at sunset, to go home at the call of your heavenly Father. To whose gracious guidance, faithfulness and love, we commend you wishing you an abundance of peace with eternal glory, through Jesus Christ our Lord. Amen."

The second circular address written in 1806, is a brief though excellent appeal to the churches, for the purpose of urging them to promptness and activity in the execution of *discipline*.

After illustrating several points in a forcible and scriptural manner, the writer concludes with the following spirited and practical appeal.

"Suffer no disorderly persons to pass unnoticed amongst you. Adopt just measures to *induce*, or if that cannot be done, to *enforce* the attendance of your members in your conferences; that you may know their standing, and lead them to greater degrees of glory and virtue. It is a time of great worldly grandeur and extravagance. *Look to yourselves;* take heed lest there be amongst you some hurtful mixture, —some undue conformity to the world—some root of bitterness—some cursed thing in the camp, as the cause of the present painful complaints. As saith the apostle, *we stand in doubt of you lest we have bestowed on you labor in vain,* and commending ourselves to your consciences in the sight of God, we make the following inquiries. When the people of the world are ambitiously seeking honor one of another, *are you not pushing for popularity too ?* When they are at frequent and great expenses to support a grand parade, do you not increase your bills to be like them? When they change their modes of dress do not some of you alter yours too? When their women clothe themselves so thinly that the shame of their nakedness does appear, do not some of yours clothe themselves or their daughters, in the attire of an harlot? *If to these inquiries you answer, no :* then we ask, whence are the ensigns of mere grandeur in your houses? The intemperate use, *or rather abuse*, of the conveniencies, but especially the luxuries of life? The frequenting *wicked*, though called *polite*, assemblies and other places of public resort, mixed with the rabble or the guilty great of the world? Whence is it that there are among your women, *bare* elbows—*naked* arms—*exposed* breasts—*shorn* heads—*ruffled*, or shamefully *tight* dresses, connected with a light, airy deportment, and vain, carnal conversation?

"Dear brethren, these things ought not to be once named among you as becometh saints : But be ye rather transformed by the renewing of the Holy Ghost. Cleanse yourselves from these vanities, and keep your garments unspotted from the world. Search the scriptures, that you may know what the will of the Lord is, with full purpose of heart to do whatsoever he has commanded you. * * * * * You profess to be Bible Baptists;—be Bible Christians. Let the spirit be in you which also was in Christ Jesus, and let the ornament of a meek and quiet spirit be in your eyes, what it is in the sight of God, *of great price;* rather than the baubles and gewgaws of the world. Be harmless and like the Redeemer, separate from sinners; that you may be perfect and entire, wanting nothing. And so an abundant entrance shall be ministered to you into the everlasting kingdom of our Lord and Saviour Jesus Christ. Now, unto him that is able to do exceeding abundantly above all that we can ask or think, according to the power that worketh in us, unto him be glory in the church, by Jesus Christ throughout all ages, world without end,—Amen."

In the Circular of 1811, the writer, in a very pithy and condensed argument, presents his reasons for regarding the administration of baptism by Pedobaptists, though in the proper mode, as *invalid*. The author first lays down and illustrates the following propositions:

"I. The APOSTOLIC CHURCH, continued through all ages to the end of the world, is the only TRUE GOSPEL CHURCH.

"II. Of this church, CHRIST is the only HEAD, and true source of all ecclesiastical authority.

"III. Gospel ministers are servants in the church, are all equal, and have no power to lord it over the heritage of the Lord."

From these propositions, satisfactorily established, as the author conceives, he draws the following inferences, "*as clear and certain truths.*"

"I. That all churches and ministers, who originated since the apostles, and not successively to them, are not in gospel order; and therefore cannot be acknowledged as such.

"II. That all, who have been ordained to the work of the ministry without the knowledge and call of the church, by popes, councils, &c., are the creatures of those who constituted them, and not the servants of Christ, or his church, and therefore have no right to administer for them.

"III. That those who have set aside the discipline of the gospel, and have given law to, and exercised dominion over, the church, are usurpers over the place and office of Christ, are against him; and therefore may not be accepted in their offices.

"IV. That they who administer contrary to their own, or the faith of the gospel, cannot administer for God; since without the gospel faith, they have nothing to minister; and without their own, he accepts no service; therefore the administrations of such are unwarrantable impositions in any way.

"Our reasons therefore for rejecting baptism by immersion, when administered by Pedobaptist ministers are,

"I. That they are connected with churches clearly out of the apostolic succession, and therefore clearly out of the apostolic commission.

"II. That they have derived their authority, by ordination from the bishops of Rome, or from individuals who have taken it on themselves to give it.

"III. That they hold a higher rank in the churches than the apostles did, are not accountable to, and of consequence not triable by the church; but are amenable only to, or among themselves.

"IV. That they all, as we think, administer contrary to the pattern of the gospel, and some, where occasion requires, will act contrary to their own professed faith. Now as we know of none implicated in this case but are in some or all of the above defects, either of which we deem sufficient to disqualify for meet gospel administration, therefore we hold their administrations invalid."

Upon the subject of apostolic succession, alluded to in the above extracts, the author makes a few additional remarks.

"But if it should be said, that the apostolic succession cannot be ascertained, and then it is proper to act without it; we say that the loss of the succession can never prove it futile, nor justify any one out of it. The Pedobaptists, by their own histories, admit they are not of it; *but we do not*, and shall think ourselves entitled to the claim, until the reverse be clearly shown. And should any think authority derived from the MOTHER OF HARLOTS, sufficient to qualify to administer a gospel ordinance, they will be so charitable as not to condemn us for preferring that derived from Christ. And should any still more absurdly plead that ordination received from an individual is sufficient; we leave them to show what is the use of ordination, and why it exists. If any think an administration will suffice which has no pattern in the gospel, they will suffer us to act according to the divine order with impunity. And if it should be said that faith in the subject is all that is necessary, we beg leave to require it where the Scriptures do, that is, *everywhere.*"

In the Circular of 1816, the writer takes occasion to urge upon the churches some of those important duties which arise from their social compact as fellow-citizens with the saints, and members of the same redeemed family. Some extracts from this letter will be found in a subsequent part of the volume.

The Circular Letter of 1821, is the longest and the most elaborate of the series. It contains many sterling thoughts, but space cannot be afforded for a full analysis, nor for many lengthy extracts. The subject is the UNITY and DEPENDENCE *of the Churches of Jesus Christ;* which the author thus defines. "By the *unity* of the churches, we mean that they are all under one head, all members of one body: and by *dependence,* that necessary connexion which forms them into the same body, to which they owe their greatest competency for practical and virtuous excellence; and their highest felicity in perfection and beauty."

From the practical remarks with which the letter closes, the following are selected:

"We pray you to walk charitably towards those, who, in Christian profession, differ from you in faith or practice. And though you cannot reasonably hold communion with them at the Lord's Table, * * * * yet, dear brethren, we exhort and admonish you to carry yourselves towards them as Christian professors; engage with them, and invite them to engage with you, in exercises of devotion and enterprises of usefulness; go with them freely as far as you can preserve a good conscience and the fellowship of your brethren, and stop where you must according to the scriptures; evince to them that the reason why you do not yield an entire and cheerful compliance with their wishes in communion, is not founded in prejudice or ill-will, but in a conscientious regard to the views you entertain of truth and propriety; extend to them your brotherly watch-care, and invite theirs over you; reprove and admonish them in love when you overtake them in a fault, and endeavor to reclaim in the spirit of meekness; and thus, by an affectionate intercourse, and a dispassionate, free, and candid interchange of sentiments, combined with a friendly use of Christian discipline, lessen, if you cannot annihilate, the unhappy differences which are between you and them. This course, accompanied by the blessing of God, we think is the only anchor of hope for the union and communion of the present contending religious denominations.

"Furthermore, brethren, we exhort you carefully to cultivate in yourselves views of extended and general usefulness. Dismiss, for ever banish from your hearts, that God-dishonoring and soul-starving sentiment, that your Christian obligations are restricted to the church to which you in particular belong. Recollect that 'what the Spirit saith to the churches,' is bound on the observance of 'him that hath an ear.' Feel as you ought to feel, as 'members in particular' of the whole body of Christ, and bound by his authority in the same ties of brotherly love to all and to each member of that body 'as you have opportunity to do good,' and 'always abound in the work of the Lord, knowing that your labor shall not be in vain in the Lord.' And we also admonish you to esteem very highly, as your most gospel attitude, the medium of your highest privileges, and the source of your most extended usefulness on earth, your associated union. Here you are 'like a company of horses in Pharaoh's chariots,' and 'terrible as an army with banners,' prepared for united and powerful effort. What cannot be done in your individual capacity, may receive its highest accomplishment in your associated union. Divided strength is weak, but united strength is powerful. Do not treat the resolutions and advices of the association with neglect and indifference, as the counsels of a mere 'advisory body,' with which you have no connexion, but as decisions and advices of your own body, composed of your 'messengers, who are the glory of Christ.' If the counsels of the association are consonant with the word of God, you are bound to observe and obey them on Divine authority, as well as from the bond of union which holds you together 'in one.' Study agreement, and endeavor through your associated connexion, to come at a uniform practice in the order of your religious affairs. Be ready, not as a matter of constraint, 'but of ready mind,' to act in concert, like the churches of Macedonia, of whom the apostle bears this honorable testimony, that 'they are willing of themselves' even 'beyond their power,' in any matter of general utility, whether benevolent, charitable, or religious. Attempt whatsoever God in his word has instituted to be done through the instrumentality of his church on earth, and fear not. Keep in mind you are not alone: even in your associated body you are but one detachment of the thousands of Israel's hosts. The strength of opposition against you is 'an arm of flesh;' but with you is the Lord your God to help you and to fight your battles. And what may be done by united and vigorous effort of all the churches of Christ in his name, will never be known until the experiment is made; but when that experiment is made, the result will be, that the whole earth will be full of the glory of God. Let each heart hail the day in adding a double Amen.

"Finally, dear brethren, 'whatsoever things are true, are honest, are just, are pure, are lovely, are of good report,—if there be any virtue, if there be any praise, think on these things.'

"And may 'the God of all grace, who hath called us unto his eternal glory, by Jesus Christ, after that ye suffer awhile, make you perfect, establish, strengthen, settle you to do his will; to whom be glory and dominion now and for ever—Amen.'"

In the body of the above paragraphs, the author had included, in a long parenthesis, a condensed argument against mixed communion; which it has been thought best to detach from its original connexion, and present by itself. He urges his objections to mixed communion in the following manner:

"1. Because the union is broken and the dependence lost between you and them, so that communion would be a shadow, without any proper substance— too pretensional for sacred and sincere christianity. 2. Because there is no discipline instituted amongst the denominations, the influence of which can preserve such an attempt at communion from the grossest impositions and wildest disorders; and of consequence must be absurd, until some regulation be established among the parties, and they all agree 'to walk by the same rule,' and 'speak the same thing.' 3. Because you and they are not, and in the present state of religious affairs, cannot become, members together of the same body, which is a capital requisition in the gospel to a meet communion. And, 4. Because the principles and practices, which first produced, and still prolong, the difference of denominational character among professed Christians, are so heterodox and discordant, that the maintaining of the one is of necessary consequence the destruction of the other. To attempt communion in such a state of things, would be to form a religious chaos, and to promote envy and strife as the legitimate tendency. This may be exemplified immediately by reference to the ordinance of baptism: if the Pedobaptists establish their baptism as true, yours is absurd; but if yours be maintained as the gospel ordinance, then theirs is no baptism at all. It must then be improper and disloyal to attempt communion until these discordant principles are done away, and the parties conciliated in Christian love and union."

It is now something more than forty years, since an effort was made to combine the strength of the denomination in Georgia for wise and benevolent purposes. At the session of the Georgia Association in 1800, the following interesting resolution was adopted, viz.: " That as a spirit of itineracy has inflamed the minds of several ministers, who are desirous to enter into some resolutions suitable to carry into effect a design of travelling and preaching the gospel, a meeting be, and is hereby appointed at Powel's Creek, (Powelton) on Friday before the first Sunday in May next, for that purpose; that the same day be observed as a day of fasting and prayer to Almighty God for prosperity on the design, and for a dispensation of every new covenant mercy in Christ Jesus."

This proposition, which we shall soon see, resulted in some important measures, originated with Mr. Mercer. In accordance with the appointment of the Association, the meeting was held at Powelton, and after consultation and prayer for divine direction, a letter was drawn up and addressed to the Association at its next session, which " called the attention of the Association to the propriety and expediency of forming a Missionary Society in the state, for the purpose of sending the gospel amongst the Indians bordering on our frontiers, which was *unanimously and cordially approbated.*" Thus it appears that our early fathers were men of a missionary spirit.

Another ministerial conference was held at Powelton in May, 1802, to deliberate upon the subject of an Indian Mission, at which meeting it was proposed that a General Committee of the Georgia Baptists should be formed, consisting of three members from each Association in the state; the leading object of which should be to meet and confer with other Christian societies, in order to remove differences, and if possible, bring about a more general and close union of real Christians on the principles of eternal truth." The Georgia Association, at its next session, approved of the recommendation, and appointed Elders Marshall, Walker, and Mercer, to meet that Committee at Powelton on Saturday before the first Sabbath in May, 1803. At that time and place, the " General Committee of Georgia Baptists" was formed by some eighteen ministers. The leading objects at first were itinerant preaching, and the establishment of a school in the Creek nation; though at their next annual meeting, they enlarged their designs, and resolved upon measures for the establishment of a Baptist College in Georgia.

The legislature of the state refusing to grant a college charter to the Baptists, the General Committee was much discouraged and crippled in the prosecution of its benevolent designs : still it continued to hold its annual meetings for several years, for the purpose of devising and executing liberal plans for Zion's enlargement. Speaking of the subject of this biography, says Mr. Sherwood, "he was a master spirit in the doings of the General Committee from 1802 to its dissolution about 1810; was frequently the Secretary, always in attendance, and in 1805, wrote the circular. In this he overthrows the objections against the efforts to establish a college, and against a ministry of more improved minds. He was then laboring shoulder to shoulder with Sanders Walker, Abraham Marshall, James Mathews, Ross, Bledsoe, Talbot, Holcombe, Clay, George Franklin, Benjamin Mosely, and other choice spirits, the fathers of the denomination in the state, men friendly to missions and education; but of late years the charge has been publicly made, that missions and education were new schemes, and that Jesse Mercer, in patronizing them, had abandoned the scriptural path, and the doctrines and practice of those who founded and nurtured our churches in early times."

Our sketch of Mr. Mercer's useful services would be very imperfect without referring to his connexion with the "*Baptist Convention of the State of Georgia.*" The germ of that body seems to have been a resolution drawn up by Mr. Sherwood, and presented by Charles J. Jenkins to the Sarepta Association at its session in 1820, and which, with a slight amendment, was adopted in the following words: "Resolved, that we suggest for our own consideration, and respectfully that of sister associations in this state, the propriety of organizing a General Meeting of Correspondence." The Ocmulgee Association approved of the design, and appointed messengers to meet such brethren as might be delegated from other bodies. The Georgia Association also, at its meeting in October, 1821, was highly favorable to such an organization, and appointed messengers. The brethren appointed by the two last named bodies, (the Sarepta having discovered at last that there was no need of such a meeting, and declining to send messengers,) met at Powelton in June, 1822, and organized themselves in a formal manner as "The General Baptist Association of Georgia," and adopted a constitution. In 1826, the constitution was so modified as to admit delegates from Auxiliary Societies, as well as from Associations; and in 1828, the name of the body was altered to that of "The Baptist Convention of the State of Georgia."

The eleventh article of the Constitution explains the objects of the body; and is in these words : " The following are the specific objects of this body, viz. :—
1. To unite the influence and pious intelligence of Georgia Baptists, and thereby facilitate their union and co-operation. 2. To form and encourage plans for the revival of experimental and practical religion in the state and elsewhere. 3. To aid in giving effect to useful plans of the several Associations. 4. To afford an opportunity to those who may conscientiously think it their duty, to form a fund for the education of pious young men, who may be called by the Spirit, and their churches, to the Christian ministry. 5. To correspond with bodies of other religious denominations, on topics of general interest to the Redeemer's kingdom, and to promote pious and useful education in the Baptist denomination."

The Convention, as has been seen, commenced a very feeble body, embracing only two of the Associations in the state, (one of which afterwards withdrew;) and its designs were looked upon with much indifference by a large portion of the churches. At length it encountered the most determined opposition, and even from some who at first approved of its plans, were active in its formation, and for a time in its subsequent support. But it has gradually, by the fostering care of heaven, advanced in efficiency and numbers, until now it embraces amongst its constituent members, about twelve Associations, besides several respectable Auxiliary Societies. Eternity alone will reveal the good which has already resulted, and is yet to result from the labors of this active and useful body; yet it might not be improper, in this connexion, to glance hastily at some of the more obvious fruits of its exertions. A permanent fund of about $25,000 has been gathered up for education purposes; about the same amount has been collected and disbursed for the support of Foreign Missions; a considerable number of Domestic Missionaries have been employed in destitute sections of the country, by whom an amount of labor has been performed which would require the constant service of a single individual probably twenty years, and by whose instrumentality many churches have been established in the upper, western, and south-western portions of the state. Many hundred volumes of valuable theological works have been put in the hands of our ministering brethren by the funds of the Convention; between twenty and thirty beneficiaries have been sustained for longer or shorter periods at different institutions of learning; and under the auspices of the body, a seminary for literary and theological instruction has been reared up with a respectable endowment, which has already conferred great benefits upon the denomination and the country at large, and with the blessing of the Almighty, will be a powerful auxiliary to the cause of religion and learning for generations to come. A much greater amount might have been accomplished, if the entire denomination in the state had put forth their best endeavors; but enough has been done to afford delightful evidence that God has approved of the labors of his servants, and to remind us that we cannot place too high an estimate upon the toils and sacrifices of our venerable fathers, who have been pioneers in this good work.

Mr. Mercer was not, perhaps, as fruitful as some others in devising new and important plans; nor did he possess as much executive energy as some in carrying forward a plan, in its perplexing details, into practical operation; but how few could judge with more accuracy of the merits of any scheme when proposed; or were more ready to sustain it in every reasonable way, when it commended itself to him as wise and useful; or by prudent and well-timed suggestions could more readily prune off excrescences, supply defects, and thus mould it into a proper and practicable shape; and at the same time defend it against the short-sighted judgment and eccentric zeal of its erring friends. It was in this way, that he impressed his image upon all the leading measures of the convention; thoroughly identifying himself in their development and successful progress, and standing forth to view, in his wisdom, prudence, constancy, and untiring benevolence as, in a very important sense, the bright and strong centre of this useful and respectable body. He was regularly chosen the Moderator of the Convention till the session of 1841, when his feeble health and domestic afflictions rendered his attendance impossible. He watched over the interests of the body with untiring vigilance; took every suitable opportunity to explain its objects, and defend it against the assaults of its enemies; never allowing himself to become damped in zeal, or alienated in feeling, in consequence of any difference of opinion which might exist between him and his brethren; and never shrinking from any reasonable service, which might at any time be imposed upon him. He was a member, ex-officio, of the Convention's Executive Committee: the meetings of this body were frequent, and the business often laborious; but on all needful occasions he was ever found at his post.

Mr. Mercer prepared and read before the Convention (in 1825,) "An Exposition of the first seventeen verses of the 12th chapter of Revelation," which, in connexion with other essays presented at the same time, was published in pamphlet form, and circulated pretty extensively amongst the churches.

The pages of the Convention Minutes were often enriched by the valuable and important productions of his pen. In the minutes of 1829, appears his "*Dissertation on the Prerequisites to Ordination ;*" of 1830, an "*Essay on the Scriptural Meaning and Manner of Ordination ;*" of 1831, a circular on the "*Importance of an elevated standard of Christian Morality ;*" of 1833, a dissertation on "*the Resemblances and Differences between Church Authority, and that of an Association.*" The circular of 1831 will be found entire in a subsequent chapter of this work; some extracts will also be made from the essays. It may be proper here to state, that to the dissertation of 1833, as it was republished in the Index, there was appended a short "*Essay on the Independence of the Churches.*"

CHAPTER VIII.

Mr. Mercer's efforts in behalf of education.—Mount Enon.—Columbian College.—Attempts at co-operation with South Carolina. —Mr. Mercer's views on the subject.—His aid to Mercer University.—Brief history of the institution.—Project of a college at Washington, Wilkes co.—Sermon on Education.—Extracts from the same, and from Christian Index.

The cause of education ever found in Mr. Mercer an able, indefatigable, and successful advocate. His father, as we have seen, was an early and zealous patron of learning; and it may with safety be said that never, for a moment, were his principles and example in this respect reproached by his distinguished son. As a prominent member of the " General Committee," he exerted himself to disseminate correct views on the subject amongst his brethren; and in the attempts that were made to establish upon a permanent basis a respectable literary institution at Mount Enon in Richmond county, he took an active part. This academy was opened in 1807; for several years it progressed with encouraging prospects; but becoming at length encumbered with pecuniary embarrassments, it came to a sad and untimely end.

The failure of the Mount Enon enterprise cast a deep gloom over the prospects of education amongst the Baptists of Georgia; but this disaster did not in the view of Mr. Mercer, diminish its importance to the interests of the denomination, and the general welfare of society. The Baptists, as constituting an important portion of the population of the country, and holding large pecuniary resources in their hands, he conceived were under a commanding obligation to contribute their portion to the education of the public mind; and deeply did he feel the necessity of their establishing seminaries of learning, which might afford to their own children the means of a good education, and under such circumstances as would naturally prevent their becoming alienated from those sentiments which, as a *Baptist*, he considered in accordance with the word of God. Especially was he impressed with the importance of a well educated ministry. The progressive intelligence of society furnished, in his view, a strong reason why there should be a corresponding improvement on the part of those who were to be the public instructers of the people in sacred things; and he plainly foresaw, (what subsequent events have sadly verified in numerous instances,) that the superior intelligence in the ministry of other denominations, would give them the decided ascendancy in many of the most important places in the country, and that many of the children of Baptist parentage, preferring the ministrations of educated men, though less inclined at first to their sentiments, would gradually attach themselves to their congregations, and finally become identified with all their denominational movements. And aside from all such considerations, he regarded it a sacred scriptural requisition, that "the priest's lips should keep knowledge;" that every minister should, if possible, acquire that general information which would tend to secure for him respect and influence; and especially such an enlarged and accurate knowledge of the scriptures, as would render him a workman that needeth not to be ashamed, able rightly to divide the word of truth. After all, however, ardent piety in the ministry he deemed paramount to every thing else. A graceless preacher was, in his estimation, a character to be abhorred. None were more anxious than he to guard by every possible means, the avenues to ministerial preferment against the intrusions of those who, from carnal, sordid, earthly motives, would thrust themselves into the sacred desk. If at any time, persons have uttered or entertained a different opinion in regard to Mr. Mercer in this respect, they have most egregiously mistaken his principles.

From the first, he was much interested in the efforts which were made to establish a college in the District of Columbia. His name was enrolled amongst the trustees of the institution; in the midst of its long and distressing embarrassments, he clung to it with a steadfast affection, and contributed to its support with a bountiful hand. Seldom, if ever, was an appeal to him for assistance made in vain. And in no small degree may it be attributed to the example and influence of Mr. Mercer, that such liberal contributions were raised in the state of Georgia in aid of the college. He deemed it the true policy of the denomination to concentrate much of their bounty upon this institution until it should be raised above its embarrassments, and secure an ample endowment; fearing that the many local movements which were commencing in many of the states, would greatly cripple its operations, if not hurry it to certain ruin.

The Baptist State Convention of South Carolina, which originated about the same time with that of Georgia, took early measures to establish a literary and theological institution. It was the anxious desire of many that Georgia might be brought into cooperation with that state in the support of this important measure; and several ineffectual efforts were made to this end. Mr. Mercer, though he considered the effort premature, was, on the whole, favorable to the union of the two states in this enterprise, provided it could be secured on proper principles, well satisfied that concentrated action was far preferable to that isolated policy which was beginning too generally to prevail. His views, however, were not favored by his brethren. Insurmountable difficulties, growing out of local, state partialities, on both sides of the Savannah, prevented that co-operation which was in itself, so important and desirable. In the following letter addressed to a ministering brother, Mr. Mercer's sentiments on some of these points are clearly expressed.

"*Washington, March 11th,* 1831.
"MY DEAR BROTHER M.

" There is no saying more true, (for it is truth itself,) than that of our Saviour, 'out of the abundance of the heart the mouth speaketh.' No wonder, as you are recently from South Carolina, and yet full of South Carolina matters, especially those of *vital importance,* whether there or here, that you should stick to your old objects, 'like a puppy to a root.' And such adherence to good objects is not to be ridiculed by the odious epithets of '*bigotry or selfishness.*' But to be more serious; on the subject of yours of the 4th inst., I had been addressed by brother Manly before the S. C. Convention, and since. I have answered him, and can only say to you that I am of opinion that union of effort in the education business would be more efficient: and, taking an abstract view of the subject, I am fully of the belief that it would be best to unite; and taking a single view for myself alone, I am on that side. But still, I am very doubtful whether it is practicable. In the first place, Georgians are like other people, *selfish*, and vain in their imaginations, and I am slow to believe they would be gotten to agree to give their money for a union institution of any kind. But secondly, I fear if it was attempted on this side or on that side of the river Savannah, we could not agree in the provisions, objects, and minutiæ of the institution. There is a still greater difficulty with me, one evil into which our brethren are constantly running; 'tis one for which the people of this country are said to be famous, that is, 'to be always doing too much or too little.' It is to me certain we *all* are not yet prepared to do what *each* is disposed to do. I have always been opposed to these *forward steps*. I was opposed to the commencing the Furman Academy, because the Columbian College was not settled firmly on its base. The same difficulty is yet on hand. If, when that institution was undertaken, all had continued at the wheels, it might now have been a flourishing college. But New-York must have its Hamilton College, Massachusetts its Newton Theological Institution, Virginia its College, South Carolina its Furman Academy, and now Georgia must have its Working Establishment, &c. &c.; and I know not what next. The proposals as laid down by you and brother Manly are fair, quite fair; but it might prove a great inconvenience to one or the other. If we begin together, it must be near the river. Now suppose this should be broken up in a few years, and South Carolina, or Georgia, should begin to 'nib for herself,' in what an awkward situation would it leave the other? in a much worse than if the connexion had never existed."

From the foregoing letter, as well as other letters inserted in a previous chapter, it appears that the establishment of a manual labor school had become a favorite scheme with many of the Baptists of Georgia. At the annual meeting of the Convention at Buck Head, Burke county, in April, 1831, the following resolution was adopted : "*Resolved*, that as soon as the funds will justify it, this Convention will establish in some central part of the state, a *Classical* and *Theological* School, which shall unite agricultural labor with study, and be opened for those only preparing for the ministry." At the next meeting of the Convention, the plan of the institution was so amended, as to admit others besides students in divinity, under the direction of the Executive Committee. Although this plan did not originate with Mr. Mercer,[*] and he feared that the movement on the part of his brethren was rather premature ; yet no sooner had their wishes and purpose been definitely expressed, than he embraced the enterprise with his accustomed promptitude and zeal, and from the very first became one of its most devoted and munificent patrons. Indeed, the part which he took in the nurture and endowment of this Institution, may be considered the most important and prominent of the many and useful benevolent services of his whole life. As it was determined by his brethren that the seminary should bear his honored name, and from its first establishment it engaged his unremitted solicitude ; as very much of its respectability and success, (whatever they may have been,) must be attributed to the liberality

[*] The plan seemed to have originated with Mr. Sherwood. In 1832 Mr. S. established a small manual labor school on his own premises, near Eatonton in Putnam county, by way of experiment.

of his contributions, and the wisdom of his counsels; and as it was constituted, by his last will and testament, the principal heir of his large estate, it would seem proper that a more particular account of its origin and early progress should be imbodied in his biography. The writer feels happy in being able to present this account in the language of that worthy and indefatigable brother, who for seven years presided over the Institution with uncommon ability and success. The following extracts are from Mr. Sanders' "Valedictory Address, delivered before the Trustees, Faculty, Students, and Friends of the Mercer University," 12th December, 1839.

" The origin, the design and the progress of our Institution to its present state, may be proper subjects of reflection on this occasion. At a meeting of the Baptist Convention of this State in 1829, it was reported that a Brother Josiah Penfield, of Savannah, having died, had left a bequest of $2,500, to aid in the education of poor young men preparing for the Ministry, and to be under the direction of that body, upon the condition of their raising an equivalent sum for the same object, the interest only of which should be used. The equivalent was at once subscribed by the brethren and friends present, although it was not until the beginning of the year 1833, that the legacy was paid over to the Convention, and the equivalent made collectable.

" In prospect however of realizing this amount in a short time, and already in the possession of small sums received from Associations and benevolent societies for the same object, it was thought expedient by the Convention in 1831, to establish a school, Theological and Literary, connected with manual labor, at as early a period as practicable, in some convenient and central part of the state. To effect this without delay, the Executive Committee of the Convention, whose province it is to transact all its business during its recess, was directed to procure subscriptions, to examine locations, to receive propositions, and to report to their next annual meeting.

" At the meeting of the Convention in 1832, a subscription of $1,500 was reported, and the respective advantage of a variety of locations that had been examined. The one we now occupy was selected, the purchase ordered to be made, and the school to be gotten into operation, if practicable, by the beginning of a new year. The Committee, with whom it was a maxim 'not to go in debt,' speedily made the best arrangements *the means in hand* would admit. These arrangements consisted of two double cabins with a garret to each, for dwelling, for dining, and for study, for both teachers and students. With these limited accommodations and with one assistant, I opened the Institution in January, 1833, with thirty-nine students, having thirty-six of them to board in my own family. Among those were seven young men preparing for the Ministry.

"I shall ever remember, with lively emotions of pleasure, the patience and cheerfulness with which the students of this year sustained the privations and trials, to which they were subjected by their cramped circumstances. They may be truly said to have borne hardness like good soldiers. While living as in a camp in their midst, and burdened with the charge and responsibility of the Literary, Theological, laboring, and boarding departments, I found no little support in all my cares and labors, from witnessing, that while they lived upon the cheapest fare, had no place for study but the common school-room, no place to retire to for rest but a garret without fire in the coldest weather, and labored diligently three hours every day, no complaint was heard, but that the most entire cheerfulness ran through all their words and actions.

"In a word, those favorable indications of the success of the enterprise, soon began to inspire its friends with confidence, and to animate their efforts for the extension of its advantages. An amount was soon raised to erect another large wooden building, with eight comfortable rooms for dormitories, and a brick basement for chapel and school-rooms.

"The second year's operations were commenced with increased accommodations, with an additional teacher, and eighty students, seventy of whom boarded in commons. During the second and third years, the building of a larger and comfortable dwelling, a commodious dining-room and two society-halls, abundantly increased both the comforts and conveniences of the Institution.

"Thus did its interests advance from year to year, by the multiplication of its friends, and the increase of their bounty, under the superintendence of a Committee, whose watch-word was, 'Owe no man any thing,' until 1837, the fifth year of its operations. During this year, two circumstances occurred to give a strong impulse to the advancement of its prosperity. Just at this period, a project that had been gotten up for a Baptist College, to be located at Washington, in Wilkes county, was relinquished, after nearly one hundred thousand dollars had been subscribed for its accomplishment. This event was promptly improved by the Executive Committee of the Baptist Convention, charged with the interests of this Institution, and a resolution was at once passed by them to elevate it by the addition of a Collegiate Department. An agent was appointed to obtain, if possible, a transfer to it of the sums that had been subscribed to the contemplated college at Washington. In the execution of this labor he was peculiarly successful, and to the Convention of 1838, he made a report of the transfer of between 50 and $60,000.

"During this year also, a town was laid out around the Institution, and named after the donor of the first contribution, which had laid the foundation for its existence. Several thousand dollars worth of lots were at once sold, with a condition prohibiting the admission on them of gambling-houses or tippling shops, on pain of forfeiture of title. The number of lots sold, as well as the prices, were abundantly increased by a judicious arrangement of the Committee appropriating $3,000 of the avails, to build a Female Academy in the town.

" Arrangements were now also made to have the Male Institution transferred to a separate Board of Trustees, to be appointed by the Convention once in three years, and required to make annual reports of the state of the Institution. By the Convention of 1838, that Board was appointed, and shortly after met, and organized, and made the necessary arrangements for the commencement of the operations of the Institution in its elevated character, under the title of the *Mercer University*, in the beginning of the present year. That board I now have the pleasure to address. It is well known to many of you, my brethren, with what doubtful apprehensions of duty, and with what consequent reluctance, I gave up the more general and active labors of the Ministry, to take upon me the charge of this Institution in its infancy. Yielding, however, to the strong impressions of my brethren, that, as its more immediate and especial design was for the improvement of the Ministry, it would afford one of the best opportunities of promoting Ministerial usefulness; and encouraged moreover, by my own convictions of the importance of early attention to the religious sentiments, and ideas of duty to be entertained by young men entering into the labors of the Ministry; I eventually consented to take charge of it, until a suitable opportunity might be presented of having the office supplied by another.

"After laboring six years in the complicated, oppressive, and responsible duties of Principal of all the departments of the Institution, and after it had, in the dispensation of Divine Providence, been so promoted as to justify the division of its several departments, and the appointment of a separate officer to the charge of each, I supposed, the occasion had occurred that would justify my retirement. I consequently availed myself of it, and obtained your acceptance of my resignation. But, being unable to procure the services of the officer of your choice to preside over the Literary department, I was again induced to consent to your wishes, in assuming that charge, till the office could be otherwise satisfactorily filled.

"The desired arrangements have now been made. You have been able, in all departments, to obtain the services of officers of proven abilities to fill their respective appointments, and I now with pleasure again resign my charge into your hands. In retiring from your service as an officer of the Institution, permit me to assure you, that the testimonies, which I have received from time to time, of the satisfaction which my services have given, have constituted no small share of the reward of my labors.

"Permit me here to recount some of the principles upon which your Institution was first organized, and on which it has since been conducted by its founders; principles which have no doubt contributed eminently to its past success, and in favor of which evident indications of Divine approbation have been manifested. In the first place, it was a principle with them to deliberate maturely on every subject of investigation, and to examine well the ground about to be occupied, before they took their position. So far from being hasty in their conclusions, or rash and precipitate in their acts, they took care to satisfy themselves fully with regard to the merits of every subject that presented its claims to their attention, before they put forth their labors in its behalf.

"This they did, not from a belief in the pernicious doctrine, that a good end will justify any unhallowed means. Such a doctrine they would have individually spurned, however it may be entertained by some great men of the day. But this they did, from the conviction that it is the duty of rational and accountable beings, to have their principal energies directed towards the accomplishment of great and important objects, that they may the better obey the injunction 'whatsoever thy hand findeth to do, do it with thy might.' This principle they by no means overlooked in the subject of our present reflections. As a Classical Education of candidates for the ministry had long been, and still was, reprobated by many, it was the more necessary that they should make a careful and thorough examination of the subject, before they engaged in its promotion. But the more carefully and thoroughly they examined it, they were but the more fully persuaded, that it was an object worthy of the prayers and labors of all the friends of God or man. Their efforts therefore, made in the prosecution of this object, have not only been with an approving conscience, but with unrelaxed energy and ardent prayer, and have not been in vain in the Lord.

"Although since the origin of this Institution, there have been but few among us entering the ministry, yet it has, no doubt, been the means of abundantly enlarging the sphere of usefulness of a portion of that few, not only from our own state, but also from neighboring states. It has aided about twenty young brethren in their preparation for their labors, and fifteen of them gratuitously. Several of these are now engaged acceptably and successfully in the field of labor. Their efforts have already been abundantly blessed, in promoting revivals of religion in the different sections of country to which they have been called, as well as in advancing the benign objects of christian benevolence.

"2d. Your Institution has also been built upon the faith of that divine principle of truth, 'that except the Lord build the house, they labor in vain that build it.' Its founders have not stopped at making sure of a good object and then laboring diligently for its accomplishment. In all their efforts, they have acknowledged God, and sought his blessing in earnest prayer. How often and how fervently have they, in the language of the pious Psalmist, prayed, 'Establish thou the work of our hands upon us, yea, the work of our hands, establish thou it.' And the Lord hath graciously heard their prayers, and wonderfully granted their desires, and exalted their Institution to an elevation of character and usefulness, transcending in so short a time, the most sanguine anticipations of its warmest friends. In retrospecting its history, we are called upon to recognise the hand of God, not only in building up the interests of the Institution, and giving it favor in the eye of the people, but more particularly in the frequent revivals of religion, with which he has been pleased to visit it; and these, mostly through the instrumentality of the young brethren here preparing for future labors in the ministry. Here the Lord has said to them, cast in your nets for a draught, and in so doing, they have enclosed, to their astonishment, a multitude of fishes. This they had little expected, and have been willing to receive it as a divine acknowledgment of the acceptance of their labors. It has become to them a verification of the promise, 'and, lo! I am with you always,' and an antepast of the blessedness of an instrumentality in the salvation of immortal souls. By the founders and contributors to the institution, this may be regarded as a demonstration of the importance of the work in which they are engaged, as an expression of the divine approbation of the labor of their hands, and a striking evidence of the answer of prayer. To all future officers, members and patrons of the Institution, it affords a lively encouragement to labor with diligence, and to pray without ceasing.

"It is a heart-cheering subject of contemplation, that but one year out of seven has passed away without more or less religious revival among the students; and that nearly one hundred of them, have here hopefully been translated from the kingdom of darkness to that of light; some of whom are already actively engaged in the labors of the ministry. Who can tell the influence these may have on the destinies of the world, through the instrumentality of their labors and their prayers?

"3d. Another principle, early laid down and firmly adhered to by the founders of your Institution, was 'to keep out of debt.' The Convention of 1832 passed a resolution, 'that no debt shall be contracted by the Committee or Trustees on the credit of the Institution, without funds in hand to pay; otherwise, in every such case, it shall be on their own individual responsibility.' The wisdom of this policy cannot be too highly appreciated.

"Mount Enon in our own state, and the Columbian College in Washington City, were beacons of warning for our denomination; and well have they improved the melancholy lessons of instruction that had *here* been taught them. Instead of embarrassment, and perplexity, and loan, and abatement of funds by usury, you have now before you, the free and unfettered use of all the property and funds of your Institution.

* * * * *

"4th. Another important principle with the founders of your Institution, was, 'to *go more for substance than for show, and more for sense than sound.*' In digesting systems, in erecting buildings, in arranging studies, in selecting teachers, in a word, in every operation of the Institution, this principle has had its influence. It was the high consideration in which this principle was held, that recommended so strongly to them the manual labor system of education. They could readily see that if thoroughly carried out, it was well calculated to make effective practical men:

men, not only able to understand, but also able to perform whatever service might be necessary to promote the interest of their country or their own prosperity. It is on this principle, that the instructions of the teachers have been addressed to the understanding of the pupils, and not merely to the memory, and that public examinations have been required to be thorough and undeceptive; and on this principle it is, that more attention has been paid to the solid branches of mental and moral improvement, than to any of the forms of fashionable etiquette.

"The result has proved that honesty is the best policy; that however the world may labor to deceive, it is not willing to be deceived; and that its imitators in hollow show, are not the objects of its confidence and respect. While on this subject, I would remark that if I have understood the views of this board, they are in entire harmony with this principle; that they consider it a matter of more importance to have good instructers, than fine buildings; that the elevation of character and usefulness of a college depends more upon the talent and learning and moral principles of its faculty, than on the number and splendor of its edifices."

Mr. Sanders was succeeded in the presidency of the Institution by Rev. Otis Smith, who conducted its affairs for the three successive years. The Rev. Mr. Sherwood, now President of Shurtleff College, Illinois, was for some time connected with the Institution as Theological Professor.* It has been highly grati-

* Besides the individuals already named, the following have been connected with the Institution for longer or shorter periods, as instructers: E. Moyer, J. O. M'Daniel, John F. Hillyer, W. D.

fying to the friends of the University, that the number of theological students has of late increased, thus brightening the hope of realizing the accomplishment of the most prominent design for which the Seminary was founded. On account, however, of the late unparalleled pecuniary embarrassments of the country, the destruction of the principal building by fire, and other causes, the Institution has been much impeded in its operations; yet it would be wrong to relinquish the hopes which its past success has inspired; and still more criminal for the denomination to withhold their vigorous support from a seminary so needful for their prosperity, and upon which so much prayer, and labor, and pecuniary bounty have been bestowed.

In the preceding extracts from President Sanders' Address, and also in one of Mr. Mercer's letters to Mr. Bolles, in the 6th chapter, there is reference to a plan for a time entertained, of establishing a Baptist college at Washington, Wilkes county. This was suggested to the minds of one or two pious brethren, at that place, upon the final determination of the Presbyterians to establish their Institution at Medway (near Milledgeville) rather than at Washington, these two places being strong competitors for the honor. Mr. Mercer favored the suggestion, and indeed, sustained it with a zeal and devotion uncommon, even for himself. It was, however, feared by many that the Mercer Institute and the Baptist College

Cowdry, J. W. Attaway, Robert Tolefree, A. Williams, R. J. Miller. The present faculty are as follows: Rev. John L. Dagg, Professor of Theology and President pro tem.; B. O. Pierce, Professor of Natural Philosophy and Chemistry, S. P. Sanford, Prof. Mathematics; Rev. P. H. Mell, Prof. Languages; T. D. Martin, Tutor.

could not both be properly sustained at separate locations; and at last it was resolved by a majority of the Trustees of the College, that the project should be abandoned, and the charter given up. Seldom, if ever, was Mr. Mercer known to manifest so much sensitiveness and mortification at any decision of his brethren. It was evident that a gourd had been smitten, in whose shade at least in anticipation, he had reclined with uncommon interest and delight. And it was a rare occurrence indeed, that the opinion and influence of Mr. Mercer should be overruled in any matter in which he had taken such a decided stand. Under such circumstances, some men would have become permanently alienated from the councils of their brethren, and settled down into a state of sullen disquietude, if not of disgust. Not so Mr. Mercer. He acted the part of a truly magnanimous christian. "*I cannot work alone*," was his emphatic declaration, "*I must go with my brethren;*" and before the close of the year he subscribed *five thousand dollars* for the endowment of the Collegiate Department at Penfield. From that time he turned towards the Institution in its remodelled character, the full tide of his good feelings and princely munificence; thus, presenting an example worthy the consideration of all, especially of such as are ready to falter and draw back, if in all things *they cannot have their own way.*

It would be tedious to enlarge upon all the useful services rendered by Mr. Mercer to this important Institution, aside from his numerous and liberal contributions. His frequent visits to the field of its operations, and often when he was oppressed with bodily infirmity; his cheerful conformity to the genius of the establishment at its first origin, when, for example sake, and to relieve others pressed with many cares, he would stoop down and *make up his own bed;* his unwearied attention as a member of the Executive Committee, and of the Board of Trustees, to all necessary business; his calm and patient endurance in times of trial; his wise, seasonable, and apparently indispensable counsel in matters of special doubt and difficulty; his many and fervent prayers, in which he would so feelingly and appropriately seek the direction of the Father of Lights, and commend the Institution to his Almighty protection—all these things, and many more which might be specified, are deeply engraven upon the minds of his surviving coadjutors; and as they rise up to recollection, cannot fail to remind them how highly they were favored whilst they enjoyed his presence and aid; and how much they have lost by his lamented death. The beneficiaries, and other students in the seminary, will long remember how often his venerated form was seen in their midst; with what tender care he watched over their welfare; and how often and how affectionately he urged upon them his rich, paternal counsels.

In speaking of Mr. Mercer's exertions in behalf of the cause of education, a reference might be proper to a valuable discourse on this subject, which he delivered before the Convention in 1834. It was published by request of the body, and is entitled "*Knowledge indispensable to a Minister of God.*" It is founded on a selection from the 4th and 6th verses of the 6th chapter of 2 Corinthians. "*Approving ourselves as the ministers of God—by knowledge.*" In this discourse, two important questions are discussed:

"1. *What knowledge is necessary to a minister of God?*"

"2. *How is it attainable?*"

* * * *

As to what knowledge is necessary to a minister of God, the author remarks, " To this inquiry we unhesitatingly answer—THE KNOWLEDGE OF THE TRUTH. For we know of *no truth*, the knowledge of which would be *unimportant* to a minister of God. We should like, dear friends, you would now throw your thoughts over the universe, and see if you can discover *any truth* which would be unnecessary to be known by a gospel minister. If it should be said by any, that it ought to be restricted to the knowledge of the truth *as it is in Jesus;* then we answer again, that we know of no truth which is not in Christ Jesus. The scriptures declare, ' It pleased the Father that in him all fulness should dwell.' He it is ' that filleth *al in all.*' ' He is head over all things to the church.' And ' by him all things consist.'—Then we ask, what truth is not in Christ Jesus? But the whole may be summed up in *the knowledge of God and his works.* —Nay, God is only to be known through his works of nature, grace, and providence."

* * * * * *

"We conceive a thorough knowledge of God in his natural and moral perfections, (on which the scripture places the highest value,) is of the utmost importance to the minister, to fill him with a holy reverence, and to guard him against fanciful constructions of scripture, and the forming of false systems of theology. The standard of truth is in the God of truth. The most fruitful source of error is ignorance, or vague notions of God. But if God be truly known and kept in view, it regulates all the thoughts of the heart, and fixes the sentiments of the soul accordingly. Whatever, therefore, is in strict accordance with God's nature and perfections, must be truth; and whatever is inconsistent therewith, *however plausible,* must be false."

In considering the question, how is this knowledge attainable? the author makes some plain common-sense observations. A few sentences only can be copied. " This knowledge, then, we say is to be attained only by a close application *to the study of the works of God.*

* * * * *

"It is to *be sought as silver.* How do men act, when they lay themselves out to get money? Why, they engage in some mechanism, profession, merchandise, or agricultural pursuit, in which they ply themselves with untiring diligence to gain their object; so all good men, but especially ministers of God, ought to apply themselves to the acquisition of knowledge. But Solomon uses a bolder comparison. He says, it must be *searched for as for hid treasures.* Here reference is had to the anxious solicitude—the patient and indefatigable perseverance, with which men dig after the precious metals and other valuable substances, hid in the bowels of the earth; which can be better conceived than described. But as knowledge is more precious than silver, or gold, or rubies, it ought to be sought not only with equal, but superior application and untiring diligence; and then we have the encouraging promise of attaining the precious boon. And here we would ask, why God hid his most precious natural treasures in the bowels of the earth, or rather why he did not spread them over its face, so that the inhabitants of the world might just go out and gather up what they needed, as the children of Israel did the manna round about their tents? Why, for this simple reason, it did not suit his plan. He formed man for labor, and constructed every thing accordingly: so that if man obtained them, he should dig deep for them: and the harder for the more precious.—And thus, says Solomon, in the acquirement of knowledge, 'This sore travail hath God given to the sons of man to be exercised therewith.' And it is evident, that the most deep and valuable treasures of wisdom and knowledge are gained by the most patient and persevering efforts of the mind."

* * * * *

"Jude, in describing these same persons, [false teachers,] says, verse 10, 'These speak evil of those things which they *know not;* but what they *know naturally*, as *brute beasts*, in those things they corrupt themselves.'

"Here observe, these false teachers are reproached for *knowing nothing*, but what they know *naturally*, as *brute beasts*.—In order, brethren, to perceive the full force of the contempt and derision thrown on these pretended teachers by the apostles, it is necessary to conceive rightly, how *natural brute beasts* acquire knowledge—namely, by instinct, or the force of habit.—Now, then, it is plain that these apostles thought it ridiculous for any man to pretend to be a teacher who *knows nothing*, but what he knows *naturally* as *brute beasts*, by infusion or force of custom; without an effort of the understanding, or the exercise of the reason. 'Tis true, a man residing in a learned community, will drink in the knowledge of the society he keeps, and may seem to be learned; at least he may use many learned words; but not having exerted his understanding and reason in obtaining it, but having received it as a brute beast does, cannot use his knowledge understandingly, but rather as parrots do, and therefore is ever subject to expose himself, and the cause he attempts to advocate, to contempt, and his hearers to deception. The Lord save us from an *ignorant* ministry!"

In the conclusion of the discourse, the author answers some objections.

" But objection is made to schools for the education of young ministers, on the ground that the instruction afforded is *human* learning. To see the weight of this objection, it is requisite to know what the objectors intend by *human* learning. If they mean instruction in *human* inventions, in which the knowledge of God and his works *are not taught*, then we join heart and hand with them to put it down: but if they intend to object to all learning, which is received by *human* instrumentality, then we most sincerely pity them as ignorantly opposing the institution of God; for we think no man can read the scriptures, and not see that God requires knowledge to be imparted from the parents to the children, and from the wise to the simple. But we presume the objection proceeds altogether from a mistaken notion of the nature and design of the instructions given in those schools. They have heard of geography, geology, chemistry, history, astronomy, philosophy, and theology; * * * but what is the study of these, but the study of the works of God, in creation, and providence, and grace ? For instance: Is the *earth* the Lord's ? *Geography* describes it, in its extent, with its different soils, climates, and productions—its inhabitants, with their various religions, laws, and customs.

"*Geology* gives a view of its state, and teaches the nature of its pebbles and mighty rocks, stupendous mountains and majestic seas: where the wonders of God are seen.

"*Chemistry* enables us to discover and separate the peculiar properties of all natural bodies, and learn their various uses.

"*History* teaches us the events of time—the rise and downfall of nations and kingdoms, together with a minute account of those facts which have transpired under the providence of God, in the successive generations of earth; so indispensable to a right understanding of scripture.

"*Astronomy* teaches us of the heavenly bodies—the sun, moon, and stars—their distances, magnitudes, and velocities—wherein is declared the glory of God, and shown his handiwork.

"*Philosophy* teaches the nature and reason of things. It is the system in which general causes and effects are explained; and mind, both human and divine, with all its natural properties and moral powers, is examined and exhibited in its dignity, beauty, and moral excellence.

"*Theology* teaches of divine things. It is the study of the Bible—a critical examination into its language—the modes and figures of speech employed in it—the manners and customs of the times in which it was written—and the best rules of construction, in order to come at the truth, taught in that sacred volume.

"Thus you see, brethren, the instruction given, under these and such like heads, in the schools, are not about the inventions and theories of men of corrupt minds, but of the truth of God as displayed in his works of nature and grace; and *as such* proper, that the mind of a minister of God should be deeply imbued with it.

"Again, objection is made to the Convention, as opposing *a call* to the ministry, and designing *to rear up* a set of *graceless* preachers. In reply to the first cause of complaint, we say the Convention believes that no man ought to attempt, or be encouraged to preach the gospel, until he has a full satisfaction in his own conscience, that God requires it of him, and can afford his brethren the same satisfaction in regard to it. And as to the second, we say, that one of the first requirements for admission is, that the applicant must be licensed to preach by the church of which he is a member, and be approved by surrounding churches—so that if the Convention should unfortunately contribute to raise up a set of graceless ministers, the churches shall share in the first blame.

"And now, dear brethren in the ministry, let us enjoin on you the acquisition of knowledge; by the right use of which you may approve yourselves *as the ministers of God*. We urge this on you, that you may understand the Bible—the Bible is a learned book, and cannot be understood well without much pious knowledge and learning. He who now addresses you regrets that he knows *so little* of the Bible. After reading and studying it for near half a century in some sort, he has to make this humbling confession, that he knows *to his shame*, comparatively but little of the Bible. This he does not say for his own sake, but for yours, *young* brethren, that you may devote your youthful days to the acquisition of all possible useful knowledge. Give yourselves to reading and study, that you may be approved unto God, and that your profiting may appear to all; to the honor of God and the advancement of the kingdom of Christ. Amen."

A few remarks of Mr. Mercer on the subject of education, which appeared under the editorial head of the Christian Index in August, 1834, will close this chapter.

"Education is not, *in the least*, designed, so far as we know, among Baptists, by any who are engaged to promote it in the ministry, to usurp the place or take the power of any of those gifts, talents, or mental endowments which God by his holy Spirit imparts, and without which no man has any right to pretend to be a minister of God. But only to assist him, in those qualifications which it becomes him to possess, in order to discharge the duties incumbent on him by the gifts and appointment of God. Can ministers be considered, in regard to divine influence and power, what a cork is to the stream on which it floats—having no care, no interest, no duty or concern as to how their ministry is performed? Or are they to be viewed as ambassadors, whose duty it is to prepare for, and endeavor to perform the duties of their appointment in the best manner possible? The scripture will decide the question in the affirmative in accordance with the voice of reason and common sense.

"Education is *in nowise* designed as a mere endowment or accomplishment, whereby the man by the use of high and learned words, may raise the admiration of his hearers; or by the excellency of speech and enticing words of man's wisdom, gain the applause of the great of the world. These are motives utterly unworthy the minister of Christ. But to enable him, in the use of right words, to set forth the truth to his fellow men, in the most plain and forcible manner. We consider education to the minister, what clothes are to a man. They have no power in them to make the man, yet they are very necessary both to his comfort, and to render him acceptable to his fellow men. So education is very necessary to the happiness and acceptance of a minister in the course of his ministry. Suppose God was to call a poor young man to go and preach the gospel; and he had no suitable clothes, nor means to get them, would it not be right for his brethren who were able, to supply them? Doubtless it would. So also, should God call a poor young man destitute of the learning which would render him an acceptable preacher, would it not be proper to put him to reading and study, in order that his profiting might *appear* to all?

"Again: The minister is a workman for God, and words are *his tools*. A mechanic, to do good work, must have a variety, and a knowledge of the use of tools. So a minister, to do good work in preaching for God, must have a fund, and be acquainted with the right use of words. But how shall he attain to *this right use* of words, unless he studies it? Does God give the knowledge of language now? It would seem that many think, the less a man is educated, the more plain, forcible and useful he is as a preacher; but the fact is exactly the reverse. It ought to be apparent to every one, that the less a man knows, the poorer must be his stock of words, and the less his capacity to use them advantageously. The man of understanding and wisdom alone can use knowledge aright. He that knows the power of words, can use them to express his ideas plainly; and this is the proper use of education. The learned minister of God, under the influence of a right spirit, will use his knowledge to present truth, not floridly, *but clearly;* not in the eloquence of human wisdom, *but in the simplicity* of demonstration, commending himself to every man's conscience in the sight of God.

"We close these remarks by saying, that the argument drawn from the gifts and promises of God to *inspired men*, in favor of the advantages of ministers *now*, is, in our judgment, a very deceptive one; because the analogy is not true. Prophets and apostles doubtless had a peculiar degree of inspiration, by which their writings constitute the INSPIRED SCRIPTURES; but will any man pretend that ministers are *now* inspired *so* that their sermons may with equal propriety be styled *inspired sermons?* If so, the scriptures are not the *only* rule of faith and practice, but these sermons have equal claim. We think the absurdity of such a sentiment will fully refute the argument, and lead us to depend *alone* on the holy scriptures for all our knowledge of the mind and will of God, in all matters of faith and duty."

CHAPTER IX.

Mr. Mercer's efforts in the Missionary cause.—Formation of the Powelton Mission Society.—Mission Board of the Georgia Association.—Mission to the Creeks.—His favorite argument for Missions.—Letters in defence of benevolent plans, from the Index.—Letter to Mr. Shuck.—To Mr. Bolles on the Abolition Excitement.—Remarks from the Index on the same subject.—His kind feelings towards the northern brethren.—Skeleton of a Missionary Sermon.—Letter on the "Imprisonment of the Missionaries to the Cherokees."

The blessed cause of Missions was ever dear to the heart of Mr. Mercer. It might be said that he was, in truth, an active and efficient domestic missionary for nearly thirty years, a large portion of that time being actually spent in itinerant labor. An interest in foreign missionary operations was roused in his bosom at an early period, by the accounts which reached this country through Rippon's Register, in relation to the labors of the English Baptists in India. After the return of Mr. Rice from the East, he soon caught the fire which was scattered abroad by that wonderful man, and communicated it to his churches. Thence the sacred leaven soon found its way into the Georgia Association. In the minutes of that body for 1814, is found the following record: "According to a suggestion in the letter from the Whatley's Mill Church, Brother Mercer presented and read the Circular and Constitution of the 'SAVANNAH BAPTIST SOCIETY FOR FOREIGN MISSIONS,' and then moved for the approbation of the Association, which was given most *willingly* and *unanimously.* Whereupon it was thought proper to recommend the subject, *for its evi-*

dent importance, to the consideration of the churches; and Friday before the first Sabbath in May next was named as a day on which all, who were *individually* disposed, as well of other Associations as our own, might meet at Powelton, in Hancock county, to form a Society, and digest a plan to aid in the glorious effort to *evangelize the poor heathen in idolatrous lands.*"

Pursuant to this notice, a number of brethren and friends assembled at Powelton on the 5th of May, 1815, and formed " The Powelton Baptist Society for Foreign Missions." Of this highly useful and respectable Society, Mr. Mercer was President, and Gov. Rabun, Recording Secretary. The amount raised the first year for missionary purposes, was nearly five hundred dollars. The following is the conclusion of a brief account of the origin and first year's operations of the Society. "In the conclusion of this brief sketch, the Board of Directors cannot forbear expressing their gratitude to the Father of Mercies, that success has attended their exertions, far beyond their most sanguine expectations; and although the friends and patrons of the Institution have been obliged to encounter the frowns of some and the prejudices of others, we still believe the cause is God's, and must ultimately prevail. For we recollect, that when the Lord inspired his people with a disposition to rebuild his temple, he inspired the hearts of many others to assist in furnishing the means: And notwithstanding a *Sanballat* and *Tobiah* were permitted again and again to hinder the work, yet the most ample success crowned the efforts of the feeble few. And can we believe that less certainty will be manifested in the erection of the great spiritual temple, the materials of which are now scattered abroad in all parts of the world? No; we cannot, we will not indulge the ungenerous thought, but will rather look forward and hail the approach of the glorious period, when the great trumpet shall be blown, and those who are ready to perish shall come from the east and the west, and from the north and the south, and shall sit down at our Emmanuel's feet, and learn and feel his grace."

The same year, (1815) the Georgia Association *unanimously* agreed to co-operate with the Baptist Board of Foreign Missions, and resolved itself into a body for Missionary purposes, and appointed a Committee, of which Mr. Mercer was chairman, to digest rules for its regulation; to address a circular to the churches upon the interesting and important subject, and to hold correspondence with the Foreign Missionary Board.

At the session of 1816, the above named Committee reported a system of Rules for the regulation of the Missionary operations of the body, which with some amendment were adopted. By these regulations, the Association was required to choose annually seven Trustees, to be denominated "THE MISSION BOARD OF THE GEORGIA ASSOCIATION," and to be a component member of the General Missionary Convention, and also the organ of domestic missions, according to the openings of Providence, the means in hand, and the instructions of the Association; or as their own judgment might direct from time to time.

The Mission Board, regularly appointed in accordance with the above regulation, prosecuted its business with much success for many years, assisted in the establishment of a Mission amongst the Creeks, received and disbursed considerable sums of money, kept up a correspondence with the General Board, and presented to the Association from year to year spirited and animating reports of their proceedings, and of the general condition of the cause of missions. Mr. Mercer was uniformly appointed as a member of this Board, was generally its President, and invariably one of its most liberal and efficient supporters. In 1820, and 1826, he represented this body in the General Convention. At length the Georgia Association concluded to dispense with the separate agency of their Board, and merged their operations in those of the State Convention.

In 1820 a plan for Indian reform was organized under the direction of managers appointed by the Ocmulgee, Georgia, and Ebenezer Associations. These managers were denominated "The Board of Trustees of the co-operating Baptist Associations, for instructing and evangelizing the Creek Indians." Of this Board, which continued in operation some years, and at one time had several missionaries in its employ, Mr. Mercer was an active member, and for a while, the corresponding secretary.

Mr. Mercer often preached on the subject of missions, to his churches, at the anniversary meetings of the various associations which he attended, and at other convenient times on his numerous excursions through the country. Multitudes will long remember with what sweetness, pathos and power he would expatiate upon the last commission of the ascending Saviour, and point out the future glories of the Redeemer's kingdom, as delineated on the pages of prophecy. Upon many portions of Isaiah he dwelt with peculiar delight. A very favorite argument with him, was one that he drew from Acts 13 : 47, compared with Isa. 49 : 6. "Notice," says Mr. Mercer, "the language of Paul and Barnabas after having declared that, in consequence of the wilful rejection of the word of God by the Jews, they would turn to the gentiles, they add, '*For so hath the Lord* COMMANDED *us;* saying, *I have set thee to be a light of the gentiles, that thou shouldest be for salvation unto the ends of the earth*.' Now observe, that what these inspired men present to our view in the form of a command, we find in Isaiah, from which they quote it, in the character of a simple prediction : we have, therefore, inspired authority for this inference, that *old-testament* PROPHECY is *new-testament* COMMAND. Thus we are to regard all the predictions of the prophets in relation to the advancement of Christ's kingdom, and the salvation of the world, as invested with the power and authority of divine commands, requiring us to labor and pray for their accomplishment." To one who beheld imbodied in every line which exhibited the future triumphs of divine truth, the majesty of unalterable law, who heard, as it were, the commission of the Saviour, "*go ye into all the world, and preach the gospel to every creature*," bursting from the lips of every prophet who had spoken of the glory of the Messiah's kingdom, the bible must have been indeed a *missionary book;* and the individual that would act in accordance with such convictions, (and so did our venerable father,) could be nothing less than an untiring and zealous defender of the *missionary cause.*

Strange to tell, there have been many opposers. Some of them, Mr. Mercer had reason to fear were influenced in their opposition by unworthy motives; but as many honest and pious persons were led astray by the unscriptural arguments, erroneous statements, and unhappy examples of their leaders, he did not deem it an unworthy or needless service to meet, both from the pulpit and from the press, the various cavils and pretended arguments which, from time to time, had been raised against the missionary enterprise. Its opposers, with strange misconception, or as some would think, with strange effrontery, claimed for themselves the honor of being *primitive* or *old school Baptists !* How *just* and *honorable* their high claims appeared under the scriptural arguments and historical facts poured upon them by Mr. Mercer, need not here be stated. He that may have seen a millstone fall upon the little moth, or the swollen torrent bearing away upon its wave the trash of a summer stubble field, can well understand the merits of this controversy.

From a series of letters, published in the Index early in 1836, for the purpose of meeting the inquiries of a christian brother, the two following are selected. They do not seem to be confined to the missionary cause exclusively, but embrace the various objects of benevolent effort.

"DEAR BROTHER A.

"In my last to you, I proposed to make '*the new schemes and their tendencies*' the subject of a future reply; and now I proceed to the performance of it.

"It is plain, from a review of H.'s inquiries, that by '*new movements—new plans*—and *new schemes*,' he intends the various social operations of *these days;* such as Bible, Missionary, Tract, Sunday School and Temperance Societies. These are considered as *evil*, not only in themselves, but because they are *new*.—

Hence, they of the opposition, call themselves '*Old School Baptists.*' But such an insinuation indicates the belief, not only that the Baptists had, in their operations to further, *instrumentally*, the kingdom of Christ in the earth, attained to perfection; but a lamentable want of *scriptural* knowledge. I suppose, however, the first will not be *seriously* pretended; and by the latter, it will be shown that the *path-way* of the Lord's people through the wilderness of this world, is as the shining light, *that shineth more and more unto the perfect day;* (Prov. 4 : 18); and that *in the ages to come*—the dispensation of *the fulness of the times*, God will make known *by the Church*, his manifold wisdom; or the exceeding riches of his grace by *new* and increased labors. (Eph. 2 : 7. 3 : 10.) There will then be something *new* constantly transpiring. For instance, when *the mountain of the Lord's house*, (or the church,) *shall be established in the top of the mountains, and all the nations shall flow unto it*, (Isa. 2 : 2,) there will be something *new !* And when '*the kingdoms of this world shall become the kingdoms of our Lord and his Christ ; and his dominion shall be from sea to sea, and from the river to the ends of the earth ;*' then will there be something *new !* (Rev. 11 : 15. Zech. 9 : 10.) Moreover, when the earth shall be filled with the knowledge and glory of God, then there will be something gloriously *new !* (Isa. 11 : 9. Ps. 72 : 19.)

"Again; when '*Israel* (the church,) *shall blossom and bud, and fill the face of the world with fruit,*'— there will have been done something *new*. (Isa. 27 : 6.) And when the church shall have enlarged the place of her habitations, and broke forth on every side, so as that her sons shall make the desolate cities of the gentiles to be inhabited by the redeemed of the Lord; there will have been done something gloriously *new!* And when the people of the saints of the Most High shall *take* the kingdom and possess it, because *it shall be given to them*, in the greatness thereof, *under the whole heaven;* then there will have been done something *wondrously new!* (Dan. 7 : 18 —27.) God declares emphatically, '*Behold, I make all things new!*' And it must be very evident to any sober bible reader that *new* things will be transpiring in every generation of men, until the final consummation of all things. And it will be as readily seen, that as new dispensations succeed each other, and as changing vicissitudes arise, it will be indispensable *to concert plans of action* to suit the exigencies of the times and accomplish those things which may be requisite for the carrying forward of the cause of Christ in the earth. It is obvious too, that no community can move in concert in the performance of any work, *but by counsel.* Solomon says, 'Where no counsel is, the people fall: and without counsel purposes are disappointed: but in the multitude of counsellors they are established—there is safety.' (Prov. 11 : 14. 15 : 22.) If Christ has constituted his people the light of the world, and commanded them to let their light *so shine;* or to make known the riches of his grace *among all nations* for obedience to the faith; and at the same time to wage an interminable war with the powers of darkness; it follows, as a matter of necessary consequence, that they must meet in Convention, and by *wise counsel* adopt such plans as shall be judged best adapted to effect the objects in view. Accordingly, the Apostles assembled at various times, passed resolutions for different purposes;

and finally they in conference assigned to each other their sphere of labor in effectuating their Master's great command; "*Go ye into the world and preach the gospel to every creature.*" See Gal. 2 : 6—9. Those useful schemes or plans of operation, which were established in his day, Paul enjoins it on Titus to urge and affirm constantly, that they who have believed in God might be careful *to maintain* good works.—And again; 'Let ours also learn to maintain *good works* for necessary uses, that *they be not unfruitful.*' (Titus 3 : 8, 14.) Now, what are these *good works*, which are to be urged on the observance of the brethren with so much care, but those plans or institutions, which were established as best calculated to promote the general interests of the kingdom of Christ, and the good of all men? And what is it *to maintain* these good works, but to give aid and support to them, so that the ends proposed may not fail? But *without counsel purposes are disappointed, and the people fall!!* If this be true, should not our brethren, who oppose in toto, the schemes of benevolence now in operation, fear the consequences of their own temerity? But why do they oppose them? Is it because they are calculated to do evil? Is it because it is an *evil* work to supply the *unregenerated* world with the bible—or to endeavor to send the gospel *by the living preacher* (as near as can be come at, *called of God to the work*) to all the nations of the earth, *that they may be saved*, (1 Thes. 2 : 16)—or to write pieces on important subjects, and send them abroad; or to direct them to certain individuals—or to combine to raise our children in the *nurture and admonition of the Lord*—or to unite to suppress iniquity in any shape; but especially in that odious and most destructive form—DRUNKENNESS? Surely not!! Perhaps they will say 'yes; we will have our churches and associations; but we will have nothing to do with these societies.' That is, they will have *nothing to do* in publishing the word of God to the world—*nothing to do* in furnishing a preacher to those who sit in the region and shadow of death, that they may hear of a precious Saviour, believe and be saved; (Rom. 10 : 11, 15.) *nothing to do* in giving them *any means*, not even a tract by which *they may be saved ;* (Rom. 11 : 14;)—*nothing to do*, in having their children taught in the scriptures by suitable teachers in Sunday schools—*nothing to do* in reforming the intemperate, or in making an effort to save a poor *deluded and infatuated* fellow man from a drunkard's grave, and a miserable family from ruin. I ask in the name of common sense,— *What will they do?*

"But, pressed for time and perceiving that I shall stretch out my reply too long, I beg leave to pause here, and make 'the tendencies' the subject of a separate number.

"I am, dear Brother A.,
"Yours, truly,
"JESSE MERCER."

"DEAR BROTHER A.

"I proceed to consider some of the supposed *tendencies* of the 'new schemes,' patronized in our days.

"It is asked ' whether they have not uniformly operated to produce dissatisfaction, and destroy fellowship? I think it quite probable they have ever had this tendency *in a greater or less degree.*

"The *new movements* of our Lord and his apostles

had this tendency. The nature and influence of his miracles induced many to become Christ's disciples; but when they heard his doctrine of salvation by grace alone, and his requisitions of self-denial and practical godliness as indispensable to discipleship; they were offended, and went away and walked no more with him. Christ told his disciples not to think that he was come into the world '*to send peace; but rather division—a sword.* (Matt. 10 : 34. Luke 12 : 51.)

"But why was all this? Because, not only that the unregenerate heart of proud man, could not submit to his doctrine of *the new birth;* but also many of the *religious* Jews, however pious, were not prepared to admit his '*new measures;* and therefore opposed them, they being of the *old Mosaic school.* And we find that the same spirit of opposition to the *new schemes and movements* of the apostles, to carry out the commands of their Lord, to establish his kingdom *in all the world*, was ever and anon stirring up strife and exciting contentions and divisions amongst the churches. Although the prophets had before declared that the name of the Lord should be made known in all the earth, by the rising of Zion, to whose light the Gentiles should come, and kings to the brightness of her rising; (See Isa. chapters 42 and 60) and Christ had in accordance therewith, commanded his disciples to preach his gospel to the ends of the earth; yet, such was their overweening prepossessions in favor of Judaism, that they strenuously opposed every attempt to preach the gospel to the heathen that they might be saved. For instance; even Peter was so prejudiced against going to the Gentiles, though his Lord and Master had commanded him (with the rest) to *go into all the world and preach the gospel to every creature*, that a vision from heaven must descend to convince him of his duty; and when by this extraordinary occurrence, he was constrained to go, on his return to Jerusalem, his brethren called him to a severe account for it.

"Now it is quite evident that the apostles called a convention, and held a conference on this subject, (Gal. 2 : 6, 9;) and when they perceived that it was the will of God, and that he. had called Paul and Barnabas to that work, (a fact not to be overlooked,) they gave them *the right hand of fellowship* that they *should go unto the heathen;* not only as a token of approbation but of confirmation. Nevertheless, there was opposition still. For while Paul was at Ephesus, he says (1 Cor. 16 : 9,) '*a great door and effectual is opened unto me, and there are many adversaries.*' And in Thessalonica the Jews rose up *forbidding the apostles to preach to the Gentiles, that they might be saved.* (1 Thes. 2 : 16.) And still more pertinent— There were certain brethren, who went among the Gentiles for Christ's sake, taking nothing of them for their support; whom Gaius had received and relieved. For this act of benevolence, Gaius is commended very highly by the Apostle John (3 John;) and then he adds, '*We therefore, ought to receive such, that we might be fellow-helpers to the truth.*' Receive such, How? but as Gaius had done; affording them that support, they had refused to take of the Gentiles; or else how should we, *in receiving them*, be fellow-helpers to the truth, in their ministry? The apostle wrote to the church on this account, no doubt stirring them up to this duty. But there was one *Diotrephes*, who loved to have the pre-eminence among them, received not the apostle, *in this apostolic letter*, nor these missionary brethren, and forbade them that would have received them, and *cast them out of the church.* How picturesque! How often has this high handed opposition been acted out in more modern times? How many letters and other writings on missionary subjects, have been refused a reading, and thrown under the table? How many of the brethren, *of the effort cast*, have been refused the use of meeting houses, and *cast out;* or excommunicated as far as practicable, by declarations of non-fellowship, &c.? All such, I take to be of the household of Diotrephes. However, I cannot envy their pre-eminence arising from this relationship; but rather give me an humble connexion with the excellent Demetrius.

"But do the preachers, who are opposed to these *new plans*, preach the same doctrine that Abraham Marshall and Silas Mercer did? I presume they do, *essentially* preach the same doctrine, with this shade of difference; they are *more generally* on the doctrine of the covenant and predestination, and less practical. But I believe the soundness of their faith has never been called in question. But do the advocates of these '*new movements*' believe and preach as did those able ministers of the New Testament? I think they *substantially* do. With this difference; they do not preach as *controversially* as some of those venerable ministers did, because there is not the same cause for it *now*, as in their day, when the fundamental principles of the Baptist faith were assailed, by all the force of the *Arminian* host. But do *you* preach as you used to do? This question I have answered several times in the Index; and if it was not believed then, why is it asked again? But for the sake of those who may not have given themselves the trouble to read heretofore; or who may not have noticed it, I repeat, that I have undergone no *fundamental change in faith from my forefathers.* I believe *now*, and always preach in perfect accordance with the faith adopted by the Georgia Association, and from her (so far as I am informed) the other Associations in the state. But is not the preaching of those who advocate the *new plans*, too *practical, too Arminian?* I do not think so. I speak as to the great body of those who are the advocates of the benevolent operations of our day. Of individuals I cannot say any thing. By far the great majority of those engaged in *benevolent efforts* are *strictly Calvinistic.* I use this word in its common acceptation. Those professedly *Arminian* are far in *the rear* of the *Calvinists* in those operations. And I suspect the idea, that the patronising of the benevolent institutions tends in the least to arminianism, has been gotten up from some isolated cases, of persons being suspected of arminianism, being very active in advocating these measures; and not from any solid ground.

"It seems to be taken for granted that all those venerable fathers, who founded the Baptist denomination in this state, were as stern calvinistic preachers as are the opposers of the *new plans*. But this is altogether a mistake. Some of them were so—seemed to be set for the defence of the gospel. Of these, Silas Mercer and Jeptha Vining were the chief. Abraham Marshall was never considered a *predestinarian* preacher. To use his own figure; he used to say, 'he was *short legged* and could not wade in such deep water.' He, with several others, was considered sound in the faith, though *low Calvinists.* Peter Smith and some others were thought rather *Arminian;* some *quite* so. But no division was thought of till Jeremiah

Walker adopted and preached openly the doctrine of *final apostacy*. Then a division ensued; but soon after the death of Mr. W., the breach was healed. And here it may not be amiss to add, that the Baptists in the upper parts of South Carolina, in those days, comprehended mostly, it is believed, in the Bethel Association, were general provisionists. I think the most of their ministers preached what is *now* called *General Atonement*. But this was never thought of as a bar to correspondence, or even Christian communion. Well, then, if there is no fundamental difference between the opposers and the advocates of the *new plans, why not unite?* I know of *no substantial reason* why they should not. I believe the friends of benevolent societies have never agitated or even wished a division with their brethren on account of their not seeing proper to patronise these societies. And I am not able to see any thing in these benevolent Institutions which can justify their opposers to declare non-fellowship with their advocates. Nor do I believe that any will pretend that these operations are wicked in themselves; but when they condemn the promoters of them, it is by censuring their motives or designs, so as to make them wicked. But as in doing this, they break one of the laws of Christ, they must account for it at his bar.

"Is there no way for the Baptists to come together and be united? I think there is. 'Let them love as brethren; and *not judge one another any more*, but judge this rather, *that no man* put a stumbling-block, or an occasion to fall, *in his brother's way.*' But how would a convention of all the churches do? If such a conference, or a meeting of the principal ministers, could be had *in the spirit of meekness*, I should hope it might have a good effect. At least it would be worth the trial. But this has been already proposed, again and again, and *nothing has been done!*

"In conclusion, I say for myself, that it appears as if the Lord had in his righteous displeasure, shut us up in prison houses, so that we cannot come forth; or has mixed a perverse spirit in us, *because he will destroy us.* It is high time we should humble ourselves under his mighty hand, and beseech him to take away from us *an evil heart of unbelief,* and put into us *a right spirit.* Let all who have hearts to do so, remember the first Thursday in April next, the day set apart by the Georgia Association, and concurred in by the Sarepta, as a day to afflict our souls on *this very occasion,* and implore of the Lord his restoring mercy and cheering grace.

"In hope of better times by the Grace of God,
"I am, dear Brother, yours, in
"Christ Jesus our Lord,
"JESSE MERCER."

Mr. Mercer watched the progress of our Foreign Missionary operations with the liveliest interest, held frequent correspondence with the leading members of the Board, of which he was the honored President from 1830, till the meeting of the Triennial Convention in 1841, and into whose treasury he poured his bounty with an unsparing hand.

A letter addressed to Br. Shuck, of the Chinese Mission, through the columns of the Index, may be properly introduced in this place.

"Washington, Ga. April 6, 1838.

"Dear Brother Shuck,

"'As cold waters to a thirsty soul, so is good news from a far country:' so your very kind letter from Macao, (China,) refreshed and comforted my spirit. I hastened to lay it before the readers of the *Christian Index,* and suppose a few words in reply will not be less acceptable through the same medium to you, and may be gratifying to them. Truly the short 'acquaintance and intercourse' had at Richmond, (Va.,) were pleasant and interesting, and left an impression on my mind, which has led me to read in the *Religious Herald* all the communications from you with particular interest. It was peculiarly engaging to my feelings to witness with what devotedness and disinterested zeal, you and others appeared before the Board of Missions to make known the impressions which had led you to the conclusion, that it was your duty, *from the Lord,* to engage in the ministry; and especially those, which disposed you to a foreign field, where you might 'preach among the Gentiles the unsearchable riches of Christ.' And this you did, *without asking or receiving* a promise of one jot or tittle of earthly emolument. All you asked, and all you received, was the approval of the Board, and a promise of *aid and support !*

"It is truly a consideration which 'affords no small gratification to know' that through the providence of God, oceans and continents have made us antipodes, yet we 'can meet at a common Mercy Seat,' and there enjoy 'intercourse and commune with each other in prayer,' and by writing those things, which the grace of God has wrought by and in us, for the furtherance of his cause on earth, and which lead 'the soul in holy contemplation towards the brighter developments of celestial bliss,' where personal intercourse and enjoyment will be uninterrupted and eternal.

"I consider it an amazing wonder, my dear brother, 'a consideration of overwhelming and painful interest, that while the hearts of so many thousands in America, (and other Christian countries,) beat high with a Christian's joy, and swell with a Christian's hope,' so little is felt for the millions (of China and other nations) who are sitting in the regions and shadows of death, and perishing for the lack of knowledge! If, that 'some (men) had not the knowledge of God,' was spoken to the shame of Christians in Paul's day, what must be spoken of Christians in these days! O, when will Christians wake up to the importance of 'keeping the commandments of God!' And it is still of more amazing and painful concern, that so many professed Christians, like the Jews in Paul's time, rise up '*forbidding us* to preach (the gospel) to the Gentiles, that they may be saved.'

"I agree with you, that every church should act as a missionary society, and that if, at the concert meetings, some one or two of the members would prepare themselves to make some brief remarks relative to some case, history, or interesting incident of the missionaries, it would give a 'heightened interest' to those meetings, and to the cause of missions generally. It would also excite attention to the history of missionary operations as they transpire. We need very much in our denomination an *increased taste* for reading. Any thing which would tend to increase this desire, would benefit the cause, by developing and rendering familiar, the labors, difficulties, and situations of the Missionaries; and doubtless, at the same time enforce the moral and personal obligations of giving the gospel to the Pagan world.

"I rejoice that the prospects before you were encouraging—that you have made such progress in the acquisition of the language, as to be able to write a tract in Chinese, which was soon to be published. I have great hope, by the grace of God, on the circulation of tracts. They are silent and unobtrusive, and will get admission where a Missionary would be rejected. I am happy also to learn that 'the Portuguese government has somewhat altered its policy,' so that Missionaries can now reside in any of the precincts of the 'Celestial Empire.' Those parts where the prohibitory laws of the Emperor cannot affect the cause are so extensive, that if the word of the Lord should take deep root in them it would easily spread into the interior. But why speak in this casual strain? He who touches the mountains and they smoke, and the hills and they skip, can say to the haughty and imperial Throne of China, 'be thou removed,' and it shall vanish away like smoke, or yield obedience at once to the King of nations!

"I am acquainted with Brother I. J. Roberts. While I wish him all grace and success in his undertakings, I can but regret his isolated condition. If the Board should make Macao a permanent station, (and under existing circumstances I see no reason why they should not,) I trust you may find in him a true yoke-fellow in the great cause of evangelizing (by the blessing of God on your labors) the Chinese, and bringing them to the obedience of faith.

"As to sending you more laborers from Georgia, it would rejoice my heart to see many young men rising up, like the zealous and devoted Isaiah, and saying to the call of God, each for himself, '*Here am I—send me!*' But alas! we have a *great deficiency* of pious, devoted, and faithful ministers in this state, and there seems little spirit of prayer in the churches, to the Lord of the harvest, that he would send laborers into his harvest, which is truly large.

"It will give me pleasure to send you, my brother, any thing—Minutes, and the Index, which may afford you and those with you, any consolation or strength.

"With Sister S. I have no acquaintance, but what I have gained from her letters, &c.—but it has been quite sufficient to give her an interest in my best wishes for her happiness and prosperity in the great enterprise in which she has, as your *help meet*, engaged. My most sincere gratulations to her and Brother Roberts. May grace, mercy, and peace be with you all, and give you success, is the prayer of one who is deeply interested in the Missionary enterprise.

"JESSE MERCER."

The movements of the Abolitionists, which at one time seemed to threaten the disruption of the north and south, gave him much concern. He looked upon the separation of the denomination as a result greatly to be deplored, inasmuch as it must necessarily embarrass, to a fearful extent, our foreign missionary operations, and portend great evils to our common country. In a letter to Mr. Bolles, he expresses his sentiments on this exciting subject with great candor and freedom.

"*Washington, Oct. 21st*, 1840.
"My Dear Brother Bolles,

"Yours from Philadelphia was duly received, and I was gratified in reading its contents. I have also received an address to the missionaries, the sentiments of which I approve. I have all along intended to write, but continued and increased affliction has led to procrastination; and so it is, I have not undertaken it till now. But now it seems to be imperious on me to speak. The address of the Anti-slavery Convention held in New-York last spring, with E. G. as president signed to it, and certain copies of the Reflector, have been sent to almost all our ministers and pastors of churches, and other prominent persons among us, and, I suppose, through all the Southern States; and have acted as fire brands through all our parts. Our abolition brethren are exceedingly mistaken in the case they have undertaken to remedy; and therefore, their measures can only operate a *bad influence;* and the tendency will inevitably be to break up all our united operations, and, I seriously fear, our *civil* union also. They ought to consider that the institution of slavery is a *civil* and not an *ecclesiastical* one; and that it is not one of our (the present owners') making; that we, as a slaveholding people, are mostly the inheritors of them from our forefathers—that they came into possession under the prejudice of early education. We have been taught from our cradles that they were *our money*, that we had a right or title to them. This has grown with our growth, and strengthened with our riper years. Now be this right or wrong, it ought to be kept in mind that this prejudice is not to be removed by any immediate cause, nor by hard words, or by arbitrary condemnation. These can only excite to a fiery resistance, and, of course, rivet the chains of the prejudice (above stated) the tighter, and strengthen them by the influence of that interest which blinds the judgment. The terms on which the address proposes the continuance of christian fellowship are altogether *impractical*. If we would, we cannot comply. We are, as a community, both classes, as a *tangled* hank, so tangled that we cannot be *severed* in the way proposed. We have no alternative, therefore, but to yield to their sentence (bull) of excommunication. I suppose before you receive this, you will have received an address from the Executive Committee of our Convention, (a copy of which has been sent me,) on this vexatious subject. I exceedingly regret the necessity of this movement in our Board, but under the circumstances, I must justify them in it. I was not able to attend our session of the Association, nor the meeting of the Executive Committee. I too regret the alternative to which the present crisis subjects the acting members of the Board of Foreign Missions. They must disavow any connexion with or approval of the *ultra* movements of the Abolitionists, or lose the southern interest in the Foreign Mission cause. Our people talk of a southern Board; but that to me is just equal to an entire separation from the cause itself. The Board will have to look to the north and northwest for its supplies, and the south will cease to do any thing, or turn their benefactions some other way. * * * *

"Dear brethren, we have fallen on stony places, and some of us will be sorely tried. A few, with myself, would prefer to continue our union and co-operation, Abolitionism notwithstanding; but what can the few do against the many? The consequences of a dissolution of our missionary co-operation will be deleterious, if not ruinous. We must reflect on our obligations to our missionaries. This obligation is of the most serious character, and ought not to be broken without paramount considerations. But I leave all these things to be digested by your wisdom and prudence.

"I have written the above with considerable pain, and must ask the prayers of the Board to God for me and wife, who is paralytic both in body and mind, that we may be able to endure as beholding him that is invisible, ready to help. With sentiments of affectionate regard,

"I am, dear brethren, yours in the kingdom and patience of Jesus Christ.

"JESSE MERCER."

A short time before the meeting of the General Convention in 1841, he thus speaks upon the same subject through the columns of the Christian Index.

"I am of opinion we are making quite too much of their puffings and loud noise. If they are disposed to roar, let them roar on, *unheeded* by us; for to be disquieted and alarmed is just what they want— the more they can disturb and discompose us, the better they will be pleased. Now let us care as little about all their 'sound of words' as a company of shepherds would the howlings of wolves on the opposite side of an impassable river. Let them alone, and their long and their loud soundings will die *harmless*, in the distance.

"It may be asked what shall we do in this distressing case? I give as my advice, to sacrifice *feeling to principle*, and hold on. To continue the union of the present effort in the General Convention, to me is palpable and all important. A division of the southern brethren from the northern, would, in my view, be deleterious, if not totally ruinous to the whole concern. Some talk of a Southern Board, but this to me is visionary and futile. We have no southern intercourse with India, and should have to send our funds through the same channel they now go, and that would defeat the very object for which a Southern Board would be gotten up. I see no way that a Southern Board could support missionaries in Burmah, or other places in the East, without trusting their funds to northern conveyances, and whom would they sooner trust than the present tried members of the Board of Missions? I hope our southern brethren will never think of it.

"But before I close this article, I must say something about the approaching Triennial Convention. Many North and South, are looking to that meeting with great expectation. Well; I hope something will be done then, tending to settle the agitations which now threaten the dissolution of the missionary compact. For myself, it is my settled conviction, that to pretend to investigate *the right or the wrong*, the *merits or the demerits* of slavery, would be worse than folly. Who can amuse himself with the idea, that that question could be decided in a public controversy? Nothing could be the result but '*strifes of words*, whereof cometh envy and perverse disputings of men of corrupt minds.' I think nobody, North or South, on mature reflection, can desire such a dispute, except Abolitionists, and I suppose it would be *marrow and fatness* to their souls. Something, however, should be done in that meeting to harmonize the feelings of the South, and to direct the energies of all united in the missionary enterprise, in *one sacred effort* to send the gospel to the heathen. I cannot persuade myself, but that there will be a great majority of those who shall form that body, that will have no *hesitancy to unite* in the sentiment, that for any Baptist minister or set of ministers, however large, to judge and condemn others, *unheard*, as guilty of most base crimes, and to pass resolutions of disfellowship in relation to brethren over whom they have no disciplinary jurisdiction, is undenominational and contrary to the plain dictates of the word of God; and therefore, not to be tolerated in any belonging to the Convention, much less any member or members of the Board itself."

Mr. Mercer had enjoyed an opportunity of cultivating considerable acquaintance with his northern brethren, and though he most decidedly condemned the course of a few unreasonable and erratic men, yet he placed a high estimate upon the prudence, piety, and zeal of the great body, and especially of the more prominent individuals concerned in the management of our missionary affairs. There are some who will, no doubt, recollect the ingenious, and yet kind and paternal manner in which, at one of the meetings of the State Convention, he softened down a discussion in which there had been thrown out some rather unkind intimations against the brethren of the north. The following is about the substance of his remarks. "Brethren, allow me just here as I am sitting, to relate a little anecdote: though it has something to do with myself, yet I hope you will nevertheless excuse it. In my younger days, and when I was also young in the ministry, I had occasion to pay a visit to Charleston, S. C. I went to the place with many prejudices against the brethren in that place, taking it for granted, that as they lived in a large city, they were a proud, formal, fashionable people, and had very little religion. I did not expect to be pleased with them. But after a few days intercourse with them, I found them a very kind, humble, spiritual people; and I left them with the conviction *that they had a great deal more religion than I had.* Now in regard to our northern brethren, let me say I have been with them, and have had an opportunity of judging of their spirit; and brethren, *they are a better people than we are.*" If this disposition to lie at our brethren's feet, and to esteem others better than ourselves, were universally prevalent, how much bitterness, jealousy and strife would be banished from the church of Christ.

The following brief notes on Matt. 28 : 19; " *Go ye therefore and teach all nations,*" were found among Mr. Mercer's manuscripts, and may serve as a specimen of his *longest* skeletons of sermons, of which, however, he prepared but very few.

"The gospel is of God. Its glorious design travails with infinite benignity to the praise of his grace in the salvation of men. It exhibits a system of means, reserving the efficient cause to God alone. The humble beneficiaries are constituted its instruments. It is of grace they are so. A failure of success in their labors, admits of no discouragement.

They have received more than they have rendered back; and their Lord was ever beforehand with them, and they were originally unworthy. Privilege never comes alone; it is always accompanied by obligation. God gives something in the privilege, which he never fails to require again, according to his own wisdom and counsel. Hence the vows of God are upon us. 'Where the word of a king is, there is power.' And this power must be felt when Jehovah-Jesus speaks. When He who has all power in heaven and earth commands, 'go ye therefore, and teach all nations,' who will be inattentive, or disregard his authority?

"My brethren, let us spend a little time in contemplating the command of God to teach the nations.

"I. Whose duty it is.

"II. What it involves; and

"III. The ground of encouragement to those who are making one sacred effort to obey the command.—And

"I. Whose duty it is.

"The eleven were present only; but it could not have been restricted to them, for then the ministry would have ceased with them. Christ says of himself, 'I am the light of the world as long as I am in it.' If then the command rested with them, both the work and the authority for it must have ended with them, and the world is now wrapt in moral and spiritual night! But they must have been the representatives of all ministers of Christ till the end of the world.

"*In proof of this.* The commission itself extending to the end of time. The mode of expression by Mark, and the manner of Christ's addressing in relation to the end of the world, and of his second coming, and how they ought to be found of him, are in point. Also the apostolic rule of expounding prophecy to be command.

"They must also have been the constituents of the Gospel church. In proof of this, what Christ says of them in his sermon, and the figurative illustration he gives of them and their duty, answering only to the church of Christ, is in evidence. But if the prophecies are commands, then the question is at rest for ever. It is the church's duty, including all, not without ministers, to teach the nations. The church is the pillar and ground of the truth, &c. The prophecies being commands, taken together with the examples of the first churches, will show that the duty of teaching the nations lies on the church and ministers.

"II. What it involves.

"1. The publication of the scriptures. In proof of this, urge the example and command of God—the prophetic declarations in Isa. 2 : 3. 4 : 12. 42 : 4. 49 : 22. 62 : 10.

"2. The translation of the scriptures. The reasonableness and necessity of it. The giving of tongues and ceasing of them—the choice of the Apostles to publish the New Testament in the Greek, being the most popular language then in the world; and Paul's sentiment for plain words.

"3. The sending of men to teach them. The appointment of the Prophets and Apostles is sufficient to prove this point. But Ps. 68 : 11. Dan. 12 : 4. It is declared in Isa. 66 : 19. Ps. 45 : 16. Isa. 60 : 11.

"4. The use of money, and a great deal of it. The service of God in Israel required a great deal of money, &c. The prophecies show that presents and gifts should be brought unto Zion for the service of God, and the first churches did abound in liberalities, &c.

"III. The encouragement afforded

"Lies in the commander's having all power in heaven and earth, whereby the free use of all means, the employment of men and angels, and the fulfilment of all the promises are sure.

"*Inferences.*

"1. The propriety of being ready for the work.

"2. Unity in the effort—and

"3. Courage and strength in the work."

The following piece originally published in an April number of the Christian Index, 1832, when edited by brother W. T. Brantly, in Philadelphia, may here be allowed a place as a kind of appendix to this chapter, since it has some bearing upon the missionary cause. As it embraced some topics of a different character, the biographer did not think best to break the connexion of the preceding portions of the chapter, by inserting it in its proper chronological order. It refers to the unhappy affair of Messrs. Worcester and Butler, missionaries of the American Board of Commissioners for Foreign Missions, who, refusing to submit to the laws of Georgia when the state saw fit to extend her jurisdiction over the Cherokees, had been arrested by the civil authorities, and confined in the penitentiary. Many distorted and erroneous representations of the occurrence were circulated far and wide to the injury of the reputation of the state; and some respectable Baptist publications (without any evil purpose, it is presumed,) assisted in giving them currency. The design of this communication was to present the subject in its proper light, and to aid in allaying the ferment of the public mind. If it failed in fully exonerating the authorities of the state

from blame in the view of all, it showed clearly that
they had been greatly misrepresented, and that the
character of Georgia had found a very able and zealous advocate in the person of Mr. Mercer. The writer believes he is correct in stating that the offensive
piece complained of by brother Mercer, which appeared in the Baptist Magazine, was not published by
the sanction of the Board. In a manner worthy of
all commendation, that highly respectable and efficient
body have ever kept themselves aloof from all matters irrelevant to the one great object for which they
were appointed, *the superintendence of our Foreign
Missionary work.*

" *Imprisonment of the Missionaries to the Cherokees.*"

"BROTHER BRANTLY,

"In regard to this subject, the editors of periodicals seem to me to have made themselves busy-bodies
in other men's matters, understanding neither what
they say, nor whereof they affirm. It is truly to be
regretted that such an event should have ever transpired. But before Georgia should be criminated, it
ought to be demonstrated to be the legitimate result
of her laws; and not the sheer consequence of insubordinate feelings, and unloyal conduct in the missionaries towards them.

"The right of Georgia to extend her government
over that part of her state which was in the occupancy of the Cherokees, I do not pretend to determine;
and it seems to come with a very ill grace, from any
individual, unhesitatingly to denounce the judicial
proceedings of a sovereign state, as 'unconstitutional,
unjust and wicked.' But it may, however, be asked,

what right that was which Georgia conveyed to the United States by the cession of 1802? And whether the United States did not take jurisdiction over the territory ceded, and all the Indian tribes therein, by virtue of said contract? If so, then it was always right in Georgia to exercise the same jurisdiction within that part of her territory not so ceded; and the United States could constitutionally have no control over it but by her consent. Under this consent, impliedly yielded, the United States have had a governmental agency over the Cherokees, till they attempted the establishment of an independent, national government within the limits of Georgia. Now it is believed no state would look on such a government rising up within her bounds, with approbation. Georgia did not approve of it, and has resisted it. And who can blame her?

"They who know any thing of the affairs of the Cherokee country, as it lies under the agency of the United States, know that no white person (except he belong to the nation,) was permitted to reside among the Indians, without a license both from the United States and the Indians; and that yet intruders were constantly insinuating themselves among them; not only to serve themselves of the Indians, but to eat the fat of the land; and that the United States' troops had frequently to scour the country and drive them out. It became Georgia, therefore, in taking the government of her territory, to act on the same principle, and to see that no white person (not otherwise authorized,) should reside therein, who was either disposed to gratify his own licentious interests, or was inimical to her cause. This was necessary, both for the safety of the Indians, and the good of the state.

It was therefore provided by law, that after a given time, all white persons residing among the Indians within her jurisdiction, (United States' and states' agents, persons renting improvements of Indians emigrated west of the Mississippi, all females and children excepted,) should have obtained a license or permit from the governor or his agent, for that purpose; and have subscribed the following oath: 'I, A. B., do solemnly swear (or affirm as the case may be,) that I will support and defend the constitution and laws of the state of Georgia, and uprightly demean myself as a citizen thereof, so help me God;' or on failure thereof, should be deemed 'guilty of an high misdemeanor, and upon conviction thereof, shall be punished by confinement in the penitentiary at hard labor, for a term not less than four years.' This is the obnoxious law, to which the missionaries not yielding, as pious christians should, a quiet submission, but opposing their resistance, have fallen under its penalty, and are imprisoned in the penitentiary. But, brother Editor, what can there be in this law, so offensive to these missionaries? Its requirements bind them to do nothing but what all good men are morally bound to do; and to which all the disinterested motives inducing these men to engage in the missionary enterprise, should have influenced them to yield a ready compliance; not only because the law of God requires it, but because the very constitution and laws they would thereby bind themselves to support, do guarantee to, and defend them in 'the inestimable privilege of worshipping God in a manner agreeable to their own conscience.' Thus it will appear, these men were only required to support the laws, which in turn would have supported them in their missionary labors. Why then resist them? And why is Georgia denounced as highly criminal in this affair, even by christian editors?

"I have seen in the 'Pioneer' of the West, some harsh and even cruel things on this subject, which would have better suited an infidel paper. I had thought the editor, a brother of more candor, and dispassionate argument.

"But, more than all, I have sickened at reading a piece, under the above caption, in the 'American Baptist Magazine.' The publishers are men of undoubted worth, deep and liberal piety. And it is the more to be regretted, that they should have been led to publish this libel on Georgia, so derogatory to the genius and objects of the Magazine; but especially as they had its refutation, not merely within their reach, but in their very grasp! It would have been less painful if they had no missionary in the same territory, and subjected to the same laws; but he promptly met the requirements, and so far from sinking, he stands higher in the estimation of all parties; so that they had a practical demonstration, under their own patronage, that the evil complained of was neither in the design, laws, nor administration of Georgia; else their Missionary would have been imprisoned too!

"They say, 'the periodical publications have furnished the disgraceful fact, that Dr. Butler and Mr. Worcester, Missionaries among the Cherokees, have been sentenced to the penitentiary in Georgia, for residing among the Indians.' This is part true, but to a stranger it conveys what is not true. These men were not sentenced to the penitentiary, merely for residing among the Indians; but for residing within the jurisdiction of Georgia, in defiance of her laws: but whether this is a disgraceful fact to Georgia remains to be proved. If, however, it is wicked in a state to execute her laws, and cause them to be respected within her own bounds—if Missionaries, as such, are unaccountable to any laws, human or divine, and if it is virtuous in them to despise dominion and speak evil of dignities, then it is a disgraceful fact, that Georgia has reduced them; but if otherwise, then these nominal Missionaries are suffering only the reward of their own temerity!

"The managers of the Magazine have adverted to 'the imprisonment of Mr. Judson, in Burmah, and of John Bunyan, in England,' as analagous, it should seem, not only the more to disgrace Georgia, but to 'arouse feeling of the most decisive disapprobation in the breasts of every Christian and patriot,' against her. But is there any parity in the cases? Is the government of Georgia a despotic barbarism? Has she made any laws 'forbidding ministers to preach the gospel,' or to prevent Missionaries 'remaining on the Indian lands, and exercising their missionary functions? If she has, the fact is disgraceful; but, if not, then they should have remembered what that means— I will have mercy and not sacrifice.

"But they further say, 'perhaps no event has occurred in the country, which has excited greater surprise and displeasure among good men, than the degrading manner in which the Missionaries of the cross have been arrested, conducted in chains to trial, and consigned to the penitentiary.' But it remains to be proved, that these professed 'Missionaries of the cross' received any mal-treatment—especially that they were 'conducted in chains to trial;' as the conducting officer assures me, there never was a chain on them, except while in bed, and that only for safekeeping, as the other prisoners were.

"The managers seem to take for granted what is not true, and therefore have been led into error; that is, that Georgia has passed laws forbidding missionary operations among the Indians; and have condemned these men as Missionaries. But no such laws exist, nor has any judicial proceeding been had with these men, in any other character than white men, offending against her laws. Georgia regrets, we all regret, that they were Missionaries.

"Since writing the above, I have been informed, that the Supreme Court of the United States, (or a majority of the Judges presiding,) have sustained the writ of error against Georgia, and decreed that the sentence of the Superior Court here should be reversed, and the prisoners released. But this decree makes the case neither better nor worse in a moral point of view: circumstantially, it may make it a great deal worse. It will be viewed in Georgia as an interference with her internal rights, which has no constitutional basis; nay, as a direct infringement of her constitutional right, and an infraction of her sovereignty within her own judicial bounds. As the Governor and Legislature of Georgia considered the writ nugatory, and confiding in the wisdom and justice of the Supreme Court, determined not to appear in the case, it is probable her Judges will pay as little attention to the decree. If so, and it should be attempted to be enforced, none need be surprised, should it prove the scissors that clips the cord that binds our union, and the pen that writes Ichabod on it for ever.

"Dear brother, I tremble while I write, at the prospect before us. I have always been an unionist, and have resisted all ideas of dissolution as desperate. But when I hear Solomon say, 'Surely oppression maketh a wise man mad;' and James, 'Behold how great a matter a little fire kindleth;' I can but fear the signs of these times! I hope, however, that there may yet be 'a redeeming spirit' in the United States, 'and that she may adopt a course, which may allay the just excitement which exists in the public mind' of Georgia, and preserve our beloved Union. Our last, and only sure resort, however, is—

> 'God is our refuge in distress,
> A present help when dangers press;
> In him undaunted we'll confide;
> Though earth were from her centre tost,
> And mountains in the ocean lost,
> Torn piece-meal by the roaring tide.'

"JESSE MERCER."

CHAPTER X.

Mr. Mercer and the Temperance Cause.—At first stands aloof.—His reasons for this in a letter to Mr. Brantly.—Mr. B.'s editorial comments.—Finally takes the pledge.—Establishes a Temperance Paper.—Opposes the use of wine.—His opinion on the traffic in spirits.—Remarks from the Index.—Sketch of a Temperance Discourse —Short notes on the Wine Question.

It would not be proper to pass over in entire silence Mr. Mercer's relation to the great Temperance Reformation. For several years he took no active part in its support, and it is highly probable that many of his friends and admirers, by the influence of his example, were induced to withhold their names from the temperance pledge. And as he was in the habit for many years, in accordance with the advice of physicians, of using *Cogniac Brandy*, in moderate quantities, we are not required by charity to discredit some reports which crept into circulation, that now and then an inveterate drinker, with an air of complacency and triumph, would quote the example of Mr. Mercer in his own vindication. The following extracts from a letter of Mr. Mercer, published in the Columbian Star and Christian Index, in 1829, may be read with some interest, as it explains the ground occupied by him at that time. The letter was intended to rebuke what he considered the unguarded and intemperate zeal of some of the friends of the Reformation, and also to present his reasons for not connecting himself with a temperance Society.

"It becomes the members and *real* friends of temperance to be moderate, forbearing and tender; not to offend, but conciliate. To bear much without retort; to go forward without conflict; to gain the vantage ground by non-resistance. I am (if non-members can be) friendly to the anti-intemperance societies. I have been informed, however, that my example has been quoted on the opposite side. *This I deeply regret.* I am sure this was done without knowing any justifying reason, except, that I still used spirits, and had not become a member of some temperance society. For the sake of such I will state my example and the cause why I am not an actual member, &c. 'When it pleased the Lord to reveal his dear Son in me,' and to impress me with the worth of immortal souls, I was made deeply to deplore the ravages of intemperance, and to inquire what was the source of this wide-spreading evil: And I soon came to the conclusion that the tippling shops, and other places of public resort for drinking, were the most, if not the true and only cause of intemperance; and I have ever avoided them *as the snares of death*. No man can, with truth, accuse me of entering, or visiting one of these places and calling *for a gill or half pint*, to this day. I have, in days when temperance societies were unknown, recommended this as an example to others; but with what success, the day of final decision must make known. It may be asked, why I am not a member? It is not because I think 'it degrading to a Baptist to become a member of a temperance society,' but that my brethren have *now* gone rather too far for me, and more especially, because I wish to be *consistent* in the view of my beholders. 1. I have not yet been convinced that the *use* of spirits is *in itself* a sin. Convince me of this and I will be a member, or come to 'the desired result.' But, 2d. I have been in bad health for years past, as you know, and after using many celebrated and prepared medicines, without effect, to restore the tone of my intestines, several of the most eminent physicians, at different times and places, recommended to me the *habitual use* of Cogniac brandy. This course I adopted *reluctantly*, but with apparently good effect. I now use it medicinally; but this cannot be *generally known*, and therefore, I do not join the society. But the main object—*to promote temperance, by suppressing intemperance*, I most cordially patronise and wish to promote. But I fear it is likely to suffer in the hands of its friends."

Upon the letter, from which the above is extracted, the Editor, Rev. W. T. Brantly, who by the by was an ardent friend and great admirer of Mr. Mercer, made some rather severe, though entirely well-meant, and good-natured comments. They excited many a pleasant smile at the time, rather at the expense of the venerable brother; and the Editor's expressive figure, "*Brandy Bay*," soon became a standard phrase amongst the people. The following are his remarks:

"We can never dissent from any opinion or practice of our dear MERCER, without suspecting and scrutinizing the accuracy of our own views. He is so uniformly right and good, that we might be almost tempted to pick up, and preserve, the very errors which he *lets fall;* but in the present case he has dropt from the rear wallet, more of this commodity than we can honestly pocket, and more we apprehend than he himself will, on reflection, think worth preservation. The use of *Cogniac* in his own case for *medicinal purposes*, we pretend not to question. Let it be so in his case and in all other similar cases. If it be an essential article in the *Materia Medica*, we have no quarrel with it. But we should remember, nevertheless, that if our use of *calomel* or *arsenic*, which are potent medicines, should be likely to make our neighbors and families so fond of the poison as to endanger their lives, though we ourselves might be wise enough to avoid danger from it, yet on their account we should banish the snare. I have a good vessel and steerage, and am an expert sailor, and can therefore cruise about in *Brandy Bay* without being drawn into the whirlpool of intemperance, but some of my less skilful neighbors, seeing me sail so pleasantly, may be tempted to go a pleasuring upon the same deceitful Bay, and may be lost. If my example encouraged them to the venture, I should have cause of regret."

Satisfied at length that his example was doing injury, under the influence of the sacred principle laid down by the Apostle Paul, that "*it is good neither to eat flesh, nor to drink wine, nor any thing whereby thy brother stumbleth, or is offended, or is made weak*," Mr. Mercer determined to abandon his little moderate excursions on "*Brandy Bay*," though rendered somewhat needful as he supposed, by his declining health, and draw up his boat and fasten it for ever upon the safe and dry shore of *Total Abstinence*.

He soon became a thorough and able advocate of the cause, was appointed the President of a Temperance Society in the town where he resided, and established a temperance paper, which, though sustained at a pecuniary loss to himself, had considerable circulation, and was the means of doing much good. The paper was transferred with the Index office to Penfield, where it is now published by Mr. Benj. Brantly, not however, as the paper of the Convention, but as his own individual concern.

Should any be anxious to know what effect the entire disuse of *Cogniac Brandy* had upon Mr. Mercer's health, the writer feels authorized to state, for he heard it from his own lips, that his abstinence was rather beneficial than otherwise, and that he was satisfied at length the *medicine* he had been using tended, on the whole, to aggravate the disease it was designed to mitigate.

It will be recollected that for many years the use of wine was tolerated by most temperance societies, but that at last the propriety of this began to be questioned, and finally that it became pretty generally a settled point, that the temperance reformation demanded for itself a radical *reform*, inasmuch as its great designs could not thoroughly and universally be accomplished upon any other principle than that of total abstinence from all kinds of intoxicating drinks. At the early stage of this *second reform*, Mr. Mercer was found amongst its warmest advocates; and he was no less ready to warn the people of the dangerous shoals of *Madeira Lake*, than he had been for many years to point out the fatal *whirlpools* of *Brandy Bay*.

Mr. Mercer's opinion of the traffic in ardent spirits may be learned from an answer which he gave through the Index to the question, "What is to be done with a church member who traffics in ardent spirits?" It is as follows:

"In this case we are of opinion, the church should be as *kindly affectioned* towards such a brother, as the case will permit, and endeavor by brotherly love to dissuade him from his course. His duty however is plain. He should immediately forsake the traffic which is *offensive* to his brethren, *as his bounden duty*. Read Rom. 14 : 13. 15. 19, 20, 21. 1 Cor. 8 : 10–13. The scripture requires us to walk circumspectly. It ought to be noticed, that public opinion is changed, and changing very fast on this subject. And the traffic in ardent spirits cannot be entered into now, as safely as it could some years ago. It is *now* satisfactorily ascertained that there is *no benefit* whatsoever in ardent spirits. It must therefore be *morally* wrong to offer for sale, that which the vender knows can do the buyer *no good*. It must be worse to offer for sale that which he knows, while it can do him *no good*, may do him much harm. We regret very much that any Christian brother should allow himself, under any pretence, to engage in a traffic which would make it his interest to encourage his fellow-men to ruin themselves for time and eternity. And such must be the interest of those who enter into the traffic of ardent spirits."

The annexed piece from the pen of Mr. Mercer, appeared also in the columns of the Index. It contains some solid and judicious reflections.

"A MATTER FOR SOBER CONSIDERATION."

"*Now consider this, ye that forget God, lest I tear you in pieces, and there be none to deliver.*

JEHOVAH.

"It is wise and safe in man to study the will, and endeavor to walk before God *to all well pleasing*. To be indifferent to his honor, must be offensive to his majesty and provoking to his wrath. We are commanded that *whether we eat or drink, or whatsoever we do, to do all to the glory of God.* This teaches us that the little affairs of life and the pleasures of taste should all be regulated by this rule: for we may offend in eating and drinking. This must depend on the motives we have, and the extent to which we indulge them in eating and drinking. Our Creator made us dependant on wholesome aliment for growth, health and beauty; and has graciously given us appetites and cravings for it. The gratification of these natural desires so far as consists with the ends to be secured, must be according to the pleasure of him who *gave us richly all things to enjoy;* but all beyond this must be injurious and offensive—must be intemperance, gluttony and debauch. This evil state will be produced by losing sight (in part or in whole) of the meet ends to be attained in eating and drinking, and in seeking to satiate those appetites which are excessive, and which in their indulgence become insatiable; and thus men plunge themselves into licentiousness, dissipation and perdition.

"There is another circumstance which aggravates this sore evil among the people. It is the preparation of food, or the invention of new articles of food, to suit the cravings of the vitiated palate, or to please a debased taste, which, instead of improving the strength, pleasure and usefulness of the body, only tends to enervation, disease and death. Among this last class, are those articles of food which have in them no nutriment at all, and are used only for certain relishes which they possess, suitable to gratify the palate and regale the taste, and which are, therefore, the better adapted to increase dissipation, misery and ruin in society. Here it may be proper to inquire, whether this was not, most probably, the very purpose for which intoxicating liquors were at first introduced *as a beverage*, into common use? It could not have been on account of any nutritious quality they had; for universal experience has proven that they contain no such quality. It must, therefore, have been from some medical virtue found in them, or their tendency to excite and please a vicious taste their use had created; or to animate the feelings and arouse the baser passions of the heart. It may be asked if they can in no way be lawfully used? We answer yes: in just so far as they can be satisfactorily proven to be needful, either for the good of the user or the happiness of the community; otherwise their use will be injurious, and, by the dictates of common sense, ought to be declined. But it may be further asked,—does not the bible allow their use; Yes—just so far and no farther than they are beneficial. The bible does not permit their use for food; for there is no sustenance in them. It cannot allow their use for the fulfilment of any but the innocent and natural desires—but there are no such desires for them to satisfy. There is nothing in them that can gratify any natural propensity of nature. The bible, then, allows their use only so far as they are medical. That is in cases of disease, where the patient '*is ready to perish*,' and sinking nature needs some artificial excitement, or when pining sickness, or hysteria, and other disordered affections (heavy hearts,) or a complication of complaints (often infirmities,) make their use needful to sustain, invigorate and assist the body in regaining its health.

"But we are fully of opinion that the bible *indirectly*, at least, forbids their use as a common beverage, because that use is practised only to gratify a desire or taste which is unnatural, and unnecessary for the benefit of the body, but altogether artificial, and which, in the attempt to supply its cravings, proves itself *insatiate* and vicious. Let it be carefully determined to what class of desires mentioned in the bible, the desire which leads to the use of spirituous liquors, belongs. Can it be classed with those desires for nourishment which are common? No—because these always have something good, and capable to give the satisfaction in view; but there is no such capacity in those liquors to afford gratification, and the desire for them does not belong legitimately to human nature. Does it in any wise associate with the desires of the child of grace, who is prompted by the spirit to seek spiritual nourishment? No—for these are holy; and the more they are fulfilled, the more spiritual, holy, heavenly and godlike do their possessors become; but not so with the desire for alcoholic drinks, for the more it is fed, the more *earthly, sensual and devilish* do its possessors become. It cannot belong to these. But we think it best associates with *the desires of the flesh*, in which they *who are dead in sins*, walk. These desires are called *lusts*, because of their vicious character; and they are declared by the apostle to be '*corrupt.*' And what habit tends to more corruption, individual and social, than that which is constantly, in regard to ardent spirits, like the horseleech's daughters, *crying, give, give*,—and like *the fire that can never be satisfied?* They are also pronounced 'deceitful.' And what desire in its gratification can be mare *deceitful* than this? It constantly is promising something good and pleasurable to its votaries, and yet deals uniformly in disappointments, wretchedness and death. They also are said to '*war against the soul.*' And what desire or lust can strike a more deadly blow at every interest of the soul, whether for time or eternity, than this?

"If the desire for alcoholic liquors must be classed with the lusts of the flesh, and we cannot see that it can be placed in any other company, then the bible must be at war with the fulfilment of it, because its tendency is as much, if not more than any other, *to fill the world with corruption.* And if God is at variance with the causes of sin, and strikes at the roots of iniquity, he must be opposed to this, *as a most fruitful source of all moral evil*—of all unrighteousness and ungodliness in the earth. To suppose him to be favorable to the gratification of this desire, *any more than he is favorable to the practice of sin*, would be to suppose him the accomplice of the workers of iniquity, and to have fellowship with the fruitful work of unrighteousness; which would be palpably derogatory to all the attributes of his nature, and counter to all the tenor of his word. It cannot be.

"And now to conclude this long article, permit us to address among our readers, the professors of religion. We request every christian brother whose eyes shall fall on these lines, to ask himself, as in the presence of God his Saviour, whether it is right to use any thing, not necessary to his well-being, which tends to generate a thirst, the gratification of which is dangerous to morality, piety, and religion? And whether it can be right to fulfil the desires of that thirst when excited, since it only leads to disorder, misery, and death? You have professed to be converted from sin, to have turned to God and joined his armies, warring against all unrighteousness and ungodliness in the world. Truly it may be said of those who indulge in potations to slake this vicious thirst, *that they have not resisted unto blood, striving against sin;* but they have by their example and influence, been building up the strongholds of the kingdom of darkness. Alas! alas! for this inconsistency. We are astonished that christian professors have slept over this glaring sin so long. That they have not opened their eyes and looked on the prodigious strides which iniquity is taking by means of this vice, encouraged by their example, leaving behind it nought but tears, wo and despair. We trust they will soon take the warning, and arise to the rescue. That ministers of the gospel will, with one voice, 'Blow the trumpet in Zion, and sound the alarm in God's holy mount,' until all shall unite in the pledge of total abstinence."

Brief sketch of a temperance discourse found amongst Mr. Mercer's manuscripts.

"Rom. 13 : 10. Love worketh no ill to his neighbor; Therefore love is the fulfilling of the Law."

"I. Love—what is it?

"Love fulfils both tables of the law. Matt. 22 : 35—40. But more particularly the second. Matt. 7 : 12. Love to ourselves fixes the standard of moral conduct. It is a principle of nature. Rom. 2 : 13—15. It secures us from harm. Eph. 5 : 29.—and leads to happiness and praise. Ps. 49 : 18. ('Men will praise thee when thou doest well to thyself.')

"This principle will secure our neighbor from injury, (see the text,) and seek his good; Rom. 15 : 2. It will forego its own pleasure to save its neighbor from suffering injury; Rom. 14 : 21. It will even abandon what is lawful, *lest* it should do harm, &c.; 1 Cor. 8 : 9—13.

"It appears from the foregoing, that all men are bound not to injure themselves or their neighbor; but to do good both to themselves and their neighbor. This is the law of nature and nature's God. And this, love to God and love to man will secure.

"II. Having fixed the true principles of morality, let us now apply them to the subject before us.

"Let us inquire whether intoxicating liquors can be used as a common beverage, without injury to ourselves and others?

" 1. To ourselves. They are unnecessary. Unnatural excitements must do harm. They may infix [evil] habits; create [improper] relishes, and produce diseases and death.

" 2. To others. The use of intoxicating beverages will influence society for evil.

" The effect on the reforming inebriate must be destructive. Intemperance will increase as any intoxicating drinks are indulged in.

" Motives to total abstinence. Love of ourselves—love of country—love of our family—love of our neighbor—and lastly, love to God and immortal happiness, should secure us against this besetting sin."

To the above may be added a few short notes in reference to the objection which is sometimes urged against total abstinence societies, viz. that the scriptures allow the use of wine.

" 1. The bible seems to show the proper use to be restricted to the faint and weary. See the case 2 Sam. 16 : 1, 2. and the case of Lemuel, Prov. 31 : 4—6. These are high examples.

" 2. The *disuse* is commended—In the case of the Rechabites, Jer. 35 : 18, 19. In the case of Daniel, &c.; Dan. 1 : 5. 8. 15. In the case of John the Baptist; Luke 1 : 15.

" 3. Total abstinence is enjoined in the case of the priests in the sanctuary; Lev. 10 : 8—11. Of the Nazarites; Num. 6 : 1—4.

" 4. It is considered a curse. See the case of Hannah; 1 Sam. 1 : 14—16. Micah 2 : 10, 11.

" 5. The history of wine in the bible, is the history of sin and death."

CHAPTER XI.

Mr. Mercer's pecuniary contributions to benevolent objects.

Mr. Mercer was a man of unbounded liberality. "I am persuaded," said he, in a letter to a christian brother, "the day will come when christians will have no other object in making money, but to give back again to the Giver, in some useful way." Few men have acted in more strict accordance with this sentiment, than the author of it himself. His liberality was not under the control of sudden, variable, and undisciplined impulses, but was regulated by sound judgment and established principle. He felt that he belonged to the Lord, that all which he possessed was the Lord's, and how well he fulfilled the duties of his stewardship, his unwearied acts of benevolence for a long series of years bear ample testimony. In his career of liberality and well-doing, "he walked by faith." He exercised an habitual and strong reliance upon those promises which connect the blessing of heaven with the judicious and bountiful appropriation of our substance to the cause of Christ. "He used to relate," says a brother that knew him well, "many instances in his own history, of the Lord's willingness to remunerate those who gave for his cause. He had been one winter handing out his five dollars to several benevolent objects as they had been presented, till he thought prudence dictated that he should do no more at present. In a day or two the claims of the Jews were brought before the community at Powelton. Notwithstanding his fears about duty, he again threw in his five dollars. That night he took from the Post

Office a letter containing twenty dollars, from an unknown person. Several instances of this kind were within his own knowledge." It might be proper here to state, that the circumstance just related occurred at a time when his means for giving were limited in comparison with what they were at a later period of his life.

It was a matter of great grief to him that so many of his brethren withheld their pecuniary aid from the cause of Christ, and that so many who pretended to give, measured out their bounty with such a parsimonious hand. He used occasionally to say, "we have a great many *dollar men* amongst us. Present to them a subscription for the preacher, and they will put down a *dollar;* hand them the missionary subscription, and they will put down a *dollar;* ask them to aid the Sabbath school cause, and they will give a *dollar.* This seems to be their standard, when many of them, if they had the disposition, might just as easily give their *fives,* their *tens,* and their *fifties.*" Brother Mercer was not a *dollar* man. He gave by hundreds and thousands, and tens of thousands. It would be very difficult, if not impossible, to make out a full and accurate list of his more public benefactions; and still more so, to write the history of his private bounties. It is probable that many and large amounts were distributed by his right hand, which his left was forbidden to know, and which will not be known to men, till the judgment shall reveal the secret charities of the faithful.

There is reason to believe that for a long series of years, most of the compensation which he received from the churches for his ministerial labors, was appropriated to charitable purposes; the addition which he made to his estate, being derived mainly from the sale of books, and other sources. After the death of his last child (in 1814,) he seemed to have lost sight of every object for the accumulation of property, but the cause of the blessed Redeemer. Some of his occasional donations to benevolent objects will now be specified.

The Columbian College shared largely in his bounty. On one occasion he gave $750 to that Institution; at another, $1000.

He aided the Mercer University by numerous and liberal contributions. To defray the current expenses at the outset, he gave say $150; for the land first and last, $550; for one of the buildings, $1000; for another, $400; For the library and apparatus, he also gave $400; and he gave his note for $5000, the interest to be appropriated to assist in the support of the faculty.

To the Female Academy in Washington, under the control of the Presbyterian denomination, he gave $300; to the Baptist church in that place, he gave a house and lot for a parsonage.

The Christian Index, press, type, and outstanding dues, he turned over to the Convention; and he also gave to the Georgia Association all the unsold copies of his history of that body, amounting to one thousand or more, to be disposed of for any purpose that his brethren might deem proper.

To the bible cause he was a liberal contributor; Tract, and Sabbath school institutions found in him a ready and bountiful patron; indeed, there was scarcely any object of benevolence placed before him, which commended itself to his judgment as proper and deserving, which was dismissed without his prayers and his alms.

His noble contributions to sustain the missionary enterprise, are well known to the christian community. Besides his regular annual contributions, which were generally large, he gave at one time to the Baptist Board of Foreign Missions, fifty shares of United States Bank stock, worth at the time, *five thousand five hundred dollars.* The enlightened views which he entertained when determining the specific application to be made of this generous donation, will appear from a short extract from a letter to Mr. Bolles the corresponding secretary. "I hasten to reply in reference to the endowment of a permanent fund. I am not of the number who believe the funds designated for missions, must not be applied to any purpose but the operations in the fields, but to all the needful means for putting those operations into motion. The support of those officers whose services are needed *all the time*, must be provided for, as well as the laborers at the stations. I am therefore, as cheerful to consecrate my bequest to that fund, the interest of which is only to be used in paying the salaries of the officers of the Board, whose services are as above, as to any missionary purpose; as the one is indispensable to the other, and will as well forward the general design."

In relation to this liberal donation, the corresponding secretary, in the closing part of a lengthy communication to Mr. Mercer, writes as follows, under date of Oct. 12, 1835. "Since writing the above, the Board has held a special meeting, and acted on the subject of your munificent donation. They were deeply impressed with the Christian and fraternal spirit which all your letters in relation to it indicate, and the enlarged views taken by you in assigning it the direction you have. The following extracts from the minutes of the Board will show their sentiments and purpose.

"'1. The corresponding secretary read a letter from the Rev. Dr. Mercer, enclosing as a donation to the Board, fifty shares of the United States Bank stock.

"'2. Also another letter from the same, specifying that the above named shares are to be a perpetual fund, the nett proceeds of which shall be applied to the support of the Secretary (or Secretaries,) and Treasurer of the convention.

"'3. Resolved, that the Board gratefully accept the above donation on the conditions specified by the donor.

"'4. Resolved, that the Cor. Secretary be requested to address a letter to the Rev. Jesse Mercer, D. D. President of this Board, expressing our high sense of his kindness and liberality, accompanied by a copy of the resolutions adopted in relation to it.'"

To some of his brethren who were on terms of confidential intercourse with him, it was known many years before his death, that he intended to bequeath the principal portion of his estate to the cause of Christ. He had many relations, and some of them in limited circumstances, who would, no doubt, have been gratified to have received a liberal portion of his substance; but the question with this conscientious and holy man was, "in what way can I dispose of that which God has given me, so that the greatest amount of good will ensue, and the Lord be most glorified?" When his Will was opened, it was found that the purpose which had been long and calmly resolved and firmly settled in his mind, was carried faithfully out. All, all that he had to dispose of, with some trifling exceptions, was bequeathed to the Saviour, who had bought him with his blood. The following extracts from his last Will and Testament, exhibit the details of his final, pious benefactions.

" As it hath pleased God to take my beloved wife, Nancy Mercer, to himself, I now proceed to make such distribution of the property now left in my hands, as voluntarily and mutually agreed upon when we first came together in marriage. We having seen, as we thought, an evil rather than a benefit, in bequeathing property to relatives; that even the expectation of receiving such gifts, often nourishes evil propensities, &c. concluded that when we should no longer need the use of our temporal effects, they should be disposed of to benevolent and literary Institutions, according as might seem to be most advisable. I therefore, for aiding and assisting in the operations of the following benevolent societies and institutions, give and devise, to wit:

"1. I give and devise to the Baptist Convention in the United States, for Foreign Missions, fifty shares of the capital stock in the bank of Augusta, Georgia.

"2. I give and devise to the Baptist Publication Society, twenty-five shares of the capital stock in the bank of Augusta, Georgia.

"3. I give and devise to the American and Foreign Bible Society, twenty-five shares of the capital stock in the bank of the state of Georgia.

"4. I give and devise to the American Tract Society, twenty-five shares of the capital stock in the Bank of Augusta, Georgia.

"5. I give and devise to the American Baptist Home Mission Society, chiefly to aid in their operations in Texas, twenty-five shares of the capital stock in the Bank of the state of Georgia.

"6. I give and devise to the trustees of the Columbian College in the District of Columbia, twenty-two shares of the capital stock in the Bank of the state of Georgia: provided, however, that if the debts of the said Columbian College remain *unpaid* six months after my decease, and the Institution still embarrassed, then the twenty-two shares of bank stock to it devised, shall be given to the Baptist Convention for foreign missions, in addition to that bequest made in No. 1 of this will.

"7. I give and devise to the trustees of the Mercer University, Penfield, Green county, Georgia, one hundred and twenty-five shares of the capital stock in the Georgia Rail Road and Banking Company, for the support of the Faculty of said Institution, and such other purposes as the said Trustees may find necessary: the dividends or annual income only, to be used.

* * * * *

"I make the further bequests:

"I give and devise to the Trustees of the Mercer University, at Penfield, Georgia, one hundred shares of the capital stock of the Bank of the state of Georgia, and the whole residuary of my estate, which may remain after the payment of all my just debts and necessary claims thereon, and what may hereafter be bequeathed. This amount is to constitute, with the sum of the professorship made by the Central Association, a professorship of Sacred, Biblical Literature, or Theological Learning. The annual income of which only, to be used.

* * * * *

"My library I wish also to be turned over to the University, and all other books which may remain undisposed of at the time of my decease, to be disposed of as the Trustees may direct."

How pleasant to the pious heart to contemplate such pure and bright examples of enlarged and disinterested philanthropy. They are rare indeed, but their moral influence upon the church cannot but be salutary and lasting. Each one is a portion of precious leaven thrown into the great mass, which in due time will work out a sure and blessed result. Covetousness, which has so long been the sin and curse of the church, must sooner or later yield up its sway under the increasing light and power of gospel influence. But the benevolent heart is pained in reflecting how long it will probably be, before this auspicious era will arrive, and the universal church fully realize the sweetness and glory of the Saviour's words, "IT IS MORE BLESSED TO GIVE THAN TO RECEIVE." Is there one amongst a hundred, nay, one amongst a thousand of the Baptists of America, who, as to his pecuniary sacrifices for the spread of the gospel, has a right to share the honor of her that anointed the Saviour for his burying, of whom it was said, *"she hath done what she could."* There are about sixty thousand Baptists in the state of Georgia. Were they all to be warmed with pentecostal fire and love; were the grace vouchsafed to the Macedonian churches, which, in their deep poverty, abounded still in their charities, and to their power, and beyond their power, imparted of their substance to relieve their suffering brethren; we should soon see an amount brought forward for benevolent purposes, equal, perhaps, to the present annual contributions of the entire denomination for Foreign and Domestic Missions. It would no longer be necessary to beg and implore, and argue, to gain their consent to give, but with joyful haste would each and all come forward, "praying us with much entreaty that we would receive the gift," and bear it speedily to the needy and perishing. There are half a million Baptists in the United States, who could give annually, from fifty cents to one thousand dollars for the dissemination of gospel light. Yet there are thousands, whom God has blessed with plenty, and who profess to have been purchased with the blood of Christ, and to be heirs of a heavenly crown, who have not a mite to give; and of those that do something, how many are *farthing* men, and *dollar* men, who would be the happier and the richer for increasing their bounty a hundred fold. When our brethren shall all begin to feel that the highest and noblest object they are to have in view in making money, is "*to give it back again to the Giver, in some useful way,*" when they shall all begin to associate the claims of Zion with the daily wants of their wives and children, and plow, and sow, and reap for the Lord and his cause, rather than for the gratification of their own pride and covetousness, and love of ease; when each shall settle it in his mind to do what he can, certainly, systematically, and from established and deep-seated principle, then will abundant means flow in for all needful objects in our own, and every foreign land; nay, it might soon be necessary to say to the churches, as was said to ancient Israel when contributing for the Ark and the Tabernacle, "*the people bring much more than enough for the service of the work.*" It is high time for us, as a people, to bemoan our sins, and repent in dust and ashes. What poor returns have we made to the Lord for all his benefits! The examples of Judson, and Cobb, and Withington, and Mercer, reprove us; especially are we reproved by the example of our blessed Saviour, who, "*though he was rich, yet for our sakes became poor, that we through his poverty might be rich.*"

CHAPTER XII.

Unhappy divisions in the churches.—Mr. Mercer's opinions as to the causes.—His Circular Letter published in the Convention Minutes of 1831.—Usefulness at ministers' meetings.—Extracts from his sermon on ministerial union.—Letters to Mr. B. and Mr. L.

For twenty-five or thirty years previous to 1829, the Baptist churches of Georgia had lived in great peace and harmony. Some occasional difficulties, it is true, had occurred, but they were generally confined to narrow bounds, to inconsiderable numbers, and were of comparatively short duration. The years 1827 and 1828 were signalized by a remarkable outpouring of the spirit upon many of the churches, and by uncommonly large and rapid accessions to their numbers.

This period of unexampled prosperity was followed by extraordinary efforts on the part of the adversary of the church, to sow the tares of strife and confusion. A great reaction in the zeal of many of Christ's ministers and people seems to have taken place; practical godliness was too generally neglected; those continued and well directed means, which are so essential to perpetuate and multiply the happy results of powerful revivals of religion, were greatly neglected; and of course we need not be much surprised that the efforts of the enemy were so sadly and extensively successful. The writer would gladly avoid all reference to this unpleasant topic; but a narrative that should entirely overlook it, would not be a full and faithful record of the life of Mr. Mercer. Whilst, therefore, a sense of duty compels him to take a cursory view of some events which cannot be called to mind but with the deepest sorrow, he trusts that he will not be suspected of the most distant intention to afflict the feelings of a single christian brother, or to rend afresh those wounds which are now so rapidly healing under the gracious care of the great Head of the church.

A disposition on the part of some of the associations to interfere in what was considered an arbitrary and unscriptural manner with the affairs of the churches, was one of the most fruitful sources of the many distressing evils which so long afflicted the Baptists of Georgia. The encroachments of associations were met with prompt resistance on the part of many of the churches, mingled, oftentimes, no doubt, with a spirit not the most lovely and conciliating; this, in some instances, was followed by attempts on the part of the associations to justify their previous course, and by further acts, which the churches deemed an unwarrantable interference with their rights. The result of these proceedings was, that some of the churches withdrew from the associations, and some were withdrawn from; whilst others were sadly divided amongst themselves, and rent into fragments. In many cases, associational correspondence was laid aside, ministerial friendship and intercourse were entirely suspended, and the communion and the fellowship of the churches broken. Bitter jealousies, evil surmisings, and uncharitable accusations were multiplied; whilst the occasional attempts which were made to bring about a more desirable state of things, seemed for a time, only to aggravate the disorders they were intended to cure. In the mean time, the anti-missionary spirit, which it is to be feared had been secretly operating for several years, burst forth in great violence, and by its rending, non-fellowship policy, increased still further the work of strife and confusion. It was one of the greatest afflictions of Mr. Mercer's life, that some of the brethren with whom he had co-operated on terms of christian confidence and affection, became alienated from him, and from those noble, benevolent objects which he had so long been engaged in sustaining, and that some even went so far as to accuse him of a departure from the gospel faith.

Under such peculiar circumstances, it seemed that important duties devolved upon the intelligent and influential members of the denomination; and especially, upon the venerable father whose counsels had ever been so much valued in times of difficulty and trial. It was of great importance to ascertain and exhibit the causes of these multiplied afflictions, and also to search out and unfold the appropriate remedies; to place in a clear and convincing light, before the churches and associations, the established principles of the denomination, and wherein these principles had been lost sight of; and not only to bring back the erring to correct principles of discipline, but, as far as possible, to assuage exasperated feeling, and restore divided and alienated brethren to each others confidence, fellowship, and affection. In the efforts which were made to accomplish these desirable ends, Mr. Mercer, as might have been expected, took a conspicuous part. His faithful exertions at associational meetings, his private labors with brethren by epistolary correspondence and personal intercourse, his able circulars and essays, together with his numerous editorial communications in the Index, in exposition of the faith and practice of the denomination, and his prompt, indefatigable labors at important ministerial convocations, all go to illustrate the ardent zeal with which he toiled for reconciliation and peace, as well as the great utility of the services which he rendered.

The disunion of the churches had been charged by some to the objects and operations of the Baptist State Convention. In reference to this accusation, Mr. Mercer makes the following judicious remarks. "Before any acts can be considered 'fellowship-destroying,' they must be ascertained to be either immoral in themselves, or evil in their tendency. But what immorality or evil tendency was there in the objects of the General Association? For instance, what *immorality* can there be in an effort to *unite the influence* and *pious intelligence* of *Georgia Baptists*, so as thereby to facilitate their union and co-operation? Or what evil can there be in *forming* and *encouraging* plans for the revival of experimental and practical religion? Or can there be any sin in *giving effect* to the useful plans of the several Associations? Or can it be thought a bad thing to *furnish the means* for the education of *young, pious* and *indigent* men, who are *approved* by their churches as called of God to the gospel ministry? Or can it be regarded by any as an immoral thing *to promote pious and useful* education in the Baptist denomination? We cannot conclude that any man whose mind has been in any wise imbued by that wisdom which *is necessary to direct*, will pretend there is any cause in any of these objects to break the union of the churches."

Some of Mr. Mercer's views as to the real causes of the unhappy divisions complained of may be learned from one or two extracts from his editorial communications.

"All divisions are the fruit of contention and strife, originating in pride and ambition, the agitating of '*unlearned questions*,' or departures from the true faith and order. There is no evil against which we are more advised and cautioned in scripture, than this; which shows, not only the evil of party strifes, but the unhappy bias under which we naturally tend to divide and break asunder the cords which bind us together in unity and peace; and against which we ought therefore to keep up a most strenuous guard.

"I consider the causes of these divisions, which have rent our churches and spoiled our beauty, as a denomination, are to be found in *the neglect of a godly discipline*, and the consequent results.

"Our Lord has laid down a few plain rules of government, and established a tribunal in his church, at which all offences are to be tried and decided; and from which *there is no appeal*. I believe it is adopted by all regular Baptists as the doctrine of Christ, that his church is his kingdom on earth; that he sits in judgment there; and that when a gospel church is sitting *in gospel order*, for the transaction of disciplinary business, *there is not a higher court on earth;* and that such church *is arraignable at no other, or foreign bar:* because her Judge is in her midst, and has commanded her implicit obedience. Now any departure from these rules, and any appeal from this authority and tribunal, will, can do no other than produce amongst Baptists, strifes and divisions."

Again he observes:

"The Lord has laid down those rules by which a godly government can be kept up, and all the separations or distinctions placed between the righteous and the wicked, which are necessary for all the purposes of godliness in the world. Now any rules set up, other than his, are stumbling blocks set up, by which brethren are made to fall. When churches or associations establish rules which the scriptures nowhere require, and make the observance of them necessary to fellowship; then they *cause divisions and offences contrary to the doctrine we have learned*. We think our brethren have gotten into the habit of placing too great stress on particular points of doctrine, and even on a *particular* mode of construing them, and are determined on forcing a uniformity of faith by associational union.—If so, they will cause divisions, and not union. Union between christians, is like the coming together of two straight edges, it readily forms a joint; or it is like the going up of the temple, where no tool of iron was necessary to bring any thing to a joint. Force will never make a union among christians; but force will drive them out of joint. Where force is used, therefore, to keep the unity of the faith, it will always *cause divisions and offences, contrary to the doctrine we have learned.* When will our brethren learn the *easy way* of keeping *the unity of the faith in the bond of peace?*"

In the following extract, Mr. Mercer glances at an evil which had become unhappily prevalent amongst some of his ministering brethren, and which he reproves in the spirit of christian kindness.

"Among the ministers of Christ, there is a diversity of gifts, and of course, different strains of preaching. Some are set, like Paul, for the defence of the gospel, or the establishment of the saints in faith; others, like James, to excite christian professors to every good word and work. In this strain of preaching there may be an appearance of heterodoxy in its tendency, which is not real. And still *more so* in the strain of the evangelists, who are sent *to call sinners to repentance.* There must then be great care taken in such cases, lest *the oil and the wine be hurt.* But should it be satisfactorily clear that the tendency is too heterodox, then the church (or rather those brethren who notice it and are best able to judge,) should converse freely, and admonish such an one tenderly and faithfully; and if this does not remedy the evil, he should be reproved sharply by the pastor or elders: and if this fails, he should be called before the church, and if he refuse to be subject to the church's counsel, his gift must be taken from him, and if he refuse to lay it down, or otherwise carry himself disorderly and incorrigibly, he must be excluded.

"We take this occasion to state our conviction that there is utterly a fault among the ministers of Christ; that is, instead of each one pursuing his proper calling, according to the gift he has received of the Lord, and all laboring in different parts of the same field together, to obtain the same great object, they too often fall out and accuse one another of some supposed error, or inconsistency in their matter or manner of labor; each one at the same time sacrificing so far to his own drag, as to condemn his fellow servants because they do not labor *precisely* with him. Thus the *high* predestinarians accuse the *low* with arminianism; and in turn the *low* accuse the *high* with antinomianism. Now this may be in some cases true; and proper steps should be taken, *in the spirit* of christian meekness, to remedy it: but this spirit of crimination and recrimination cannot be right. Let not him, therefore, that preaches the covenant and all things *ordered in it* and *made sure*, despise him that preaches that men should repent, and exhorts, admonishes and beseeches them to turn to God through Christ; nor yet him that *dwells* on practical godliness, because he does not preach election in every sermon; and let not those despise him that preaches the purposes of God in the salvation of his chosen people, as the theme of his ministry, for God may have accepted them all in their different spheres of labor.

"We most affectionately exhort and admonish all our brethren in the ministry, to cease to look on each other with an *evil* eye, and to speak of each other with *harsh* words. But let us all rather take the Apostle's advice in Rom. 14 : 13. in view of the most solemn and interesting fact that *every one of us shall give account* OF HIMSELF TO GOD. 'Let us not therefore judge one another any more: but judge this rather, that no man put a stumbling block, or an occasion to fall, in his brother's way.'"

A Circular from the pen of Mr. Mercer, and published in the Convention Minutes of 1831, has a direct bearing upon the topics embraced in the present chapter; and it contains so much sound and valuable instruction, as to entitle it to a prominent place in these biographical sketches.

"MEN AND BRETHREN,

"Having obtained help of God, we are now assembled, according to appointment, and for the time we have been together, have had much pleasure in meeting and enjoying each other's company, harmony in deliberation, and comfort in the prospect before us; though, at the same time, mingled with sorrow, for the desolations of Zion: And, therefore, beg leave to address you, in a few unvarnished remarks, on the importance of a *more elevated* standard of christian morality among the churches and ministers of our denomination.

"The standard of christian morals, in itself considered, is THE TRUTH, *as it is in Jesus;* and is incapable of either elevation or depression: but in our present design, it means the *public* estimation and *practical* regard, in which it is held; and will be *higher* or *lower*, according to the views *truth* obtains in the denomination; and to which the practice of the churches will conform, and will be *elevated* or *depressed* accordingly. Just as water seeks its own level, or as the conduct of a community accords to public opinion; *so* will christians' morals be influenced by the standard of piety and godliness, as held sacred among the churches. This will be strikingly illustrated by reference to the one only point, in which, we think, this standard is sufficiently raised among us, that is, it is *universally agreed* that immersion, and nothing *but immersion is* BAPTISM; and the practice is everywhere, in the denomination, *one and the same*—there is no difference—no dispute about it. Now if the standard was equally elevated in every other point of faith and duty, the churches would be in all points, in *the same* practical unity and peace; and tending fast to perfectness. Just as rays of light converge, as they approach their centre, so we, in following this standard, when duly elevated, shall approximate each other, as we approach THE TRUTH, *as it is in Jesus;* and losing all asperities in assimilations to him, who is *the truth* itself, be swallowed up in light. But as rays of light, flying off from their source, diverge as they fly, till they lose themselves in regions of unbroken darkness; *so* we, in pursuing a depressed standard of piety, must *widen* and *separate*—become less and less ardent in christian affections, and losing all sense of vital union, merge into bitter animosities and destructive feuds, and, lost in ourselves and to each other, be disembogued in the blackness of that darkness which is *reserved unto wandering stars for ever.* That the standard of christian morality is deplorably low among the ministers and churches of our denomination, is too obvious to be concealed.

"*Beloved friends and brethren*, to bring your minds to bear on this lamentable case, permit us to ask you a few plain questions.

"Are there not many professors among us, whose spirit, life, and conversation, *illy* become the gospel of Christ—worldly in their views, and mercenary in all they do, *so*, that if they were not seen in church meeting, or at the Lord's table, they could not be told from *mere* worldlings? And yet, do they not go unreproved?

"Are there not many, who, to the entire neglect of all family religion, seldom attend church meeting, and habitually live *irreverently*, if not *immorally?* And are they not suffered to go undisciplined?

"And others there are, who, in the plainest sense, are *drunkards*.

"And though *no drunkard hath any place in the kingdom of God and of Christ*, yet do they not by some means—by feigned repentance, or empty and vain resolves, continue from youth to old age in the church, frequently, if not habitually, drunk? And are there not many such cases?

"And more, is it not common, that *mere* negative goodness is all that is requisite to constitute a member *in good standing*, and to recommend him, *as such*, to a sister church?—But does not the parable of the fig tree reprove this practice? since the tree was not threatened to be cut down for bearing *evil* fruit, but because it bore none!

"And moreover, is there not evidently a want of *union* and concert among both ministers and churches of our denomination?

"Have not instances occurred in which some churches have disciplined their members *for what* others have winked at, or even commended in theirs? And have not censured, and even excluded members of some, been received and nurtured by other churches?

"And have not ministers gotten into *heated and*

hurtful controversies with one another—breathing towards each other the most crude asperities and cruel animosities? And is it not true, that *one* has preached *what* another, in, and to the same congregation, has contradicted and exposed, as *unsound and dangerous;* by which questions which *gender strife*, have abounded? And has not all this passed off too, without any effort to correct the evil, or to reconcile these *inconsiderate* brethren?

"Does it not then, brethren, behoove us to inquire, *with great earnestness,* for the causes of these afflictions? And on close examination, will they not be found, *mostly, if not altogether*, in the following particulars?

"1. In *a want of carefulness* in the admission of members.

"By a cursory review of the New Testament churches, it will be readily seen, that they were all constituted of believers in Christ *alone*, such as were called to be saints—all of *one heart and one soul:*— that the first churches were patterns for all others, which should be built up. Hence the church in Thessalonica was commended, for becoming followers of those which were in Judea. That they kept a close guard at the door of admission, whose vigilance the unworthy and designing had to escape and creep in unawares; but they soon found themselves *in so hot a bed*, that they went out of their own accord. And such would have been the effect *even till now*, if the standard had been kept up equally high. But alas! even in the apostles' days, the mystery of iniquity was at work; and the standard of godly practice was soon lowered, *so* that men of corrupt minds and loose morals could live in the churches; and they were corrupted in their pristine simplicity, unity and beauty, they had in Christ, and became the subjects of severe rebukes, and were even threatened with extinction!

"Now were not all these things written for our admonition, to the intent that we should be careful to admit into the churches of Christ, *none but such* as give good evidence of being *one spirit with the Lord, and members in particular with his body?*—lest we should incur the displeasure they incurred; and that too denounced against Israel, (probably the churches in our day were in the prophet's eye,) Ezek. 44: 6, 7. *Thus saith the Lord God; O ye house of Israel, let it suffice you of all your abominations; in that ye have brought into my sanctuary, strangers, uncircumcised in heart and uncircumcised in flesh, to be in my sanctuary, to pollute it, even my house, when ye offer my bread, the fat and the blood; and they have broken my covenant, because of all your abominations. And ye have not kept the charge of my holy things.* This last complaint plainly shows,

"2. The want of a close and goodly discipline.

"Christ, as head of his church, has constituted the power to govern *in the body*, according to his laws, for *edification*, and not *destruction;* for the preservation of the churches in *purity, unity, and peace.* But when discipline is neglected or loosely executed, the exact opposite state of things must ensue. Corrupt men, suffered or tolerated in the churches, will seek their own level, and like *the old leaven*, will corrode and corrupt the whole body, and tend *to more ungodliness;* till, by their number and influence, the church, *at this or that place*, may become a *mere worldly sanctuary*, or a *synagogue of Satan.* These deleterious effects, it is believed, will be found to grow very much out of,

"3. An inefficient ministry.

"The gospel ministry, in all its grades, was given to, and constituted in, the church, to bring all *in the unity of the faith, unto the stature of the fulness of Christ.* But it must be obvious to any one, that such an end can never be accomplished by a *weak, contentious, and divided ministry.* Say what we may of the church's power to govern, and even to govern her ministers; and yet *it will be true,* that ministers give *tone and impulse* to public feeling, *direction and energy* to public spirit, and *power and efficiency* to public effort. The corruptions and errors of Israel are charged on her prophets, who, refusing to speak *the word of the Lord faithfully, saw vain visions of peace, and taught out of the imagination of their evil heart.* And the *divisions and offences,* which rent, with fierce controversies, the churches at Antioch, Corinth, Galatia, Cappadocia, Bythinia, and Asia, are charged to those ministers who preached doctrines contrary to *that* taught by the apostles. Against *these,* not only foreign, but also of *their own selves,* the churches were cautioned, warned, reproved, and even threatened. And shall we be inattentive to these things? Similar causes will produce similar effects. Therefore, as is the ministry, such will be the churches. If ministers are inefficient, the churches will be *weak and wavering:* if ministers are in controversy among themselves, the churches will be *in confusion:* if ministers break asunder, the churches will *divide,* and fall *into party feuds.* And are not these things *so?* Have we not, brethren, reason to take the apostolic caution :

if ye bite and devour one another, take heed that ye be not consumed one of another? Surely, in the plaintive strain of the weeping prophet, we should inquire: *Is there no balm* in Gilead; *is there no physician* there? *Why then is not the health of the daughter of my people recovered?* Let us examine prayerfully and practically, and see if the health of the churches cannot be found in,

" 1. A more careful regard to *an elevated standard* of faith and piety, in the experience and character of those who are received to membership among us.

"All bodies derive their qualities from the elements of which they are composed. No church, therefore, can be more righteous and holy, than the members *individually* are. Then if the church is *the beauty of holiness*, the members must be *beautified with salvation*. If the church is *one body*, each member must have *one heart and one soul*. If the church is *the Lord our righteousness*, the members must all be *one spirit with the Lord*. And if the church is *the light of the world*, and *the joy of the whole earth*, each member must be *light in the Lord*, and glow *with a sacred passion* to make him known to the ends of the earth.

" When due care is had that the members of the churches *are all righteous;* and discipline is everywhere duly executed in the right spirit, then the standard of *holiness to the Lord* will be elevated, and true godliness promoted, till a state of efficient, practical piety will exhibit the churches as *a company of horses in Pharaoh's chariots;* and *terrible as an army with banners.* But to effectuate this, we believe will require,

" 2. A more careful attention to *the qualifications*

and faithfulness of those who are preferred among us to the gospel ministry.

"Nothing can be more certain, than if the churches are ever raised to be *holiness unto the Lord*, the ability and fidelity *requisite*, must be sought for in the constitution of ministers.—And wherever this is neglected, the consequences must be most deleterious to the purity, unity and peace of the churches. Let none say, 'God will qualify his ministers—he will give them *matter and form.*' This, we fear, is the very spirit that ruined Israel; they *cried peace, peace; when there was no peace!* Something must be *practically* and *efficiently* done to remedy the evils among us. It is now generally conceded, that both miracle and the inspiration of the truth, ceased with the Apostles. If so, ministers now have no just dependence on inspiration for what they preach: only as they are *instructed* to understand the truth, from the inspired scriptures. This shows the importance of education, which seems to be the scripture plan. Those sent out by the Apostles incurred blame, in that they *taught* what they were *not commanded;* proving plainly enough, that they were authorized to preach nothing but what they were taught.—Thus Paul *instructed* Timothy and Titus *to preach and teach the things* (not with which they were inspired, but those) *they had heard and learned of him;* and to commit them to those men only *who were able and faithful to teach others also, as they had been taught.* And Christ lays down the same rule in Matt. 13 : 52. *Every scribe instructed* (not inspired) *into the kingdom of heaven,* (or the gospel of Christ,) *is like unto a householder, who bringeth out of his treasures things new and old.*

"And surely, it is just as senseless to send out a man to preach the gospel which he had never been taught, with any expectation of his teaching it correctly, as it would be to employ a man to teach all the branches of a refined education, who had never studied their elementary principles.—But it may be asked—does not God do more for the one than for the other? Yes, blessed be his name! he does.—He gives to the man he calls into the ministry, *his holy Spirit* to impress and lead his mind to the work, to elevate and open his understanding in the study of the scriptures, to know and receive the truth, and aptness to impart it to others. And to secure *faithfulness* in the discharge of the duties of this *highly responsible* office, HE gives, not only *the spirit of fear, but of power, and of love, and of a sound mind*. But that man might as well be expected to know and explain all the beauties of nature, whose eyes had never been opened on its volume, as for a minister to preach the truth *as it is in Jesus,* who neither knows nor studies the scriptures. Nor can he else preserve *the ministry from blame by knowledge, or show himself approved unto God, a workman that needeth not to be ashamed, rightly dividing the word of truth.*

"Besides, the results to be had by the gospel ministry, are such as can never be attained, unless *purity* in knowledge, *unity* in design and purpose, and *fidelity* in practice be first found in the ministers. They must be taught all *to speak the same things ;* they must become sensible to mutual obligations, and the importance of unity in effort. And when ministers, of every degree, shall be found in unity, all *workers together with the Lord,* all pulling at once, and the same way; none too selfish to receive help—too proud to be taught—too wise to learn—too independent to submit—nor too great to be least; but all studying *to be prepared* to do the work of the Lord— meditating diligently on *the things* taught in his word —and *wholly giving themselves* to them, that their *profiting* (not their greatness) *may appear to all;* then the standard of christian morality will be elevated, and the churches will all fall into regular ranks under its flying banners; and '*onward*' shall be heard from every camp of our Israel, till they all come, *in the unity of the faith, and of the knowledge of the Son of God, unto a perfect man,* UNTO THE MEASURE OF THE STATURE OF THE FULNESS OF CHRIST.

"' Pastors and churches then,
All with united ken,
Wrap'd in seraphic flame,
God and the Lamb to praise,
Shall shout through endless days,
The long—the loud amen.'

"JESSE MERCER, *Moderator.*"

In consideration of the important service rendered by Mr. Mercer to the cause of Christ, by his able exposition from time to time of the principles of gospel discipline, a silver medal, containing appropriate inscriptions, was presented him by some of his brethren in 1836. Subjoined, is an extract from the letter which accompanied the medal.

" *Talbotton, May* 1, 1836.

"BROTHER MERCER,

" Inclosed, is a small medal which has been committed to my care for you. It was prepared by the direction of brethren in the Central Association, and sent by them as a token of their regard for you. Though the medal is marked as from 'the C. A. &c.,' it is truly from certain brethren of that body, as stated above, and not from the body itself. We hope you will accept it with this explanation, and receive it in the same spirit of *friendship* which prompted us to offer it.

* * * * *

"Yours truly,
"J. H. CAMPBELL."

The discussions which were carried on for several years, through the columns of the Index, and other channels, and in which the subject of this memoir took a distinguished part, tended greatly to settle the churches in correct views of many important principles, and particularly those relating to church and associational powers; still it was evident that something farther was necessary to remove deep-seated prejudices, soften down excited feelings, and bring the scattered ranks of the brethren into useful and affectionate co-operation. From time to time, suggestions were made in favor of a general ministers' meeting, in hope that by the united prayers and counsels of such an assembly, some effectual balm might be found for Zion's bleeding wounds. For a while, these recommendations received but little attention; but at length, they were revived and urged in such a manner as to secure a respectable meeting of ministers at the village of Forsyth, in July, 1836. Mr. Mercer's feelings were much enlisted in the meeting; he brought to it the unimpaired strength of his great mind, the aid of his golden counsels, and the unction of a sweet and heavenly temper. If any good resulted from that meeting, (and that its influence has been salutary and lasting, no reasonable doubt can be entertained,) much of it may justly be ascribed to the prudent zeal and matured wisdom of Mr. Mercer. Though the attendance was not as full as could have been desired, and some little incidents occurred during the progress of the meeting, not altogether the most agreeable, yet on the whole, it was a memorable occasion. There was a free and profitable interchange of views upon many important subjects; the mingled tears of penitence and christian affection were seen to flow; mutual acknowledgments were made by many, and mutual forgiveness sought and extended; and many fervent prayers ascended to the God of Israel, that the hurt of the daughter of his people might be healed. "It was a sight on which angels could not but look with peculiar delight, to see those, who, for years, had been cold and distant, who had thought and spoken hard things against their brethren, and even cast out their names as evil, acknowledging their errors with tears, and begging pardon. The readiness with which it was granted, melted all in the house. Every eye was wet, and every heart *full*. The feelings of that hour more than compensated for all the toils and difficulties of attending the meeting. All seemed to feel, 'I'm glad I come.'"* From that time, the work of conciliation has been steadily and successfully progressing; ministers, and churches, and associations, have gradually flowed into pleasant correspondence and fellowship; so that at the present, with the exception of our antimissionary brethren, and a comparatively small num-

* An extract from the minutes of the Forsyth meeting.

ber of churches who lean to free-will sentiments, the Baptists of Georgia present, in a highly encouraging degree, the aspect of a harmonious and united people.

Several other ministers' meetings were held from time to time, attended with consequences more or less beneficial; and in which the aid of Mr. Mercer was still conspicuous. He was much in favor of a permanent organization, which should imbody, as far as possible, the Baptist ministers of the state, and bring them regularly together for the purpose of pious consultation and fraternal intercourse. He was well convinced, and upon the most conclusive grounds, that the strife of the churches had originated mainly in the contentions of ministers, and that no better expedient could be devised to draw together the scattered flock, than to secure unanimity of feeling, sentiment and action amongst the shepherds of the flock. A State Ministers' Meeting was organized at Eatonton, in October, 1838; but it was found exceedingly difficult to secure a general attendance at any of its subsequent sessions, and in two or three years, it languished into non existence.

In accordance with a previous appointment, Mr. Mercer preached a discourse at Eatonton, at the time above specified, on " the importance of union amongst ministers of the gospel;" and at the particular request of the meeting before whom it was delivered, it was afterwards published. The sermon is founded on John 17 : 11. "Holy Father, keep through thine own name, those whom thou hast given me, that they may be one as we are one." It abounds in rich and original thought, and forcibly illustrates the nature of that union which should exist amongst ministers, and the great importance of maintaining it in full and constant vigor. A few of the concluding pages are here subjoined.

" To conclude,—If the position taken at first, namely, *that ministers form a distinct class in the church of Christ, with separate and peculiar obligations and duties*, has been established; and the nature and extent of their unity have been correctly defined, as suggested in the text, then it must be obvious to the slightest review, that the manner of rearing up ministers, and of the general course of the ministry in our denomination, in Georgia at least, has been very defective. Theirs has been, for the most part, an *isolated and individual* course, *thrown* entirely on *personal*, or at most, on *ecclesiastical* responsibility. This *defected* state of things among us, I will attempt to illustrate by the following similes. And

"1. A king stations a garrison well officered and defended, in the midst of a revolted colony, in order to redeem and bring back by *kindness*, his rebellious subjects to loyal submission. He commits to these officers the terms of peace, and gives them authority to establish new garrisons, and commission other officers, as the case might require. These officers proceed on their mission, with due deference to the honor of their sovereign; and many of the colonists return to their allegiance; and new garrisons are settled, and officers are commissioned. All things for a while, went on very well. In appointing to office, they were careful to select such men as gave full evidence of a sound reformation, and a just regard for the laws, government, and honor of the king; and who possessed such abilities and dispositions as fitted them for the execution of the duties of their office, and an honorable association with themselves in sustaining the government, peace and happiness of the realm. But in process of time, the officers who were in those days, *became careless* in this department of their duty, and commissioned *any* who were presented to them by the garrisons, who, in like manner, had become indifferent, with little regard to their qualifications for office, or their attachments to the government and honor of the king. So the garrisons were satisfied, *all was well*, throwing the whole responsibility on the incumbents and the garrisons.—Thus the officers soon became vain, self-conceited and proud. Strife was engendered among themselves and the garrisons; and the garrisons soon enlisted for their respective partizans; and so the whole colony was filled with internal broil and confusion. How picturesque of the present state of things among us!

"Have not many Presbyteries ordained men to the gospel ministry, *purely* on their own and the responsibility of the churches to which they belonged, with very little, if any inquiry into their qualifications for the sacred office; or the obligations they felt for the honor of God, or the ministry into which they were being put? And

"2. I ask, if our ministry do not present a likeness to a drove of pack-horses on an Indian trail, each going *in his own chosen path*, rather than a well harnessed and orderly team, moving in concert?

"Permit me here to state some of my own reflections: I was much impressed at the Ministers' Meeting last summer, at Harmony, and still am, with one feature of Israel's backslidden state, as alleged by Isaiah 53 : 6. 'All we, like sheep, have gone astray; we have turned *every one to his own way*.' If, thought

I, being turned *every one to his own way*, was descriptive of a revolted state in Israel, what must be now the state of the ministry in our denomination in Georgia? May it not be said with great propriety, that we have turned *every one to his own way?* Have we not lost all union of effort? Our brethren cannot be prevailed on to come together for ministerial consultation and co-operation, even in these days of Zion's afflictions. And why? even because they are turned, *every one to his own way!*—Each one has his own appointments to fill, and his church-meetings *must* be attended; and so he cannot go to a ministers' meeting. But let me ask each brother, in brotherly kindness, and let him answer in the spirit of candor: if his secular business pressed him to go to market, would he not leave all and go? And if he had relatives at a distance, or in another state, and he felt a strong inclination to visit them, would he not leave all and go? And even if he took it into his head to go a land hunting, (perhaps on speculation,) would not some of you leave all and go? But you cannot be persuaded to *leave all*, and attend a Ministers' Meeting, for *mutual* consultation, with a view to united, concentrated and vigorous effort to stop discord, and produce peace in the churches.

"I am fully impressed with the sentiment, that all the strife and confusion which now abound among our ministers and churches, may be traced to the want of a well organized ministerial union. Or, in other words, if all the ministers of our order in the state, had, *at once*, formed a Ministers' Meeting, with a view to maintain the unity of the faith in the churches; and had co-operated in the work of the ministry, all those distracting controversies, which have broken the peace and spoiled the beauty of our churches, would have been prevented, and the churches continued in peace and love.

"Let me then beseech you, brethren, *now* though very late, to rally around the standard of your Lord and Master. There may be yet a redeeming spirit in *the divine order*, if speedily adopted, by which the plague may be stayed, and many be recovered from its pernicious and deadly influence. What can be better suited, instrumentally, to arrest and redress the evils which are now rending the churches, than the combined union and co-operation of all the ministers in the state? Let all the ministers who are of *one heart and one soul*, not only in the great scheme of salvation by grace alone, but in the points of practice now in question, come together with one consent, and let their light shine in unison; let them bring their united efforts to bear on the cause, and by every consideration which the laws of truth and brotherly kindness can urge, endeavor to persuade and convince, and bring back their brethren to reconciliation, peace, and love: and surely it may be hoped in the Lord, that many will pause and consider, and return to good order, and seek that fellowship again, which they had so wantonly thrown away.

"I am aware of the difficulties which lie in the way of bringing about this practical union and co-operation of the Ministers in the Churches, because our young ministers have mainly had the rearing of themselves in the Churches, as circumstances provided; (for really the churches have taken but little care upon themselves about it) and they have been so long accustomed to direct their own course, according to their own counsel, that it will be hard to bring them to submit to the discipline of a *Ministerial Union*, and to act only in harmony with the body of Ministers. For many ministers, especially young ones, seem to have a peculiar fondness for a solitary course. They are seldom seen at a General Meeting; or, where they will be brought in contact with older Ministers. I suppose they *feel best* and *most free* when they *are alone*, or only in company with those whom they consider their inferiors; but surely, it is contrary to the plan of our Lord, as well as to the dictates of wisdom and common sense, and well calculated to gender strife and create jealousies and parties, and so to bring up divisions among Ministers and Churches.

"There is another evil to overcome. It is this:— *The Churches love to have it so.* On the one hand, it frees them from much labor and care, in bringing forward their licentiates into the ministry; and on the other, it gives them the privilege, nay, the *right* to control the labors of their ministers, which they will be reluctant to abridge in the least, even so as to give them the opportunity to attend a Ministers' Meeting. 'Tis true, Ministers are members in the churches, and amenable to their authority, so far as discipline and good order is concerned; but they should think this again, that Ministers were not given merely for their internal benefit; but, *for the work of the Ministry*, and the up-building of the *whole body of Christ*, and that any use they may make of them which will detract from this is wrong, and derogatory to the claims of their Lord. Although it may seem comfortable to retain ministers at home, when there seems to be so much need of them, yet if hindering them from attending Ministers' Meetings, should be promotive of discord among Ministers and Churches, will not the evil be justly chargeable on the hindering causes?

"Will not Ministers and Churches wake up to the important work which lies on them—*the work of the Ministry?* And what is it? But the whole work which God has determined should be instrumentally done, *to the ends of the world*—and which cannot be accomplished,

"'Till all the ransom'd Church of God,
Be sav'd, to sin no more.'

"In the accomplishment of this sacred design, the Father and the Son are at work; and all ministers, as laborers together with them, are called upon to be up and doing the work of the day, because the night cometh wherein *no man* can work. Let us then, Brethren, arise; be united *in one;* and be ready for every good word and work. And may the Lord our God be with us, and bless us, who is our only joy and strength; and to his name be all the glory, for ever and ever. AMEN."

The three following letters were addressed to a worthy ministering brother, whose mind had been much perplexed upon certain doctrinal points, and who had been seriously involved in some of the difficulties which had so long disturbed the peace of the churches.

Washington, Sept. 26, 1836.

"DEAR BROTHER B.

"I have had it in mind to write you a few lines ever since we parted at F. I was afflicted at that meeting by the spirit manifested by some brethren towards those of the N. Association; and pleased at the more Christian temper of those brethren. I hope they will not be disposed not to attend the next by reason of such treatment. Though you differ from most of the brethren in regard to faith in some particular points, I am not prepared to believe you *so far* gone as to be irreclaimable.

"As well as I recollect, the article on Election, in the system adopted by your Association, holds election through *sanctification of the Spirit*, &c. This I think is an error. If you will examine 2 Thes. 2: 13. and 1 Peter 1: 2. you will find that Election is unto salvation and obedience, which salvation and obedience are through sanctification of the Spirit, &c. But what is worse, the Association sermon, published by request, is an effort to set aside *personal* election. Now if election is not of persons, but a character, then I cannot see how any one could be saved by it; because God could not choose an *unholy* character, and no sinner could get into [a holy] one, and therefore could not be saved by it. By examination, you will see election (and its kindred doctrine, predestination) always holds an end in view. That end is *to be holy —to be conformed to the image of Christ—to be saved —obedience—adoption*, &c. Now without contradiction the act must be before the end proposed by that act; or the design must follow the purpose; so that election must be anterior to our conversion to God. And you can but see that the end or design of an act, cannot be the condition of that act. But I need not argue the case with you. I only wish you to consider the Scripture in its own light, and strive to bring your mind to a willingness to receive the doctrine taught herein without the rule of your own reason.

"Surely the truth of the Scripture, *as it is in Jesus*, is plain enough to enable those who are under the influence and guidance of the Holy Spirit, so far to agree, as that they may walk together in holy fellowship. It is always at least worth the effort to attain. And now it seems that those more *antinomian* are determined to break off on the score of missions, &c. It is then the more important that those united in the benevolent operations should *strive*, and *strive hard*, to be of one mind in all other essential truth, that they may labor together in the *great cause* of God and Christ, and human happiness.

"I am informed that many churches have determined, and declared non-fellowship with all benevolent societies; that Br. M. has taken sides, and aided if not induced the O. Association to so declare. This measure will divide and tear to pieces their own ranks! I hope this very thing will be the means of opening the eyes of many who have heretofore been blinded by the cry of 'faith! faith!'

* * * * *

"Now brother, do lay aside every stumbling block, and come up to the meeting at C.; influence as many of your brethren in the ministry to come as you can, and come in hope of better treatment; or if you should meet worse, to bear it as good soldiers of Jesus Christ. Come any how.

"I have written to Br. S. and entreated him to come. I long after you all in the Gospel.

"I am, dear brother,
'Yours in Christ,
"JESSE MERCER."

"*Washington, June* 28, 1838.

"DEAR BROTHER B.

"Your very kind and affectionate letter of 18th inst. was received and read a day or two since, with great interest. This was because, *first, I love* you, and secondly, because I find you in perplexity, and know not what to do. And now, my dear brother, what shall I say to you? You are not satisfied with the U. Association; well, I fear they are gone too far in opposition to the truth, as well as become negligent and careless as to measures necessary to a return of peace. The —— brethren who remain, are different from what they were, but I fear they (many of them) are not over *half* converted. Your best resort is to fall in with the C. brethren, as I judge. But there, a difficulty at once meets you. You would have to come up square-toed to all their articles of faith 'without note or comment.' You say, though you cannot go the full length of their faith, yet you feel no disposition to oppose, and their preaching is *as your own*. Perhaps you would (should you try it) not find so much difficulty as you fear. For my own part, I never was of the opinion, that a single point or article of faith should be made a test of fellowship. *Opposition* to any point would break fellowship; but so long as a good brother would admit, though he could not understand a doctrine in a particular way, I should be in favor of holding him in fellowship.

"You seem to think there is a discrepance between the holding and the preaching of the Central brethren. There may be in some. But you [know that] many hold *predestination*, sovereign and eternal, consistent with man's free agency, and entire accountability. There is a state of things, as they lie before God, which is as determinate and as unchangeable as God himself; and there is another state of things, which lie in the department of the divine administration, and in which the dispensation of the Gospel proceeds, and in which men are treated as rational and intelligent beings. Now, though we may not be able to decipher and explain the line which separates these two states of things, we may find evidence sufficient of their existence, and should yield to the conviction of their truth.

* * * * *

" Dear Brother, I have written you a few crude thoughts. I fear they will do you no good; but I pray to God he will direct you in the *true and the right way*. Although I think you would do *well*, perhaps *best*, to unite with the Central brethren, yet do all you do in the fear of God, which is the beginning of wisdom. If I can be of any use to you, it will afford me pleasure at all times to do you service.

" I am yours in Christ,

" JESSE MERCER."

" *Washington, Nov.* 14, 1838.

" MY DEAR BROTHER AND LONGED FOR,

"I received your very interesting letter of 29th ult. and have let it lie by, thinking that I should write. Truly I desire peace and righteousness to abound amongst all God's people; but I find it much easier to sunder, and keep at a distance, than to come together when once parted. Asperities and bitterness arise, and an indifference even to be united; or alienation of even Christian affections springs up and grows stubborn. Big *I*, and little *you*, or selfishness, is hard to be subdued. I fear that some of the ——— brethren will never come to that humility, which is needful to a union among all the parties. Also some of those of the U. A. are in the same case of stiffness. But *all must be humbled*. I am happy to find you are so moved on this subject, and rejoice in the course you have taken. I highly approve of the efforts made and making to reconcile the churches in the vicinity of each other. This is the right way to bring about a more general union.

* * * *

"I think I am as much disposed to keep off the *rock of fatality* as you, or any one else. I believe in the doctrine of predestination and election, and the certain and sure performance of all God's purposes; and yet I believe they are to be effected strictly in accordance with the responsibilities and free choice of men, so far as they are concerned. God does not operate on men as *matter*, but as *rational* creatures; and his influences are designed to bring them to act according to the abilities which he gave them, *freely*. But I do not believe them *less sure*. As to the Missionary Baptists uniting upon the principle of *mutual* forbearance, or 'think and let think,' I should have no objection if the limit could be fixed so as that the liberty would not tend to licentiousness, and presently [mischief] break out worse than ever. We never can agree, (I speak for myself,) to a latitude of liberality, which would allow of opposition to those doctrines.

* * * *

"And what shall I more say? I know not what. May the Lord, the Prince of peace direct all our hearts into the love of God, and a patient waiting for his presence amongst us.

"Our State Ministers' Meeting is to commence on Thursday of next week, to which I intend to go, if permitted. Shall I see you there? I think it would tend to incline the ministers favorably towards you, and might give some new impulse. Wishing you much grace and blessing, I am, dear Brother,
"Yours, in Christ our Lord and Saviour,
"JESSE MERCER."

The following letter was addressed to a highly esteemed and valuable brother in the ministry, (now no more,) who, in consequence of what he deemed some improper proceedings of the Association with which he was connected, had withdrawn himself in a great measure from the society and councils of his brethren. It is to be hoped that it will be read with profit by every individual, who, under similar circumstances, might be tempted to pursue the same injudicious course.

"*Washington, Dec.* 8, 1838.
"MY DEAR BROTHER L.

"I have in 'the house of my pilgrimage' constant proof of my want of firmness; for I find I am much better to resolve, than to fulfil my purposes when made. When I was at your house, (if I recollect rightly,) I told you I had often felt like harnessing up and coming right away to see you. When I said so, I said truly; but how have I fulfilled? For a long time now I have often thought I would write, but still I have neglected it. I have been no indifferent observer of things as they have transpired, in reference to you. I assure you, brother, many an anxious thought—many an inquiry has gone up towards your dwelling to ascertain how you were doing, and what were the most probable future prospects in reference to you; for 'My brother, I am much distressed for thee; For very pleasant hast thou been to me.' I have been looking for your return from your *voluntary* exilement, and that the ancient order of things would be restored amongst us again; but again I fear I shall be deceived! O, that I may not be disappointed in this hope! I cannot think of you as dead, but still I have thought, as somewhat applicable to you, on what was said of Enoch, 'he was not.' Methinks he had been a *constant* associate with the few pious cotemporaries of his day, (rendered probably the more precious by being *few*;) and labored so assiduously in all the ways of piety and usefulness, known to them for the honor of God and mutual edification; and the warning the wicked, (see Paul and Jude,) till he obtained among them 'this testimony that he *pleased* God;' but it came to pass that '*he was not:*' that is (I presume) he did not appear in their company as heretofore. This was a conspicuous—a notable '*was not.*' His few pious brethren must have been grieved always when they *met*, to find that Bro. Enoch was not in their midst—his seat was always empty. Alas! 'he was not.' This must have been a great grief to them, but how much greater must it have been if *the cause* had been any thing else but '*God took him.*'

"From the late revival in which you shared so largely, I hoped to see your *youth renewed*, and to find you again in company; but alas! still, *he is not.* In all our meetings for the promotion of the public good, or the general weal of the church or the world, it may be said of our dear brother L. *he is not.* My brother, can you be persuaded to come up to the help of your brethren—of God against the mighty, and the many who oppose all that is good, and virtuous, and true, and of good report.

"I had also hoped that the fire of the revival at Antioch would have burned up all the old leaven, which had been working strife and division in it for years past, but in this too I fear I am disappointed. Opposition, I hear, is still working and warring in it. Does it not strike you, brother L. that it is high time 'that thou shouldest set in order the things that are wanting—and strengthen the things that remain ?' Permit me, my brother, to say that I fear, (as Whitfield said of himself to Wesley,) that you have been sinfully silent too long ! You have been hoping that things would get better, and have remained *neutral*—but your influence has not been *neutral*. It has been at work, and probably on the wrong side. When the temperance societies first began to form among us, I did not unite—not from opposition; but I was not quite ready to put in. But I found my influence operated to *encourage* intemperance ! I therefore threw myself into the society to turn my influence (let it be what it might) into a useful channel. It is proper to watch lest while we essay to do good, ' our good may be evil spoken of,' and all our efforts to be useful be hindered or prove abortive. Surely the state of our churches in these days, calls for energetic effort to settle them again in peace. To sit still and sing a requiem to ourselves will not do. We must take sides, not to fight; for direct opposition will be likely to make bad worse ! but to enlist a host that by silent influence may undermine the strong-hold of their opposition !! Some of us have thought a State

Ministers' meeting might operate such an influence, as well as cultivate unity of sentiment and feeling in the ministry throughout the State; but if we were right in this conclusion, we were baffled in our design by the non-attendance of the brethren. The brethren who engaged last year in the constitution at Eatonton, did not one half attend at Macon the last month, and few others. Does it not commend itself to your mind that you could do greater good by uniting with your brethren, and *be* with them *like a company of horses in Pharaoh's chariot?* I have a mind, as no general meeting falls on the fifth Sunday in March, to have a big meeting here. Will you come? Where is brother N.? Married—and therefore *cannot* come! However, I wish him and his second-self all possible happiness in their hymeneal union; and that his helpmeet may be a helper to him in his ministry which he has received of the Lord. I had hoped from the movements I had heard of concerning brother G. L., that he might be induced to think again and turn to his forsaken brethren. It is really a puzzle to me to imagine how a thinking Christian can take the course of the rending brethren and continue!

"I must close by saying, the time is short—it is high time to awake out of sleep. What remains to you and me to be done, must be soon done, or go undone for ever. May the Lord direct into the right way, and give strength to walk therein for his name's sake, is the prayer of one who is most

"Respectfully, yours,
"In the bonds of the Gospel,
"JESSE MERCER."

CHAPTER XIII.

Mr. Mercer as a writer.—Speaking the truth in love —His Ten Letters on the Atonement.—Extracts.—Sermon on the Excellency of the Knowledge of Christ, and extracts from the same.— Essay on Lord's Supper —History of Georgia Association.— Review of a certain Report.—Essay on Forgiveness of Sins.— Extracts from his Editorial pieces.

Mr. Mercer was less distinguished as a writer than a preacher. He very seldom used his pen until he had arrived at that period of life when his intellectual habits had become fixed, and it could hardly be supposed that he would feel much inclined to expend labor in rounding his periods, and decorating his essays with rhetorical beauties. He aimed at nothing more than a plain, concise, and scriptural exposition of his views. In this he was generally successful; and indeed sometimes the natural force of his mind, and the strong flow of thought would carry him beyond his simple aim, and impart uncommon vigor to his style, and now and then bear him into a strain of true sublimity. Few writers had equal power of condensing a logical discussion, and of compassing weighty and useful instruction in few words. In this respect his composition bore a striking resemblance to his extemporaneous effusions, and was one of the natural effects, as well as a striking evidence of his intellectual strength.

In his lengthy and studied productions, he has constant recourse to the word of God, illustrating his positions by copious and pertinent selections from this great storehouse of divine wisdom. If his frequent and lengthy quotations from the scriptures, detract from the value and interest of his productions in the view of some, others will esteem them more on this account, and especially when there is discovered in the application of scripture (as will be the case with attentive readers) not a tame imitation of commentaries and theological compends, but the work of a thoughtful, independent, and original expositor of the word of God.

In his controversial writings he would sometimes use expressions which might seem to savor somewhat of unkindness and asperity, and convey to some minds an erroneous impression of the real state of his feelings. In opposing what he conceived to be error, he was firm, independent and faithful; and in his zeal for the truth he did not weigh every expression with that care which would have been desirable; but no one could be more free from bitter and malignant feeling. His heart was deeply imbued with the spirit of love, forbearance and Christian kindness. In referring to some strictures on two of his brethren which had given offence, he remarked in a letter to a Christian brother, "If I might judge for myself I never wrote any strictures on any brethren with more kind feelings towards them. I was endeavoring to refute what I conceived to be mischievous errors, and not in personal abuse. It has been one of the first desires of my heart to be in a Christian sense, *a good man*, but to *breathe a bitterness of temper abhorrent from the Gospel*, is so abhorrent from my best wishes, that I am exceedingly pained to be thought to have it." In the same communication, referring to his connexion with the Christian Index as Editor, he observes; "The place of an Editor is very responsible and difficult. He must judge of the communications sent from his patrons for publication, and give his mind and be faithful as one that must give account, and yet be kind, courteous, and brotherly towards all. O that I may ever *speak the truth in love* "

SPEAKING THE TRUTH IN LOVE ! This is indeed a blessed maxim for the regulation of all the communications of Christ's professed followers, whether they proceed from the pen, or from the lips. Were the spirit of this precept to insinuate itself into all their religious discussions, what a multitude of hurtful evils would be turned away from the cause of Christ. Bitterness brings no aid to the truth, and unkind words will not reclaim an erring brother. The heart should ever be full of Christian tenderness, and the lips should speak with prudence and moderation. In defending truth and opposing error, a man should be candid, faithful and fearless ; but he is still to remember that candor should be blended with courtesy, faithfulness with love, and boldness with a meek and humble spirit. It may be said that in extreme cases severity may be needful ; but even then it should rather be the severity of truth and argument, of sound speech that cannot be condemned, than of keen and irritating words. The truth of these reflections must be obvious to all ; and yet they are uttered at this time under the full persuasion that they are not as deeply felt by our brethren as they should be. Can it be denied that our denominational difficulties have been greatly aggravated by a want of proper conformity to these sentiments ? Even where there has existed the kindest feelings and the best intentions, harsh and unguarded expressions have fallen from the pen or the lips, which have given origin to new resentments and new complaints; or torn open some old wound that was just ready to heal. Our editorial brethren are often too caustic and too peevish; speaking sometimes as Jesus would not speak, and as Paul would say was not "lovely and of good report." If in some of these respects it may be said that our beloved Mercer was not altogether faultless, it certainly becomes all others less wise and holy, to watch with diligence and pray without ceasing that they enter not into the same temptation.

Mr. Mercer's writings consist principally of Circular Letters, Essays on various subjects; a few occasional sermons and controversial pieces which appeared from time to time in pamphlet form, or in the columns of periodicals; with his various editorial effusions, and a few manuscript sermons which have never been published.

In the preceding pages several of his productions have been briefly noticed, and numerous extracts from them presented to the reader, but there are others which claim a few passing remarks, and from which such further extracts will be made as may give a more ample view of his various religious opinions.

It is not to be supposed that all will concur with Mr. Mercer in every theological opinion which he has expressed. He has left a record of his sentiments on a variety of subjects, some of them of acknowledged difficulty, and in regard to which, sentiments more or less dissimilar have been entertained by the wisest and best of men. It is presumed however, that the anxious inquirer after truth will consult the opinions of Mr. Mercer with interest and respectful attention, happy to find any of his own views confirmed by the conclusions of one so honest, original and profound;

and scarcely willing to adhere to an important opinion that might conflict with the sentiments of one so uniformly correct, without carefully reviewing the ground upon which it rests.

About the close of 1829, Mr. Cyrus White published a pamphlet on the atonement which contained sentiments that were deemed unscriptural, and of a decidedly arminian tendency. As Mr. White had previously been employed as one of the missionaries of the Convention, the publication of his piece was considered by some of the opposers of that body as evidence in favor of their free and bold assertions, that the supporters of the benevolent plans of the day, were unsound in the faith. For the purpose of wresting this argument from their hands, as well as discouraging the circulation of sentiments which he considered unscriptural, Mr. Mercer wrote and published, in 1830, his Ten Letters on the Atonement.

Every candid reader will be ready to admit that this is the production of no ordinary mind; and that its author has presented many weighty and important views upon a subject of momentous interest, and in some of its aspects of great difficulty.

Mr. Mercer's general views of the atonement may be learned from the following extracts from his second Letter:

"In my last, I promised you some examination of your views on atonement. And first, you identify atonement with propitiation. This, though common among commentators, is in my mind, to confound *cause* and *effect*. Propitiation is what Christ is, as the Saviour of sinners—atonement is what he has made by the offering of himself to God for us. Propitiation is the great plan of mercy itself—atonement is that reconciliation and peace, which he has obtained by his cross. Propitiation is the victim for sacrifice—atonement is the acceptance of that victim in the place of the transgressor. Propitiation is the redemption price—atonement is the acceptance of that price for the deliverance of the lawful captives.

"These words have a strong and indissoluble connexion in scripture, and constitute the great scheme of mercy, as it is both by and through our Lord Jesus Christ; and may sometimes be synonymously used, nevertheless they are strikingly different in signification. The original import of these words, as they occur in the New Testament, is distinct—though it is said, that in the Hebrew, they are both derived from words signifying to cover, *as a lid*, like the mercy-seat did the law in the ark of the testimony. Paul in Rom. 3 : 25. uses the very word for *mercy-seat*. 'Whom God hath set forth *to be* (hilasterion) the propitiatory' which is to be approached 'through faith in his blood.' Thus Christ is the antitype of that grand symbolical system of divine communion made in the institution of the mercy-seat. John uses in his 1 Epis. 2 : 2. and in 4 : 10. a kindred word (hilasmos) which is the victim, or sin-offering itself. But atonement is made by the offering of that victim acceptably to God. Thus in Rom. 5 & 11 chaps. (where the word alone occurs in the New Testament) (katallagen) the word usually rendered reconciliation, is used, and is expressive of what we receive by Christ through faith, and is evidently the effect of his propitiatory sacrifice. Your manner of treating it therefore, as a provision of life and pardon offered to sinners in the gospel, is not just; for it is that very life and pardon obtained by the blood of the cross."

After referring to the sacrifices of the old dispensation, the author adds:

"I know of not an instance, where the sin-offering is called *the atonement;* but always it is said to be made by the offering of it unto the Lord. Now then as atonement is received from the Lord Jesus Christ, it must be something which he has, as mediator, to bestow; and may be understood under the following different terms. 1. It is called *reconciliation.* Dan. 9: 24. 'To make *reconciliation* for iniquity.' Heb. 2: 17. 'Christ an High Priest in things pertaining to God to make *reconciliation* for the sins of the people.' 2. It is called peace. Col. 1: 20. 'And having made *peace* by the blood of his cross.' 3. It is called *salvation.* Heb. 5: 9. 'And being made perfect (through sufferings) he became the author of eternal *salvation* unto all them that obey him.' Lastly. It is called *redemption.* Rom. 3: 24. 'Being justified freely by his grace, through the *redemption* that is in Christ Jesus.' Heb. 9: 12. 'Christ by his own blood having once entered into the holy place, obtained *eternal redemption* for us.'"

After having laid down the scripture account of what he conceives atonement to be, Mr. M. then proceeds to examine its *relations.*

"1. It relates to God. If Christ was set forth a propitiation through faith in his blood, to *declare* the righteousness of God in the remission of sins (Rom. 3: 25.) and if it became him, *in bringing many sons* TO GLORY, to make the captain of their salvation perfect through sufferings, (Heb. 2: 10.) without controversy the atonement was necessary, in some way, *that God might be just* and justify the ungodly, (Rom. 4 : 5.) I do not like very well your idea that 'the atonement must be *that*, in its nature, which will *render God propitious*.' Strictly speaking, God was never *unpropitious*. But sin was not only *an offence* to him, but had thrown obstructions in the way of his mercy. The atonement, therefore, must be *that* in its nature which will honor him in the view of all rational intelligences, in the vouchsafement of pardon and acceptance. This is fully established in the following texts. 'Christ hath loved us and given himself for us, an offering and a sacrifice *to God*, for a sweet smelling savor.' (Eph. 5 : 2.) 'Who gave himself (*to God*) for us, that he might redeem us from all iniquity.' (Titus 2 : 14.) 'How much more shall the blood of Christ, who through the eternal Spirit offered himself without spot *to God*,—purge your consciences from dead works to serve the living God.' (Heb. 9 : 14.) 'Christ is also said to be High Priest in things pertaining *to God*, to make reconciliation for sins.' (Heb. 2 : 17.) These texts are in perfect accordance with the whole ritual service, where it will be seen, that all the offerings for sins were made *to God* to make reconciliation, or atonement for the transgressors. Thus says Fuller, 'Atonement has respect to justice, and justice to law, or the revealed will of a sovereign, which has been violated; and its very design is to repair its honor.' (See vol. 4. p. 266.) Thus Christ is the end of the law, *or the fulfilment of it*, for righteousness, *or the atonement*, to every one that believeth.

"2. It relates to God, in reference to the sins of those who are atoned for. As the scriptures connect the sins and the persons of those for whom atonement is made, I choose to put the two together, where the scriptures have placed them. And which will be seen clearly in the following texts. 'Surely he hath borne *our griefs*, and carried *our sorrows*. He was wounded for *our transgressions*, he was bruised for *our iniquities;* The *chastisement of our peace* was upon him, and with *his stripes we are healed*. All we like sheep have gone astray—we have turned every one to his own way; and the *Lord* has laid on him *the iniquity of us all*. When thou shalt make his soul an offering *for sin* he shall see *his seed*—He shall see *the travail of his soul* and be satisfied: For he shall *bear their iniquities*. Because he hath poured out his soul unto death: and he was numbered with the transgressors; and he *bore the sin of many*, and made *intercession for the transgressors*.' (Isa. 53d chap.) Seventy weeks are determined *upon thy people to finish the transgression*, and to make *an end of sins*. (Dan. 9 : 24.) Christ was delivered *for our offences*, and raised again *for our* justification. (Rom. 4 : 25.) And I delivered unto you, that which I received, how that Christ died *for our sins*, according to the scriptures. (1 Cor. 15 : 3.) Because Christ also *suffered for us:* Who his own self *bare our sins* in his own body on the tree, that we being dead to sins, should live unto righteousness; By whose stripes ye were healed. For Christ also hath once suffered *for sins, the just* for the *unjust*, that he might *bring us to God*. (1 Peter 2 : 21, 24. 3 : 18.)' Thus the atonement is complete. It being a full satisfaction to the claims of divine justice, through the violated law, by the offence or demerit of sins. This complete satisfaction of the mediation of Christ is expressed by—*Christ's* being the end of the law—fulfilling the law—magnifying and making honorable *the law.* And the entire and full extent of Christ's sacrifice for the redemption of transgressions made under *the law,* being expressed by *making reconciliation for iniquity, an end of sin, finishing transgression* and *purging* OUR SINS *by the cross.* The fulness of the atonement is not to be measured by the *number saved;* but by its *competency to save one sinner.* Since it is not to be imparted by *parts,* but as A WHOLE. If it is capable *amply to save* ONE SINNER that believeth in Jesus, then it is *of the same capacity* to save to the uttermost all that come unto God by him. So that to talk of a limited atonement, is to talk of an atonement short of the requisitions of Justice, and which leaves sin partially atoned for! and which of course can save no one—or it is to suppose it is administered by drops and that the merits of Christ can be exhausted; which I presume none will admit."

In regard to the atonement's being considered in the light of a commercial transaction, Mr. Mercer makes the following observations in his third letter.

"I do not mean to contend for the atonement, as a commercial transaction: but I mean to oppose the idea of a vague atonement. I must contend with Fuller that though we cannot view the great work of redemption as a commercial transaction betwixt a debtor and his creditor: yet the satisfaction of justice, in all cases, requires to be *equal* to what the nature of the offence is in reality—and to answer the *same end* as if the guilty party had actually suffered. And for Christ, as our substitute, to have suffered *less* for us than we should if the law had taken its course, would be no atonement at all, and leave us in our sins. I do not admire the distinction; nor do I believe any thing is really gained by it. It seems however, better calculated to fritter down the sufferings of Christ within the grasp of our comprehension—to show they were not, in reality, what was required for sins, and to make them a shade, or representation of what justice required, rather than to present them in their full view of infinite value. It ought, too, to be recollected *what is impossible with men is possible with God.* We poor limited creatures cannot tell what calculations infinite wisdom can make, nor what doings Almighty power can effect. The Scriptures do employ terms taken from commercial transactions to teach us our obligations on the one hand, and the greatness of salvation on the other. Our sins are figuratively called debts—the blood of Christ is our redemption price, and redemption itself is a commercial transaction. I see no reason, therefore, why we should depart from it, nor any thing in it that renders Atonement impossible."

Respecting the question whether the sinner has a right to *claim* salvation, as a matter of justice, on the score of the full atonement made by the Lord Jesus Christ, the author in the same letter thus expresses himself:

"A. is cast into prison to suffer the just demerit of his crime. B. his Father, King and Judge pities him, and would release him, but the nature of the case forbids it. He has one only elder son, amiable, honorable and beloved, he proposes the case to him with its difficulties; C. ponders the matter. He loves his Father—and pities his unfortunate brother, and undertakes for him. The stipulations are all laid down and made sure between B. and C.;—then C. throws himself into the breach betwixt B. and A; assumes A.'s place and answers to all the claims of law and justice against him—sustains the honor and dignity of B. as King and Judge in this case, and lays the ground for peace and order in the kingdom. The application of this scale is easy to every one, who understands the gospel plan of redemption. Here full and complete satisfaction is made, but yet carries no claim of deliverance to A.; he has had nothing to do in the matter, it is all grace to him. The scheme of his deliverance originated with B. his Father and King through the compliance of C. heartily yielded to the will of his Father. And though it is a matter of justice, according to the covenanted agreements, promises, and fulfilments between B. and C.; and these C. may of right plead, yet it leaves A. in all his sin and misery and under law and condemnation. Now you may see, though 'the debt is *fully discharged*'—the satisfaction for sin *is fully* made, yet it affords to sinners no 'claim to heaven on the principles of justice;' because it originated not with them, but with God, on whom they had no claims for compassion. Indeed, if they had procured for themselves a good and acceptable surety, who had made full satisfaction for their sins, they would—they must have had a just right to deliverance. But since they had no part in the scheme, but it was all of God—OF HIM *are ye in Christ Jesus*, WHO OF GOD *is made unto us wisdom, and righteousness, and sanctification, and redemption*, both the plan and the application of it are clearly of God, and is therefore, a matter of the *merest* mercy and *free* grace to sinners justly condemned under the law, and lying under its curse till they are quickened and made alive in Christ. Thus though their 'debt is fully discharged,' in the plan of Redemption as it lies with God, yet the Holy Ghost can, and does in conviction teach sinners, 'that they are *justly condemned*, and that if they are saved, it must be by God's mercy alone.' For the Divine Spirit does not first teach men what they are in Christ Jesus, but what they are in themselves and under the violated law, and then, he presents to them Christ the propitiation, 'that by faith in his blood,' they may see the righteousness of God sustained in the remission of their sins."

A sentence or two from the seventh Letter will give some of the author's views on the subject of human obligation and ability. After referring to some of Mr. W.'s peculiar views, he adds:

"From all which, it is evident you believe, that sin has destroyed in man the principle of responsibility; else he could not be free from obligation to obey God in any case; for the want of *natural* ability *alone*, destroys moral obligation. If so, then sin has rendered disobedience *no crime!* But is this true? If there be *no* obligation on man, as a sinner, then, there is *no* duty; and where there is *no* duty, there is *no* law; and where there is *no* law, there is *no* transgression; and where there is *no* transgression, there is *no* blame; and consequently impenitence and unbelief are *harmless* things!"

Farther on, he remarks;

"It would be well to observe, there is a *natural* and a *moral* ability. The one constitutes us accountable beings; the other consists in well disposedness towards God, our Maker, and fits us for duty. The loss of one destroys responsibility and frees from blame—the loss of the other makes us sinners and subjects us to guilt and condemnation."

Mr. White professed to be of the sentiments of Fuller; but it is evident that he did not fully understand the views of that profound theologian. Many of what Mr. Mercer regards as W.'s objectionable views, he fully answers by lengthy quotations from Mr. Fuller's controversy with Mr. Button and Philanthropos.

In the conclusion of his ninth Letter he makes the following observations on Fuller and Gill.

"From the above it appears, that Mr. Fuller is not so opposed to Dr. Gill as many have thought. All that Fuller contends for, as to the *infinite* worth of the atonement, is comprehended in Gill's view of the scheme of redemption. What Gill places in the covenant transactions, and considers as *past and done* in the eternal mind, Fuller resolves into '*the sovereign pleasure of God*, with a regard to the application of the atonement; that is, *with regard* TO THE PERSONS *to whom it shall be applied*.' What then is the difference? A mere shade—a difference *only* in the *modus operandi* of the great plan. They are in perfect harmony in the *totality* of human depravity—the necessity and efficiency of divine influence—the fulness and sufficiency of the covenant provision for, and the certain application of them to the salvation of the elect *only*.—The difference then, betwixt them is only speculative; the *agitation of which* is much better calculated to promote those *oppositions of science falsely so called*, or that *philosophy and vain deceit*, from which Paul so much dissuades, rather than *Godly edifying.*"

Space can only be allowed for two or three more short quotations from this work : they are from the last Letter.

"You represent the atonement precisely *the same* 'to all the unbelievers in the world,' as 'to the believers;' nay, more, as applying 'in the same sense,' to all those '*dead and in hell*' as to those '*dead and in heaven* before the Saviour died!' This is the same as to say, that all who have been *hanged*, since the provision was made, in the law, to reprieve criminals, were, *just as much* interested in that provision, as those who were reprieved; which is *to affirm* against fact, reason, common sense and truth. It makes the application of the atonement a *nullity*, and puts the believer and the unbeliever upon the same footing: and as it leaves unbelievers exposed 'to the impending storm, which will burst with fury upon their heads in the awful day of accounts,' so it must leave all believers *equally* exposed to wrath! Besides, it removes that line of difference, which the Scriptures have laid down between the righteous and the wicked: and subjects you to the severe rebuke of the rulers of Jerusalem. 'Her priests have violated my laws, and have profaned my holy things; They have put no difference between the holy and profane, neither have they showed the difference between the unclean and the clean.' (Ezek. 22 : 26.) This is a very serious charge!"

* * * * *

"There is one other point, to which, I must call your attention before I close : It is the manner in which you treat *a personal interest* in the death of Christ. There is no subject so fraught with comfort to the Christian soul, *as the dying love of Jesus :* No *feeling*, so full of pleasure as *a consciousness* of interest in that love. When faith, working by love, is in full exercise, the happy soul sings for joy

> ' He hath loved me, I cried, he hath suffer'd and died,
> To redeem such a rebel as I!'

"This was the joy of the ancient saints : ' Rejoice greatly, O Daughter of Sion ; shout, O Daughter of Jerusalem ; behold *thy King* cometh unto thee : he is just, and having salvation ; and riding upon an ass, and upon a colt the foal of an ass :' Zech. 9 : 9. This was the glorying of Paul. ' God forbid,' said he, ' that I should glory save in the cross of Christ ; who loved me, and gave himself for me.' (Gal. 2 : 20. 6 : 14.) It is the joyful, and triumphant song of the redeemed both in earth and heaven ; ' Unto him that loved us, and hath washed us from our sins in his own blood, and hath made us kings and priests unto God and his Father ; to him be glory and dominion for ever and ever. Amen. And they sung a new song, saying, thou art worthy, for thou wast slain, and hast redeemed us to God by thy blood out of every kindred, and tongue, and nation, and people.' (Rev. 1 : 5, 6. 5 : 9.) But the view you take of this delightful subject, saps the foundation of all this holy joy : for if Christ has died equally for those in unbelief, as in faith, for those in hell, as for those in heaven, there can be no propriety in the joys of those who are saved, because

Jesus had died *for them*, when he had died '*in the same sense*,' for those who are perished! Common rights should never be the reason of peculiar joys."

* * * * *

"That the sheep of Christ have a glorious interest in their shepherd's death, over the world, which lies in wickedness—that a believer has a part in the atonement, with which an infidel—a stranger, intermeddles not, is spread all over the face of Scripture. There is nothing plainer in the sacred pages than that men, before faith in Christ and the inspiration of his Holy Spirit, are *dead in sins, under the law and curse* of God, *without Christ and without hope and God in the world;* and as such, liable to eternal death! It is false and deceptive to address men, in unbelief and impenitence, as the objects of Christ's death, as if they had a *personal* interest in him, and were redeemed by his blood, any further than it regards them *as sinners*. It is true there is an objective fulness in Christ, of infinite worth, able to save *to the uttermost*, all that come unto God by him; which forms the *glad tidings of great joy*—the substance of the gospel message—the object of faith—*the fulness of the blessings of the gospel of Christ*. But whatever this is; it is in the Bible of God restricted to them that believe. Thus, Christ is set forth to be the propitiation *through faith* in his blood. The gospel is the power of God unto salvation to every one *that believeth*. Christ is the end of the law for righteousness to every one that *believeth*. But he *that believeth not* shall be damned."

It may here be proper to notice a discourse of Mr. Mercer's published in 1839, in the Southern Baptist Preacher, entitled the *Excellency of the Knowledge of*

Christ Jesus the Lord. It is founded on Phil. 3 : 8. The author considers the excellency of the knowledge of Christ as dependent upon the excellency of Christ himself, and illustrates that excellency as it relates, 1st, to his personal dignity; and 2dly, to the value of his sacrifice. In discussing the 2d branch of his subject, he takes occasion to present some important thoughts upon the nature and design of the atonement. A few extracts are here subjoined, which in connexion with the selections already made from his Ten Letters, will give something like a general outline of Mr. Mercer's sentiments on this interesting and momentous subject.

"As the Apostle informs us, in his epistle to the Hebrews, especially in chap. 10 : 1—10. that Christ offered his body once for (or in lieu of) all sacrifices, we are safe in concluding that all *the good things* which were held forth in shadows to the family of Israel, are found essentially in Christ's atonement, and exhibited in the dispensation of the gospel to mankind. Let us examine the Levitical Economy, and see what atonements were made therein, and their uses, and then search for their analogies in the atonement made by our Lord. And

"1. There were sacrifices offered to make atonement for the sins of the whole house of Israel. This was done to preserve the nation, to avert divine judgments, and to establish among them the institutions of mercy. See Lev. 16 : 33, 34. Num. 8 : 19. 16 : 46—50. 25 : 10—13.

"2. Sacrifices were offered to make atonement for persons and things, to consecrate and sanctify them, and to make them suitable to be engaged in the work of God. See Lev. 16 : 16—19.

"Sacrifices were offered to make atonement for the sins of individuals. This was done to open a door of hope to those who were sensible of their sin, and burdened with their guilt before God, that they might seek and obtain pardon of sin, and peace of mind. See Lev. 1 : 4. 5 : 6—13.

"Now all these benefits will *in truth*, be found in the dispensation of the gospel to mankind, 'Through the redemption which is in Christ Jesus.' There is in all this a main design, which is the certain salvation of all God's spiritual Israel. Other things, no less obtained through the atonement, made by the shedding of the blood of Christ, must be considered as 'scaffoldings to the main design.' And

"1. Atonement was made in Christ for the sins of the world. Let none be surprised at this position, till it is well considered. Although atonement always has reference to sin, yet it relates to sin under different circumstances and obtains satisfaction for it in relation to different ends.—When the scriptures speak of the taking away of the sin of the world, or of the world's being saved, we are not to understand *eternal redemption;* but the reconciling of the world as such, and its preservation from deserved wrath until the redemption of the purchased possession. This is obvious too, from the fact that God does not design to save men by worlds, or nations, but only by individuals. In this particular sense, the sin of the world may be taken away, and yet every man be still in his sins; and will be so until the atonement is applied to him by faith for the pardon of his own sins.

"2. Through the atonement made by the offering of the body of Christ once for all sacrifices, has been obtained a divine influence to consecrate, set apart, and render fit all persons and things, which might be employed in the service of God. As in the type, no person or things could be engaged in the ritual service, without atonement made, so all fitness for any service in the kingdom of God, is derived from the atonement of Christ.

"In this view Christ said to his disciples, (and it is of general application,) 'without me ye can do nothing.' And hence he prayed for them 'That they might be sanctified through the truth,' or be set apart to the ministry of the word in the world. John 15 : 5. 17 : 17, 18. In accordance with this view, Paul (for himself and his fellow ministers) disclaims all efficiency in themselves, but avers 'our sufficiency is of God.' And therefore, gives thanks to God for all their successes. 2 Cor. 3 : 5. 2 : 14.

"This doctrine is more generally taught, 2 Tim. 2 : 21. 3 : 17. But

"3. By this atonement is secured the complete and final salvation of all the elect, or church of Christ. This Paul affirms, Eph. 5 : 25—27. He says, 'Christ loved the church and gave *himself for it;* that he might sanctify and cleanse it with the washing of water by the word; that he might present it to himself a glorious church, not having spot or wrinkle, or any such thing; but that it should be holy and without blemish.' And in Heb. 10 : 14. 'For by one offering he (Christ) hath perfected for ever them that are sanctified.' Or set apart by said offering to such an end. This is the main design.

"And now the question very naturally comes up, was the sacrifice of Christ offered as a sin-offering to law and justice, without regard to any persons whatever, but only to make an atonement which might justify the offended God in the pardon of such persons as he might see proper afterwards to apply it? Or, was it made with a special design for those who were afterwards to be benefited thereby? I cannot admit of this impersonal atonement, 1. because it does not show any justifiable or legal reason for the death of Christ, or why it pleased the Father *to bruise him.* If he died for sin, it must be the sin of somebody, or else it establishes the vague notion that sin can be punished in hell and the sinner saved in heaven. But 2. The scriptures connect so often and so fully the suffering of Christ with those for whom he suffered, that I cannot resist the conclusion that Christ died specially for those who shall be the heirs of eternal salvation."

In support of this view of the subject, the author quotes John 10 : 11. 15. Rom. 5 : 8. 1 Cor. 15 : 3. 1 Thess. 5 : 9, 10, and various other parallel passages, and then proceeds as follows:

"Under this department of atonement, lies the special and efficacious operations of the Holy Spirit, and all the measures of divine grace necessary to effect and bring about all the purposes of God in the full and final salvation of his people. And for this purpose Christ is constituted, 'the Head over all things to the church.' To him is given all authority and power in heaven and earth; and in him it has pleased the Father that *all fulness should dwell.* So that he, as king, rules in the midst of his enemies, and reigns in his church, dispensing his grace, and shedding abroad his love. He influences, directs and renders efficient the uses and operations of all means and instruments he may see proper to employ in his work, and nothing is sufficient of itself without him to do any good thing, so it is, that he *is all and in all.*

"In conclusion, let us observe that the different departments of the great atonement form but one mighty scheme of mercy. Though some parts are, as I said before, scaffoldings to the main design, yet they are all necessary to that design, and properly belong to it.

"As the atonement made for the whole house of Israel, procured to individuals who were sensible of their guilt, an opportunity to come and offer a sacrifice to make atonement for their own sins, and obtain pardon, see Lev. 1 : 2—4. 4 : 27—35. so the death of Christ, by the dispensation of the gospel to the world, has opened up a way whereby guilty sinners under conviction, may come and seek the pardon of their sins by faith which is in Christ Jesus. And there is something in this process analogous to the guilty Israelite's obtaining pardon under the law. A convicted soul in coming to God through Christ, as it were, brings Christ and presents him by faith to God as his sin-offering, lays his hands on his head, confesses his sins over him, and slays him, and sees him offered a sacrifice to God for a sweet savor, and feels his sins forgiven him, through the shedding of his blood which cleanses from all sin.

"I admit that the provisions of the general atonement, by which the kindness and love of God to man appeared, through our Lord and Saviour Jesus Christ, who abolished death and brought life and immortality to light through the gospel, accompanied by the common or general operations of the all-pervading Spirit of God, are sufficient for all the purposes of man's salvation, and all men, wherever they are dispensed, would be saved, were it not for that alienation of heart, which has everywhere estranged man from God, and filled him with that enmity which is not subject to his law, neither *indeed can be;* but God, foreseeing that *no man would receive the testimony,* John 3 : 32. and that all men would turn away from the holy commandment delivered to them, whereby all men are without excuse, has, in the plenitude of his mercy, determined, in the riches of his grace, according to the sovereign counsel and good pleasure of his own will, (Eph. 1 : 10, 11.) to exercise a power sufficient to effect the purposes of his grace in the salvation of his own chosen people. By the display of this power, his enemies are changed into friends, Ps. 111 : 2, 3. and they that hated him bow before him and give him glory. In the exercise of this power there is nothing arbitrary or absolute, for it is the fruit of love; but is all conciliatory and effectual. And thus, by influences perfectly congenial with human capacities and responsibilities, men are constrained to turn unto God with their whole heart, and subject themselves unto his reign and become the people of his praise."

In 1833 Mr. Mercer published an essay on the Lord's supper, based on 1 Cor. 5 : 7, 8. in which he runs an analogy between this gospel ordinance, and the Jewish passover. It contains much judicious and well-timed instruction, and would, no doubt, be useful to the churches if more generally circulated and carefully perused. Space can only be allowed for one or two paragraphs from the concluding part of the essay.

" From the foregoing, it is palpable that open, unrestricted communion has no place in scripture ; has not the least shadow of propriety, and is perfectly untenable. It is truly to be regretted, that so much should have been said on a subject on which the scripture is entirely silent; and therefore can only distract the weak and wavering, instead of edifying and confirming their souls in the right ways of the Lord. The plea on which open communionists rest their arguments, is 'christian *liberality ;*' a cause for which we are nowhere in scripture required to commune. If then we commune together at the Lord's table to show our *christian* love to one another, we pervert the ordinance of the Lord, and subject ourselves to the keen rebuke of 'who hath required this at your hands ?' Though church members to hold a *pure* communion, must be in christian fellowship, formed into *a new unleavened* lump, *in sincerity and truth*, yet they are nowhere required to commune to show their union, love and affection to each other; but to their Lord—to keep a holy memorial of his sufferings, and to show his death till he come.

" Christian love, or *liberality*, is a fundamental prerequisite, without *the manifestation* of which, no body of believers can be in that state of union and fellowship which will authorize them to commune at the Lord's table. This love is everywhere, in scripture, required to be manifested by believers in Christ, one towards another; not indeed, by any ceremony, but by practically abounding in the works of benevolence, brotherly kindness and charity; when, therefore, any body of Christians have gained gospel union and fellowship one with another, by the manifestations of fervent love towards each other, then, and not till then, are they prepared to give an expression of their love and affection to Christ, in a participation of the memorials of his sufferings and death. No set of believers can be practically brought to this state of christian unity and fellowship, without the pious use of a godly discipline, and therefore, none can sit together, with gospel propriety, at the table of the Lord, but those who are subject to its control; for if discipline guards the table of the Lord, then none can gospelly sit around it, but those who are under its banner."

In 1836, Mr. Mercer published his History of the Georgia Association, a work that was prepared in accordance with the request of that body. It is proper, however, to state, that most of the labor of preparing the volume was performed by the Rev. W. H. Stokes, associate editor of the Index; Mr. Mercer furnishing the materials, and taking the general oversight of the work as it progressed. Mr. Mercer therefore held himself responsible for the accuracy of the historical details, whilst the merits of the composition, whatever they may be, except as to those documents which are introduced in the language of others, are to be put to the credit of his esteemed and worthy co-laborer. The work is divided into *four* parts:—The *first* embraces some account of the churches previous to the formation of the body; an account of its organization, its articles of faith and decorum, compilations from the Minutes of the body, and some of the reports of its Missionary Board, &c. The *second part* consists of the most important *queries* that from time to time were propounded to the body, with the answers given. The *third part* embraces a selection from the Circular Letters of the Association, and constitutes rather more than one half the volume. Amongst the names of the various authors, are found those of Silas Mercer, Jesse Mercer, Abram Marshall, Wm. Rabun, James Armstrong, J. P. Marshall, W. T. Brantly, Jack Lumpkin, Adiel Sherwood, Otis Smith, B. M. Sanders, and many others, whose names are dear to the Baptists of Georgia. The *fourth* and last part is made up of short, yet interesting biographical sketches of some of the venerable departed fathers in the ministry; who had either been connected with the body, or labored usefully in gathering more or less of the materials of which it was afterwards composed.

It is to be regretted that this volume has not met with that ready sale which its inherent value would have justified. A large portion of the work would be edifying and instructive to ministers and private members of the church; and the entire volume valuable as a work of reference. The future historian cannot fail to turn over its pages with pleasure and advantage.

In 1837 Mr. Mercer published a Review of a certain Committee's Report, which appeared in the 12th number of the 1st volume of the "Primitive Baptist," a violent *anti-missionary* paper, published in North Carolina. This Report, in giving its version of certain church and associational difficulties, which had been the occasion of much controversy and bitter feeling, impugned unjustly, as Mr. Mercer supposed, the Georgia Association and the State Convention. " To disabuse the public mind, in reference to the two bodies above named, to exculpate them from the misrepresentations and ill-demeanors laid to their charge, and to set some facts stated in a more clear light," was the design of this Review. As the pamphlet is mostly devoted to affairs of a local and temporary interest, a particular notice of its contents may not be necessary here: it is due however to the author to say, that it was prepared with much ability, and was well adapted to the design for which it was written. The following are the closing sentences of the pamphlet.

"Say not that this distress is produced by missionary and kindred societies. Those existed long before this discord arose—and all were in peace—all admitting that each brother should use his liberty in these things, to act or not as he choosed. And thus all was, up to that very day when the Associations assumed the right to adjudicate the churches. But from that day, fierce contentions, bitter animosities and divisions have increased amongst us. Will not the brethren wake up to this fact, and come up, with one heart and united hands, to the help of our bleeding Zion? As said Paul in another case, '*he that letteth will let, till he be taken out of the way;*' so we may say in this case. *The cause which has produced our strife and divisions, will continue to produce confusion and discord, till it be taken out the way.*—And I can see no way by which peace can be restored to our Churches, except our brethren will give up their Associational jurisdiction, retract their decisions, and restore to the Churches their plundered rights.

"May the God of peace, send peace; by leading all his people to do that which is well pleasing in His sight, for the sake of the Prince of peace. So prays the friend and fellow servant of *all who love our Lord Jesus Christ in sincerity.*

"JESSE MERCER."

At a Ministers' Meeting in Powelton, held in Nov. 1839, Mr. Mercer read an essay on the query, "*Is the cause of Missionary Societies and other kindred institutions, as advocated by the Georgia Baptist Convention, the cause of God?*" The writer, of course, endeavored to establish the *affirmative*. After presenting a few appropriate and remarkably condensed scriptural arguments, he thus concludes : "If the societies complained of are not fulfilling the scriptures according to the purpose of God, set forth in prophecies and command, there is no operation now fulfilling, or pretending to fulfil them. Can this be supposed!"

Early in 1841, appeared in the columns of the Index an essay in three numbers, from the pen of Mr. Mercer, on the *Forgiveness of Sins*. In these numbers are considered the *Source* of forgiveness; the *Medium* of communication ; *how it is dispensed*, and *how it is received ;* and also its *occasions*. Under the last head he presents his views upon a subject which has been much controverted of late years in certain sections of the country.

"These texts (Mark 1: 4. Acts 2: 38.) have been used by some as if remission of sins was dispensed in baptism, and that believers were now to be baptized in order to receive the remission of their sins. If these passages were all that the Bible contained on the subject, there might be a shadow of difficulty in the construction of them; but as the Scriptures are elsewhere indubitably clear, that pardon is dispensed by the Holy Spirit, and received by faith, as all other gospel blessings are, the sense in these texts must be differently understood. And I am fully persuaded that the true meaning is, that baptism is to be submitted to, as all other obedience is to be done, in *reference* to the remission of sins. The true sense in these passages, depends on the meaning of '*for*,' as used in them. Webster, in his late Dictionary, among many other renderings, has the two following. ' *On account of*.' And '*towards the obtaining of*.' I think all will agree it must be in these texts used in one of these senses. It either must be that believers are to be baptized in order *to the obtaining* the remission of sins, or it is to be performed on *account of* the remission of sins.

I take the latter ground of construction as the *true one* in these declarations; because the scripture ascribes it to a different cause; see Acts 10 : 43. in reference to Christ crucified, the prophets all gave witness 'that through his name, whosoever believeth in him, *shall receive remission of sins.*' This is conclusive. For if forgiveness of sin is received through the name of Christ, by faith in him, it can't *be received* by baptism, nor any other act of gospel obedience. A critical observance of the text in Acts 2 : 38. will show that Peter did not intend to convey the idea to those convicted, inquiring souls, that they on being baptized should *receive* the remission of their sins; for then he would have placed '*receive*' before the remission of sins, and then it would have read thus :— 'Repent and be baptized every one of you in the name of Jesus Christ, and ye shall receive the remission of sins and the gift of the Holy Ghost;' but *receive* being placeed bfore *the gift of the Holy Ghost*, plainly excludes the remission of sins from the reception; and shows he designed the forgiveness of sins to be considered the great reason *on account* of which they were to be baptized. I think any one may perceive a marked difference between Christ and the Evangelists in the use of this little word '*for;*'— Christ said to his disciples at the supper-table, (Math. 26 : 28.) ' For this is my blood of the New Testament, which is shed for many *for* the remission of sins.' Who doubts but Christ intended *for the obtaining of* the remission of sins ? But the Evangelist and Peter use it evidently, in my view, in the sense of, *on account of*, and shows that baptism is to be received in joyful regard to Christ, by whom we received the atonement.—Once more and I close. Baptism is a figurative representation of Christ's death and resurrection *for the remission of sins*, wherein the baptized show their faith in Christ and hope of salvation through him, and must have the remission of sins already in their joyful possession; and of course, submit to the ordinance in view of their *being forgiven all trespasses*, and in hope of a triumphant resurrection with their ascended Saviour, to that inheritance which is reserved in heaven for all those who look and wait for his coming."

A few extracts from Mr. Mercer's shorter pieces that appeared from time to time in the Index, under the editorial head, will exhibit his opinions on various important subjects, and furnish a proper conclusion to this chapter.

Justification and Sanctification.

"1. Justification is an act of God the Father *as Judge;* sanctification is by the operations and influences of the Holy Ghost. 2. Justification is opposed to guilt and condemnation; sanctification is opposed to the corruption and the pollutions of the heart. 3. Justification is by the righteousness of Christ imputed; sanctification is by the graces of the Holy Spirit implanted. 4. Justification gives a title to heaven; sanctification fits and prepares for heaven. Thus Christ *on us* is our justification, while Christ *in us* is our sanctification and hope of glory."

Free Agency.

"This term is used by theological writers to express the state of men as creatures vested with power every way suited to yield obedience to the laws of their Maker, while at the same time they were left *free*, or liable to 'turn from the holy commandment delivered unto them.' The word *agent*, in this connexion, simply describes man as capable of action, and *free* is used to show that that action was the result of no compulsory coercion, but produced wholly by the volition of its agents, or that men act according to the most prevailing disposition of their hearts. This *free agency* is that whereby men are the proper subjects of moral law; bound to obey the voice of their Creator, because he gave them in their creation, the ability to do so, and therefore requires them to *love him* with all their heart, soul, mind and strength; but never coerces them to this obedience—for this would be to render their service a matter of necessity and not of choice, void of virtue and incapable of giving him any honor. In order that men's obedience might be voluntary, virtuous and honoring to their Creator, they must be *free* to disobey if they choose to do so. 'Tis this that renders them responsible for their actions—the subjects of praise or blame. Without this they could not be blessed in their obedience, nor condemned for their sin.

"The fact that men have sinned, has no tendency to alter, or change, or abate the claims of their Creator on them, or their obligations of obedience to him, in the least. He has created them the subjects of moral government, and commands them accordingly; and it is their duty to obey; but their foolish heart *being fully bent in them* to do evil, they *will not*.

They choose their own evil ways and doings, and refuse to return. Therefore they are without excuse, and justly condemned, and would all perish in their own corruption, if God was not better to them than they are to themselves.

"But God, in the infinite provisions of his mercy, has purposed in Christ to employ such divine operations and influences as shall, in perfect accordance with the *free agency* of men, make his people *willing in the day of his power*. It is believed that all the *saving* operations of God in men, are to bring them to this willingness, and so to be saved. That God in these operations, never does any violence to the will of men, but always seeks to change it from its evil inclinations, and so to turn them to himself. The evidences of God's favor towards any are, therefore, not to be sought in *forcible* restraints, but in the drawings and sweet inclinings of their hearts to seek the Lord, and to obtain his favor. Nor are we to think these sweet drawings are *the less certain*, because they do not rise to coercion. The Lord who formed the heart, knows best how to govern it, and form it anew to love and serve him with true delight."

Atonement and Reconciliation.

"While I was at the Georgia Association, I received from a highly esteemed brother, the following note. 'My dear brother,—In reading your letters on the atonement, I find on the 4th page, 1st column, *it is called reconciliation*. Are atonement and reconciliation synonymous expressions? If so, I will thank you to remove a difficulty resting on my mind; it is this: the atonement was made say eighteen hundred years ago; its effects reached back to the first real penitent, and forward to the last. J. M. was hopefully reconciled to God, say 1787; what influence had the atonement before this period? If atonement and reconciliation are the same, he must have been reconciled while his life and heart gave abundant evidence that he was unreconciled: or in other words, he was reconciled and yet in rebellion; which to me is absurd! You will oblige me by removing this dilemma.' It may be that other brethren are puzzled with this dilemma, and for their sakes as well as his, I request you will insert in the Star and Index,* the following solution.

"Reconciliation is the making peace between parties at variance. God and men are at variance, and reconciliation relates to both parties. From God it removes the offence; from men, *sin*, the cause of it. The offence is removed from God by the death of his Son—by the blood of his cross, &c. Sin is taken away from men by the operations and influences of the Holy Ghost, giving them faith in that death and blood. In reference to God it is atonement; in reference to men it is regeneration and conversion. Paul uses the word in both these senses in one verse, Rom. 5 : 10. 'For if when we were enemies, we were *reconciled* to God by the death of his Son; much more, being reconciled, we shall be saved by his life.' The same idea is expressed in verse 8: 'In that while we were yet sinners, Christ died for us.' Now, as Christ really died *for us* eighteen hundred years ago, and in purpose from the foundation of the world, reconciliation must have rested in his mind coeval thereto, and so, while men lay in sin, and were rebels.

---

* The paper was published at Philadelphia when the above was written.

"The same may be said of redemption and even of pardon; indeed, pardon is of necessity some time with God before it is received by us: and so, we may be said to be pardoned, and yet not pardoned.—I believe that Gill, Scott, Brown, Doddridge, Buck, and Henry, all agree in reconciliation and atonement being synonymous, as they relate to God. I can't see any other sense in the texts I have cited. If this is correct, the doctrine is established, whether the 'dilemma' is removed or not."

Predestination and Free agency.

"The knotty question—How predestination in God can consist with free agency in man? is more puzzling than edifying. We may affirm the fact, though we cannot explain the manner; for the scriptures plainly teach us both, and '*they cannot be broken.*' We do not, however, see any particular difficulty in harmonizing them together, unless it could be thought that seduction or inducement could exonerate its subjects from responsibility; but if that could be allowed, it would apply as well to *temptation* as to *divine influence*, and *so* render man *a mute;* neither the subject of praise or blame. But if man may be tempted, or induced to act *in a certain way*, and yet be accountable, we see not why God might not foresee how the various temptations and trials, *he would please to suffer*, would operate on man, and *determine* to employ such counteracting operations and influences as he might see good to effect a *certain* end, and yet he remain *righteous* and man *responsible*. For instance: If God, having created man a rational and intelligent moral agent, should determine to place him in circumstances, and suffer him to be tempted by all the inducements, the best suited to test his integrity, would he be thereby freed from responsibility, *in case he sinned?* Certainly not. Can it be supposed, that such a case would possess any difficulty *to an infinite mind,* in perfectly comprehending the results of such a trial? We think not. Well then, should God predetermine to oppose to the sinful inclinations of men, such restraints and influences under his providence, as would overcome them, and dispose him to choose and adopt that course which would terminate in *that end,* which would, (all things considered,) be most for his glory and the greatest good of the universe; would that in any wise destroy man's free agency? It surely could not. Then it is easy to see how God could consistently with the perfect accountability of man, 'declare the end from the beginning, and from ancient times *the things* that are not yet done, saying, My counsel shall stand, and I will do all my pleasure?'"

Duty of Man and Purposes of God.

"We presume the difficulty of these brethren *in reconciling* the purposes of God with the duty of man, arises from viewing duty *only* in relation to its agents, and as dependent *alone on uninfluenced* human volition. Their minds therefore revolt at the idea of resting the purposes of God on conditions *so* precarious and uncertain. But this difficulty will wholly vanish, when it is considered that these agents and all their works *are in the hand of God,* Eccl. 9 : 1. and *directed in truth* to the ends designed, Isa. 61 : 8. That God has connected the operations of his people with the designs of his grace, is as certain as he has commanded them; but in appointing the duties of his servants to be the means of subserving his purposes, he also has appointed his Holy Spirit to be the superintending Lord over them, their works and the things to be accomplished. But we are not to suppose that God always makes known his designs, with the requirements of those duties, which he intends to make instrumental in the accomplishment of his purposes, or that his people are always conscious of the effects which will follow their obedience. In this respect they are often left in great obscurity, while God plants his footsteps before them, in the deep waters, and makes darkness his pavilion round about him; and they are left to be impelled on only from those motives and honest considerations which are conducive to all holy obedience, arising from the fear, love and authority of Him who commands their respect. Thus Christians should be diligent in the discharge of those obligations which are clearly intimated from the commands of Scripture, the indications of divine Providence, and the operations of the Holy Spirit in their hearts—humbly looking to God for the desired results."

Conditional Election.

" Mr. Wesley, in his zeal to establish his favorite scheme of *conditional* election, notwithstanding all his learning and skill as a controversialist, yet lays down a scheme which fixes on the elect *personally*, and secures their salvation, from eternity as absolutely sure, as the knowledge of God was perfect or his faithfulness unchangeable. He lays down his position thus— *God from the foundation of the world, knowing all men, believing or unbelieving, did according to his foreknowledge choose, or elect all obedient believers, as such, to salvation; and reprobated or foreappointed all disobedient unbelievers* as such, to *damnation; not without, but according to his foreknowledge of them and all their works* from the *foundation of the world.* Here it will be noticed that Mr. W. admits the all comprehending and infinite understanding of God, and makes it the base of his position. According to this perfect knowledge of God, of all men and their individual characteristics, they were disposed of for eternity, from the foundation of the word. Now we ask any man, free from prejudice, that if God foresaw *me* as an *obedient believer,* and elected *me,* as such, to glory, can I *fail to attain to it ?* Or if *I* was seen, from the foundation of the world a *disobedient unbeliever* and reprobated, or foreappointed as such, to damnation, can *I* possibly escape it? It will be easily seen that this scheme renders the destiny of every man absolutely sure from the foundation of the word, without the possibility of a change, unless it could be shown that there had been some error in the foreknowledge of God. But the worst-feature in the conditional scheme is, that it divests the doctrine of every particle or vestige of grace. What grace is there in God's choosing worthy persons to glory? Is there any wonder in God's loving and choosing *the righteous ?* But the astonishment of men and angels has been called forth in that God loved us, and Christ died for us *while we were enemies.* In scripture the doctrine of election is considered as a matter of amazing gratitude and thanksgiving. See Ephe. 1 : 3, 4. 2 Thess. 2 : 13. 1 Peter 1 : 3. and whoever holds or feels towards it in any other light, holds it not in accordance to scripture."

Persons are sometimes improperly accused of Arminianism.

"Although Mr. Fuller writes much on the responsibilities and duties of men to believe the gospel when it is preached to them, yet he argues fully, the total depravity of fallen men, and that they can be saved only by sovereign grace, through the application of the atonement, by the Holy Spirit.

"Some expressions, dropped by Judson and other missionaries, have been caught up, and construed into *Arminianism :* such as, if Christians had done their duty, *what multitudes of heathen might have been saved ! Or, what multitudes of heathen are perishing every day, for lack of that knowledge, which Christians have failed to propagate among them !* These and all similar expressions, which connect salvation with the use of means, are to be understood in *the light of means,* and no further. And in that light they are perfectly scriptural. In Matt. 11 : 20—24. our Lord upbraids the hard hearted and impious Jews, because they repented not at his mighty works; and declared that if they had been done in Tyre and Sidon, and in Sodom, they would have repented long ago, and remained to that day. Again, he said to those who persecuted, and would have killed him, John 5 : 34. 'These things I say, that ye might be saved.' Also 20 : 31. 'But these things are written, that ye might believe that Jesus is the Christ, the Son of God; and that believing ye might have life through his name.' Paul declares to the Gentiles that the design of what he said, Rom. 11 : 14. was that—' If by any means he might provoke to emulation, them which are my flesh, and might save some of them.' And in 1 Cor. 9 : 19—22. he says : 'I made myself servant unto all, that I might gain the more.' And says he, 'I am made all things to all men, that I might by all means save some.' And he even expresses the same connexion between his efforts, and the salvation of the elect in 2 Tim. 2 : 10. 'Therefore, I endure all things for the elect's sake, that they may also obtain the salvation which is in Christ Jesus, with eternal glory.' If then, the missionaries in the sentiments above were Arminians, then were Christ and Paul Arminians!!

"But we presume, the whole complaint springs out of a mistaken notion of what Arminianism is. Or from a wish to stigmatize whatever is opposed to their antinomian notions.

"Arminianism rightly understood, is comprehensibly expressed in universal provision, made in Christ for the salvation of all men; and a corresponding ability in man to accept the offered mercy and live by it. Or, if we mistake not, as expressed by Arminius himself, that it consists in '*All free grace* in God, and *all free* will in man.' The doctrine inculcates, that Christ as the second Adam, represented all mankind, and restored all to a state of initial salvation. So that all men are born with a seed of grace in them; and stand justified free from the condemnation of Adam's sin. That God freely dispenses his calls and invitations to all, and that his Spirit operates on all—but on none irresistibly; so that all are capable at all times to resist the grace and be lost; or cherish the influence, and be saved.

"But appeals to men, in regard to their danger or duty, must not be considered inconsistent, either with their condition in sin, or the eternal and unchangeable purposes of God; because the scriptures abound with them. Divine purposes form no rule for human action. They are rather the rule of the divine operation. The *holy commandment* is the rule for the obedience of men. And all men are bound to obey God, in all his dispensations of law or gospel. They who have right notions of God's purposes of grace and men's responsibilities, will never confound them together. All duties, whether yielded to command, invitation or exhortation, must be considered only as duties, and done as necessary to some usefulness, and for the honor of God. Salvation always comes from God, through the redemption that is in Christ, according to the riches of his grace. But it may be received in the way of duty. It is God's way, first to call men to repentance which issues in obedience; and then to faith in our Lord Jesus Christ that they may be saved through him. Therefore, the scriptures abound in exhortations, invitations, and even commands to repentance and faith. It is right then that men should be taught their obligations to God, and exhorted, and urged, and even expostulated with, that they turn from the evil of their ways, and seek the Lord while he may be found, and call upon him while he is near; lest they sink from the dark mountains of their error, and perish for ever. All this, however, must be kept distinctly within the sphere of means and duty; or only as ways in which the Lord may be found, *in whom alone is all grace*. If any man has ever inculcated the efficiency of means and instruments *in themselves considered*, he is worse than an Arminian. The effort-brethren, so far as we are acquainted with them, hold with the apostle, that while they 'plant and water,' it is God *alone* 'that giveth the increase.' They feel it to be their duty to do their endeavor to fulfil the ministry which God *has entrusted* to them, but they look to him for all their successes. To God, therefore, be all the Glory."

For whom are the invitations of the Gospel particularly intended ?

"Although the invitations of the gospel are full and free, answering to every case of distress, which convinced sinners can feel or the fulness of Christ relieve; yet we know of no command which requires a minister of Christ, or even justifies him, in inviting *thoughtless sinners* to come to him for salvation. And why should he? They neither know nor feel their need of the blessings he has to bestow. It appears to us the first duty of a gospel minister is to teach men the ruined state they are in by reason of sin, and the provisions of mercy God has made for their recovery in Christ; then to warn them of their danger, then after that to call them to repentance and faith, and then last of all to invite the perishing, helpless and dying to come to Christ and live. The invitations of the gospel are predicated on some circumstance of distress, which the blessings of salvation are suited to remedy. The most free and general invitation is, '*And* whosoever will, let him take of the water of life freely.' But we presume, all will admit this *will* is *desire*, and even involves *thirst* for these waters, with anxious fears of being denied, else why invited to take them *freely*. Should it be said the thirsty in the 50th of Isaiah, evidently intend those who are athirst for carnal or worldly pleasures—then we ask, is there any thing in the waters of life to satiate this *sinful* desire—to allay this *burning* thirst for sensual gratifications? We answer no: the causes of this sinful thirst must be removed by soul-stirring convictions, and the place filled with 'hunger and thirst after righteousness.' And then, and not till then, the invitations will apply.

"Should any inquire why sinners are preached to *at all*, if they be '*blind, deaf, dumb?*' We reply, because, God has *commanded us to preach unto the people*. And we should obey as did the prophet, when commanded to prophesy to the *dry bones* in the valley. And rationally, because they are *alive* in all that renders them accountable beings; but *dead* in all that fits them for acceptable, evangelical obedience. And therefore theirs must be a guilty *blindness, deafness and death*, about which they ought to be *preached to*."

The doctrines of Grace favorable to Godliness.

"The doctrine of divine grace, according to *eternal* purpose, which God purposed in Christ Jesus before the world began, is a doctrine according to godliness; and when rightly held and taught, tends to promote comfort, zeal, and perseverance in all holy obedience, from a sense of gratitude; and in nowise interferes with the obligations and responsibilities of men; but when made a party question, and run out into extremes, (to which controversy leads,) it becomes a snare to many souls—a nurse of inaction, and a conductor to the ruins of Antinomianism. The opposite extreme should as assiduously be guarded against.—Dwelling on practical religion, and insisting on the duties and obligations of men, without keeping in constant view their moral and guilty disability, and the sovereignty of God in affording salvation to them, as unworthy, helpless sinners, as directly tends to the *bogs of Arminianism*. The truth of the gospel, rightly held and taught, is that which turns men from darkness to light, and the power of sin to serve the living God, by faith which is in Christ Jesus our Lord."

Sincerity.

"Sincerity may be defined, *the exact agreement* of a man's conduct, *with the feelings and designs* of his heart. If then hatred to God and man cannot be justified, nor even excused because *it is sincere;* the sincere belief of error cannot apologize for its votaries, in its practice. It is not sincerity, but truth, which can justify any one in his faith or practice. If otherwise, all kinds and forms of religion would be equalized. For doubtless there are *sincere* Jews and Pagans, Infidels and Idolaters, as well as Christians. But who will ever excuse Jews, Pagans, Infidels, Idolaters or Christian errorists, *because they are sincere?* None! we presume. But nevertheless, sincerity is an indispensable trait of a godly man's heart. It is the true and genuine characteristic of a real christian, and which distinguishes him from, and opposes him to a hypocrite. The true christian therefore, sincerely believes the truth, and does it; because it is the truth, and not because it suits his convenience, or fosters either his pride or pleasure."

Submission to God, not always followed with immediate comfort.

"And we inquire, if there is not in christian experience a crisis beyond which there is no opposition to God's justice or his mercy, and yet there is no comfort and peace in believing? But on the contrary, a mighty struggle, an awful suspense! This *struggle* is not with God to induce him to pardon sins—no *enlightened* sinner does that—but he is in strife in himself, to know whether God will, or even can pardon him. What does the Saviour mean when he says *strive to enter in?* does he not, so far as prayer is concerned, mean the *importunity* he recommends, and what is that but a mighty struggle at the throne of grace? Christ says that God bears long with his own elect which cry unto him day and night. Is it likely they at such times have no struggling to enter into rest? We are of opinion that there is in the dispensation of God's grace to men, a season in which after they are convinced and humbled, that they are left to seek, and mourn, and wait before God, to obtain his pardoning mercy, and that during this time they have many fears and tremblings, and we may say many *strugglings* lest they should be finally cast off!"

Comment on Rom. 8 : 19, 20, 21.

"This is reckoned among Commentators, one of the most difficult passages in the epistle, to understand and explain satisfactorily. The reason, we think, is that they mostly adopt a plan of construction, which is wide of the apostle's theme of discourse. They are very much divided, and it does not appear that they have yet come to any agreement as to what is the true meaning. We have consulted all the expositions we have at command, and cannot find any with which we can be satisfied.—Some make '*the creature*' to mean the *brute* creature, others the *heathen* creature, others the *inanimate* creature, and others *the creation*. But these meanings all represent the apostle, as suddenly breaking off from a most interesting subject, to a different one without any just cause; and besides, we cannot see the propriety of attributing to these the strong expressions of desire and hope ascribed to the creature by the apostle. We shall therefore give our own opinion and leave our friends to make their own.

"As the apostle assigns what is contained in these verses, as a reason for what he had said in verses 17 and 18, we think it best to understand him to intend by the creature, *the child of God*. The new creature in Christ Jesus. (See 2 Cor. 5 : 17. where the same

Greek word is used for creature.) Paul having come to the conclusion that the sufferings endured by christians in the present world, were not worthy to be compared with the glory that would be revealed in them, assigns as a reason for this conclusion, that the *earnest expectation* of the child of God, waited for this glorious reversion; and though now, for a season, it might be needful for him to suffer the afflictions which his heavenly Father had appointed to him as trial, or chastisement, yet he was taught to believe that he should be delivered from this state of bondage into the glorious liberty of the sons of God in light. The verses may be thus paraphrased. For the earnest expectation of the child of God waiteth for the time when all the children of God will be manifested in their true character. For he was made subject to vanity, or the state of suffering in which he remains, not by his own will or desire, but because it is the will of his Father in heaven, that he should continue in this transitory state of disappointment and sufferings. But in doing this, hope has been given him as an anchor to his soul, sure and steadfast, to enable him to endure his trials till his redemption come. And he shall be delivered from this bondage of corruption into the glorious liberty of all the children of God in the heavenly kingdom. And to encourage the brethren to endure their sufferings with patience, the Apostle alleges, as a known fact, that all the *new creation*, or people of God in the past ages, groaned and travailed in pain for this deliverance; and not only those who had lived in the more dark dispensation, but even we, the apostles, who have received the richer degree of the spirit of adoption, groan and wait for the redemption of our body. Hence the apostle would have his brethren rather to count it all joy when they fell into many temptations and trials, knowing 'that tribulation worketh patience ; and patience experience, and experience hope, and hope maketh not ashamed, because the love of God is shed abroad in our hearts by the Holy Ghost which is given unto us !"

Trinitarian arguments for John 5 : 17. and on.

"To understand the paradoxes of Scripture in reference to Christ, his twofold state, or complex character, as *son of man* and *son of God* must be kept constantly in view. Without this many texts are perfectly inexplicable. As *son of man*, in which exists his mediatorship, he is a servant, obeys, suffers, prays, and dies ! In this character he declares himself to be inferior to the Father.

"As *Son of God*, he thinks it no robbery to be equal with God, is the express image of his person, and the very brightness of his glory, and affirms himself to be *one* with the Father.

"Unitarians endeavor to establish the creatureship of Christ, in order to destroy his godhead. A man would argue just as conclusively, who, on proving man to be a frail and dying mortal, would triumphantly affirm that he was not *immortal*. But to the point in question. Our Lord had declared himself to be the *Son of God* in such a manner as made the Jews charge him with blasphemy, in making himself *equal* with God. In all that Christ replies to this charge, his *essential, indivisible* and co-existent union with his Father is asserted. In any other view of the divine Personalities they could work separately. If Christ was a creature he could act without his Father, as angels and men have done in committing sin. But as he is one of a co-ordinate and inseparable existence he cannot work of himself or alone. So when the Father works he also works. For what things soever the Father doeth, *these* also doeth the Son likewise. This is not imitation, for then there would be a double set of works, but it is the work of indivisible unity. It is therefore that the Son is entitled to the same degree of honor with the Father; which if he be not God, *is idolatry.* Now whatever is said to be given to him, is '*because he is the Son of Man.*' In this sense all is communicated and derived.

"It is hoped the above may serve as a clew to direct the thoughts of those bewildered, in the intricacies of this very mysterious doctrine. Our advice to all is to build their faith on the *plain*, and not the *obscure* portions of Scripture. On the rock of divine declaration, and not on the sand of *human* conjecture."

The true Christian and deceived soul.

"Many a *sincere* child of God and lover of Christ has inquired with anxious solicitude, under conscious defects and short-comings, "*can I be a christian?* Surely *I must be a deceived soul!*' And one has lately asked us with earnest concern, ' what are the exercises of a *real christian,* and some of the most striking marks by which he may be distinguished from *a deceived soul?*'

"We now in compliance with the request thus earnestly made, will endeavor to place a few of the exercises and most obvious marks of a true christian in contrast with those of a deceived soul; for the benefit of those who have *little* faith and tender consciences.

"1. A christian is a believer in Christ, whose *sole* dependence for salvation is in Him; and who, from a sincere regard for his person and honor, is endeavoring to follow his precepts and examples.

"A *deceived soul*, while he may admit that Christ Jesus is the procuring cause of salvation for the human race, and that it *originated* all in grace, yet does not wholly trust in him, nor on divine grace, for that salvation, but in something else, either in, or done by himself, or by somebody else for him; and he is not careful to follow Christ as *his Lord and Master*, but only as he may think it' necessary for his own happiness and final safe arrival in heaven.

"2. A christian loves God. 1 John 4 : 7. 'Every one that loveth *is born* of God.' Which may be known by an exercise of holy and reverend fear of him, leading to eschew evil and do good from a pious and devout regard to his honor.

"A deceived soul does not love God, only in *so far* as he thinks he sees something in him, which has a direct bearing on his own happiness, and enables him to cherish his hopes of salvation founded on his own imaginary goodness; he has no fear of offending God, except as he supposes his safety is concerned.

"3. A christian loves his fellow-professors, just in that proportion in which they give evidence that they are born of God.—1 John 3 : 14. 'We know that we have passed from death unto life, because we love the brethren.' The motive of this love is in the love of God their heavenly Father, as laid down in 5 : 1, 2. 'Every one that loveth him that begat, loveth him also that is begotten of him. By this we know that we love the children of God, when we love God and keep his commandments.' So that the love a christian has to professors of christianity, marks him to be a *child* of God, just so far as it springs from the love he has to God, which is evident from its issuing in a sincere endeavor to keep his commandments.

"A deceived soul loves professors of religion either *nominally*, without distinction, because it is counted *liberal* and *popular*, and is highly commended among men; or *denominationally*, because they are of his own sect or party, or because they hold in matters of religion precisely as he does.—His motives for the love of the brethren, are never drawn from so remote a source as the love of God and the keeping of his commandments.

"4. A christian has a knowledge of himself, which at once distresses and humbles him. He views himself *without Christ*, totally depraved, Rom. 7 : 14. 18. His heart is a sink of sin; Jer. 17 : 9. He knows its plague, 1 Kings 8 : 38. and bitterness, Prov. 14 : 10. He often reproaches himself as vile and unworthy; and the greater his discoveries are of the holiness and greatness of God, the more he abhors himself in dust and ashes; Job 42 : 5, 6. Prov. 30 : 2, 3. Isa. 6 : 5. He is often disappointed in his fondest hopes and anticipations in happiness and success in duty; Rom. 7 : 15. to the end of the chapter, compared with Gal. 5 : 17. He is also exposed to many and fiery temptations; 1 Peter 1 : 6. 4. 12 : 13. But he rejoices in hope of deliverance. Ps. 34 : 19, 20. Rom. 8 : 18—25.

"A deceived soul trusts in himself that he is righteous; Luke 18 : 9. Puts dependence in his own heart, or in man, or some set of men; Prov. 28 : 26. Jer. 17 : 5. Ezek. 13 : 6. And is not in trouble as true believers are; Ps. 73 : 5.

"Deception does not consist *so much* in erroneous exercises and practice in religion, as in a misguided dependence for salvation, and selfish motives in regard to the service of God. The *deceived* soul cannot love Christ for any intrinsic value, or supreme excellence he sees in him, and therefore cannot trust to his righteousness for justification, but chooses to depend on his own inward holiness, and to poise himself on his own good frames and feelings. But true and vital piety consists not *so much* in frames and feelings which may be had, as in a well grounded dependence on Christ for acceptance with God, and a deep rooted disposition of heart exercised towards God in reverence and godly fear. The child of God loves Christ supremely, and can trust his righteousness *and nothing else*, for justification with God. He can have no confidence in himself, for in him (that is in his flesh) he knows dwells no good thing. Phil. 3 : 3. Rom. 7 : 18.

"'But, brother Editor, I thought, should I ever be a christian, I would be a *holy* one, but have been entirely disappointed—I fear instead of growth in grace, my life is retrograde. I perform no duty as I ought. My attempts to pray are often with a mind *so void* of feeling, *so* wandering, *so* little impressed with a sense of my wants or necessities, that were I to approach an earthly judge *in the same manner*, I know he would spurn me from his presence.'—Well be this all true, and why lament it, if not a christian? 'Tis a mercy that christians know their errors, and mourn over them, and are *humbled* on account of them. Ps. 19 : 12—14. Lam. 3 : 19, 20. We cannot close this article better than in the words of the excellent Newton.

"'If I love, why am I thus?
Why this dull and lifeless frame?
Hardly, sure, can they be worse,
Who have never heard his name!
Could my heart so hard remain,

Pray'r a task and burden prove,
Every trifle give me pain,
If I knew a Saviour's love?
When I turn my eyes within,
All is dark, and vain, and wild;
Fill'd with unbelief and sin,
Can I deem myself a child?
If I pray, or hear, or read,
Sin is mix'd in all I do;
You that love the Lord indeed,
Tell me, is it thus with you?
Yet I mourn my stubborn will,
Find my sin a grief and thrall!
Should I grieve for what I feel,
If I did not love at all?
Could I joy the saints to meet,
Choose the ways I once abhorred,
Find, at times, the promise sweet,
If I did not love the Lord?
Lord, decide this doubtful case!
Thou who art thy people's sun,
Shine upon thy work of grace,
If it be indeed begun!
Let me love thee more and more,
If I love at all, I pray;
If I have not lov'd before,
Help me to begin to-day!'"

The following is a connected list of the principal writings of Mr. Mercer.

1. Circular Letter of Ga. Association, 1801. 2. Do. do on Discipline, 1806. 3. Do. do. Invalidity of Pedobaptist Administration of Ordinances, 1811. 4. Do. do. Various Christian Duties urged, 1816. 5. Funeral Discourse on the death of Gov. Rabun, 1819. 6. Circular of Ga. Assoc. Unity and Dependence of the Churches, 1822. 7. Exposition of the first 17 verses in 12th ch. Rev. 1825. 8. Dissertation on the Prerequisites to Ordination, 1829. 9. Scriptural Meaning of Ordination, 1830. 10. Ten Letters on the Atonement, 1830. 11. Circular Letter of the Bap. State Convention, 1831. 12 Resemblances and Differences between Church authority, and that of an Association, 1833. 13. Essay on the Lord's Supper, 1833. 14. Education Sermon,—Knowledge indispensable to a Min-

ister of God, 1834. 15. History of the Georgia Association, 1836. 16. Review of a certain Report on Church and Associational Difficulties, 1837. 17. Sermon on the Importance of Ministerial Union, 1838. 18. Sermon on the Excellency of the Knowledge of Christ, 1839. 19. Essay—The Cause of Missionary Societies, the Cause of God, 1839. 20. Essay on Forgiveness of Sins, 1841. 21. Hear what the Spirit saith unto the Churches, 3 numbers, 1841. 22. A Manuscript Sermon on Baptism, founded on Acts 10 : 47. 23. Manuscript Sermon on Missions, from Matt. 28 : 19.

CHAPTER XIV.

Narrative of Mr. Mercer's Life resumed.—Letter to Mrs. R.—Severe indisposition.—Address to patrons of the Index.—Letter to the Georgia Association.—Letter to Mrs. R.—To Heman Lincoln.—Death of Mrs. Mercer.—Letter to Mr. M.—Letter of Mr. Curtis to Mr. Mercer.—Mr Mercer's reply.—" Hear what the Spirit saith to the Churches," 3 Nos.—His feelings in view of his approaching end.

We now return to something like a more connected narrative, for the purpose of giving a hasty sketch of the declining days of Mr. Mercer. This account may be introduced very appropriately by a letter to an esteemed sister in the Lord, with whom he kept up an occasional correspondence for many years. It speaks of increasing infirmities.

TO MRS. R.

" *Washington, March* 27, 1839.

" DEAR SISTER DOLLY,

" I acknowledge my fault in not replying to your former letter. I am too apt to procrastinate till I forget : pardon my neglects.

"As well as I can recollect, you requested in your former letter, that your marrying should make no difference to us. I considered that you were free to marry whom you chose, and of course we ought to be content; so you need give yourself no further concern about that. In your last you speak of old times. Truly I often throw my thoughts back on days gone by, and many recollections pour in upon my mind, rather with a mournful pleasure. Oft have I thought of the days of your conviction. That meeting we had at Brown's Meeting-house—O what days those were! If it should come in my convenience, it would be as much as ever my joy to call and stay with you. But my going abroad has become pretty much a matter of necessity—of business, and I go where I must.

"I think I can say with you that I am as ever determined *to be* and *live* for God; but O my infirmities seem to increase upon me, and I am like Samson when he had lost his strength. I cannot do as aforetime, but when I would do good, evil is present with me. I feel more and more the need of divine help. I always felt as is expressed by Oliver Hart in one of his hymns.

> 'Some long repent and late believe,
> But when their sins' forgiven,
> A clearer passport they receive,
> And walk with joy to heaven.
>
> Their pardon some receive at first,
> And then, compelled to fight,
> They feel their latter stages worst,
> And travel much by night.'

"I should have said I always felt the spirit of this last verse, and often called it *mine*. But I now find it still more and more appropriate. But still I do not despair. My motto is, *trust in the Lord and go forward.*"

Though Mr. Mercer was occasionally the subject of bodily infirmity, yet during his long ministry, he was seldom compelled, by disease, to suspend for any considerable length of time his useful labors. He was particularly favored in being allowed with great punctuality to attend all the most important meetings of his brethren. Advancing years, however, brought with them their attendant infirmities, and Mr. Mercer found at length his natural force sensibly abating. The annual session of the Georgia Association in the fall of 1839 was denied the presence of the venerable moderator; a violent attack, attended with some distressing and alarming symptoms, confining him at home. Never before were his brethren so deeply conscious of the strong hold which this good man had upon their respect, veneration and love. The absence of their long-tried and faithful friend, upon whose countenance they had often gazed with so much delight; and whose counsels and instructions they had learned so much to value, left in their midst a broad and mournful chasm. The countenances, the conversation, the prayers of the brethren clearly indicated the deep sense they had of their bereavement, and how tender and strong were their sympathies for the venerable sufferer.

To Mr. Mercer this affliction was rendered peculiarly trying by the consideration that this was the first time for a long series of years that he had been absent from a meeting of the Georgia Association. He bore it however with exemplary patience, and after a few weeks was so far improved in health as to be able to resume in a measure his accustomed labors.

The last of November he attended a ministers' meeting at Powelton; his patriarchal form was again seen in the prayer-meeting and in the pulpit, and occasionally he communed with his brethren through the pages of the Index. But his outward man was evidently yielding to decay, and it seemed mournfully obvious to his brethren, that a few more rude shocks of disease must necessarily close his earthly career. In May, 1840, he was able to attend the meeting of the Convention at Penfield; and though the labors of the occasion were too much for his enfeebled health, yet he gave strict attention to all the important business of the session, and aided as usual by his paternal counsels. Some of the brethren were particularly struck with the sweet and heavenly minded spirit which he exhibited, remarking that he seemed fast ripening for a better world.

The following communication appeared in a June number of the Index, and will probably be interesting to the reader of this volume. The writer refers in an affecting manner to his own personal afflictions, and also to the distressing complaints of his estimable wife. It is to be hoped that his exhortations to his brethren "*to hold fast to the Index,*" will not be forgotten now that he is no more; and that the paper, amply sustained by "*the right sort of zeal,*" will long continue to defend the cause of truth, and diffuse religious intelligence far and wide amongst the churches.

" *To the Patrons of the Christian Index.*"
"OF OURSELF."

" *Dear Brethren and Friends,*—In the providence of God, I was laid aside from business by a severe illness for several weeks, last October,; and when I had recovered so as to go out, I still found myself laboring under a pining intestine complaint, and which has continued *varyingly* till now. What this case is, I am hardly able to say. It may be, as a knowing physician said to me, *a kind of rheumatic, gouty* state of the bowels. This affliction, combined with the increasing infirmities of age, has rendered me altogether unfit for the discharge of the duties of the editorial department of the Index; and it has fallen for the most part on the junior editor. Finding I should of necessity be obliged to give it up, and being desirous that it might be continued *in the south*, I came to the conclusion last fall, to place it under the care of the Georgia Baptist Convention, as the most sure method to secure the continuance of its publication. I therefore made a proposition last winter to the Executive Committee to receive it for the Convention, and to proceed forthwith to provide for its publication under their superintendence; but the Committee thought it might be assuming too much responsibility, and resolved to lay the proposition before the Convention at its next meeting. This was accordingly done at the late meeting at Penfield, and was accepted; and an order passed that I should be entirely relieved as soon as practicable. And it was further resolved that the Committee should adopt measures to remove the Institution as soon as convenient for publication to Penfield. Thus the work will soon, *as to necessity belongs*, pass from my hands, I trust into better. But for the present I am not, nor do I see how I can be entirely released, if God shall continue my life and strength, until the close of the present year. Then it is pretty certain it will go into the hands of the Committee to be published at Penfield, under the supervision of some persons, who will doubtlessly be appointed as a publishing Committee, &c.

"And now, my dear friends and brethren, let me exhort and admonish, nay, let me beseech you *to hold fast to the Index.* That such a publication is needed in the south is acknowledged by many, but too few feel the right sort of zeal in the cause. I have made many personal sacrifices of convenience, ease and pleasure both to myself and family, and hundreds of dollars to sustain the paper amongst us; and now, will you not take a little extra pains to perpetuate its publication in the hands of the Convention? I do trust, that those who have been its warm supporters, will not only continue themselves, but make a strong effort to induce others to do so. Cannot every subscriber, who feels a wish for the prosperity of the paper, obtain each another subscriber for the paper next year? It will require a considerable increase of good paying subscribers, to sustain the paper as it should be sustained, and especially in view of the expenses which will, of necessity, be incurred in its removal, &c.

"FURTHER PERPLEXITIES.

"It is known to many that while I was absent last year, attending the Convention in Twiggs, my wife was stricken with palsy. On returning home I found her in bed, unable to walk. Her entire right side was paralyzed—but from this she slowly recovered, so as to walk about the house, and attend to her domestic concerns in some measure. But her other side became quite painful, and gradually the joints were so affected that she was less able to get about. This was her situation when I left home to attend the late Convention in Penfield. But on returning from that meeting, I had the distress to find her again in bed, by a recurrence of palsy in the left side, so as to be entirely unable to walk a step. But through the mercy of our Heavenly Father, she is again little amended—she can now begin to sit up, and with help walk across the room. Putting this increase of affliction in the scale with an increase of my own, since the meeting in Penfield, bars, not only my doing much in the editorial labors of the paper; but my further going abroad to attend the principal meetings of my brethren, or much more mingling with them in public service of the cause of our Lord and Saviour Jesus Christ; and indicates that I must soon bid them a *final farewell!* To them I now say, Be strong IN THE LORD, and in the power of his might—and be ye faithful until death, and ye shall receive a crown of life, which fadeth not away.

"JESSE MERCER, *the aged.*"

The continued afflictions of himself and wife prevented his attendance at the meeting of the Georgia Association in 1840. Anxious however to manifest his affection for his brethren, and to do all in his power to promote the cause of the Redeemer, he addressed a letter to the body, in which he urged upon their attention some matters of great interest to the churches. Most of that communication is here subjoined.

"*Washington, (Ga.) October* 6, 1840.

"TO THE GEORGIA ASSOCIATION, AT BETHESDA.

"DEAR BRETHREN,

"I have cherished with fond anticipation, the hope that I might be permitted to be with with you at this your annual meeting; but the Lord seems to have determined otherwise. If my own afflictions would permit, (which however can hardly admit it,) those of my palsied wife added, form a complete barrier. I think, under the prospect which lies before me, it is very problematical whether I shall ever meet with you again, in your present capacity on earth. I therefore, in this way, wish to press upon *your* attention, and *through you* upon the consideration of the *churches*, the importance of a few particulars. We have not yet, according to the Apostle's exhortation, gone on *to perfection* in those godly practices, which are by Jesus Christ, intended to glorify God, and fill the earth with his knowledge and glory. There are two things especially, which should be urged upon the consideration and practice of the churches, in order to their being prepared, fully, to even bear any competent part in the instrumentality of this great and glorious design of mercy. The one is, a more frequent and proper observance of 'the Lord's day.' The Apostle (Heb. 10 : 24, 25.) condemns the manner of some, *in forsaking to assemble themselves together.*— Now is it not the manner of the churches, who fail to meet together three Sundays out of four, to forsake the assembling of themselves together in the sense of the Apostle? The churches therefore ought to be urged, yea, *provoked* to this love and good work. I shall not attempt a labored argument to prove the change of the Sabbath to *the first day of the week.* Let it suffice, that it was changed and has been so observed, by the churches, from the Apostle's days till now. Our Lord left in charge with the Apostles, to teach their disciples ' all things whatsoever he had taught them.' And these Apostles have taught us that we have them for *our examples.* Now how is it, that the first churches came into the universal observance of the *first day of the week* as their day of public worship; and how is it that all christian nations have established it by law, if it was not at first established by the authority and example of the Apostles themselves? But there is another view of it. The Apostle (Rom. 14 : 6.) commends him that *esteemed one day above another*, in that he *regarded* it *unto the Lord*. Now then, as all the churches have professed to esteem '*the Lord's day*' above all others, the obligation is imperative *to regard it unto the Lord:* that is, to devote it entirely to his service. Such works of mercy, as are stated by Christ in Mat. 12 : 11. and of necessity, as in Luke 13 : 15. are lawful to be done on the Lord's day. But do not our churches suffer their members to start and drive their teams to market or other *particular* business; or set out on contemplated journeys and travel on the Lord's day, in which they employ themselves, their servants and beasts of labor as they would on any other day? This I take to be equal to harnessing up and going out to ploughing in the field; for he that offends in one point is guilty of all! These things must be remedied. —For if the day is not *regarded unto the Lord*, it must be a profanation. I fear this guilt lies upon all our churches.

"The other point to which I solicit the special notice of the Association, is, the assembling of the churches every Lord's day (familiarly called Sunday) for the purpose of religious worship and service. I suppose the practice of monthly, instead of weekly meetings, grew up out of sheer necessity; but has not this custom continued long since that necessity ceased? Whether the churches have settled Pastors or not, they should assemble at their own places of worship for the instruction of their families, the raising up of their children in the nurture and admonition of the

Lord, and the training their young men to religious habits and usefulness.

"There is one prominent feature and custom in our Lord's character, that has been totally overlooked by the churches. It is recorded Luke 4: 16. 'And he came to Nazareth, where he had been brought up: and, as *his custom was*, he went into the synagogue (or place of worship) on the Sabbath day, *and stood up for to read.*' From this it appears, that the child Jesus, from the time when he went down with his parents to Nazareth and was subject to them, was in the constant habit of going *every* Sabbath day to the synagogue *to read to the people*. Why should not our churches adopt the custom of going up to the house of the Lord every Sunday and employing their young men in reading to the people? This would tend, I apprehend, to another, and a very important result—the settling of regular Pastors in the churches. Why should not the churches now speedily return to the Apostolic plan, and the practice of the first ages? This consideration cannot be pressed upon the attention of the churches with too much earnestness.

* * * * *

"And now in conclusion, I hereby individually present my christian love and salutations to each member of your body, and request an earnest interest in the prayers of each and all to God for *us* in our low estate, that we may be able to submit ourselves under the mighty hand of God, with the Spirit of the suffering Jesus.

"Wishing you the presence of the Lord at your session and at all other times,

"I am, dear brethren,

"Yours in indissoluble bonds,

"JESSE MERCER."

TO MRS. R.

"*Washington*, Feb. 26, 1841.

"My dear Sister Dolly,

"I have received a friendly letter from you every now and then, but as I was burdened with my editorial labors, and you as it were, heard from me every week, through the Index, I did not answer; but now I am not connected at all with the Index, and have recovered a little from my decline, I have concluded to reply to yours of the 22d inst. I thank you for kind and christian remembrance and prayers; I hope these will ever continue while there may be any use for them. You say that you had heard *yesterday* I and wife had been sick. 'Tis to me strange that you did not know our afflictions before that. I have enjoyed no good health since October was a year, and Nancy has been palsied since May was a year. Until last May it was in the right side only, and she could hobble about a little in the house, and with help in the yard, and even in the garden; but in May last she was stricken in the other side, since which time she has not been able to walk at all. But this all is trifling compared with the state of her mind. It is palsied as much as her body, and gives us much more distress. Her health is, however, in some sense good: she eats with good appetite, &c. In her weakness of mind, she is often under the most deceptive perceptions, and is not convinceable. She becomes *mad*, and is the most distressed creature you can imagine to yourself.

"I have been in decline more rapidly since about November, and till two or three weeks past I have been laid aside from all active business, and confined for the most of the time to my room and bed. I have not written any letters that could be dispensed with, and some of these *I got written*. For two months I have not been to the meeting-house till last Sunday, and had thought it probable I should never go again on earth. But afflictions spring not from the earth. It is the Lord, let him do with *me* and *mine* as seemeth him good, and I *submit*. O pray I may be able by the help of God, to do it with a *good grace*. I want the Spirit of Christ in this case.

"Dear Sister D., I remember you with pleasure from your youth up. Scenes at Brown's meeting-house and thereabouts, have not been effaced from my endeared recollection, and ever since in all your changes of life, I have had a tender sisterly feeling towards you. And I hope the Lord of your youth will be the God of your riper age and last days on earth, and preserve us both unto his eternal kingdom.

"I am yours in Christ,
"JESSE MERCER."
" *Kindest love to brother R.*"

TO MR. HEMAN LINCOLN, OF BOSTON.

"*Washington, April* 11, 1841.
"MY VERY DEAR BROTHER LINCOLN,

"Your very acceptable letter of 27th ult. was read with much gratification. I was very glad to know that your visit and interview with the Executive Committee at Penfield, had resulted in a better state of feeling; and I do hope and trust by our heavenly Father's good pleasure, will ultimately produce a good effect. It was well that you 'escaped the flood' and made your way in safety. I trust the same good hand will be with you to your journey's end, which had preserved hitherto. But you said nothing of your meeting with dear Mrs. L., or how you found her. I suppose in good health, at least for her, or you would have said something about it.

"Your visit to me was the more appreciated, from the adverse weather through which you made it; though the little time which was left you to remain, was regretted much by me. I would be thankful that you suffered nothing from your exposure to the severe inclemency through which you came and went. I suppose, in all probability, we may never meet again on earth; but while on earth, I trust we shall be prompted to remember and pray for each other by this renewal of our intercourse, and that we may, through grace, be so happy as to meet in that world where no sorrow is, but joy and everlasting consolation.

"As to the *confidential* part of your letter, so far as it relates to myself, I accord entirely with you. I suppose you may remember that I wrote the Board at its last election, *not to continue* me their president any longer; I then thought it most probable that I should never be with them more on earth, and that any how, it would be better for some one who could attend at least oftener, to fill that place. I had come to the conclusion to decline a re-election *positively* should I be continued one of the Board at the next election, before you suggested it. And now *through you* I say to the brethren who may be elected to the Board, if my name should be found among them, not by any means appoint me again to that office. I am *too* old, and now *too* much afflicted to do any good in such a place. Indeed, I hope and request that you will ask the president of the Committee to let it be known that I wish not to be a trustee, or one of the

Board of Managers; as I am altogether unable to do any good for the cause abroad. At home, I shall, as I may have ability, do what I can in the good cause.

* * * * *

"The Lord grant to the Convention a good meeting at Baltimore, and give such a direction to all the business of that body, as may be for his glory.

"My most christian affection to Sister L., and to all the dear brethren connected with you in the arduous labors of spreading the gospel to the ends of the earth.

"I am, dear brother, yours in the kingdom and patience of Jesus Christ,

"JESSE MERCER."

"P. S. My health is, through mercy, still a little better. Wife is nothing better. *The Lord have mercy on us.*"

The afflictions of Mrs. Mercer, so frequently mentioned in the preceding letters, continued with only some occasional mitigations, bidding defiance to all the attempts of friendship and medical skill to relieve them. They were of such a nature as greatly to oppress the feelings of her most affectionate and sympathizing husband, at the same time that they deprived him in a great measure of the society of his brethren, even at his own house, and by keeping him in a constant state of confinement, greatly aggravated his own bodily complaints.

On Friday the 21st of May, it pleased the Lord to cut short her sufferings, by removing her, as is confidently believed, to a better world.* The following letter was written the day after her interment:

---

* For a Sketch of the Life and Character of Mrs. Mercer, see Appendix C.

"*Washington, May* 23, 1841.

"My Dear Brother M.

"It is now some time since any thing has passed between us. The occasions which you used to have to write every now and then have changed to Penfield with the Index, and I have been for the most part all winter unable to write except what was indispensable, and some of that I got written by others. Nevertheless, I do desire to have some direct intercourse between us kept up. I have rejoiced to find how amicably the *vexed question* went off at Baltimore, when once the brethren had an opportunity of *personal* conversation. I too am happy that our own Convention was ultimately so harmonious and pleased in the Report of our Delegates on the subject. I do hope *now* all will go on more peacefully and successfully in the great and best of causes,—in the promotion, so far as instrumentality goes, of the kingdom of our Lord Jesus Christ. We must make an effort to redeem the time and money lost last year by the agitation of the subject of slavery amongst us.

"My health has been so bad, and my confinement so great, that I could do but little except at home; and indeed I need not expect to do much at my time of life, and in affliction and increasing infirmities. A month ago I thought I was in a fair way to be restored, as far as my health was concerned, but I have rather declined again. Still I hope there is a radical change in the cause of my affliction, and I may yet be able to meet my brethren at their more important meeting, other things *being equal*.

* * * * * *

"My dear brother M., I am this day in quite a changed state from that which I have occupied for nearly two years. It has pleased the Lord to end the confinement under which I have been 'like a poor prisoner bound,' by taking to himself my dear wife. Yes, she is gone to her *long home.* We placed her remains in the house appointed for all living, yesterday afternoon, in our meeting-house yard, beside which it is designed I shall be laid, when it may be the will of God to call me away. You know somewhat how to sympathize with a poor widower. I find that

'One evil to another cries,
Billows on billows roll.'

"Now that the troubles of a poor distracted wife are removed, straightway the solitude, cares, and burdens of the future pour in upon me with an almost overwhelming power. Pray the Lord for me, my dear brother, that I may be sustained, and kept from the evil of my remaining days. My Christian love to your lady, and be assured I am as ever,

"Yours in a precious Redeemer,
"Jesse Mercer."

The following letter, addressed to Mr. Mercer by the Rev. Mr. Curtis, on hearing of the death of his wife, deserves a place in this volume, as well as Mr. Mercer's answer, which immediately follows.

"*Penfield,* 29*th May,* 1841.

"My Dear Brother,

"We have heard here from several quarters of the removal, and even of the funeral, of Mrs. Mercer; so that, without direct tidings, we conclude that this event has transpired.

"You have been mercifully *prepared* for it. Af-

flictions are workmen, as the blessed book tells us—
and they 'work *together*' or in an important, mysterious *union* of operations, or they would do us little
'good.' Your *past* trials in this case—all its peculiarities of *trial* were meant to prepare you for the present trial, and thus became *mercies* in relation *to it ;*
'working *together* with' it. You could not have borne
the *parting*, if the union had not become no longer
hopeful and help-full. You could not bear so well
your *solitude*, if the company of a late beloved object
had not become the source of much pain. Afflictions
are both *light* and *heavy*, according to the skill or
ignorance, that we may regard as directing them.
Heavy afflictions do little or light good to the careless
and the unbeliever. '*Light afflictions which are but
for a moment*' work out for us, in the skilful hands
and management of the divine mechanist, '*a far
more exceeding and eternal weight of glory.*' For he
can apply that power of a lever by which a feather
will lift a ton. And afflictions are light and heavy according to the scale on which we regard them. What
so heavy as death, even a believer's death, when we
consider it on an earthly scale, or *what* is removed.
What so light when we consider it in the scale of
God's divine plans for his people. It is but an inconceivable transition-point—a moment! I cannot
doubt that the believer often first *wakes* in glory, with
entire surprise at the gentleness of his passage, the
kind *manner* in which the change has been effected,
the little *friction*, so to speak, of the momentous movement.

"All these reflections, however, will be familiar to
you, I only pen them to assure you of a comparative
stranger's sympathy. 'Jesus wept,' I suppose, by a
contagion of friendly tenderness. *He* knew what he

would do for his friends, but *they* did not. Therefore *they* wept, and *therefore* he. So he sweetly *partook* all the infirmity belonging to the case. You will find him, I doubt not, the same compassionate Redeemer in yours. To his almighty—ever well *timed* grace, I would commend you.

"The brethren here talk of urging you to come over, if possible. It will give no one more satisfaction to see you than the unworthy pastor of the church. See whether the scene of many of your hopes, prayers and liberal efforts, may not be providentially within your *reach* to re-invigorate your powers. For we must go on trading, *spending* and receiving some little *more of returns* for the Master, until he calls for the account you know.

"Your condoling, affectionate brother in the Lord,
"THOS. CURTIS."

"*Washington, June 8, 1841.*
"MY DEAR BROTHER CURTIS,

"Yours of the 29th ult. was duly handed me, by brother S. I thank you for it. Though 'a *comparative* stranger,' you have hit on a right expedient. Your sympathy and consolation came in the proper time, and gave me help in need. I had not thought *so well*, what God was doing with me, and for me. I had reflected on the cause of my afflictions, and asked the Lord, I hope *in humility*, the reason why? but it had not occurred to me that God was by *previous lighter* trials, preparing me for the last and greater 'trial.' Indeed, I do not know how I could have borne the parting with the dear departed object of my affections and solace in life, had it not been for those distressing causes which rendered the 'union no longer *hopeful and helpful.*' In this light affliction, are '*mercies*' in disguise. Of our heavenly Father it may be truly said

> 'Behind a *frowning* providence
> He hides a smiling face.'

"'Afflictions are workmen.' Truly they work, and always under the skilful direction of infinite wisdom and goodness, yield to the poor sufferers who are exercised thereby *the peaceable fruits of righteousness*. All we have to do is to

> 'Judge not the Lord by feeble sense,
> But trust him for his grace.'

"'Afflictions are workmen,' working together, one with another, and with the ultimate design, or end in view, or they surely would do us little good: but as they are ordered by the Lord, they work out for us *an eternal weight of glory*. What a wondrous product, from such unpromising seed! But this is God's way with his children: he puts on them light afflictions, *only for a moment*, and then gives them an eternal weight of glory—everlasting consolation and unmixed, unalloyed pleasures at his own right hand.

"O, how light and short are all our afflictions here, when weighed in this scale! But these 'workmen' are working for us a *present* and valuable result.—They always, however severe, are kind, they come in love, and design to make us partakers of the divine holiness—to bring us nearer to our *Just God and Saviour*, and conform us more and more to the heavenly standard.

"Truly afflictions are *heavy*, if they come alone, and work singly in their own simple character, and thus they must come to all the unbelieving, who know not God, and love not our Lord Jesus Christ. And afflictions are *heavy* even to a believer, so long as he contemplates them on an earthly scale, or views them in their own nature and tendencies. The *alleviation* lies beyond the veil of flesh and sense, in the gracious and eternal results which they are 'working together' by 'a mysterious union' to produce; and is realized in considering them as parts of God's plan of *merciful* economy with his children. When God's exceeding great and precious promises are viewed with believing eyes, the suffering child of grace may glory in tribulations; rejoice in this dark vale of sorrows and triumph even in death! Afflictions, though roughly clad in vestments of camel's hair, must be viewed as the harbingers of everlasting peace and rest; and contemplated on this scale, the man of God is not only able to endure them *patiently*, but in the *meekness* of his suffering Forerunner, he welcomes them, as indispensable to the fulfilment of God's plan of mercy towards him, and necessary to the perfecting of his eternal inheritance in heaven.

"The sympathy of Christ our Saviour is also a rich source of *peculiar* comfort to an afflicted saint. 'Jesus wept.' How consoling the reflection that in all our afflictions he is afflicted; that in his love and pity he bears us up; and strengthens us on the bed of languishing. Our High Priest and Mediator is touched with a feeling of our infirmities; yea, what is wonderful! he was made perfect through sufferings, being tempted in all points, that he might know how to succor them that are tempted, in all their afflictions.

* * * * *

"Your brother in Christ,
"JESSE MERCER."

TO MR. HEMAN LINCOLN.

"*Washington, June* 23, 1841.

* * * * *

"I suppose you have seen, or heard of the death of my *dear wife*. When you were at our house she was in one of her best times, calm and somewhat reasonable and capable of taking a degree of pleasure in the rehearsal of former things which in their enjoyment had interested her; but she soon became disordered and distressed and distressing; and so continued with short intervals to be more palsied in her limbs, and more lost to herself. No mortal can conceive what she suffered in her mental feelings. She was perpetually in a labyrinth of imaginations the most inconsistent in themselves, and the most harassing to herself. This continued to increase till the 16th May, when she had a slight turn of apoplexy, from which she mainly lost her power of action : was mostly disposed to sleep. On Tuesday she at times seemed to know those about her; and expressed herself as quite to herself. The friends present thought she was *so*, and if she could have talked, she could have satisfied us she was. Indeed she did say so much, late that evening, as gave me to believe she was *dying in hope in the love of Jesus*. She never spake after Wednesday morning, nor opened her eyes, no not in death! which occurred Friday night about forty-five minutes after ten o'clock. I am in desolate widowhood; in this you and dear sister L. can sympathize with me. My health, which had somewhat improved when you were with me, soon began to degenerate, and I am not much amended yet. I have it in view to go up to Penfield and spend a little while with friends there ; and after the commencement, go up the country higher; and see if change of place and company will not have some good effect on my health: but the will of the Lord be done. I wish above all things I could know the *will* of God concerning me, and do it, or suffer it in a Christ-like manner, to his honor while I live. O pray, my dear brother, that the spirit of the Lord may still be my guide and comforter till death; that my little remaining time may not be spent in uselessness and pinings.

"Tell brother Bolles that I received his letter in reply to mine on the subject of 'the vexed question.' But as all things in reference to the Board's actings on that question were going on, as I thought, well, I did not think it necessary to write any thing further on it. Besides, I was at that time under circumstances which rendered it very inconvenient to write any thing. I trust and hope the Board will be able now to carry forward all their present operations if they cannot enlarge them. Though the times are very trying in pecuniary matters, the crops are rather promising, and if they should turn out good, I think we shall be able to make up our loss.

"I see brother Davis has been with you. Brother Peck says *he* added considerable interest to your anniversaries. I hope he may be useful wherever he goes by the good Spirit of our God upon him.

"You will make my best christian regards to sister L. and all the dear brethren of the Board.

"I am, dear brother, yours in much affection and in the kingdom and patience of Christ our Lord,

"JESSE MERCER."

It must be evident that Mr. Mercer's protracted afflictions rendered it impossible for him at this time to give much attention to his ministerial labors. His lack of service in this respect was very usefully supplied by brother C. F. Sturgis, a highly esteemed brother in the ministry, who had been chosen early in the year as co-pastor of the church at Washington.

Occasionally however, as his circumstances would allow, he mingled with his beloved flock in the sanctuary, to encourage them by his prayers, exhortations and instructions in the ways of righteousness and peace. He had a place in their tenderest affections; his presence always afforded them delight; yet a delight now blended with the mournful reflection, that their beloved and venerated pastor, fast sinking under the weight of years and disease, must soon bid them farewell. It was but a few times that he was able to ascend the pulpit, during the last ten or twelve months of his life; his occasional addresses to his people were below, and when speaking, such was the feeble state of his body, that he frequently found it necessary to remain in a sitting posture.

Mr. Mercer manifested a commendable solicitude for the spiritual welfare of the colored portion of his flock. Though during his last days he was not able to give much personal attention to them, yet he encouraged his co-laborer Mr. Sturgis, and the most active members of his church, to hold religious meetings on all suitable occasions for their benefit. These efforts were not in vain. In May a work of grace commenced amongst the blacks, which seemed to advance with happy consequences for one or two successive years. As has been previously stated, the number of members reported in 1840, was 87; in 1843 it was 181. This increase was principally from amongst the blacks, and furnishes a pleasing view of the results of the work of grace, to which reference is now made.

It was the ardent desire of Mr. Mercer, to be useful as long as he lived. In a letter to an esteemed brother he says, "I have deprecated before God, a *worn out, useless and sinful old age.*"

Though cut short by the hand of God in his ministerial labors, he roused himself up from time to time to such efforts with his pen as he thought might be acceptable and useful to his brethren. His Essay on the Forgiveness of Sins, already noticed, was written in the midst of his great domestic afflictions. At a subsequent period he prepared three numbers for the Index, which were published under the caption, "*Hear what the Spirit saith to the churches.*" They were his last efforts with his pen intended for the public eye; and as they may be regarded as the valedictory, the dying counsel of this Father in Israel, they properly claim a place in these pages dedicated to his memory.

"*Bro. Stokes,*—I have concluded to send your readers a few more Nos. on a subject which I deem of vital importance to the churches. I fear many of them are *settled on their lees;* or are living in great remissness, and neglect of duty; that they do not consider well the obligations they are under to preserve their own purity, or fitness for the acceptable discharge of the duties required of them. I write to stir them up to a more lively sense of what *they ought to do*, if possible to provoke them, by plain scriptural representations, *to love and good works.* I do this, the rather, because, though I wish I could do better, I am obliged to say, with Newton's kite,

'But ah! like a poor prisoner bound,
My *string* confines me to the ground.'

"It seems to be the good pleasure of God still to confine me, by continued affliction. I cannot *indulge* in the hope of getting out and doing any thing of greater utility, and therefore, give vent to my desires *in this way.* I hope and pray my effort may be acceptable to the churches, and for the use of their edification. I am both theirs and yours in Christ.

"JESSE MERCER."

"*Washington, March,* 1841."

"*Hear what the Spirit saith unto the Churches.*"

No. 1.

THE INTRODUCTION.

" The sacred injunction is placed in the close of each epistle, sent from Jesus Christ, the great Head of the Church, by his servant John, to the seven churches which were in Asia. The reiteration was doubtless designed to give weight and importance to the divine mandate, and to engage the particular attention of *each* and *all* the churches to the momentous things spoken. The command to hear, or attend to the things which the Spirit spake, must not be limited to the seven churches in Asia, but considered as equally binding on the observance of all the churches of Christ in any part, or age of the world. This will not be controverted. Then let it be also carefully noticed, that the requirement is made, not only of the churches collectively, but of every member particularly; '*he*, that hath an ear to hear,' is called on to hear what the Spirit saith unto the churches. And this strikingly proves, that *what is the duty of all, is the duty of each ;* or in other words, that each member has a special obligation resting on him, as well as an inviting interest, in the things taught; nor are we to understand the things commanded to be heard, as referring to what is contained in these epistles merely, but in the whole book, (see chap. 1 : 11.) and not the things written in this book only, but to all the holy scriptures; for they were all given by inspiration of the Spirit, and are required to be read, searched, preached and heard by all, that the man of God may be thoroughly furnished unto all good works.

"The Spirit teaches the churches, as well by the figures and characteristics used, as in the declarations made, and the exhortations and commands addressed. By the epithets of character assumed for our Lord Jesus Christ, they are shown how glorious is *He*, who is exalted to be their supreme Head and sovereign lawgiver. They exhibit him to be, what he affirms of himself, *One with his Father*—equal in majesty, power and glory. Thus he appeared, and announced himself to the exiled John, in the isle of Patmos, saying, 'I am Alpha and Omega, the beginning and the ending, saith the Lord, which is, and which was, and which is to come, the Almighty.' This description of character belongs to God alone, and is unlawful to be assumed by any creature. Therefore, this declaration, together with the characters given him in the beginning of each of these epistles, fully proves him to possess all authority and dominion, and worthy to be worshipped by angels and men, as *God over all, blessed for ever*.

"This appearance was most heavenly and divine. Christ here manifests himself in his mysterious union of natures, in his mediatorial and God-like characters. His dress indicates his kingly and priestly offices. His robe and girdle are rather vestments of the priesthood. His head and hair, white as snow, show him to be 'the ancient of days.' His eyes being like a flame of fire, denotes the terribleness with which he flashes vengeance on his foes, and beams his love on his friends, and proves to all the churches, that it is *He, that searches the reins and hearts.* His feet, like burnished brass, may signify the firmness of his going forth, and the brightness of those dispensations, in which he treads down his enemies, as mire in the street; or comforts his people with salvation. His voice, as a trumpet—as the sound of many waters, indicates the exceeding greatness of his power, the dreadful majesty of his speech. Let Sinai tell the awful tale—let the red sea and Jordan repeat the story—let Moses and Habakkuk bear their witness—let John testify this solemn truth. His countenance, like the sun shining in his strength, may show the infinite blessedness of his favor, which is life, and his loving kindness, which is better than life.

" How terrible must this sight have been to John; yet how delightful! how dreadful, yet how joyful! So dreadful was Christ Jesus to look upon in his heavenly habiliments, that John fell at his feet *as dead;* but his Lord and beloved Master, who had lost nothing of his tenderness, drew near and laid his right hand softly on him, and said, as it were, It is *I.* Be not afraid. I am Jesus, who *was dead !* but *I live !* and behold *I am alive* for evermore. Amen.

" How comfortable must this visit of Jesus Christ have been to his servant John, in his desolate and dreary solitude. He was then indeed, in pressing need of comfort; and Jesus did not prove unmindful of his promise to his disciples, (John 14 : 18.) but came to his beloved disciple in distress, and comforted and blessed him greatly. And are not the churches, (and all believers individually,) taught and encouraged by this wonderful display of glory and grace to trust in the Lord in all their deepest afflictions and severest trials; and confidently to believe that it shall be well with them, and that they shall not be forsaken in six troubles, and in seven no ultimate, or final evil shall be suffered to come nigh them? For thus saith the Lord, 'when thou passest through the waters, I will be with thee; and through the rivers, they shall not overflow thee; when thou walkest through the fire thou shalt not be burned; neither shall the flame kindle upon thee.' Again, 'as thy days, *so* shall thy strength be—The eternal God is thy refuge; and underneath are the everlasting arms.' Again; 'The Lord is thy keeper; The Lord is thy shade upon thy right hand. The sun shall not smite thee by day, nor the moon by night. The Lord shall preserve thee from all evil; he shall preserve thy soul. The Lord shall preserve thy going out, and thy coming in, from this time forth, and for evermore.' Truly, the Lord has given his people exceeding great and precious promises for their consolation in trouble.

"The characters in which our Lord Jesus is manifested in scripture, as having all power in heaven and earth, and head over all things to the church, inspire hope, without doubt, and confidence without fear, that all these promises will be faithfully fulfilled. His means are ample. Among these he has given his ministers to strengthen and encourage them; saying, 'comfort ye, comfort ye my people, saith your God.' And (speaking of things that are not, as though they were already done) he saith, 'Cry unto them, that their warfare is accomplished, that their iniquity is pardoned;' for they have received of the Lord's hand, instead of punishments for their sins, double the amount in blessings. What wondrous goodness and mercy!

But let none judge of the Lord's ways by feeble sense. The method of fulfilling his promises, God has reserved, with the times and the seasons, under his own power. God will be trusted, *as faithful*, and waited on *as sovereign*, by his people. He often bears long with them, to try their faith and integrity, and to draw out their prayer and importunity at his throne of grace. But I must close these prefatory remarks, and ask your readers to wait till next week for my next No."

"*Hear what the Spirit saith unto the Churches.*"

No. 2.

THE CANDLESTICKS.

"The considerations which have been suggested in the introduction, plainly show the weighty obligations under which the churches lie, to obey the voice of Him who spake from heaven, and the dire consequences of disobedience. I therefore most earnestly solicit them to attend carefully to what may be said in the following essay.

"The Spirit teaches the churches some useful lessons by the use of the candlestick as a figure, to represent the churches. It seems that this is the appropriate figure which God has chosen to represent his church on earth; to show its nature, consistency and design. It was a part of the furniture of the Tabernacle, and shown to Zechariah in vision. And Christ in his sermon, brings it into view in its proper use, to hold up the candle of the ministry he was about to light up, to illuminate this dark world. And here the seven candlesticks represent the churches which were in Asia.

"The precious material of which the candlestick

used in sacred figure was composed, shows the preciousness, nature and consistency of the church of Christ, as *it is in the divine estimate,* and what all churches ought to be *in practice,* as near as the frailty of human wisdom, and careful endeavor will admit. Moses was commanded to make the candlestick of *pure gold.* That shown to Zechariah was *all of gold.* And here the seven were *golden* candlesticks. This quality in the candlesticks must have been designed to represent some special trait of character in the churches of Christ, and it is easiest to conceive that which it is most appropriate to show, that is, of what the churches are composed, their preciousness and durability. And,

"First; *of what the churches, according to the divine purpose, are composed.*

"It is altogether reasonable to conclude that God, on determining to make himself a residence on earth, would choose out and build it of such materials as would do him honor. Accordingly, we find all the figures and prophecies of the Old Testament, relating to this subject, show that the house whose foundation and builder is God, is framed of such materials as constitute it '*the perfection of beauty.*' This view, the choice materials and exquisite workmanship of the tabernacle, and afterwards, the still more excellent materials and the acuter workmanship of the temple, illustrate and confirm.—The Zion of God, *which he loved,* was accordingly composed only of the sons of God, who were comparable to *fine gold,* yea, to *most fine gold.* They were his *sanctified* ones— his jewels, whom he had reserved to himself to show forth his praise. Of this ecclesiastical characteristic, the first church constituted by the apostles, was a fair exemplar. It was built up in '*the apostles' doctrine and fellowship,*' that is, they were constituted in *the belief of the truth, taught* by the apostles, having gained fellowship with them, by the profession of it. And it is also evident that they had gained fellowship *one* with another, for *they were of one accord, of one heart and one soul.* This apostolic example forms the true pattern for the constitution of all after churches. We are not informed of the particular ceremony used by the apostles in the constitution of this church; nor indeed are we of the form used in the constitution of any of the New Testament churches; but the account given of those churches, leaves no doubt but that they were regularly constituted, as was the first church, in '*the apostles' doctrine and fellowship.*' It cannot be questioned for a moment but that *they* who believed, repented and were baptized, on the day of pentecost, were imbodied as a church of Jesus Christ, else how could others have been daily added to them as such? And that none but true converts were joined to them, is evident from the fact, that the Lord added to them, and only such as should be saved. And such were the solemnities thrown around those who were invited in fellowship, that it is said, ' of the rest durst no man join himself to them; but believers were the more added to the Lord.' Paul speaks of those who should be built up in church union, as gold, silver, and precious stones; and Peter as *lively stones*, built up a *spiritual* house. It is plain the scriptures nowhere admit of a mixture of membership in the churches of Christ. It follows, therefore, that all churches (so called) built upon any other principle, or formed together on any other model, or consolidated on any national foundation, are only human establishments, and fail of the true consistency of the churches of Jesus Christ.

"Secondly. *The preciousness of Christ's church.*

"To show how precious the church is to Christ, I need to say nothing more than that he *gave himself* for her. The worth of any thing is to be estimated by the value of the price it costs. Then in this case, the value to be set upon the church must be infinite; for he did not redeem her with silver and gold, but with his own precious blood—and who can calculate the worth of Christ's blood? O how precious must the church have been to Christ! The interest which he takes in his people *passeth knowledge.* Paul represents it as '*the riches of the glory* of his (Christ's) inheritance in the saints.'—But who can estimate *the riches of his glory?* Who can put a value upon unsearchable riches?

"There is another view in which Christ's people are precious. That is complacently. This is in regard to what they are by his grace bestowed upon them, and the purposes of mercy designed to be accomplished by their instrumentality. By his grace he forms them for himself. The design which Christ had in view when he *gave himself* for his people, was that he might present them to himself *a glorious church.* And for this purpose they were chosen in him; and he is made of God unto them *wisdom, and righteousness, and sanctification, and redemption.* And in accordance the church sings, 'I will greatly rejoice in the Lord, my soul shall be joyful in my God, for he hath clothed me with the garments of salvation, he hath covered me with the robe of righteousness, as a bridegroom decketh himself with ornaments, and as a bride adorneth herself with her jewels.' To the same end it is said, ' the king's daughter is all glorious within; her clothing is of wrought gold.'

"And again. 'This people,' saith the Lord, 'have

I formed for myself; they shall show forth my praise.' And of every one of his people, he saith, 'I have created him for my glory.' And hence the command,—'Declare his glory among the heathen; his marvellous works among all nations.' It is clearly the purpose of God, through the instrumentality of his sanctified ones, to fill the world with his knowledge and praise. And hence David prays, and every pious Christian prays,—' Let the people praise thee, O God; let all the people praise thee. O let the nations be glad, and sing for joy: and let the whole earth be filled with his glory.—Amen, and Amen.'

" Thirdly. *The durability of the church of Christ.*

" The indestructible character of the church of Christ is not only indicated by the *golden* quality of the candlesticks, but by Paul's gold, silver, and precious stones, and Peter's lively stones, showing clearly the imperishable nature of those of whom God has instituted his churches should be built. God saith, I lay in Zion for a foundation a precious stone ; and the gospel order is, that precious stones be built upon it. In perfect accordance Christ says, upon this rock, (this precious corner stone,) I build my church, and the gates of hell shall never prevail against it. The Zion which the Lord loves, he founded for himself, and therefore declares she shall never be moved. Paul in unison says, we have received a kingdom which cannot be moved; or as is said of the kingdom signified by the stone cut out of the mountain, *it shall stand for ever*. This enduring character of the church is derived from her union with Christ. From him, as her head and source of all spiritual and divine influence, she derives her life—and that is eternal life—she is made partaker of the divine nature ; and from him, as her formation, being formed in him, and fitly framed into him, she receives her strength and salvation—she is builded up a glorious church— a spiritual house, which shall never be confounded, world without end.

"But it has been said, that though the church, *as such*, cannot be destroyed, yet the individual members may. Their safety being conditioned on their faith and obedience, which may fail. They may perish. To this I allege; that, as the body is composed of its members, if they can perish, it follows as a matter of course that the body may also. The parts of any whole being destroyed, the whole must be lost also. So then the only way in which the church, *as a body*, can be secure, is in the security of each member; for if *one* member may fall, it follows so may all. But the scriptures have provided amply against this suggestion. I shall only refer to a few passages. Isaiah admits that the Zion of God may become, by various and severe afflictions, distressing and even overwhelming calamities, *a city of solemnities;* yet announces her to be a tabernacle that shall not be taken down. And then, as if to prevent the doubt that some of the parts might be injured or lost, he adds, *not one of the stakes thereof shall ever be removed, neither shall any of the cords thereof be broken.* Our Lord says *it is not the will of his Father that one* of the little ones who believe in him should perish. And again : that he came into the world, that whosoever should believe in him, *should not perish, but have eternal life.* God having promised his Son a numerous seed that should serve him and *endure* for ever, it was provided in the stipulations of the everlasting covenant, that should any of them fall away into negligence and crime, their transgression and iniquity should be visited with the stripes of the Father's chastising rod, which is always done in love, and for their profit, and in faithfulness to him, of whose travail of soul, they were to be both the fruit and reward. Now then, if the wandering will be restored, (and that they will, see the parable of the hundred sheep, and mark its bearing on this case,) the good and obedient children will doubtless be saved; and then as a matter of course, all will be saved; and our Lord will be able, with joyful acclamation, to say to his Father, 'behold I and the children which God hath given me.'

"A few reflections will close this number. How wonderful is the kingdom of God—the church of Christ on earth! glorious things are spoken of Zion, the city of God. For her defence, salvation has God appointed for walls and bulwarks. Her safety, therefore, is in the munition of rocks. Though hosts of men and devils may encamp against her, yet the inhabitants may be undismayed, rejoice and be strong and confident in this, that with their besiegers, in all the mighty multitude of them, there is but an arm of flesh, but with them is the Lord their God to help them, and to fight their battles. Their bread shall be given them, and their waters shall be sure. We may safely exclaim, happy art thou O Israel, who is like unto thee, O people saved by the Lord, who is the shield of thy help, and the sword of thy excellency. But let no man deceive himself, and conclude from hence, that he may indulge in the gratification of his lusts, and live according to the pleasures of the flesh, *and be safe:* For if ye live after the flesh, ye shall die. 'There is in the doctrine of believers' perseverance in grace, no tendency to licentiousness. 'Tis only as the fruits of faith and love abound in them, showing them to be the children of God, that they have any right to claim the joys of this salvation. Let all, therefore, who name the name of the Lord, in profession, denying all ungodliness and worldly lusts, strive to live soberly, righteously and godly in the present world, while they are looking for that blessed hope and glorious appearing of the great God, even our Lord Jesus Christ, into eternal life, which he has promised to all them that love him."

"*Hear what the Spirit saith unto the Churches.*"
No. 3.

"By the appropriate use of the candlestick, the Spirit teaches the churches their proper and imperative duty. As the candlestick holds up a lighted candle, that it may give light to all in the room, so the churches are to hold up the light of divine truth to the nations of the earth, enveloped in gross darkness. The light by which the churches are to shine, is two-fold: First—*The light of* grace which they received in regeneration, and which is supported and increased by the indwelling of the Spirit of Christ. Every believer is a lighted lamp, a number of whom being gathered into church union, makes the church a luminous body. Thus Paul says to the saints at Ephesus, 'ye were sometimes darkness, but now are ye light in the Lord.' The duty of church members, in this regard is also two-fold: First—In using their gifts, and manifesting their graces in the most impressive manner, one to another, and to those with whom they are conversant, *individually*. And secondly; in their united church state, to act in unison with the body, in making known the knowledge of Christ to the world, among whom they shine as lights. This position will commend itself to every man's conscience *at once*, that the performance of those great ecclesiastical duties, which are essential to the fulfilment of the important purposes for which they were raised up together, and made to sit together in heavenly places in Christ—even in a gospel church state, depends on a proper and faithful discharge of the sacred obligations which rest on the members as individuals. For in proportion as the members are fervent in love, holy in devotion, and godly in practice, the church will be active in every good work, abounding in all the fruits of righteousness, which are by Jesus Christ to the glory of God. But as the members are carnally minded, conformed to the world, and negligent in religious duties, or only perform them in a formal manner, as a matter of course, so will the church dwindle into insignificance, and become to the community *a curse* rather than a blessing. How important then is it, that each member should have his lamp trimmed and his light burning, that in himself, and one with the church, he may, as not being his own, but bought with a price, even the precious blood of Jesus Christ, glorify God in his body, and in his spirit which are God's! Secondly. *The light of the gospel ministry.* This ministry is Christ's *lighted candle* to illume the world with the light of the knowledge of the glory of God in the face of Jesus Christ. This, the churches are raised up to support and strengthen in the propagation of the word of life, which can be done only by sustaining the ministers thereof, as the gifts of Christ to them; for the work of the ministry, and the edifying of the body of Christ, (or the whole church of God,) till the gracious design be brought to a happy and glorious perfection. This indispensable duty requires to be discharged in two ways. First, *by a due regard to their character and standing before the public.* Ministers must have a good report from those *who are without.*—For which purpose, all who approve themselves as the ministers of Christ should be *received with all gladness* and *held in reputation;* for how can they have a good estimation among the people, unless their brethren are careful to commend them to their respectful attention!—In this most needful particular, I think many churches are very defective. They, (at least many among them, who would be thought knowing ones,) have, instead of commending in the best manner they could, rather held an evil, critical eye on their preachers, especially on those who are coming forward as candidates for the ministry. And their mistakes and slips have been waxed and magnified into faults, and these *very imprudently* have been made the topics of free remark before the multitude, no little to the detriment of the incumbents. The light estimation in which many ministers have been held may be owing, in a great degree, to the cheap rate at which ordinations have been had in many of our churches. From a pretty extensive observation, I am of opinion, that in many instances, a recklessness has been indulged in regard to scripture requirements. In examinations for ordination, the object has not been *so much* to ascertain whether the brother about to be set apart to the gospel ministry, was *able* and *apt* to teach its great fundamental and mysterious truths, and by his experimental feelings and religious views, to gain a reasonable and satisfactory evidence that God had made him by his Spirit and grace, *an able* minister of the New Testament, as to know his views on a few systematical points of doctrine, and his popular standing as a preacher, which has been taken as good evidence of usefulness.—Thus a *good slight* at declamation and exhortation has been received *as ability* sufficient to preach and defend the deep things of God, and to explain and enforce the ordinances of Christ. But where little has been required, little has been sought for or attained. And so it has turned out, that many a man, ordained of men to preach, has had neither talent nor ministerial reputation sufficient to sustain a commendation. Nevertheless, it behooves the churches, in my judgment, to see to it that their ministers always bear proper credentials and letters of commendation, at all times and in all places, where they may, in the providence of God, be placed.

"But secondly; *by affording them of the good things of this life, a competent support.* If any one will look soberly at the work of the ministry, he will see at once that the ministers of the gospel have no time to spare to labor for their own support. This the scripture has foreseen and provided for, by making it the duty of the churches to support the ministry. This has always been God's plan; and wherever an attempt has been made to change it, it has been attended with a curse.—Look at Israel after the flesh. The tribe of Levi, who were appointed to the service of the sanctuary, had no landed inheritance among their brethren, but were provided for by the tithes which the other tribes were to pay according to the statutes of the Lord; plainly indicating that the ministers of the spiritual Israel should be supported by the churches, independent of their own labors. . Let it suffice to say again, this is God's plan, and should be punctually and faithfully executed. Let us examine into *the work* of the ministry, and see what ministers have to perform, and it will readily appear that they must be supported by the churches, or the work will go undone. This will be clearly seen by a critical notice of Christ's illustration of his design, when he said to his disciples, '*ye are the light of the world.*' To give his meaning an impressive bearing on their minds, (and on ours too,) he laid down two propositions of universal admission. The first is, ' A city that is set on a hill, cannot be hid.' He alludes, doubtless, to a city with lamps burning, else the darkness of the night would hide it. But a city set on a hill, and well lighted, is not only inconcealable, but throws its light out in every direction, so that the lost and benighted traveller may find the highway which leads to safety and rest: or as a light-house, built on some projecting promontory, directs the storm-beaten and distressed mariner safely into port. This most plainly shows that Christ intended his churches, built on '*the high hill of God*,' and lighted by the glorious gospel, should throw their light on all parts of the surrounding country: so that the lost sinner, involved in worse than Egyptian darkness, may be enlightened and guided into the way to peace and salvation. But our Lord does not stop here—He adds still more impressively, 'Men do not light a candle and put it under a bushel, but on a candlestick, and it giveth light unto all that are in the house.' The house here answers to the *world* used in the statute—'*ye are the light of the world.*' And if any should inquire what is meant by the 'world,' the commission must explain it. Go ye, teach *all nations*—go ye into *all the world*, and preach the gospel to *every creature*. Repentance and remission of sins should, in the name of Christ, be preached *among all nations*. This is all plain. Our Lord in this position says to his disciples, (and to all churches and ministers,) I have lighted you as a candle, which is not to be obscured, but to be put on my candlestick —the church, that it may give light to all the ends of the earth. The duty here inculcated cannot be mistaken, neither by ministers nor churches; and they ought to consider themselves systematically united in this great work, and bound to co-operate in it.

"*Bro. Stokes*,—Just here I was arrested by increased personal and domestic afflictions, and forced to stop. I hoped I should be able to resume the work in some short time, but circumstances which have transpired since, have precluded it. I cherished the hope I should be able to do something at it at this place, but still, imbecility, both of body and mind, forbids it. I have come to the conclusion to send you the foregoing now, and promise, if God will permit, to send you at least two others. One on the independence and accountability of the churches, and the relative position of the ministry to them, and the other on their government, its extent and final jurisdiction.

"JESSE MERCER."

"*Penfield, July* 20*th*, 1841."

It has ever been a matter of deep interest (and most naturally so;) with the people of God, to know with what kind of emotions a long-tried, and eminent servant of Christ looks forward into eternity as he is going rapidly down the declivity of life. Mr. Mercer was sometimes approached by intimate and confidential brethren on this subject. His remarks in substance were; "I have no ecstatic joys; not so much of that triumphant assurance which some speak of; but an humble hope of heaven, an habitual, calm reliance on my blessed Redeemer, which enables me to contemplate my approaching end with composure, undisturbed by any very distressing apprehensions." In the following extract from a letter to a beloved ministering brother, written in January, 1841, there is an

Please bury since given my Israel as being up into the hands of God and am satisfied with disposal of me in sickness and in death, and for c- rity — My love to all the dear brethren in your hart — The Lord be graciously with thee. Farewell!

Jope Mercer

allusion to his state of mind, in view of his final change. After referring to a little matter of a somewhat unpleasant nature, and which had occasioned him some mortification, he adds, "I hope you will feel no displeasure against your humble servant—he really accounts you a good minister of Jesus Christ, and is always pleased to hear you; and I hope and pray the Lord may abundantly crown your labors in the Lord with success.

"And now what shall I say to my brother? I may never write to him, or see him more in life. Why, my brother, be strong in the Lord and in the power of his grace, and *be thou faithful unto death.*

"You may wish to know how I feel in the prospect of my departure being at hand. I can say little more than that I have no fears thus far on the path of the dark valley. I have long since given my *eternal destiny* up into the hands of God, and am satisfied with his disposal of me in sickness and in death, and for eternity. My love to all the dear brethren in your parts. The Lord be specially with thee. Farewell!"

CHAPTER XV.

Mr. Mercer's decline regarded with sorrow.—His last Sermon.—Sketch of the Sermon.—Visits Penfield.—Letter to Mr. Sturgis.—Visits Indian Springs.—Letter to Mr. Sturgis.—His Death.—Mr. Carter's Letter in relation to his death.—Resolutions of the Washington Baptist Church.—Of the Presbyterian Church.—Notice of Mr. Sturgis' Funeral Sermon.

We look with painful interest upon decaying objects which we revere and love. We even sympathize with the objects of nature around us, and often gaze upon their decline with melancholy emotions. The aged tree which stood so long by our paternal residence, which cast its grateful shadow over our childish sports, and often perhaps refreshed us in manhood's years, as it exhibited symptoms of decay, was gazed upon with a kind of filial sorrow;

> 'And when a hapless branch, torn by the blast,
> Fell down, we mourned as if a friend had fallen.'

With how much deeper emotion do we look upon the waning life of the aged man of God, who for half a century has stood before the people on a bright and commanding elevation, pre-eminent in piety, unequalled in wisdom, distinguished for usefulness, and the object of almost universal confidence, admiration and love. Such an object was the venerable Mercer; and with the deepest emotions of sorrow did his Christian brethren gaze upon his wasting form.

Early in the month of June Mr. Mercer ascended the pulpit for the last time, to address his fellow men upon the all important concerns of eternity. It being previously known in the town that he was to preach, (perhaps his final sermon,) the other houses of worship were closed, and a large assembly convened to hear his solemn valedictory. He spoke for about an hour with considerable freedom and animation; and under a very impressive sense of obligations to be faithful with the souls of the people. The discourse evidently made a deep impression; and though some might have taken exception to his pointed remarks on the subject of Christian duty, and on what he considered disorderly and unscriptural in connexion with religious excitements, yet it is to be hoped that many will long cherish a profitable remembrance of this his dying testimony. The following is a brief sketch of this discourse, as it subsequently appeared in the Christian Index.

"The text was 1 Sam. 12 : 23. *As for me, God forbid that I should sin against the Lord, in ceasing to pray for you; but I will teach you the good and the right way.*

"The introduction noticed the sin and folly of the Israelites in choosing for themselves a king. Of this Samuel had now so forcibly reminded them, that they confess the 'evil' and entreat his intercession for them with the Lord."

"The DOCTRINE sought to be established was—*The solicitude of faithful ministers for their people in cases of manifest departures from the good and right way.* They do not only pray for them, but they remonstrate and teach, &c. Jer. 20 : 8, 9. Rom. 9 : 1, 2, 3. 2 Cor. 12 : 15.

"What do they teach? The good and the right way. Wherein does it consist? First, in the way of truth and holiness, as it is the object of faith; see Jer. 6 : 16. Isa. 35 : 8. 2 Peter 2 : 2. and secondly, the way of obedience, in which only God can be worshipped acceptably. The preacher was inclined to believe Samuel had this way of obedience in view, because he subjoins, 'Only fear the Lord, and serve him in truth with all your heart.'

"In the remainder of the discourse, he wished to call the special attention of the congregation to a few indispensable particulars of the good and the right way, in which God can be truly and acceptably worshipped. To render a service, which can be good and right in the sight of the Lord, it must be done,—

1. *In Faith.* Faith is general and particular; *gene-*

ral as it embraces all revealed truth, and leads to the due observance of it; and, *particular* as it acknowledges the authority of God to command and the implicit obligation of men to obey. Heb. 11 : 6. Isa. 42 : 8. Mal. 1 : 6. Rev. 4 : 11.

2. According to the divine order or requirement, 1 Chron. 15 : 12. Isai. 29 : 13. Jer. 19 : 5. Matt. 15 : 69. He here expressed a wish to notice several points of modern church organization and practice, in which the divine *requirement* was not duly waited for. The whole fabric of a church, its materials, the mode of uniting them, independence, &c. were topics of pure *revelation*, on which he could not dwell as he felt their importance to demand. He came, however, to this point—That whatever in religious worship was based on tradition or human invention, must be condemned as 'vain' worship; because it either set aside the commands of God, or added to them.

"3. In love. Deut. 6 : 4, 5. 1 John 5 : 3.

"4. *Reverently.* Ps. 4 : 4, 5. 95 : 6, 7. John 4 : 23, 24. Phil. 2 : 12. Heb. 12 : 28. Allusion was here made to the occasional confusion in revivals as inconsistent with reverent worship, and as condemned by the apostle in 1 Cor. 14th chap.

"It may be said, however, by some, our brother remarked, that much good appears to be effected in the course of these exercises, and how can this be admitted if we may not regard them as of God? One or two extremes were specified. Here was a case of convulsions. A woman of weak nerves falls on the floor under preaching. Is this necessarily of God? Is this to be *encouraged* as a divine work? Then we hear singing, shouting, praying and exhortation, all at once, in another quarter of the assembly. Is this also of God? Will it bear the test of common reason and sound sense? *Whatever is contrary to these is not of God.*

"'Let me take you,' he continued, 'to Horeb. Thither Elijah had retired from persecution, and the Lord had designed to commission him for some very important future services—' The Lord passed by.' Observe, HE passed by. 'And behold, a great and strong wind rent the mountains, and broke in pieces the rocks before the Lord.' An earthquake and a fire succeeded, whose effects are not described, but we may suppose them to have been striking. The Lord, however, was neither in the wind, the earthquake, nor the fire. But in a 'still small voice,' that followed, his servant can recognise him. Elijah wraps his face in his mantle, in reverence. The Lord *is* there!

"'Now I do not say that in some of the extreme agitations and excitements to which I object, the effect of some approaches of the Lord upon our weak and erring natures, may not be seen. But the Lord, as I conceive, is not in them. Especially when indulged in as some *end* of a revival; something to be gloried in and promoted as in itself desirable. Revivals driven on to such extremes become, I must say, no longer acceptable. They involve that confusion of which God is *not* the author.'

"He illustrated his views from 1 Cor. 14 chap. This was a church that came behind in 'no gift.' They were enriched in all utterance and knowledge; but became very confused in their public assemblies, by a defective and irreverent management of those gifts. The apostle in rectifying this, supplies us with some simple but invaluable principles that should regulate all our assemblies. The cardinal point is—'edification'—'that the church,' the whole assembly, may receive edifying. To this end there must be order, subordination of all spiritual impulse, to a common object. There must be rationality. No spiritual gifts destroy men's natural faculties, but purify, extend, exalt them; make reason, so to speak, more rational. But when 'every one had,' and would sing or speak, his own 'psalm, doctrine, or tongue,' heedless of a brother's revelations or the common good in 'edification, exhortation, or comfort,' will not strangers 'say ye are mad?' asks the apostle—and a proper application of this doctrine to modern times is, if when direct inspiration was the privilege of the churches, (that inspiration which, as in itself miraculous and confirmed by miracles, was also *infallible*,) there was a duty of subordinating 'the spirit of the prophets' to the prophets—and that in fact, the government of reason, and the corresponding gifts of other brethren, were to be *restraints* on the whole, how much less pretence can any man now have to *ungovernable* impulses as from God—how much more carefully and reverently should we seek to exercise all *our* spiritual gifts!

"5. In view of the glory of God as its proper end; and the good of mankind as its subordinate but gracious design."

He visited Penfield the latter part of June for the purpose of spending a few weeks with his friends, and attending the college commencement, and the annual meeting of the board of trustees, both to take place the last of July.

Brother Absalom Janes and family had the melancholy pleasure of ministering to this afflicted disciple during most of his stay at Penfield. They speak of him as enjoying at the time a calm and peaceful frame of mind, attending devoutly upon family worship, though scarcely able to kneel and rise without assistance; as appearing remarkably fearful of giving trouble to the family, and of conversing upon various subjects with great mental clearness.

At the meeting of the trustees, the writer of these sketches, as well as many other brethren, saw their father in the Lord for the last time. But O how changed was the venerable man! Disease and care had reduced his fine portly frame to a mere skeleton; his clothes hung loosely upon him; his face was pallid and shrunken; his voice was feeble and faltering, and his steps trembled under his fading and emaciated frame. None could gaze upon the dying man without emotion, and hardly without tears. His countenance however, still beamed with its wonted benignity, his words were kindness itself, and his spirit seemed to be filled with calm serenity, and heavenly sweetness. The grace of God was evidently performing in his heart its last, blessed work. The infirmities of the outer man seemed to encumber the operations of his fine vigorous mind less than might have been expected; when roused by some little effort, it would beam forth with a clear radiance, like that of the western sun, which reminds us that though the orb of day is fast sinking to the horizon, it is still the same bright orb which shed upon us its meridian brightness. Several important subjects came up for the consideration of the Board of Trustees; he would occasionally, sitting in his chair, which he occupied as president of the body, briefly express his sentiments; and this was done in a very clear, connected, and appropriate manner.

A letter, written from Penfield to his fellow-laborer at Washington, may very properly be introduced in this place.

"*Penfield, July* 18, 1841.

"My Dear Brother Sturgis,

"Two pretty good things have come to pass to day. We have had a good and refreshing rain; very much wanted here and hereabouts. It is said in some settlements the corn, especially, is nearly exhausted. I hope however, it will turn out better than now feared. I have heard it was very dry and hot with you, and about the neighboring parts. I hope you have had rains, as we have seen good appearances that way. The crop is here said to be the best for several years past, so far as culture is concerned; but it must be very much pinched and stinted. But the other good thing was, a *good* discourse from our Dr.* here. He preached on the *true* personality and *real* divinity of the Holy Ghost. I think he did great justice to the subject; and drew several very weighty and comfortable considerations from the doctrine. His text was John 14 : 16.

"I am now some more comfortable than I have been since I came up to Penfield. I have been pining with an almost perpetual flatulent colic, somewhat spasmodic; and have therefore been worse off than before I left home. The symptoms have abated and I hope I shall get better. I intend to stay here among the brethren till commencement, but what course I shall then take, I have not yet determined. So far I have abode with brother Janes. I think of going in a day or two to brother Sanders.

* * * * *

"I should like you would write me how all are getting on at W. Is the work of grace going on yet

* Rev. Tho. Curtis.

among the blacks? How does Mrs. S—— do? Is she worse or better? Is any thing encouraging among the whites, young or old? I have understood that * * * has joined the P. Church. Well, if he loved father or friends better than Christ, he is as well— better than with us.

"I trust you are so recovered, as to be able to resume your usual course of public and private service; and I pray most earnestly that your labors may be greatly succeeded by divine influence. Religion here is low, and I think pretty generally *so*. Brother Sherwood has returned from his tour, with brother Thornton, and says there is very little excitement in any of the churches where they travelled.

"There were two deaths in Greensboro' last week. A promising young man, Dr. M.; and a Mrs. C——. This lady's husband had been to Washington City from Ala., and she came this far to meet him on his return home. I can't tell you any further of the particulars of the case, but it is a *distressing one*. The people in general are healthy. If it will be within your convenience and agree to your feelings, I should like you to go to my house, and see how they are getting on; especially in a religious respect. I had hoped that Charlotte had some concern on her mind about her soul's and eternity's interests, before I left home. I talked to her of those things, and *urged* her to seek the Lord and faint not. I should like to know if she makes any progress. Tell her (and all) that I have constant remembrance of them before the throne of grace, and hope she does not fail to pray for herself and children. Tell brother *Henry* I shall hope to receive a letter from him, unless he should come up to commencement. In that case it would hardly be worth while.

"Give my affectionate regards to sister S. and *all* the brethren and friends in W. as you may find agreeable to mention it to.

"I am, dear brother, yours, &c.
"JESSE MERCER."

On the 4th of August, Mr. Mercer left Penfield, and journeyed on to the Indian Springs in Butts county, hoping to derive some benefit from the mineral virtues of the water. For a while his health seemed to undergo some little improvement; but he found no radical and lasting benefit. The strength of his disease remained unbroken, and it seemed evident that without a speedy change of a favorable character he could not linger much longer on earth. The following letter to brother Sturgis was probably one of the last that he ever wrote.

"*Indian Springs, Aug.* 13, 1841.
"MY DEAR BROTHER STURGIS,

"Yours was duly received at Penfield. I was truly glad to receive the information it gave. May the Lord carry on the good work. I can but hope the course taken by Miss S. will be a blessing to others. Oh; her poor mother! The Lord of wonders have mercy on her, and suffer not the soul that he has made to perish before him! Tell the blacks that I have constant remembrance of them in prayer. I fear for the white people of W. lest the Lord may have given them over to their own ways. The church I think, has never yet been in travail. O that they would be *duly* stirred up to seek the Lord as they should *with all their heart*, and then they would be blessed with a revival indeed!

"I left Penfield on the 4th much weakened, and a

lax on me, which had followed my being relieved of the colic which so affected me after I reached P. This wasting disease increased on the way, and is still in some degree on me, but I hope I am on the mend; and may derive some benefit from this water. It is probable I shall stay here most of the month; but this depends on circumstances. However, I should like to receive a letter from you before I leave. I received a letter from brother Pope since yours, in which he informed me of the wind at my house. He did not say any thing of any other injury than that suffered by me—but was that all ? He then thought the work among the blacks as general and as great as ever. Well, may the Lord carry it on to great good; to the salvation of many. I hear from several churches in these parts of symptoms for good, but no great ingathering. I see little else about here but indifference and sin! I am well situated with brother Barlow, who keeps about a half-mile on the hill above the spring. We are very quiet, and have prayer night and morning for the most part; but this public-house keeping, is a poor business for the raising of a family, or for family religion, or any other! If you can, write me *to this place*, on the receipt of this, and let me know how matters and things now stand; how it is with those poor women, Mrs. S. and Mrs. W., and any others in particular cases; how the work is still with the blacks, &c., &c.

"I hope the Lord sustains your heart and hand, in his service, and that your strength will be *as your day requires*, and that he will give you much success!

"I hear of considerable sickness in the lower counties; about here I think there is but little. The crops are said to be good, but there is some complaint of *rust* in the cotton.

"The weather is now rainy, and the people will have a bad time probably to save their fodder. How is the prospect in Wilkes ?

"My most ardent love and desire for all the brethren, give to as many as you think it worth while; to sister S. and the Dr., and my servants, who will take an interest in hearing from me.

"I am, dear brother, yours truly,
"JESSE MERCER."

On the last Sabbath in August, he attended the meeting of brother James Carter at the Springs, and in the evening of the same day accompanied that brother to his residence, some eight miles north of the Springs, with the intention, should his strength allow, of prosecuting his journey as far as Walton, Monroe county, for the purpose of visiting his friends and relations in that place. This design the Lord did not however permit him to accomplish—he went to the house of brother Carter to die.

In a September number of the Index, the eye of the reader fell upon the following melancholy announcement.

"We stop the press to inform the readers of the Index, that our dear old Father MERCER is no more. We have just received the following note from his nephew, brother W. A. MERCER:

"'At bro. James Carter's, Butts Co. Sept. 6, 1841.

"'*Dear bro. Stokes*, I have the mournful intelligence to communicate to you and the brethren at Penfield, that my dear uncle JESSE MERCER is no more— He breathed his last this morning at twenty minutes after six o'clock, without a *struggle* or *a groan*. I reached here yesterday, and found him sinking very fast. He was perfectly sensible, and so remained untill the last. He spoke but a few words. I sat by his bedside through the most of the night. He answered several questions I asked him—I inquired if he was ready to *depart.* He threw his dying arms around my neck, and pulled me down near to him, and said—*I have no fears.* He would have talked more, but said he was unable—I have not time to multiply.'"

From the following letter of brother Carter, which was also published in the Index, the reader will learn most of the particulars of his death.

"*Eight miles North of Springs,*
Butts county, 20*th Sept.* 1841.

"DEAR BROTHER STOKES,

"Inasmuch as it fell to the lot of myself and family to take care of, and nurse our very dear brother MERCER, the last week of his life, and he having died in my house, perhaps it is necessary that I should say something to the brethren and friends generally, through the medium of the Index, in regard to this matter; and record what may be called his dying words, as well as his dying conduct. I visited him frequently while at the Springs. I always found him calm and ready to enter on religious conversation, (when his strength would permit.) He made many inquiries about the churches, and the prospect of religion generally.—He was much pleased to learn our prospects were favorable. My appointment with the church at the Springs, was on the last Sabbath in August—he attended, though very feeble. The text for that day was a part of the 11th verse of the 12th chapter of Exodus, 'Eat with your loins girded, your shoes on your feet, and your staff in your hand.' At the close of the sermon, this venerable old servant of Christ arose to his feet, and leaning on his staff, made a few remarks in regard to God's people going to heaven; he then called the attention of the congregation to this one fact, that the Israelites were to go a certain distance into the wilderness to worship; 'now,' said he, 'I wish you all to know that they that go to heaven, must go worshipping.' He dwelt most beautifully on that idea, and closed by prayer. This may be considered his last address to mankind, and the last prayer put up in the church. Oh, that the Lord would hear his prayer for us in this country. He came with me home that evening, and concluded to remain a day or two. He appeared to be entirely satisfied and at home. On Tuesday morning he thought he was much better, but before night he became worse.—He remarked to my wife and myself, that he regretted very much to be troublesome, and if he stayed another day, it would prevent me from going to my appointments the balance of the week: we both told him we were willing to have the trouble, and to do any thing for him in our power. He said he thought of that, but still regretted that I should stay on his account. I told him I knew the brethren and congregation at Tawaliga church, where I was expected, would excuse me—this appeared to satisfy him. He then said, 'I am here, and I cannot leave you, and I may die on your hands.' He went to his room, and did not from that time even express a wish to leave, but in no way cast down, but rather cheerful. I frequently offered to call in a physician, but he as often refused, and said he had had the attention of physicians who knew him, and were well acquainted with his complaint, and the medicine had not had the desired effect, and he did not think it worth while to put himself into new hands. I, however, went and consulted one, without his knowledge. When I came back and told him, he said he supposed the advice was good, but his complaint had gone beyond that remedy, and would only take such as he himself would prescribe. By his request, I directed a letter to brother W. A. Mercer, of Walton, and brothers Butler and Pope of Washington, requesting them, or such others as could, to come and see him. On Friday, I had much satisfactory conversation with him. On Saturday, he asked me if I recollected the song in the Cluster, that had these words in it, 'I did to him my all commit;' I told him I did. He then went on to say, 'that is continually in my mind. Forty odd years ago I committed my all to the Lord, before the mercy seat, and there is my dependence now.' I asked him if he was willing to go. He said, 'yes, if it is the will of God.' Whenever the question was asked, he always said he was willing. At one time he went on to speak at length in regard to the doctrines of grace and the promises of the gospel. I said to him, 'I recollect many of your views, when I sat under your ministry, and was baptized by you;' he said, 'yes, and these are my views now.' He would frequently take me by the hand, as if he was telling me farewell, looking wishfully in my face, but said nothing. Frequently asked if the brethren had come. He bore his affliction like his Lord and Master; not murmuring, and scarcely a groan was heard, only in prayer. He had his proper mind and memory to the last, asked me but a little before he died, if the brethren from Washington had come; said to brother W. A. Mercer, he had no fears. So he died almost without a struggle or groan, at twenty minutes after six o'clock, on the 6th September.

"The Macedonia church met in conference the next Saturday, and unanimously agreed to make a record of his death in her church book, in the following way, and to send you a copy, if you should see proper to publish it in the Index, as follows:

"The Church in Conference, 11th September, 1841. —*Resolved*, That inasmuch as it seems to have been the will of God, on the 6th day of this inst., to call from time to eternity, our venerable and dear brother in the ministry, Rev. JESSE MERCER, while in the immediate neighborhood of this church, and at the house of our pastor, we deem it our privilege and duty to mention this dispensation of divine Providence among us, and to make a record of the same in the following way:

"1st. That we desire to be thankful to the Lord that his usefulness and zeal were continued so long to the denomination and the world; at the same time we mourn with our brethren in general, the loss of so eminent a servant of Christ.

"2d. In the death of brother Mercer, we think the Baptists have lost one of their brightest ornaments, truth one of its ablest advocates, and the country one of its ancient and elevated citizens.

"3d. We should now feel more forcibly the weight of that command, pray ye the Lord of the harvest to send more laborers into the vineyard.

"4th. That we request our pastor to preach an appropriate sermon in reference to the above case, on the Sabbath.

"I endeavored to comply with the request from the text, 'I have finished my course, I have kept the faith, &c., to an unusually large congregation, (our house rather over the common size;) after filling the house to overflowing, the people stood at the doors and windows, with the utmost composure. The Lord came down by his Spirit, many were cut to the heart; and there is a gracious work going on, and has been for some time; baptized five that day; unavoidable circumstances required us to adjourn until yesterday; and the day before yesterday baptized five more; in all ten; and many are crying for mercy. Pray for them, and for all of us.

"Yours, &c.,
"JAMES CARTER."

The remains of Mr. Mercer were carried to Penfield, and interred in the public burying ground; at which spot, or some other one more suitable, near the University, that may hereafter be selected, with the consent of his relatives, and his devoted church at Washington, and in accordance with the general wish of the denomination, they will find a permanent resting place.*

Never has the death of any individual called forth such an expression of deep and universal grief in the Baptist churches of Georgia; and long will it be, in all human probability, before such sorrow will be felt again. A great and a good man had fallen, and there was lamentation in Israel.

The Trustees of the University, in connexion with the Faculty and students, and the citizens of Penfield, signalized the mournful event by appropriate resolutions, and also by solemn religious services.

The following resolutions contain an expression of

* A plain, substantial monument is to be erected to his memory, under the direction of the Trustees of the University.

the sentiments and feelings of the bereaved church at Washington, on the melancholy occasion.

"*Baptist Church, Washington, Ga., Sept.* 1841.

"*Resolved*, That this church feels sensibly the loss we have sustained in the removal by death, of our venerable and beloved pastor, JESSE MERCER. That in him, they, together with the denomination and the christian community, have lost an able Expositor of the Inspired Oracles, a faithful preacher of the word of life, a wise and prudent Counsellor in things pertaining to the interests of Christ's kingdom, and a munificent Benefactor, such as it has rarely been their privilege to enjoy.

"That in looking back upon the long series of years during which we, in common with the christian community, have enjoyed the services of this distinguished man of God, we feel a mingled emotion of gratitude, that those services were continued so long, and sorrow, that they are now closed for ever. And now that the hand that so long broke unto us the bread of life, is palsied in death, and the heart that even the frosts af age could not forbid to feel deeply for our spiritual interests, shall yearn over us no more in this world, we would hold in grateful remembrance all his services, and how 'He ceased not to admonish and entreat men night and day with tears,' —humbly praying that the seed sown by the hands of this servant of the Most High, may spring up and produce a yet more abundant harvest.

"*Resolved*, That we sincerely sympathize with his surviving family in the loss which they have sustained in the removal of their venerable relative.

"*Resolved*, that the expression of condolence with

us on this occasion of deep affliction, by the citizens of Penfield, is most gratefully received, and that we accord to them the same expressions.

"*Resolved*, That this Church acknowledges the truly christian spirit manifested by the Presbyterian church of this place, in the communication transmitted by their committee, and that we receive that expression of sympathy, as seasonable and highly acceptable in our painful bereavement.

"*Resolved*, That in reference to a final resting-place for the remains of our departed pastor, we believe that it was his intention to be placed beside his wife; a spot of ground in our church-yard having been granted him, (at his request,) for that purpose, and it is the desire of the church that this request be complied with.

"*Resolved*, That in the event of his final interment at any other place, this Church, as a farther expression of her regard for the memory of her deceased Pastor, cause to be procured a suitable tablet of marble, with an appropriate inscription, to be inserted in some proper situation upon the walls of this house.

"*Resolved*, That the Church do hereby request the officiating Minister to preach a Sermon in memory of our deceased Pastor, on the morning of the first Sabbath in October.

"*Resolved*, That a copy of these resolutions, together with the communication from the Presbyterian Church, be transmitted for publication in the Christian Index, and News and Gazette.

"Done in Conference, this 25th day of Sept. 1841.

"RICHARD W. JOYNER,
"*Church Clerk.*"

The following, is the Communication from the Presbyterian Church referred to in the preceding resolutions; and on account of the Christian spirit which it breathes, it is entitled to a place in these pages.

"*Sunday, 19th September,* 1841.

"Dear Brethren and esteemed friends,

"As a Committee of the Presbyterian Church, we transmit to you a copy of the proceedings of a meeting held this morning, at the close of divine service, which you will receive as a testimonial of our sense of departed worth, and a token of our sincere participation with you in your recent bereavement.

"We are your sympathizing friends and brethren,
Geo. H. W. Petrie,
A. S. Wingfield,
Lock Weems,
" Rev. C. F. Sturgis, and Deacons
of the Baptist Church."

"At a meeting of the members of the Presbyterian Church, convened this morning after service, with a view of giving a suitable expression of their feelings as a Church upon the bereavement which has afflicted their community, in the decease of the Rev. Jesse Mercer, Pastor of the Baptist Church, Dr. John H. Pope was called to the Chair, and A. S. Wingfield appointed Secretary.

" Rev. Mr. Petrie opened the meeting with a few remarks, and then offered the following Preamble and Resolutions, which were unanimously adopted :

" In view of the affliction with which Divine Providence has visited us in the loss of our venerable friend, the Rev. Jesse Mercer, we, the members of the Presbyterian Church, do adopt the following Resolutions, as an expression of our feelings on this mournful occasion :

"*Resolved*, That we sincerely and deeply deplore the heavy calamity which has befallen our community in the decease of this venerable minister of Christ.

"*Resolved*, That we tender our cordial sympathy to our brethren of the Baptist Church, in this their bereavement, in the decease of their beloved Pastor, and that we mourn their loss as our loss.

"*Resolved*, That as a testimony of the respect and esteem we entertain for the character of our departed friend, also for our brethren of the Baptist Church, our house of worship shall be closed on the morning of the first Sabbath in October, when, as we are informed, an appropriate funeral discourse will be delivered in the Baptist Church.

"*Resolved*, That a Committee be appointed to transmit a copy of these proceedings to the officiating Minister and Deacons of the Baptist Church, and through them to the members generally.

"JOHN H. POPE, *Chairman*.
"A. S. WINGFIELD, *Secretary*."

Similar expressions of Christian sorrow were made by the Georgia Association, the Baptist State Convention, and by many other bodies of our brethren in the State.

On the time appointed brother C. F. Sturgis, who as has been noticed, had the honor and happiness of being associated for a time with father Mercer, in the pastoral charge of the church, preached an appropriate funeral discourse, from 2 Sam. 3 : 38. "*Know ye not that there is* * * * *a great man fallen this day in Israel.*"

After some suitable introductory remarks, the

preacher announced the main point to which he invited the attention of the congregation; viz. "*That Jesse Mercer was truly a great man: I mean,*" adds Mr. Sturgis, by way of explanation, "*great as God's servant.*" This position was clearly illustrated by the speaker by considering somewhat at length the following particulars.

"I. The manner in which he rose to the commanding position which he occupied.

"II. The manner in which he retained that position, and continued to ascend to the very last.

"III. The strength of his intellectual powers.

"IV. His retention of these powers to the last.

"V. The plans and schemes which engaged his mind.

"VI. The manner in which he prosecuted these plans.

"VII. The influence which he exerted upon the world by his life, character and actions."

The above named topics were in the main judiciously selected, and well sustained: space cannot however, be allowed for a complete outline of the discourse. The brief sketch here given will nevertheless serve to give some direction to the mind of the reader; and by such facts as are supplied by these pages, in connexion perhaps with his own recollections of Mr. Mercer, he will be able to illustrate each particular point for himself, and move on by a sure and convincing process to the conclusion, that when this servant of Christ yielded to the summons of death, *a* GREAT *man indeed fell in our Israel.*

CHAPTER XVI.

Mr. Mercer's personal appearance.—Various traits of character described.—Mr. Mercer in his social relations.—Character of his mind and attainments.—His character as a preacher.—His gift in prayer.—His piety.—His faults.—His great influence.

The personal appearance of Mr. Mercer was peculiarly interesting, well calculated to arrest the attention of the beholder, and fix a lasting impression on his mind. None who had once seen him would be very likely to forget him. Most of his surviving acquaintances have probably a more distinct recollection of his appearance than of any other individual; such a recollection as would enable them, if familiar with the pencil, to exhibit on canvass a tolerably correct delineation of his whole person. In height he rose somewhat above the ordinary standard; in his younger days, as has already been noticed, he was spare, but in his advanced years, when his health was good, he was moderately corpulent. Time had gradually removed the greater portion of his hair, leaving at last but a few, thin straight locks on the sides and back part of his head, which still retained, however, their original dark brown color. His extreme baldness revealed to all the exact size and conformation of the citadel of his noble mind. This conformation was very remarkable. The horizontal length of his head from his eyebrows back, was very great, whilst his forehead seemed to rise upward with a gently receding slope even to the very crown, exhibiting a most striking development of what phrenologists term the organs of benevolence, veneration and firmness. His eye, which was of a hazel color, and rather small and deeply sunk, was clear and sparkling, and beamed with a sweet, mingled expression of affection and intelligence. He had a meek, kind and reverential look; and if he was not indeed a benevolent, devout and good man, then the human features never speak a distinct and intelligible language. Most of the time his countenance was considerably turned downward, as though he was habitually impressed with a sense of the divine presence; and a gentle bowing motion of the head, which was very often repeated, might suggest to the beholder that he was making, as it were, reverential obeisance to his Maker. His movements were generally calm, uniform, and deliberate, and marked with much of that sweet and quiet gentleness, which we may suppose peculiarly distinguished that divine person of whom it was said, "he shall not strive nor cry, neither shall any man hear his voice in the streets; a bruised reed shall he not break, and smoking flax shall he not quench."

To strangers, he often appeared cold, uninteresting and dry, but an intimate acquaintance could not fail to excite interest, and to render it apparent that he possessed those refined and amiable qualities which rendered him capable of tender, firm and lasting friendship. He was constitutionally reserved and taciturn, unable readily to suggest topics for remark, and to give a direction to conversation; on which account he often complained that he was illy qualified to perform properly the duties of a pastor; yet scarcely any subject could be introduced by others in regard to which he could not speak a word in season; and when interested and roused he would entertain a company with pertinent and instructive discourse, interspersed oftentimes with happy illustrations, and sparkling anecdotes. His first wife used sometime say, "if you wish to get Mr. Mercer to talking, when he comes to see you, you must lay up some subjects for him beforehand :"—" I was in the habit of doing so," remarked one of his intimate friends, "and would sometimes in this way draw from him by my fireside the substance of two or three good sermons."

He was a man of great transparency of character. What he appeared to be, he really was. He was a true Nathaniel, an Israelite indeed, guileless, simple, unaffected. He ever proposed to himself worthy and noble ends, and by honest, open, straightforward means, labored for their accomplishment, disdaining all tortuous management and secret wire-pulling.

He was sparing of his praises in the presence of those he would commend, and the spirit of peevish fault-finding, and bitter detraction, dwelt not in his bosom. With all his greatness and reputation, he was lowly and humble; he sustained his honors with meekness; knew how to bear the infirmities of the weak, to condescend to men of low estate, to render welcome to his presence and to his dwelling, the most obscure individual. His modesty was conspicuous; he sometimes appeared embarrassed from diffidence, especially amongst strangers; and it was not uncommon for him to be distrustful of his own judgment, and seek the counsel of those who would ever have esteemed it an honor to sit as learners at his feet.

Though possessed of an eminently meek and gentle spirit, he was, nevertheless, a man of uncommon firmness, and of great moral courage. In matters of principle and conscience, he was immoveable as a rock; upon what he deemed important and vital points, he was not afraid to proclaim his opinions, even if the whole world was to be arrayed against him. Yet in matters of indifference, no one was more ready and cheerful in yielding to the wishes of others, too generous and noble to stickle in trifling matters, and to contend for contention sake. "He had not that kind of liberality" (to use the language of another) "which, though it might please men, disregards the injunctions of heaven, a liberality which narrows, lessens or attenuates the commands of the bible; yet he was kind and courteous, and hospitable to all denominations."

From the calm and quiet manner in which Mr. Mercer prosecuted his duties, many might suppose that he was deficient in force and energy of character. In certain modes of action, as has already been intimated, he was, in this respect, no doubt, excelled by many. But a survey of the general tenor of his life, of his steady devotion to the great work to which he considered himself called of God, his almost unexampled punctuality in pressing on to his numerous appointments through heat and through cold, through wet and through weariness, and the unwavering uniformity with which he pursued all his purposes and duties, even under circumstances of discouragement and trial, will present to us a character by no means deficient in force and energy. Yet his energy was not that of the torrent which bears away with rapid and boisterous strength, dwellings, and woods, and fields; but the gentle, yet effectual energy of the summer shower, which crumbles the dry and unyielding soil; the noiseless and invisible force of heat, which gradually vanquishes the stubborn rock, and the impenetrable steel.

Mr. Mercer was a man of a remarkably tender spirit. His sympathetic nature enabled him most readily to enter into the griefs of his brethren and friends; and with what a gentle, engaging and paternal manner he would make their burdens his own, very many can bear testimony. He often preached with tears. A tender and affectionate exhibition of divine truth by others, seldom failed to engage his feelings, and to elicit some quiet and unobtrusive expression of emotion. Was there, on any occasion, a divine and melting influence poured forth upon a congregation; if Father Mercer was one of that concourse, he might be seen with his head bowed gently and reverently forward, weeping with the meek, unaffected simplicity of a little child. The incident noticed in the following extract from a letter of President Manly, may serve as a pleasant illustration of this trait of his character. "I saw Father Mercer but seldom. Once I saw him, (at Eatonton, in the spring of 1824,) in an aspect which I must relate, as it illustrates the simple piety and tenderness of his heart. It was on a Sunday of the meeting of the Georgia Convention. Brother S. and I were to preach. Brother Mercer sat in the pulpit with us. S. got up, and in his quaint way surveyed the assembly (a very large one) with several glances, and opened just in this way. 'Where shall we obtain bread to feed so great a multitude? as for my part, I am unprovided and penniless; but there is a lad here,' turning round and putting his hand on my head as I leaned forward in the pulpit, ' who has five barley loaves and two little fishes, which, with the presence and blessing of Jesus, shall constitute a feast.' This well nigh upset me. But it drove me to prayer. The Lord loosed my own mind, and unlocked the fountains of tears, so that it was computed that through a great part of the discourse, there was an average of at least five hundred persons continually bathed in tears. There was nothing in all this *Bochim*, that to me was so affecting as when I turned round and saw the sympathetic streams coursing swiftly down the furrowed cheeks of Father Mercer."

The following incident is furnished by President Sherwood. "When the Convention was organized at Powelton, in June, 1822, one of the ministers read a sermon, I think from 'Prepare ye the way of the Lord,' in which he portrayed the evils of sectional feelings, and need of a more extended acquaintance, such as the organization of the Convention was designed to promote. Mr. Mercer closed the exercises by an approving exhortation and weeping prayer, and in allusion to the plain truths touching the divisions and petty jealousies which had contributed to block up 'the way of the Lord,' he made hearty confession of sin in this respect for himself and brethren, and observed with stifled emotion, 'hast thou found us out, O our enemy! hast thou seen the evils that exist among us!' The whole assembly were melted into tears, and his prayer seemed to do more good than the sermon."

Another incident may be appropriately related in this connexion. "A case of discipline with the *Rev. Thomas Rhodes*, was the source of great grief and affliction. He had swerved from the path of rectitude, and several of his brethren were endeavoring to bring him to see his error; and though he would frequently make acknowledgments, his subsequent conduct impaired confidence, and opened afresh the wound that had been partially healed. Mr. Rhodes was an interesting and popular preacher. He had travelled much with Mr. Mercer, and their affection was strong for each other, like that of David and Jonathan; this made the trial severer. At meetings for healing the breaches which Mr. Rhodes had made,

Mr. Mercer has been seen to burst out into a flood of tears, and weep like a child over his wandering brother."* In the various domestic and social relations, he stood forth as a model of uncommon beauty and excellence. Why need we speak of his obliging kindness as a neighbor, his sincerity and firmness as a friend, his fidelity and affection as a brother, his integrity and truly christian patriotism, as a citizen?

Who better understood the duties of a husband? These duties he discharged with a prompt fidelity, engaging tenderness, and unwearied constancy, worthy of all praise. It was truly delightful to notice with what a kind voice and affectionate look he would respond to the assiduous attentions of his devoted companion, and with what patience, sympathy and carefulness, he would minister to her in all her afflictions.

As a master, his example deserves to be recorded in deep lines upon a tablet of gold, and suspended in every habitation. He treated his servants (of which he had but a few) with the most judicious consideration and the greatest humanity. He held them in the light, not of inanimate goods and chattels; but of human, rational, immortal beings. Their spiritual wants ever lay upon his heart. When speaking of their condition as needy, ruined sinners, he would often shed tears; often would he, with great concern, entreat the prayers of his brethren in their behalf; and when any of them manifested anxiety in relation to the salvation of their souls, it gave him the most sincere pleasure. Every morning and evening was their attendance required at family worship; and what

* Sherwood's sketch of the life of Mr. Mercer, in the Baptist Memorial.

may seem rather singular to many, he had the authority and address to secure without noise or severity, a uniform compliance with this regulation. The writer well remembers with what concern he once heard him speak of the death of one of his domestics; and with what christian propriety and tenderness he quoted, in connexion, the passage from Proverbs, "*He that delicately bringeth up his servant from a child, shall have him to become his son at the length.*"

With reference to the same event, he thus writes to an intimate christian friend: "The Lord has made a breach on us! It falls with considerable weight on us, as it not only deprives us of a great benefit, but of the *most dear* inmate of our house. Our little house girl, Mary, is now a corpse in our house; suddenly and violently taken away by *congestive* fever. She was so intimately connected with us and our happiness, that we feel it almost as the loss of a daughter. But the thought of our loss is nothing to the fear of the loss of her soul! Mary was a fine girl, brisk, willing and sensible, (so that her place will be hard to fill,) but she was a sinner, a poor, little *lying, thievish* sinner, and she is gone (so far as we can tell) in impenitence! For two days her speech failed her, so that we could understand nothing from her. But it is the Lord's doing and we must submit." In accordance with Mr. Mercer's request, brother Wm. H. Stokes preached a funeral sermon to the colored people, at the grave; and in some remarks which he himself made, he said with much feeling, "*I am afraid, my servants, that you will go to hell!*" On the Lord's day following, he preached a discourse which might be regarded as a kind of funeral sermon, with sorrow and tears often referring to the death of his servant.

Such a master would be likely to enjoy the confidence and affection of his servants. "They loved him and venerated him," (says a friend that for many years, was almost daily at his house,) " not only as a master, but as a father. * * As an instance of that kind feeling which was cherished by all his servants, I will just mention the conduct of old Manuel, a few days after his death. This old servant, it is well known, accompanied his master after his last marriage, everywhere he went. The first time I met him after the death of his master, it seemed as if by the power of association, the scenes and incidents of past days came afresh to his mind, and in the language of the deepest sorrow and affection, he exclaimed, '*what shall I do now? old master* (and here he faltered) *is no more!*' "

"Of Father Mercer's manner in his own house," (remarks the same brother,) "it may be said of a truth, that he exhibited all the attributes of true greatness in perfect simplicity. There was nothing forbidding about him, no assumed dignity. Uniformly kind, always pleasant, sometimes particularly so, especially if the conversation turned upon religious subjects, or upon the success of the gospel at home or abroad. It is true that sometimes from long application to business, he would seem a little dull, but let some questions relating to the doctrines or duties of christianity be introduced, and all was animation, all was cheerfulness and life."

"Order appears to have been the watchword with this good man. Not only was there order in his thoughts, but in all his conduct." Order and system reigned in his household. Although much of this was to be attributed to the excellent management of his wife, yet it was plain that every thing around bore more or less of the impress of the patriarchal head. He did not, as seems to be the case with many, reverse the laws of nature and convert day into night, and night into day; he rose early, and gave the day to its appropriate employment; and retired at a reasonable hour, and gave the night to repose. It would always require a very urgent necessity to induce him, either at home or abroad, to depart from this rule. He gathered his family together at an early hour for worship, requiring all secular business to tarry till God was thus honored; and seldom delaying the time for the accommodation of lingering guests. Should they happen to be late, some kind, reproving hint would be very likely to remind them that he expected his visiters to conform to the rules of the family.

After his settlement at Washington, his house was the frequent resort of his numerous christian acquaintances; and many pious strangers, attracted by the savory influence of his good name, would search out his dwelling to gain at least a hasty interview with this revered Father in Israel. These friends and strangers will long remember the unaffected kindness and hospitality with which they were welcomed to his fireside, feeling that his home was a much honored spot, and thankful that they were there permitted to listen to his voice and receive his blessing.

In the management of his pecuniary affairs, he displayed much ability and judgment. From a very slender beginning, and a moderate income in subsequent years, he was enabled, by economy and prudence, to accumulate, previous to the time of his second marriage, a comfortable estate. At that time, as has been already noticed, he received a large increase to his possessions; yet even then they did not transcend his financial ability. He no longer, however, aimed at accumulation, generally appropriating his entire income, beyond his necessary expenses, to the cause of benevolence. Though now in affluence, he was still economical, carefully avoiding all needless waste. He also avoided with no less care, the contracting of perplexing debts; aiming at great punctuality and exactness in meeting his engagements, thus leaving it in the power of none to say, as he urged upon others the duty of promptness, fidelity, and honesty in relation to pecuniary pledges, (which he often did,) "physician, heal thyself."

It is hardly necessary to repeat what has so often passed in review before the reader of the preceding pages, that he possessed a mind of high order. Clearness, strength, and originality, were its peculiar features. His powers of analysis were remarkable, giving him an easy and rapid mastery over intricate and perplexing subjects; whilst in comparison and illustration he was hardly less distinguished. The common place occurrences of life, and familiar scenes in nature around,[*] cast into his observing and tenacious mind a thousand similies, which with an aptness and simplicity peculiar to himself, he would scatter through his discourses like burning gems and glittering arrows, to give brightness, and point, and power, to the great truths of the gospel of Christ. Even a coarse and somewhat forbidding figure would sometimes be brought up; yet would he wield it in a manner so dexterous and engaging, that it would seem to lose its repulsive aspect, chime in as apparently the fittest illustration that could be used, and leave no other impression upon the mind but that of complacency and delight.

* For a few specimens of Mr. Mercer's figurative illustrations, see appendix. A.

There was something in the intellectual efforts of Mr. Mercer, particularly in the pulpit, that seemed almost invariably to arrest the attention of men of improved and elevated minds,* and this may be regarded as a striking evidence of his own real greatness. A great mind is more naturally impressed with intellectual superiority than minds of an inferior order, and is the only adequate judge of its real dimensions. A person of very ordinary intellect might judge another to be a great man, because upon some points he is superior to himself; whilst another of vastly higher mental stature than the first, might seem in his view to have scarcely any higher claims to greatness. He

---

* "I always feel," said an individual of strong discerning mind, "that when I hear the communications of Brother Mercer, I am listening to a wise man."—A young lady in company once spoke disparagingly of a sermon which she had just heard from Mr. Mercer; having confined her attention, it is presumed, rather to the manner of the speaker than to the substance of the discourse: a gentleman present, one of the most distinguished lawyers and statesmen in the country, who happened to hear the same sermon, observed, *that he had seldom listened to a more logical and sensible discourse.*—The following circumstance was related to the writer by a venerable and intelligent brother in South Carolina some twenty years ago. During one of Mr. Mercer's journeys through S. C. when he was quite young in the ministry, he happened to fall in company with several eminent clergymen at Camden, who it seems had visited the place at a time when some public occasion had brought together a large number of distinguished citizens. Dr. Flynn, a celebrated clergyman of the Presbyterian denomination, Dr. Staughton, then a young man, and perhaps the elder Gano, with one or two others of equal distinction, were some of the ministers who in their turn were called on to address the congregations that assembled from day to day. Mr. Mercer also preached; and his clear, masterly exhibition of divine truth, satisfied all present that he was no ordinary man. Though the others were more admired for the elegance of their language and the gracefulness of their manner, yet the general impression left on the minds of the people seemed to be, that Jesse Mercer *was the great man.*

seems like a person standing at the foot of two contiguous trees of very unequal height, who, by looking directly upwards, cannot judge correctly either of their real or comparative elevation. But a person who, by the exalted character of his mind, is compelled to look downward in forming an estimate of the great mass of mankind, is at once struck with those who rise above the common level, and contemplating them, as it were, in a natural, direct, and horizontal line, can easily judge of their comparative altitude. Very few men, in taking the measure of Mr. Mercer's intellectual power, have ever felt that they were compelled to look downward. Indeed, it is evident that he possessed a mind of that order which would have given him a bright and solid reputation, in almost any important pursuit upon which he might have concentrated its energies. As a financier he would have had few equals; as a jurist* he would have been discrim-

* Upon the death of Gov. Rabun, Mr. Mercer was prevailed on to take charge of an estate, upon which the former had partially administered. A question of law and justice arose, in which he differed from the previously expressed opinion of Gov. Rabun, and nearly every legal adviser that had been consulted. At length it was agreed that the question should be argued in court. Judge Dooly presided. Mr. Mercer employed no counsel, but managed the case himself. In his opening remarks he observed that he professed not to know much of the *law*, but he thought he understood something of the principles of *common justice*. As he progressed in his argument, he was listened to with respectful attention by the court and bar. The case being argued sufficiently on both sides, it was left in the hands of the judge, who found it one of so much difficulty, that he was some twelve months in making up his opinion. This was at last adverse to the opinion of Mr. Mercer. Mr. M., in accordance with the decree of court, turned over certain property without the *bond* and *security*, which he had all along contended was just and proper, and as he expected, it was soon squandered. It seemed that he had common sense and justice on his side, but the capricious law, and hoary precedents, were decided to be against him.

inating and profound; as a statesman, he would have taken an honorable station amongst the Shermans, the Macons, and the Crawfords of the land.

Mr. Mercer was not an extensive reader; nor was he *learned*, in the ordinary acceptation of that phrase. To an acquaintance with polite literature he made no pretensions. His early, though partial academic course, introduced him to some acquaintance with Latin and Greek, an acquaintance however which he never advanced to any considerable extent in future life. "His library," says an intimate friend, "was not extensive but select. His books were not so much his *guides* as his *attendants* in the pursuit of knowledge; he used them principally for the purpose of reference. The Bible with him was first and last. He generally kept lying by him on his desk a plain copy, without note or comment; this he *read*, and this he *studied*.

"Of what is styled Biblical Criticism," (continues the writer,) "he knew comparatively little; yet he could, with the help of Parkhurst, make out a comment upon certain passages in the Greek Testament with surprising accuracy. His principal canon, however, was to compare scripture with scripture. He always read slowly, and reflected profoundly upon what he read. His great intellectual strength, I conceive, was owing to this habit of reflection. By this the relations of things and events were traced out, and no matter how latent some of these relations, they were distinctly seen, and in his public exercises, brought out to open day. * * *

"In the composition of sermons, Father Mercer made but little use of paper. Very rarely did he prepare skeletons, and when he did, they were exceedingly brief. He simply marked the heads or principal topics of his discourses, and the quotations which he intended to introduce. The fact is, he could not write as he could speak. To the latter he was trained in his own peculiar way, to the former he had no training at all. The most of his sermons were noted in his mind, by his favorite mode of reflection. Some of the very best I ever heard him preach, were made up in his carriage as he rode along, without pen, ink, or paper, or even a Bible."

In his preparations for the pulpit, he was in the habit of studying *subjects*, more frequently than *texts*. He would fix upon some theme which he deemed important to present to his people, and then arrange in his mind such arguments as he could gather from the scriptures and other sources. This being done, he did not find it difficult to fix upon a text which would serve as an appropriate motto, and to which he could easily give sufficient prominence in the body of his discourse. The practice of studying subjects, rather than texts, he recommended to other ministers.

It was one of the most interesting features in the intellectual operations of Mr. Mercer, that he took plain, strong, common-sense views of almost every subject that engaged his attention. He had not a very lively imagination, but what he did possess seemed to be under the complete control of his well-balanced judgment. The fanciful, the visionary, the extravagant had no charms for him. His aim was simple, unadulterated truth; and this he sought in a direct and natural way. He had the rare faculty of looking at things as they are, and of presenting them in their native reality, in their own simple and undistorted proportions to the view of others. If he presented at any time views that were new and original, (and who so often exhibited such things,) it was still evident that his common sense had gone down with him into the mines of thought. He brought up solid and precious things which others had not seen before, yet they were still the gems of truth; if they were new, they were still natural; if they were original, they were still realities. The process would often seem so easy that the child would wonder it had not done the same thing before; the gems so bright and truthful, that it would seem strange they had remained hid so long.

Long will Jesse Mercer be held in honorable estimation, as one that was a truly able, pious, instructive and powerful minister of "the glorious gospel of the blessed God." Indeed it was in this character that he was contemplated with most interest when living; and it is in this character that he will stand forth most prominent in those recollections which are permanently to survive him. The impression which his preaching made upon the mind of a distinguished minister of the gospel, (Rev. W. B. Johnson of S. C.) whose discriminating powers, and extensive range of observation amongst men, especially ministers of the Gospel, entitle his opinions to great weight, was no doubt the impression left upon the minds of many others. "Having been with Br. Mercer," he remarks in a letter to the biographer, "at public meetings mostly, I had not an opportunity of forming a full estimate of him only as a preacher. In that character he was to me the most interesting man that I ever heard without exception." The views of President Manly, (a brother similarly qualified to judge of solid merit,) who was permitted occasionally to listen to his pulpit exhibitions, are of the same import, though he has expressed them a little more fully.

"There was so much," says he in a letter to the writer, "that was good and great about him, and his powers seemed to be so well balanced, that he was remarkable perhaps more for the contemperament of a multitude of excellencies, than for a few prominent or shining traits.

"To feel his greatness," (continues Mr. M.) "it was necessary to have *heard him preach under happy circumstances*. At other times he was characterized by a solid judiciousness in all he did or said, sanctified by a simple, fervent piety. But in his happy moments of *preaching*, he would rouse and enchain the attention of *reflecting* minds beyond any minister I have ever heard. At such times, his views were vast, profound, original, striking, absorbing, in the highest degree; while his language, though simple, was so terse and pithy, so pruned, consolidated and suited to become the vehicle of the dense mass of his thoughts, that it required no ordinary effort of a well trained mind to take in all that he said. I well remember a circumstance illustrative of what I say. At a meeting of the S. C. Baptist State Convention held at Edgefield C. H., (probably in 1823,) father Mercer preached preparatory to communion on Sunday, and Dr. Furman was one of his hearers. His text was, 'For if the blood of bulls and of goats and the ashes of an heifer sprinkling the unclean, sanctifieth to the purifying of the flesh; how much more shall the blood of Christ, who, through the eternal Spirit offered himself without spot to God, purge your consciences from dead works to serve the living God.' It was one of his happy times; and after a few of his honest shrugs, and workings of his neck and shoulders, as if to push his huge frame into his armor, he got *fairly under way*. Dr. Furman sat next me in the congregation. Although much absorbed myself, I could but notice that the Doctor, (whose unconscious and inordinate use of snuff, when excited and engaged was remarkable,) passed his hand to his pocket with singular celerity and frequency. At length, as the subject advanced and the interest deepened, the snuff box returned no more to the pocket, but remained open on his knee; while the thumb and finger plied incessantly and full-freighted between it and his nose. Father Mercer was now reasoning out, by overpowering argument, the position, that the divinity of Jesus Christ is necessary to his atonement; and when he announced the conclusion, proved and clear, the venerable saint, Dr. F. brought his hand down violently on his knee, exclaiming audibly, '*what an important thought!*'"

There was but little in Mr. Mercer's manner in the pulpit, which would come up to the exact and refined rules of oratory. His voice was not particularly strong nor distinguished for its compass and melody. When overstrained, as was sometimes the case, it had a shattered sound, and now and then, when the speaker became somewhat affected, it would glide off into a peculiar tone. His gesticulation was rather clumsy, and the fastidious might find fault with the occasional shrugging of his shoulders, and the side-way motion of the head which was so peculiar to himself; but after all, his appearance in the desk was far from being uninteresting. The fair and comely baldness of his head, his venerable mien, his portly frame, his countenance clothed with meekness, benevolence, intelligence and devotion, rendered him an object of peculiar interest and respect, wherever he stood forth

> "To negotiate between God and man,
> As God's ambassador, the grand concerns
> Of judgment and of mercy."

To those who had been long accustomed to the ministry of Mr. Mercer, those peculiarities of his manner which criticism might condemn, assumed a comely aspect; they seemed to be so essentially a part of the man, so necessary as it were, to his personal identity, that their correction would rather have been painful, and left upon the mind what would have been regarded as a defective and mutilated image of their venerated friend.

"His discourses," (to use the correct and able delineation of another,*) "though not constructed upon the scientific rules of composition, were of a *high* order. His representations of divine truth possessed great moral power. Whilst he seemed untrammelled by the laws of criticism, he violated not the principles of true taste. His sermons were, for the most part, doctrinal, yet always tending to practical results. His language had a noble bearing which made it a suitable vehicle of his noble thoughts. The accurate principles of sound logic ran through his performances, though its forms were not at all times visible. Ungodly men of cultivated minds listened to his sermons as to an *intellectual* treat. Religious men enjoyed them as affording a *spiritual* feast, as well as an intellectual treat. To the graces of oratory, Mr. Mercer made no pretensions, but there was an unction from the Holy One, that breathed from his spirit, and beamed from his sweet and heavenly eye, that enchained and animated the hearer, and thus more than supplied the absence of oratorical grace."

Mr. Mercer never preached without method, yet he seldom announced beforehand the arrangement of his sermons. As he advanced, his plan was gradually and clearly unfolded, well based upon the text, and happily connected and proportioned in its various parts. As the natural consequence of his general

---

* Brother W. B. Johnson, in the Southern Baptist Advocate.

method of preparing for the pulpit, (that is, of studying subjects rather than texts,) he would most frequently lay down some general doctrine or principle as naturally deducible from his text, and then proceed to illustrate it by strong and well defined arguments; occasionally, however, he would fall into the expository mode and follow out the leading ideas and clauses of the passage before him, in a kind of extended comment. His discourses were generally of a moderate length, varying from forty minutes to an hour. Seldom did he preach his hearers into a listless frame. Most generally would he leave them, (particularly on special subjects and important occasions,) regretting that he had not continued longer, and more especially, as it was so evident from what he had said, that the fountain of argument and illustration in his richly furnished mind was still deep and unexhausted. When excited and moving on through his subject with his full force, he seemed like a huge rock forcing its way through the compressed sides of a mountain chasm; he would not only clear away all the difficulties in his main track, but by the friction of his great mind, strike out thoughts upon incidental and collateral subjects, of much power and brightness, and which would supply the minds of the auditors with rich themes for after reflection. His power of amplification was not great; his words did not often flow down upon the people in a rushing torrent, but rather fell like a shower of massive golden apples. He never encumbered his topics with useless verbiage and vain repetitions: his language was plain, simple, appropriate and uncommonly compressed, each word seeming to occupy a suitable and important place, like a well-squared brick in a piece of solid masonry.

That peculiar feature of his mind which has already been so often alluded to, was very conspicuous in his pulpit efforts. He was, without controversy, one of the most *original* preachers of the age. His manner and his thoughts were in a peculiar sense his own; as has been well observed by another, "he tried to imitate no one, nor could any one imitate him with success." He had a suitable respect for the opinions of judicious expositors of the word of God; yet in the spirit of christian honesty and independence he dared to differ, if need be, from any or from all, thinking deeply for himself, and making every argument that he employed, pass through the alembic of his own mind. Few preachers in our country, of any denomination, have, through the uniform course of their ministry, brought into their discourses an equal amount of valuable and entertaining thought that might be regarded as the peculiar fruit of their own mental efforts.

To form a full estimate of Mr. Mercer's ability and worth as a preacher, it was necessary to have heard him often, and under various and dissimilar circumstances. There are some ministers who, on particular occasions and on special subjects, with ample time for preparation, will rise to an unusual elevation; when the average tenor of their discourses exhibits but little more than monotonous tameness and stinted mediocrity. Like a little stream, when swollen by a sudden shower, they will sometimes dash and roar; and like that stream, their ordinary flow is confined to a very shallow and narrow channel. Not so Mr. Mercer. His course was deep and wide. His preaching embraced a large scope of religious instruction, and exhibited a richness and variety quite above the common average. Long study and deep reflection had made him familiar with the great system of divine truth, and fixed in his mind innumerable scripture phrases and illustrations; whilst his regular and well-ordered habits of thought gave him, especially when roused, great command of his valuable resources. The word of Christ dwelt in him, indeed richly in all wisdom; and as a workman that needeth not to be ashamed, he was eminently qualified to divide out that word, its doctrines and its duties, its promises and its threatenings, its prophetic visions and its historical details, giving to every one his portion in due season. Many persons who had heard much of this eminent preacher, might, upon hearing him the first, the second and even the third time, experience a feeling of disappointment; but it would be like the disappointment of the traveller, who, for the first time, approaches the Mississippi, and happens to strike the stream at a point where the jutting banks and the impending forests hide half its current from the sight. "Is this the Father of Waters?" he might almost unconsciously exclaim; but a few hours journey along the banks would remove the sense of disappointment, and leave him satisfied that common fame had not exaggerated this natural wonder. So a sufficient acquaintance with Mr. Mercer would generally change disappointment into admiration, and justify the long established estimate which the public at large had placed upon his preaching.

Though he was judicious and entertaining upon almost every scriptural theme and felt it his duty to declare the *whole* counsel of God, yet there were some subjects upon which he dwelt with more frequency than others, and which afforded delightful scope for his peculiar powers. He delighted in contemplating the gospel as a scheme which *honored God and abased the creature.* Upon the majesty of the law, the exceeding sinfulness of sin, the amazing obligations of the sinner, and his total inability to rescue himself from his ruined and guilty state; the infinite virtue of the atonement, the uncontrolled sovereignty and glorious efficiency of divine grace, he was truly great. The cross of Christ was the fixed luminous centre of all his preaching. Planting his feet on Calvary as their immoveable resting place, he pointed his hearers back to the ancient and infrustrable designs of mercy, never afraid of the words, *eternal*, and *before the foundation of the world;* then traced out in a manner most clear and instructive the gradual developments of that mercy in the shadows of the Mosaic dispensation; then gazing at the hallowed ground on which he stood, with a flowing eye, and a full heart, and his noble powers roused to their full strength, would he portray with unequalled power, the fulfilment of type and prophecy and eternal counsel in the infinitely meritorious sufferings of the Son of God; thence would he advance to unfold the application of those sufferings in the subjugation of the sinner's heart by the word and the Spirit, his complete justification before God by the imputed righteousness of Christ, and the grand, certain and eternal results connected with faith in the Lord Jesus Christ. This was the general scope, the unvarying substance of his preaching. He did not of course unfold the whole system in any single discourse; but enough of it in every sermon, either in a doctrinal or practical form, to show to what school of theology he belonged. If he went off in his discussions to illustrate the various dependent and collateral themes of the gospel, (and this he often did,) the line of his argument was firmly bound to the great cardinal truths embraced in this system; he took not a single step in any direction in which he did not distinctly feel the drawing of the strong centre, and in which all other attentive minds could not feel the drawing. He was indeed eminently a gospel preacher. "How is Mr. Mercer?" said Dr. Staughton, to a gentleman from Georgia. "Well," was the answer. "He exerts great influence in that state," continued Dr. S. "His word is *law*," replied the other. "I am sure," said the Doctor, "it is *gospel*." And this, it may be safely said, would be the testimony of every intelligent, sound, and evangelical hearer.

Mr. Mercer's discourses generally made a distinct as well as lasting impression on the mind. They had form, weight, and tangibility. They were not like those smooth, pretty, impalpable, and evanescent things sometimes called sermons, which glide away without leaving any valuable impression upon the heart, or sentiment in the mind; but so to speak, they were well furnished with *hooks* and *handles* by which the people could take hold of them, and convert them to some lasting advantage. The noble fragments of many a sermon preached twenty, thirty, and forty years ago, are still floating in the memories of the people. There are some of our aged brethren whose minds recur with deep interest to a meeting of the Georgia Association, held long ago at Shiloh, when on Monday evening he delighted, melted, and enchained a congregation of three thousand or more, in delineating from a passage in the 12th chapter of Revelation, the trials and triumphs of the christian church. Amongst other things, the amazing power which the speaker gave to a short quotation from the Song of Solomon, in illustrating the *oneness* of the true church, is remembered with indelible distinctness—*there are threescore queens, and fourscore concubines, and virgins without number:* MY DOVE, MY UNDEFILED IS BUT ONE. The impression made by a discourse at Bethesda, on the *ten commandments*, which was listened to by a crowded assembly, is not yet forgotten: many intelligent professional men were present, and expressed at the close their astonishment at the profound knowledge which the speaker exhibited of the fundamental principles of law. His discourse at Washington, many years ago, on the Covenant, was a memorable effort: several of opposing sentiments, knowing what was to be the subject of discussion, carried with them their ink and paper to take notes of the sermon:—in the conclusion it was admitted that if he had not proved his doctrine, he had come nearer doing it, than had ever been done before. His sermon on Ezekiel's valley of dry bones, is still *visible* in the minds of some of his aged hearers; and also another from that sublime text, *Seek Him that maketh the seven Stars and Orion.*—Will the writer be pardoned for introducing in this connexion, in as brief a manner as possible, some of his own recollections of one of Mr. Mercer's sublime and noble efforts. He remembers hearing him preach at the meeting of the Savannah River Association at Barnwell Court House, South Carolina, in 1824. The text was a part of the 25th verse of the 1st chapter 1st Corinthians: "*The weakness of God is stronger than men.*" It was a passage admirably suited to the peculiar genius of the preacher; his mind happened at the time to be remarkably free and unbeclouded, whilst the feelings of his heart were in a very tender, devout, and propitious frame. He first illustrated what he supposed might be understood by the *weakness of God:* this he considered as referring mainly to the despised Gospel of a crucified Redeemer. He next considered in what the strength of men might be said to consist; for, said he, " the text seems to imply that men have some kind of strength with which the weakness of God is brought into conflict." He here enlarged, in a manner most powerful and convincing, upon the pride, ignorance, and deep-seated corruption of the human heart. He then proceeded to show how, by weak and insignificant means, the Lord thwarted the vain and proud designs of man, and how, especially by the application of gospel truth by the Spirit of God, the stubborn and rebellious heart was effectually and savingly subdued. It was a masterly effort of the human mind. His track was as clear as the noon. His simple and energetic language, his apt illustrations, and his invincible reasoning, rendered every thing visible. The audience could but have felt that they were in the hands of a master spirit, or rather in the hands of a glorious and almighty Sovereign, whose power was portrayed with such pungent and heart-searching strokes; and whilst their minds were led captive by the matchless argument, their feelings were evidently much affected by the holy fervor, the tender, sweet, and heavenly pathos of the venerable preacher.

Many such recollections* might be gathered up, and presented in illustration of the impressive character of Mr. Mercer's preaching. It is true, we have referred to some of his extraordinary discourses; but it may very naturally be inferred that an individual, who could in so many instances make himself remembered for twenty-five or fifty years, would be likely, in his ordinary ministrations, to present much which would leave deep traces upon the minds of his hearers; and this was eminently true of Mr. Mercer.

He depended more upon the plain and full exhibi-

---

* See Appendix, B.

tion of the various truths of the gospel to affect and subdue the sinner's heart, than upon direct and hortatory appeals; yet these appeals were not unfrequent; and sometimes they were urged with a pungency and power that rendered them irresistible. He ever aimed at blasting the vain and self-righteous hopes of the carnal heart, revealing its deep and abominable corruptions, that in its self-despair, and self-loathing, it might be prepared to welcome the consolations of the gospel. Those consolations he knew how to unfold to the weary and heavy laden, and with much of the tender, yearning, and weeping love of his divine Master, would he conduct them gently on to the fountain of life.

In illustration of the occasional power and terribleness of his appeals to the sinner, an incident might be related. He once preached from the text, *if any man love not the Lord Jesus Christ, let him be anathema, maranatha.* It happened that one of the most distinguished and gifted men in the country was present on the occasion, and was much impressed with the solemn discourse. "I could feel," said he, afterwards, "*the very curse of God running through my bones.*"

On experimental themes he was truly eminent. He had studied profoundly the workings of his own heart; noticed with great accuracy and attention the various religious exercises of the saints as recorded in the sacred scriptures, as well as many others whose instructive biography he had perused, or with whom he had formed a personal acquaintance; and he was thus prepared to accommodate himself with great readiness and success, to the spiritual necessities of believers in all the various stages of their christian experience. In his favored times, when dwelling on experimental subjects, there was a ripeness, a sweetness, a soul-engaging unction in his communications, which the writer remembers not to have witnessed in any other preacher. At such times, his words, mellowed by his own devout and tender affections, and freighted with the most appropriate and precious thoughts, would glide like heavenly oil into the hearts of his pious hearers, as it were, to the lowest depths, awakening in the bosom sentiments of holy tenderness and sweet delight. To the aged, way-worn, and afflicted pilgrim, these occasions were truly *transfiguration hours;* seasons when they were enabled, under the guidance of this skilful Master in Israel, to range "the land of Beulah," and climb "the delectable mountains."

Will the writer be pardoned for introducing here a rather amusing incident somewhat illustrative of what has just been said? It is presented in the language of Mr. Sherwood, who had it from Mr. Mercer's own lips. "An excellent Methodist brother who attended his preaching and was very fond of him, used frequently to express his approbation by a *hearty amen,* when any sentiment or expression pleased him, and these were very frequent. Mr. M. in private, kindly observed that he did not disapprove such expressions, if they were appropriate and welltimed; 'but you sometimes manifest your assent when the denunciations of God are made against the wicked,' &c. &c. This cooled his ardor for a season, and he was silent though restless. At last, when some rich doctrine of truth dropped from the preacher's lips, he exclaimed at the top of his voice, '*amen! rough at a venture.*' You may well conceive of the effect, both on the audience and speaker."

The record exhibited in the preceding pages of Mr. Mercer's religious sentiments, will justify the application to him of the term *strict Calvinist;* though perhaps the expression *high Calvinist* would convey a more correct idea of his doctrinal views in early days. Upon taking charge of the Index, in 1833, he thus defines himself:

"Its editor has nothing of which he can boast, *as though he did not receive it.* But *as of the ability which God giveth,* he is willing *to minister the manifold grace of God,* to the *building up* of the godly in Christ Jesus *on their most holy faith;* and to the convincing of the ungodly of their danger in sin; and leading them to the acknowledging of the truth as it is in Christ Jesus our Lord, and to faith, which is in him, that they may be saved. He is rather of the *old* than of the *new* school; and inclines to the *old fashioned* doctrine of *free grace,* as preached among the Baptists near half a century ago. Though he does not mean to quibble or criticise on mere modes of expression or shades of difference, where *the truth is not compromitted.* He does not fully receive all Mr. Fuller's views of the methods of divine mercy, yet is satisfied with his scheme (as now generally preached, when kept within its own bounds,) as leading to, and finally securing the same great and glorious results, as those of the most approved and (to use a common epithet,) *calvinistic* writers of his age."

In the early and middle part of Mr. Mercer's ministry, he devoted a large portion of his discourses to the doctrinal peculiarities of his faith, and not unfrequently glided off with considerable zeal, into matters of controversy; but in his declining years, his sermons assumed a more practical character, and were seldom directly controversial.

In prayer Mr. Mercer had a very pleasant and edifying gift. In this exercise he was not as fluent and copious as many; yet he was always appropriate, never tedious, adapted himself happily to circumstances and occasions; as in every thing else, was remarkably simple, generally fervent, and at times, surpassingly tender and affecting. His approaches to the throne of grace were always marked with great reverence and humility; he carried with him to this solemn duty exceedingly high thoughts of God, and low thoughts of himself; and seemed to lie, as it were, a little, sinful, dependent atom at the feet of the divine Majesty. His prayers were full of contrite confession and thankful praise; full of the merits and intercession of the God-man, Christ Jesus, and acknowledgments of entire and absolute dependence upon the aid of the Holy Spirit. He did not offer up, as many do, *preaching* prayers, but *praying* prayers. He prayed to God, and not to men. He did not seem to have any hackneyed form, either in the pulpit, the social prayer-meeting, or at the family altar; readily varying his expressions as feeling and occasion prompted; and he had fewer common-place and hereditary phrases in prayer, than almost any other man. His scriptural allusions were generally happy, sometimes remarkably so; and if there was less of the exact phraseology of the bible in his prayers than in those of some other ministers, yet the spirit and substance of scripture petitions were eminently there.

To the reader of the preceding pages it might seem superfluous to say that his piety was above the common standard. He was evidently a man of faith, and a man of prayer; deeply imbued with the principles of the gospel, habitually governed by religious principle. There seemed to be much uniformity in his religious feelings, (resulting in part, no doubt, from his equable, constitutional temperament;) he seldom rose to rapturous heights, and seldom, it is apprehended, fell into the hands of Giant Despair. He had humble thoughts of his best performances, exalted conceptions of the majesty of God; and ardent love for holiness and truth, a profound sense of the evil nature of sin, and of his own sin, as that which had greatly offended his Maker, and loaded with anguish the soul of the precious and adorable Lamb of God.

If the writer were, in a single sentence, to present the most distinct and prominent idea which he has of Mr. Mercer's piety, he would say, *there he is, a little child at the feet of the Saviour, tender, affectionate, humble, penitent, obedient and adoring; glorying in Christ as his wisdom, righteousness, sanctification and redemption, and looking with a simple faith, and a calm, serene hope for the mercy of our Lord Jesus Christ unto eternal life.*

The history of his heart, any farther than it has been developed by his long life of christian uprightness, pious labor, and disinterested zeal for the glory of God and the salvation of souls, must ever remain in a great measure, a secret to the world. He kept no diary in which he recorded from day to day the struggles between the flesh and the spirit which passed in his bosom, and the peculiar discipline by which he chastened his spirit into subjection to the will of God; nor did he dwell very freely in conversation or in his more public remarks, upon his own religious exercises. The knowledge we have of the lowly estimate which he formed of himself, would lead us to suppose that he saw but little in his own religious experience which, in his estimation, would be very important to others, or upon which, if recorded in a daily journal, he could look himself, in after days, with much satisfaction or profit. The chasm which is thus left in his religious history, will, no doubt, be a matter of regret to many; but still we should be thankful that so much of this good man still survives in a distinct and tangible shape for our instruction, reproof and comfort; and remember that after all, our heavenly Father well knows, even to an iota, how many fragments of the life and experience of his departed servants he will have use for in carrying forward his gracious designs of mercy and salvation.

It has already been said that Mr. Mercer had his faults. To deny this would be to claim for him something more than human. Yet it is believed that he was a careful observer of his own character, and that he judged of himself with greater strictness and severity, than most other persons would feel at liberty to do. "I think it has been told of him," (said Mr. Sturgis in his funeral discourse,) "that having heard something in himself spoken of by way of reprehension, he replied, 'If they knew as much of me as I know of myself, they would think worse than they do.'" He had naturally a rather high temper, as little as many persons would suspect it, a sudden flash of which would occasionally be seen through the grates of the strong prison in which he kept it guarded. His natural fondness and ability for the accumulation of property, would have betrayed him into covetousness, but for the influence of strong counteracting principles; and if the high estimation which he placed upon the good opinion of others could not be regarded as leaning to faultiness, it sometimes perhaps made him needlessly sensitive when censured by his brethren, or assailed by his enemies. He used sometimes to remark, "it is said that *peevishness* is one of the sins of old age; I feel that it is so with me, for I perceive that I am getting peevish as I am getting old." But as an illustration of that kind of *complacency* with which he looked upon the indulgence of this disposition, it might be stated that when at a certain time he spoke to a young ministering brother in rather a short and peevish manner, his generous soul had no rest until he went to the house of that brother, and made a meek and child-like acknowledgment of his error. "My own opinion," remarked Mr. Sturgis, in connexion with his observation quoted above, "however is, that what gave importance to any supposed or real indiscretion in him was, *that it was* HE." And this will probably be regarded by most as a very just remark. Whatever may have been the faults of Mr. Mercer, they were in general such as in ordinary men would not have excited much observation. Like a few small spots upon a snow-white robe, or an occasional knotty shrub and unseemly brier in the midst of an extensive and charming landscape, his errors gained their visibility and distinctness mainly from the great beauty and brightness with which they were surrounded.

It has also been said that he had his enemies. In some instances, their ungenerous attempts to disturb his peace and blast his fair name, was the source of the deepest distress that he was ever called to suffer on earth; yet on all such occasions, the dark clouds soon passed away, leaving the individual around whom for a time they had gathered, unscathed, upon the bright elevation which he had previously occupied, at the same time reflecting from their dark and angry folds as they receded, the useful and important moral, that a meek, christian spirit, secures the most honorable victory over evil, and that little is to be gained in the end by those who needlessly assail exalted worth. One thing is worthy of remark, that when malignity found occasion to assail him, it was generally through the medium of palpable falsehood, or by a disingenuous and prejudiced effort to give great importance to minor faults. What higher compliment could wickedness pay to virtue, unless it be that which was paid by Pilate to the spotless Son of God, "*I find no fault in this man.*"

The mental elevation, the distinguished piety, the ministerial excellence, which were combined in the character of Mr. Mercer, will in a great measure account for the extensive and wonderful influence which he exerted over the minds of men. Yet in connexion with these peculiar qualities, which so eminently prepared him to sway the opinions of others, there were other favoring circumstances, which must be taken into consideration. He lived long, and thus the authority of age and experience brought its appropriate, additional force. It must be remembered also that his ministerial relations were of a permanent character: from early youth he lived and labored upon the same field of action. Consequently the chain of his influence was not broken by frequent removals to new theatres of labor, where a new influence was to be created, and a new character in some sense to be formed. Though he sometimes changed the place of his immediate residence, yet he still retained his connexion with the same general organizations for pious and benevolent efforts, remained intimately associated for a long series of years with the same band of faithful fellow-laborers, and mingled, in at least his occasional ministrations, with the same mass of population, except as death and emigration effected their gradual changes. Thus he gained a prominent and well-established character amongst the churches and the people. He had time to make his mark. He had an opportunity for being fully known and appreciated. Multitudes grew up from youth to manhood, and even to comparative old age, under his ministry, and thus received his impress. The solid reputation which he had gradually secured for himself at home, was known far and wide, and opened a ready way before him, so that when he made his frequent and extensive excursions through the country, the people were everywhere prepared to receive him as one clothed with "the authority of a prophet." As he left them, having delivered his message from the Lord, they generally felt that "it was a true report that they had heard of him;" and there lingered behind a precious and lasting savor.

His connexion with the press for so many years, and the extensive circulation of many of his publications, especially the Cluster, which associated the name of Mercer with the sweet devotions of thousands, still tended to widen the influence of his opinions, and add to the authority of his name. Beside, he was, by the happy and well proportioned combination of his powers, and especially by the grace and providence of God, kept from most of those little follies, and wild eccentric flights, which oftentimes greatly impair, if not wholly destroy the influence of many otherwise shining and eminent men. How striking is the inspired sentiment of the wise man, "*dead flies cause the ointment of the apothecary to send forth a stinking savor; so doth a little folly him that is in reputation for wisdom and honor.*" There were very few *dead flies* in the composition of Mr. Mercer.

Finally, it must be borne in mind that Mr. Mercer's life was spent in the midst of one of the most densely populated regions of Georgia. From that region, a steady tide of emigration has for many years past been rolling out to numerous and far distant places; and wherever it has rolled, upon the opinions, the piety and the habits of thought which it has borne along, is to be seen more or less of the bright impress of the venerable Mercer. Thus by his exalted merit, his faithful services, his long life, his well-balanced character in connexion with propitious, providential allotments, was he enabled to gain an influence over the public mind, unequalled in the history of Southern Baptists, if not of the entire denomination in our country—an influence pure and bright and salutary, ranging in deep lines from the Savannah River, to the distant confines of Texas, nay, not altogether unfelt in many other remote regions of the land, and in distant heathen lands—an influence that, through the favoring grace of God, it may be confidently hoped will long survive to benefit mankind. Whilst the names of Bunyan, and Fuller, and Ryland, and Pearce of England; and of Baldwin, and Semple, and Furman of our own favored country shall be known and loved, so long will the name of JESSE MERCER be held in affectionate and sacred remembrance.

APPENDIX.

A

Memoranda of occasional remarks made by Mr. Mercer in his sermons, private conversation, &c.

"Whenever I see a professed Christian taking pleasure in sin, I cannot help fearing he may be a deceived soul; because the Scriptures expressly teach us that if any man be in Christ Jesus he is a new creature. Now if I were to see a hog taken very sick, and it should come very near dying, but all at once should be changed into a sheep, I could never expect to see that sheep take pleasure in wallowing in a mud hole, but would rather expect to find it in green pastures, or by the still waters."

"People sometimes say we make too much ado about the schisms which occur among the disciples of Christ, and the word is, 'let them alone, and they will all arrive at the same point at last.' But I cannot help thinking if it be true that we have all started right, and may all come out right, we are travelling more like a herd of cattle through a lane than any thing else. This is not like a company of horses in Pharaoh's chariot. This is not being all of one mind and one accord. This is not the peace and order of the gospel."

Referring to an article in the constitution of a certain association in which non-fellowship was declared against the benevolent institutions of the day, Mr. Mercer remarked, that, by the adoption of that article the anti-missionaries had not in the least affected us. It was evidently their intention, by that article, to establish themselves more firmly, and if possible to unsettle, or move the missionary brethren. "But," continued he, "the attempt has resulted precisely as would the effort of a man to move a ship from her moorings by pushing against her from a small boat; the small boat, we all know, would move and not the ship. So they in this have shifted their ground, while we remain where we were."

"There is a great difference," said he, "between an obedient and a disobedient christian. The one is like a sheep that remains near the fold, and sustained by proper food, and enjoying the shepherd's care, is kept in a fat and healthy condition; whilst the other is like a sheep that wanders far from the fold, through barren and unwholesome pastures, and amongst briers and thorns: at length, poor thing! it comes up weakly, and lank, and almost dead, its wool all torn off, and its skin dreadfully mangled."

In conversation about a preacher who had a little learning and was pretty full of conceits, he once made this remark. "He reminds me of a foolish dog I once heard of, that was in pursuit of a deer, but coming to a place where a fox had crossed the track, he left the deer and run after the fox; he had not followed the fox far, before he arrived at a spot where a rabbit had crossed; forthwith he leaves the fox and takes after the rabbit; and when the hunter came up, he had left the rabbit and was barking at a mouse-hole. Br. —— sometimes sets out after something valuable, but his folly drives him to the mouse-hole before he stops."

Speaking of persons interpreting the Scriptures, according to previously adopted creeds, he said, "they are like ship-builders, who first construct the frames of their vessels, and then employ the wedge, the screw, the lever, and every implement belonging to their craft to bring the other timbers to fit the frame so constructed. They will not hesitate to torture the text, make havoc of every principle of common sense, do violence to every canon of sober interpretation;—all this and more: their dogmas must be sustained, though truth be prostrated to the earth."

Of that spurious sort of liberality sometimes so highly extolled by professors of religion, he once remarked, "It is like a company of men setting out upon a journey. 'Come,' says one, (and perhaps he has less money than any one of the company,) 'let us all have one purse, let our expenses be paid out of the common stock.' It would be illiberal to do otherwise. In this way they that have but little fare as well as they that have much. So in regard to religious opinions. Let the denominations waive their differences, all commune together, and whatever inconsistencies are found to exist amongst them, are chargeable to the whole; and they that have the least of truth on their side, are the most clamorous for liberality."

He was once preaching from Heb. 6: 1. His main object was to impress on Christians the importance of aiming at high attainments and going on to perfection. "Unless we aim at a high mark," said Mr. Mercer, "we shall never attain to eminence, as we shall not be likely to rise higher than our aim. Some Christians are afraid to aim high. Alas! they have not as much courage as a chicken. As I was sitting in my piazza one pleasant evening last summer, my attention was drawn towards the fowls as they were going to their rest. One little chicken particularly attracted my notice. He fixed his eye upon a limb pretty high up a certain tree, and made an ineffectual effort to gain it. He then took another position and repeated his effort to reach the limb, but again was unsuccessful. Still, in no wise discouraged, he kept his eye upon the limb first chosen, and tried, and tried, and tried again; but to no purpose. Six times he tried and failed, but the *seventh* time he reached the limb.

My brethren, aim high—press on to perfection—try to have as much courage and perseverance as that little chicken."

"Christ to many is as a *root out of dry ground*. In passing through a dry and sandy region, you have noticed now and then a root connected with a stinted scrubby tree, naked and exposed. For the want of moisture and the necessary richness of soil, it exhibits a very meagre growth—it is crooked and knotty, a very unseemly object to the eye: such a deformed, unseemly, and worthless thing is Christ to the carnal mind."

"Shall I tell you how the fisherman secures the monster of the deep? He rows his little boat along side the huge fish, poises his barbed iron, takes sure aim, and hurls it at his prey. The little instrument has found its way to a sure place, and remains immoveable. The fisherman now gives rope. Off darts the wounded leviathan, and in his rage and pain lashes furiously the great deep. But the barbed iron is there, and every successive struggle leaves him weaker and weaker, until at last he yields himself up a vanquished captive, and is now easily managed as a helpless, harmless thing. Thus God by his Spirit, fixes his truth in the heart of the proud, stubborn sinner; he resists, and flounders, and hastens off—but the truth is there—a deep and sure wound is inflicted; by degrees the strength of his rebellion is overcome, he becomes weary of sinning and wandering, and at last yields himself up a willing and joyful captive to the cords of divine love and grace."

"Take another figure. See how the farmer tames that wild ox. He throws a strong rope upon his head and binds him to a tree. The animal resists and rages. But his strength and fury are unavailing; his violent and long repeated struggles to escape at last exhaust him; his savage nature yields; and finally he becomes entirely subdued and tamed, *and a little child may lead him.* So the Lord binds his grace and his truth upon the wild unsubdued sinner: his proud resistance is gradually overcome, and at last we see him a meek and gentle lamb. Thus the gospel which men pronounce weak and foolish accomplishes its blessed work, and it is seen that *the weakness of God is stronger than men.*"

"When a man professes himself converted to God, and the first step he takes is in error, what is to be thought? Is he converted? Converted he may be to religion, but it is a question whether he is converted to God. I think the Lord is doing a good work here, but it appears to me very much like a *barn-floor*, when the wheat is in the short straw and chaff, much more bulky than valuable."

When he would dissuade his brethren from projects, which required pecuniary means beyond what they had in hand, he would often say, "*let us get the fodder before we buy the horse.*"

"I recollect to have heard him (says a friend) once quote John 5: 19. 'For what things soever he (the Father) doeth, these also the Son doeth likewise.' Now said he, a boy sees his father make a plough; he falls to work and makes a plough also; but lo! there are two *ploughs*. Not so with the work of the Father and the Son. The Father makes the world; the Son does the same work, he makes the world too; there is but one result—*one world*. If God made the world, and the Son made the world, who can resist the conclusion that the Son is God?"

In preaching the funeral sermon of a pious, and venerable minister, he made the following remark: " Ministers are God's medicines for the people. When the physician begins to gather up his medicines and put them in his saddle-bags, preparatory to his departure, the patient begins to feel that his case is desperate: so when God gathers up his medicines—takes away his faithful ministers—it looks as though the condition of the people is becoming desperate."

B

Recollections of one of Mr. Mercer's Sermons, furnished the Biographer by the REV. W. H. STOKES.

Hancock Co., Dec. 19, 1843.

"DEAR BROTHER MALLARY,

I send you the following recollections of a sermon delivered by Father Mercer at Clark's Station, Wilkes Co., in the summer of 1837, from James 4: 12. 'There is one lawgiver who is able to save and to destroy.' At this distance of time, I cannot of course recollect many of the precise expressions, but I will try to present some of the thoughts advanced in that discourse.

" The venerable preacher remarked in his introduction, that God, whom we worship, is a being of infinite perfections. By his omnipotence he has produced all orders of existence, and by the same perfection of his character, exercised in connexion with infinite wisdom and goodness, he governs all that he has made. It was not his purpose, however, to notice the various instances in which the truth of this remark would appear, but to invite the attention of his hearers to some few of the prerogatives of this One Lawgiver. And

" I. It was in his power *to save*. That his hearers might understand the whole truth upon this subject, it was necessary that they should learn to think of the infinite Jehovah as the Moral Ruler of the Universe; or, in the language of the text, as the ' One Lawgiver' to the whole of his rational creation. ' But,' he added, ' you are not to suppose this great Sovereign could have given, with equal honor to himself, and equal safety to his subjects, one set of laws as well as another. This would have been to deny himself. God is infinitely *holy* as well as infinitely powerful, wise and good. A law that was unholy, or destitute of goodness, would have been unseemly, as coming from infinite purity, and therefore, unfit to guard the interests of a perfectly holy throne, and to secure the well-being of those upon whom it was to operate. No law, but one holy, just and good, was adequate to the purposes of presenting the claims of the 'Lawgiver,' or, of exhibiting the duties and obligations of his subjects.

"'Against such a law as this,' said Father M., in a tone peculiarly his own, 'we have all sinned. And it is written, *Cursed is every one that continueth not in all things written in the book of the law to do them*. A grievous curse rests upon the head of the sinner, because he is found guilty of a most grievous offence. He has rebelled against infinite majesty, and in that rebellion trampled upon the best possible law. And it would seem, nothing but hell could be the portion of one guilty of such presumptuous wrong-doing! but O surprising grace! the Lawgiver has power to save, and to save to the uttermost all that come unto him.'

"'It may be worth while,' he continued, 'for us to ascertain as far as we can, the grounds upon which this power is exercised. And in the first place, it is not by a repeal of the law. This stands for ever the same. Secondly, it is not by a modification of the law— none of its claims are waived, none of its rigors are softened. But it is because the law has been magnified and made honorable by the Son of God. By his glorious atonement, the life of the sinner may be spared and the throne of justice remain untarnished. *Him hath God set forth*, not only in the view of the world, but in view of the whole universe, *to be a propitiation through faith in his blood, to declare his righteousness for the remission of sins that are past through the forbearance of God*. According to this measure of moral government, God can be just and the justifier of him that believeth in Jesus.'

"[Here was given such a view of the nature and ends of the atonement, as nearly entranced us all. For myself, though no enthusiast on such occasions, it was with difficulty I could sit still, or refrain from shouting aloud. Not that the old gentleman was so eloquent, as some would call it, or that he was stormy; but on account of the majesty of his thoughts. I remarked to a brother at the close, that every passage in that discourse seemed as heavy as a mountain.]

"Having disposed of the first division of his discourse he proceeded in the second place to say,

"'II. The Lawgiver hath power *to destroy*. This is not a derived power. It proceeds directly from the essential nature of him who wields it. It is not a power assumed arbitrarily. Nor is it ever exerted without the best possible reason. We have heard of the *wrath* of God, and of his *indignation;* but these are figurative expressions. No vengeful, no vindictive feelings, in the strict acceptation of these terms, ever occupied the divine mind. The sinner dies—it is the legitimate result of law. *The wages of sin is death*.

'The law gives sin its damning power.'

"'He who enacts a law and makes it binding must, of course, have power to connect a penalty with such law. And we should naturally expect, in such a case, the penalty to exhibit the importance of the law, and the dignity of the source whence it came. The

Most High, in establishing the government of which we have been speaking, certainly acted a part worthy of himself, set up an institution, so to speak, free from all the imperfections which attach to things merely human, and for the support of this institution all the perfections of his nature were solemnly pledged. In order then to present his throne as worthy the allegiance of all loyal subjects, he must punish transgressors. He has power to punish them and, *he will punish them.*

"'You perceive then,' said the preacher, 'according to the nature of law and government, that God has power to destroy the sinner, to cast both body and soul into hell. But you flatter yourselves that he never will so destroy. How strangely you reason! Will a holy God prove unjust? Does not every well-arranged government pledge itself to the lovers of good order to punish the rebellious? And shall the government of the infinite God be less jealous of its dignity and honor than any other? Let not the sinner deceive himself. The fruit of his own doings will most certainly be given him.

"'But the power in question has been exercised. Fallen spirits feel at this moment the truth of this remark. Every pang ever felt in hell is woful proof of its truth. Dives, who may be regarded as the representation of all thoughtless, reckless sinners, proves it by his piteous yet fruitless wailings. Look at the divine procedure towards the old world. Look at the destruction of Sodom and Gomorrah. Korah and his company are slain. Ananias and Sapphira are stricken dead. The sword of justice is grasped by the hand of Omnipotence. The Lord JEHOVAH has *power to destroy.*'

"In some such strain did that venerable man of God proceed for some fifty minutes. I regard the whole performance as one of his most masterly efforts."

The following Obituary Notice of Mrs. Mercer was originally published in the Index; but believing that it will be generally acceptable to the readers of this volume, the Biographer has thought proper to insert it without abridgment.

"*Bro. Stokes;* Your readers have seen in the Index, a notice of the death of my dear wife, and may have wondered why no accompanying obituary appeared. My reason for this is, that I have thought for some time, that *long* publications of this kind are very useless things, because *seldom read;* and the reason of this is, first, that the deceased are little known, and for this cause, if no other, have not sufficient estimation abroad, to command attention beyond the little circle of their relatives and personal acquaintances. And secondly, and more particularly, because of the matter of those notices. The writers of obituary articles are apt to indulge feelings, which lead them to swell their memoirs with the minutia and particulars of the last illness and death of their deceased friends, which, though they may affect the hearts of the immediate connexions, have no interest for general readers.

"However, as my wife was extensively known, and by many, highly esteemed, I suppose it is due to them, and to her memory, to say something more particularly in reference to her life and death.

APPENDIX. 437

I therefore request you to give a place in your columns to the following memoir of her, and, I presume, you will oblige many of her friends and acquaintances abroad, but especially her bereaved husband, and your companion in a lamentable and distressing widowerhood.

"Washington, June 24, 1841."
'JESSE MERCER."

"NANCY MERCER, the subject of this notice, was born in Virginia, of respectable parents, on the 30th of October, 1772. Her father, Mr. John Mills, emigrated to this State soon after the close of the Revolutionary war, and settled on Little River, in this county, where he raised his daughter in the style and education of those times. Her mother was a pious and beloved member of the Baptist Church at Ebenezer, and taught her in the way of salvation; to respect religion and religious people, especially ministers of the gospel. She was married to Capt. A. Simons, February 8th, 1798. By this connexion she was rushed into all sorts of company. Mr. S. was a man of wealth and of the world; had a peculiar faculty for the acquisition of property. This he did very much by trading, which drew about him every class of men; besides, he took great pleasure in having about him gentlemen of honorable name and worldly pursuits. Mrs. S. in this way was often placed in the society of all kinds and conditions of men, which might suit the taste and convenience, or serve the interest of her husband. And although such were not the companions of her choice, yet she was always, and under all circumstances, ready to appear and serve, and on all occasions acquitted herself with pleasure to the company, honor to her husband, and respect to herself. In this condition she lived for many years, in the midst of affluence and worldly splendor; but she was not satisfied. In retirement, she sought for better joys—joys which would satisfy the desire of an immortal spirit, which she found not in the rounds of worldly pleasure. She loved to attend on the preaching of the gospel of salvation, and hence she was uniformly an attendant at all the places of preaching within a reasonable distance. Mr. S. too, was very polite and accommodating to her in this respect; often attended with her, and for her gratification invited ministers home with them; in whose company and conversation she seemed to take a peculiar pleasure. It was in those days she became the subject of deep solicitude and anxious concern about eternal realities. She found her soul was lost in sin, and she knew not how it was to be saved. She betook herself to reading, meditation and prayer, and sought to satisfy her conscience by tears of penitence. And for a while, at times, she was encouraged to hope she would be accepted for her own righteousness. But this refuge failed her, because of her short comings, and the imperfection of all her best performances. About this time she heard a minister, in whom she placed great confidence, say in preaching, "that he did not believe any one would ever obtain hope in Christ, till he acknowleged the justice of God in his condemnation.' Then, thought she. 'I shall never be converted; for I can never acknowledge that.' But it was not long before she was so exercised about the evil of her heart, as the seat of all her vile affections and wandering thoughts, and of the evil nature of sin, that she soon came to the full and free acknowledgment of what she had thought impossible. Under this conviction she knew not what to do. But in her distress her mind was turned to Christ crucified, as the only way by which a condemned sinner could be justified and saved. And by hearing and reading the word of God, and the reference of sundry appropriate promises to her case, she was gradually brought to exercise hope, and to have some joy and peace in believing. But this was interrupted by fears lest she might be deceived, which gave her excessive distress. She was called to a new source of trouble about this time, by the death of her husband, by which she was thrown into very afflictive and trying circumstances. These, added to those which related to her soul's concerns had well nigh overpowered her, and caused her to sink beneath the surges of mental grief and worldly trouble. But in her great distress she cried unto God, and made supplication to the widow's Judge, and found relief from David's soliloquy to his soul in trouble, which came to her recollection, as if some one had suggested it,—'*Hope thou in God.*' This turned her mind's eye to God, as 'the refuge and strength of the needy and oppressed in time of trouble,' and comforted and sustained *her* sinking soul for a while at least.

" Owing to the death and removal of many of her social and intimate friends in her neighborhood, she determined to remove to Washington, where her civil and religious privileges might be increased. Here she took great interest in entertaining those ministers who came to town, or were journeying by. These always found a sure and comfortable sojournment with her. From these and the ministry of the Word, on which she constantly waited, she sought food and comfort for her troubled soul ; for she was still the subject of much doubt and uncertainty in reference to her hope of salvation. Her fears, lest she might be deceived, often prevailed and filled her with deep distress.

" On the 11th of December, 1827, she was married to him, who is now bereaved by her lamented death. This connexion gave her improved opportunities of attending on the ministry of the gospel, and of conversation on the rich provisions of mercy in Christ for those who were ready to perish ; by which her faith became strengthened and her hope *so* confirmed, that in July, 1828, she united with the Baptist Church of Christ in this place, and was baptized into Jesus Christ, thereby *putting on Christ* according to the Scripture institution of that holy ordinance. In the enjoyment of the blessings of this union, and in honor of this profession, made before many witnesses, she lived until death.

" But I should do injustice to her memory, if I were not to say something more of her character, at least in a few particulars. I notice the following :

"*As a woman*—she possessed a noble spirit ; was high-minded and generous—candid, open and free in the expression of her sentiments ; having an unusual share of moral courage ; was very jealous for her good standing with her friends and brethren ; rather severe in her censures, but easily conciliated when the least advances were made by the adverse party ; liberal *to profusion ;* besides her own relatives and the industrious poor around her, and those who were brought to her knowledge as such, those engaged in building places of worship in the country around—they who have held subscriptions, or made collections for religious or benevolent purposes; several ministers who devoted themselves wholly to the work of the ministry, while their families were left in suffering circumstances, and many others could, *if living*, rise up and testify to the truth of the above statement.

" *As a wife*—she was fondly affectionate, ever dutiful, and happy to please.

" *As a house-wife*—she was industrious, neat and clean. Her house and household were always kept in an arrangement of the first order—every thing was managed with the most *noiseless* dexterity—her beds were well furnished, and free from those annoyances, which often prevent weary men from their desired rest—her table was ever crowned with plenty, without luxury—she was always affable and polite to her friends and sojourners, it being her delight to render all happy and free in her presence. All this is *recorded* in the knowledge and *embalmed* in the memory of many, very many friends, brethren and ministers, who have turned in and partook of the hospitalities of her house, if it were but for a night.

" *As a Christian Professor*—she was pious, prayerful, and orderly—she was a lover of the household of God, and of the gospel preached there—she was of a discriminating mind in hearing, and enjoyed that doctrine most which gave the *most* honor to God in the salvation of sinful men—but still *she was a weak believer*. Her sense of the holiness of God and of the whole plan of the gospel, contrasted with her sinfulness, rendered her the subject of prevailing fears and doubts, as to her acceptance. At times she was able to rejoice in hope through the precious and appropriate promises of the gospel, suited to her case. It may be said of her, that most of her religious life-time, she *was subject to bondage*, through the fear of non-acceptance on account of her unworthiness and sinful infirmities.

" In her last illness, which was long and trying, no particular change was apparently effected in the character of her religious feelings. While she was capable of expressing her desires, or exercising her affections, it was evident that they lay on the same objects of pious regard, which had for a long time engaged her undivided love.

" I presume, bro. Stokes, as your readers have known for a long time back, that she was in a very distressed state of affliction, so that I could not think of leaving her, it will be quite gratifying, at least to some of them, to be somewhat informed of the case. I therefore yield to this persuasion, and give it as follows :

" In the first week of May, 1833, she was stricken with palsy in the entire right side, so that she was prostrate for some time. From this she gradually recovered, so as to be able to walk about the house and yard, and with help into the garden. She could attend preaching (which was her chief delight) and enjoy the company of her friends. But in the first week of May, 1839, (which is somewhat remarkable,) she was stricken in her left side, by which she was aid in bed *an entire paralytic*. From this she recovered so as to sit up, and for a while to *feed* herself; but even this last use of herself soon declined, and she remained unable to walk a step, or even stand alone to the day of her death. But this is not the most *sad part* of this *tale of wo*. Soon after her last attack, symptoms of mental disorder evidently appeared, which gradually increased to an entire state of derangement. Understanding was darkened. Imagination was greatly excited, and assumed the entire control of reason and judgment. At times, she was calm and half rational, anon more of *an idiot* than a maniac, but most of her time she was *perfectly lost* to herself and all around her. Her ideas were the most wild and disorderly—her desires, not only unreasonable, but impossible to be gratified—and *so* for hours—nay, for days and weeks *at intervals;* she would cry for help, or relief in the same case, or wandering from one case to another of the same sort, in the most delirious and distressing degree. Oh! my dear brother, you, nor any mortal on earth, can conceive what that dear creature suffered in those seasons of mental anguish and bewilderment. Those times of extreme agitation and grief continued to increase both in frequency and violence, till it was pleasing to God to interfere, *mercifully*, though *severely*, by a stroke of his hand in another way, which acted on the surges of her tempest-tossed spirit, as the command of Christ on the winds and seas, and all her agitations sunk down into a perfect calm.

"On Sunday, the 16th of last month, about mid-day, she had an *apoplectic* turn, which laid her *senseless* and *speechless* for some time, and from which she slowly recovered through the afternoon. She spent the night following pretty much as usual, in a very restless and distressed condition. Towards day, she fell asleep, and awoke up the next morning somewhat composed, and continued so until the turn of the day, when she became unusually sleepy, and was put to bed at an earlier hour on account of it; and it was said by those who sat with her, that she never moved all night. On Tuesday morning I inquired of her if she was easy and free from pain; and she said 'yes.' I asked, do you want any thing, and she said 'no.' She seemed perfectly composed; and the sisters with her were of opinion that she was entirely at herself, and if she could talk she would manifest it; but by this time she could speak scarcely above her breath, or more than *yes* or *no*. I was extremely anxious to know how she felt, in view of her future state, and asking her several questions, so as to ascertain that she understood me; I said 'Nancy, my dear wife, how do you *feel*, are you *satisfied* that it will go well with you for eternity?' and she said 'no.' I replied, why! do you not love the Lord? and her eyes filling with tears, she said '*I hope I do.*' I repeated, 'I love them that love me,' and left her. In the afternoon, I again conversed with her, and found that understanding still held its place in her mind, when I said,—
'How do you *now feel*, in reference to another world, do you think you will be happy there?' and she readily replied 'yes.' I added, 'do you love the Lord?' and she said, '*I am sure of that.*' So far as I know, these were the last words she ever spake, except *yes*, or *no*, to some trivial questions asked her. On Wednesday morning she assumed the appearance of one in sound sleep. Her eyes were fast closed, and her breathing hard. In this state she continued until Friday night, when a change took place, which notified us that

her departure was nigh. Her dying strife was *so gentle* as not to awake her. At forty-five minutes after ten o'clock, her spirit was permitted to leave its tenement of clay without rending it, and fly to its long-sought rest.

> 'This earth is affected no more,
>   With sickness, or shaken with pain:
> The war in the members is o'er,
>   And never shall vex her again.
>
> 'No anger henceforward, or shame,
>   Shall *redden* this innocent clay;
> Extinct is the animal flame,
>   And *passion* is vanished away.'

" *The end of the righteous is peace.*"

D

Mr. Mercer's Opinions on various subjects connected with Church Discipline, &c.

Mr. Mercer's opinions respecting matters pertaining to church order, associational jurisdiction, and other kindred subjects, were so much valued, and so often sought, that many would no doubt consider a volume claiming to be any thing like a full Biography of this eminent man, as radically defective, that did not contain some record of these opinions. The writer has therefore thought proper to present in the appendix, some of his views upon these subjects; believing that though this portion of the work may not be as interesting to the general reader as other parts, yet that there are some who will consult it with much interest, and great advantage. If the reader is not prepared to sanction every opinion of Mr. Mercer's, which is here presented, he cannot fail of finding much that will commend itself to his judgment as judicious, solid, and useful.

Discipline.

(From a Circular Letter published in the Minutes of the Ga. Association, 1806.)

" That you may be able in this declining day, to possess your vessels in sanctification and honor before him, who has called you into his marvellous light, and in that light shine before others to his praise; we would awaken you to, and exhort you to be promptly active in the execution of discipline—*discipline*, without which there can be no union, order, peace or fellowship in the church; no, nor church itself—*discipline*, which, *in its right use*, is the church's ecclesiastical *life*—*bond* of union and peace—*spring* of order and fellowship—and great *source* of harmony and love.

"To this important duty and privilege, God opens the ear. Job 36:10. And commands it to be sealed among his disciples. Isa. 8:16. 61:4. The prophet Malachi, and John the Baptist, show that Christ, in the exercise of this office, would both purge and scourge the wicked from among the righteous, so that a clear distinction should be made and perpetuated between the godly and ungodly, the chaff and the wheat. Mal. 3:1. to the 6, 16, 17, 18. Math. 3:10 and 12. And Christ discovered both the authority and indispensability of this duty, when he made a scourge of small cords and *drove* the wicked out of his father's house John 2:15. Due attention to this rule will lend to prosperity, peace and pleasure. Job 36:11. Isa. 48:18. Gal. 6:16. But the neglect thereof is invariably chastised with *declension* and *destruction*. Luke 19:42. Gal. 5:13, to the 17, also read 2d and 3d chapter of Revelation.

"Dear brethren, in addressing you on this subject, we shall use plainness of speech, and in a simple style, place before you a few very plain truths. Gospel discipline involves two very important duties equally indispensable.

"The *first*, is that which each member should discharge towards himself. The *second*, is that which relates to the whole body. These may be likewise subdivided.

"The *former* includes, first, That restraint which a christian, *when right with God*, places on the passions and propensities of the *carnal* heart, by which he subdues and maintains the victory over them; and secondly, that government which he exercises over the members of his body, by which he sanctifies them for, and employs them in, the service of God.

"The *latter* embraces, first, that line of duty to be pursued in case of *private* or *personal* offence; and secondly, that to be adopted in case of *public* and *atrocious* crimes. *To which we attend in order.*

"And *first*, to discipline the heart, diligence is enjoined, Prov. 4:23. 2 Pet. 1:5—10, to show that it is a duty to be performed only by promptness and perseverance. It includes three things: First, the detecting and crucifying all improper passions, or desires, that is, all which on examination, (and none should pass without it,) shall be found contrary to the holiness, and incapable of working the glory of God. Luke 9:55. Gal. 5:24. Heb. 3:12. Secondly, the guarding and restraining those affections, which in themselves are lawful, but are capable of excess, for *virtuous*, become *vicious* desires in the extreme. Eph. 4:26. Col. 3:5. And thirdly, the promoting and pursuing all *gracious* emotions, as leading into the knowledge and service of God. Psa. 19:14. 1 Cor. 14:1. Eph. 3:16—19. 4:22—24

"Secondly: Your bodies are the *members* of Christ, and temples for the Holy Ghost. 1 Cor. 6:15. 19. Your whole deportment, therefore, should correspond with this consideration; and all the members of the body be *presented* as living sacrifices to God, and solely employed in his service: *or, as a modern poet teaches:*

> 'A cov'nant with your *eyes* be made;
> Your *words* be few, or fitly said,
> And season'd well with grace;
> Be *deaf*, or only hear aright;
> Your *footsteps* planted in the light,
> To run the Christian race.

Your *hands* be pure and rais'd to God;
Your taste delighted with his word;
Be every *member* his;
Delight to *smell* his rich perfume,
Which balms the air—will death o'ercome,
And adds new charms to bliss.'

"To be able to decide correctly on the affections of the heart, or the *right use* of the members of the body, it will be incumbent to cultivate an acquaintance with the laws of nature, grace, and providence; by which the natural, spiritual, and moral fitness of things will appear; so that you may approve the things which are excellent, and be without offence till the day of Christ. Phil. 1 : 9, 10, 11.

" The second part of discipline teaches the rules of procedure in cases of *public* or *private* offence; which should be pursued with great exactness, without partiality or hypocrisy.

" And first, *in case of private offence.* Be sure to follow precisely the directions of Christ given in Matt. 18 : 15, 16, 17. Taking especial care that you do not make that *public* which is, and should be kept *private*, or that you do not make yourselves guilty, in conversing on *private* subjects to indifferent persons, thereby becoming the *sowers* of discord, or *idle, mischievous* tale-bearers so offensive to God, and destructive of human happiness. Lev. 19 : 16. Prov. 11 : 13. 18 : 8. 20 : 19. 25 : 9, 10. 26 : 21, 22. This rule is particularly binding on the *offended*, commanding him to immediate *conciliatory* measures: but let not the *offender* think himself secure in idleness, nor carelessly wait for his grieved brother to come and deal with him; but let him attend to the counterpart of this rule in Matt. 5 : 23 to the 26, which shows it to be the duty equally of the *offender* to go and be active in the adjustment of all differences. *The sooner the better.* Rom. 12 : 10, 11.

" But secondly, *in case of public and scandalous sins.* The first step to be taken is to reprove, admonish, and in a *christian spirit*, endeavor to reclaim the apostate brother from the error of his ways. Lev. 19 : 17. Gal. 6 : 1, 2. Eph. 5 : 11. 2 Thes. 3 : 15. 1 Tim. 5 : 20. Heb. 12 : 13, 14, 15. James 5 : 10, 20. This duty we fear is very much neglected from some cause—the want of zeal—or perhaps from a prevailing notion that it would be improper to heal a *public offence*, by a *private conversation:* but however improper this might be, we conceive it would be *highly proper* to heal a *public offender* by any means the gospel directs. The design however of such reproof, &c., is not to cure the *offence*, but *him* who gave it; that *he* may be prepared to remove the *offence* in that way the gospel requires. But should he fail to be reclaimed by this measure, and not come to the church to meet, and in the best manner in his power, atone for his disorders; then it will be the duty of whoever is concerned in the case, when the church is setting in her official capacity, to bring such person before her bar, or make report of the case to her, whose duty it will be to *call for*, and reckon with him according to Matt. 18 : 24 and 31. But *in case of gross enormity*, under which the cause of God and the church particularly suffers, it may be expedient to proceed more promptly according to the case recorded in 1 Cor. 5th chap., which seems to have been done without sending for, or attending to the delinquent in any way.

"The great object of discipline is *holiness to the Lord*. With a view to *ecclesiastical* holiness, it commences cautiously in the reception of members; and ends gloriously in consummating them in the beauties of *practical* holiness. In receiving persons *carelessly*, or at the instance of *passion*, you may corrupt the church, dishonor God, and involve yourselves in much distress, confusion, and sin. Be careful, therefore, to receive none but those to whom the gospel gives a right; Matt. 18 : 3. 5. Acts 5 : 13, 14. 1 Cor. 6 : 17. That the church may be *visibly* what it is *really*, THE PILLAR AND GROUND OF THE TRUTH, and be presented a *chaste* virgin to Christ. 1 Tim. 3 : 15. 2 Cor. 11 : 2. But we are aware that discipline may be so managed as to defeat its own design, and instead of unity and peace, produce divisions and strife. A government by majority *naturally* tending *in important matters*, to make parties, and breed confusion, should be studiously avoided. Rather be of the same mind and judgment; espouse the cause of the weak, or be invariably on the part of the aggrieved, whether *major* or *minor;* and let UNANIMITY be the bond of your peace. Psa. 133 : 1. 1 Cor. 1 : 10, 11. 13. Eph. 4 : 2."

Private Labors should generally precede Church action.

(From the Circular of the Georgia Association for 1816.)

"It has been a custom pretty widely practised, to bring all cases of a public and offensive character, whether *facts* or *reports, first* before the church, that they might be met and treated in a manner correspondent with their general and infectious consequences. *This rule we think exceptionable.*

"1st. Because it is *defective :* for while it provides a remedy of the public *effects*, it proposes no means for the removal of the *cause* of offence.

"2d. It fosters *neglect :* 'Tis founded on the suspension of personal intercourse, and consequently on the suspension of brotherly love and christian care.—The duty commanded by Paul and James to '*convert* and *restore* such an one,' is totally neglected and set aside by this rule. What the Apostles make to be the proper burden and duty of an individual, is hereby thrown on the church, while the members content themselves individually, to be of the number who live in error.

"Perhaps it may be asked, shall we *all* go? Indeed, brethren, that might be the better state of the case. For admit '*such an one*' should be among you; and you *all, one by one,* should make him a visit, 'in the spirit of meekness,' on that account, in the course of a few weeks, would not his heart be broken for his sin? or would he not be left without excuse? And would not that be much better than to pass him by, or treat him with neglect? Surely you will answer, *it would be better.*

"3d. It is *uncharitable :* it is *so* distant—*so* cold—*so* unfriendly, that it is more likely to disgust than reclaim—to harden than soften—to exclude than restore. But,

"4th. It promotes *tale-bearing*. In the spirit of the rule contested, you feel at liberty to speak freely of such cases among your selves, and even to others; by which you become '*tatlers, whisperers*,' and the *sowers* of *discord*, rather than '*peace-makers*.' We need not tell you that in modern, as well as in ancient times, there are many who say, '*report* and we will report it.'—That many *false* and *virulent* tales are often circulated, with celerity, to ruin the characters, and hinder the usefulness of the *best* among men. By the rule in question, you may become the abettors, and forward the designs of the most cruel and inveterate men.

* * * * * *

"Exclusion should never be regarded as the result of our endeavors. Every idea of union—the best feelings of the heart, recoil at the shocking thought. 'Tis the resort of despair—the dreadful alternative in case of incorrigibleness, like the amputation of a mortal limb, to save the body from its ruinous consequences.

"There are, however, a few cases which justify and require a resort to this severe measure, with much less ceremony than others: as when a man brought before the church for some notorious crime, makes great pretensions to humility and godly sorrow; and being forgiven, goes out and in similar cases, carries himself with ingratitude and hardness of heart towards his brethren, or in any other way proves his acknowledgments before the church to have been *hypocritical*, he may be presented to the church without any personal regard shown him, because he has destroyed all confidence in himself. As suggested in Matt. 18 : 23, to the end. Also when a *hypocrite* among you does what proves him *so*, like Simon Magus, 'in the gall of bitterness and bonds of iniquity,' he may be cut off without any endeavors to reclaim him, because there is nothing, *properly*, to which he can be reclaimed.

"Likewise, when a man forms any illicit connexion, or commits offences which prolong their effects, and which no sudden concessions can remedy; as in the case of the incestuous man, he should without waste of time be 'delivered to Satan for the destruction of the flesh,' and that his reformation and the proofs of it might be made manifest."

Are all cases of discipline to be managed and settled by Matt. 18 : 15—17 ?

"To this question we answer no, because other scriptures require a different treatment. It is evident as there are different causes of offence, so there must be a variation of management and termination. The above rule, we conceive, provides only for personal and entirely private offences; or cases which lie alone between two brethren. For why should secrecy be enjoined in a case, which is known openly? Here private intercourse is enjoined in the first step, and only to be made public as the case might require. And we are of opinion, that if this rule was strictly regarded in all such offences, many of those cases would be nipped in the bud, or healed in the first intention, which, for the want of it, break the peace, and distract our churches with confusion and party strife. But we think it would be manifestly for the dishonor of Christ and contempt of religion, to attempt to settle cases of public and scandalous offences by this rule. However, we are fully persuaded that all cases, as a general rule, should commence in personal labors. The following texts lay this down clearly. Gal. 6 : 1, requires, that, if a brother 'be overtaken in a fault,' (i. e. caught,) the other members should restore him. And by what follows it is plain that it must be done in a tender, careful, sympathizing manner, which cannot be done without personal endeavor.

"This is also inculcated in the allusions made by Paul to the mutual sympathy and care which God has given to the members of a natural body. 1 Cor. 12 : 25, 26 which cannot be fulfilled, but by the most careful and prompt attempt to remedy the cause of suffering, according to the laws of brotherly kindness. To this endeavor to restore an offending brother, the Apostle James encourages in his Epistle, 5 : 19, 20. Here the work of converting an erring brother must require personal labor. But though every case must be begun in personal intercourse; yet it is not to end there. Should the labors of brethren succeed in restoring the offending brother, he will as a matter of course, seek to redress the evil consequences of his sinful course, which will require him to come before the church to answer publicly to the charges against him, so that the scandal may be removed from the church and cause of Christ. Should the well timed, and well meant endeavors of the brethren fail, the delinquent must be hailed before the church to answer for his offences. This is clearly indicated in Math. 18 : 32. In 1 Tim. 5 : 20. The Apostle directs that, they that sin (openly doubtlessly, as private sin is otherwise disposed of) are to be rebuked before all, that others may fear."

"There are a few cases which may be pleaded as an exception to this rule. They are cases of such enormity as makes 'a speedy execution of discipline necessary to sustain the honor of the cause and the church, by making the offender an example of summary punishment. The instructions to the church at Corinth in regard to the incestuous man are in point But we think the cases are few and very peculiar, which would justify a personal neglect of the offending brother, to restore him to his forfeited standing and lost comforts."

May a church receive testimony from men of the world ?

"It should be kept constantly in mind, that the Church of Christ is a body of light, whose office is to shine to those *who are without.* The Apostle tells us that *whatsoever maketh manifest is light.* But how can the church shine unto them, if she shut herself up from them, and refuse their testimony without reason? Would such a course be walking towards them either *honestly* or in wisdom? The object for which testimony is received at all, is to ascertain the truth; but if a church refuse all testimony from without, she will in many cases refuse valid evidence, and so obscure the truth, and injure the cause of union and fellowship in herself. We will state a case. Suppose a member is accused of drunkenness and blasphemy, under circumstances which, if true, would break fellowship with all the other members, but the witnesses are two of the most respectable *non-professors* in the neighborhood, whose veracity has not been questioned by any—but because they are not members they are refused. Now, does this refusal do away the effect of their testimony from the minds of the church? Not at all. Then the fellowship of every member in the church is lost with this man, but he cannot be excluded, because there is no admissible evidence against him. This would be an intolerable case. The better way is to hear all, and hold fast to that which appears just and good. The church is by no means bound to believe all the testimony which may be brought in, but should act wisely in weighing the evidence, in ascertaining the truth of the case on trial, and coming to a righteous decision."

Have females a right to vote in the church in matters of discipline?

" To the law and to the testimony then let us go. In 1 Cor. 14 : 34, 35, Paul lays down the following order: ' Let your women keep silence in the churches; for it is not permitted unto them to speak; but to be under obedience; as also saith the law.—And if they will learn any thing, let them ask their husbands at home: for it is a shame for women to speak in the church.' And again he saith, 1 Tim. 2 : 11—14: ' Let the woman learn in silence with all subjection. But I suffer not a woman to teach, or usurp authority over the man, but to be in silence. For Adam was the first formed, then Eve. And Adam was not deceived; but the woman, being deceived, was in the transgression.'

" From these verses, it is generally agreed that women are debarred any participation in the public ministry, and this is the uniform practice with one solitary exception) of all the denominations. But are they not *as fairly* debarred participation in any exercise of authority, or government, which would even put them on a par with male members? There is a sense in which women are not permitted to speak in the churches; and yet there is a sense in which they may speak. Now in what may they not speak? In teaching and governing. For these obvious reasons : 1. The law requires it. 2. Adam was first formed, then Eve. This gives the man the rule and government. 3. The woman, being deceived, was in the transgression; indicating her weakness, and affording a reason ever afterwards for her being under obedience with all subjection. But in what may they speak? In *praying* and *prophesying*, see 1 Cor. 11 : 5. Acts 21 : 9. But this *prophesying*, when used by women, must not be *teaching*, but only for *edifying*. FOR IT IS NOT PERMITTED to a *woman* TO TEACH. Now, then, if women are not permitted to teach and exercise authority in the churches, how can they vote in matters of discipline which is government? We are (and have been long) of opinion, that women are in the verses above, debarred the right of voting in the churches in all matters of government, because they cannot use this right without being on a par with men, and in many instances taking the ascendancy, which is at palpable variance with *the obedience and subjection* which is required of them.

"We suspect it is the general practice in the churches of our order, to allow women this use. But whenever a case of this kind has come under our observation, we have noticed an obvious reluctance in adopting it. And within the sphere of our administration they have *modestly* declined it. We have never had any difficulty on this subject with us, and we hope for the sake of the female christian character, women in no churches will ever make a difficulty of it; and if men should attempt it, in view of honoring them, they will have grace enough to rise up with one consent, and pour the waters of pious, modest, and humble contempt upon it and quench it at once."

Is it gospel or duty for one church to receive persons excluded from another church simply on account of their being friendly to benevolent institutions?

"On the above query we have endeavored to reflect with cool deliberation, and the result of our thoughts leads us to answer it in the negative. Exclusion from a regularly constituted church, is in itself right. It is the execution of a sentence on the authority of Christ, by the only authorized body, and ought to be respected by all orderly churches. But as in all human affairs there is a liability to err, even churches may become disorderly, and abuse their power, which was given for edification, by using it for purposes of destruction. The power to exclude may be used improperly in two ways; first it may be executed on proper subjects without a proper cause; and secondly, it may be exercised on those over whom there was no jurisdiction. In either case the act is disorderly. In the case before us, it should seriously be inquired whether exclusion for the causes above stated, is legitimately gospel order? If it shall be judged, (and we think it must be) that exclusion cannot rightly lie against any member, otherwise orderly, for uniting with such societies, or being friendly towards them, then it must be disorderly to exclude persons for such causes. The case, then, upon this hypothesis, presents an act of violence and disorder in its origin; and as one act of disorder may excuse, if not justify another, we are led to the conclusion in this, and such like cases, it would be to choose the least of two evils, to receive such persons, not as an orderly, but as a necessary act of indemnity against oppression."

What is the minority of a church to do when the majority (or a part of them) become notoriously immoral?

"In reply to this question, we are constrained to say that such a state of things in a church, *once regular*, is the sheer neglect of a godly discipline. For if, when the church was in order, the members all sympathizing with each other, the first buddings of immorality in the *enormities* stated, had been plucked off by the gospel rule, such a state of misrule should never have existed. So that the pious minority must be deeply involved in the guilty causes of such a case. Now, therefore, they, repenting of their past negligence, should address themselves patiently to the work of reformation. In this, they should be encouraged, by the promise made to any member in the Laodicean church (when in a similar state of decline) to enduring, persevering efforts. If these efforts sufficiently tried, fail, let the neighboring churches in good order, be called on to labor, to secure the desired end: but if, after all, the majority remain incorrigible, and refuse to be corrected, then let the minority come out and be separate from them, as not being worthy to be acknowledged a church of Christ; but rather as a synagogue of Satan."

Is it right to exclude an offending brother from the Church by a Committee, and for the accusers and witnesses to compose a part of that Committee?

"We give it as our opinion, that many cases of difficulty which come up in churches, may be *as well*, if not *better*, adjusted by a committee of judicious brethren, than by the church assembled; but a committee should never be allowed *final action* in any case of discipline. Committees should always report their actings and doings to the church for her confirmation or rejection. And we should think common prudence would select others on the committee than those concerned in the case to be examined. We are surprised that any body of brethren, worthy to be called a church, should place in a committee the accusers and witnesses in the case to be investigated; and especially when that committee was vested with power to excommunicate the supposed offender."

Ought brethren to go to law with each other? 1 Cor. 6 : 1—8.

"It is evident the apostle's object in these verses, was to admonish his brethren against going to law one with another, and to advise them to adjust all their civil disputes amongst themselves by reference; and we are by no means disposed to encourage brethren to go to law; but rather settle their differences among themselves by reference. But at the same time it ought to be recollected, that the time and change in civil affairs, which seem to have been anticipated by the apostle, have long since taken place. Our laws and courts are founded on Bible principles. They too are enacted and created by us as a republican people. Why, then, should we complain of ill usage in being brought before the bar of our own country, to be tried by the laws of our own enactment? Although, as we said, we would by no means encourage brother to go to law with brother, yet we cannot see any thing in this passage which forbids it, under present circumstances. At least, we think, before the churches could with any propriety, withhold their members from seeking their rights at the tribunals of their country, they ought to establish an adequate system of administering justice in civil and pecuniary affairs within their own bodies."

What is valid baptism?

"On the general principle, we say, as the best conviction of our own mind from the scriptures, that the only qualification in the subject of baptism, required in the Bible, is a credible profession of repentance towards God, and faith towards our Lord Jesus Christ. And as to the administrator, the New Testament lays down directly nothing about it; but it is fairly to be inferred, that he should be a man ordained to minister in holy things; of orderly walk and gospel faith. But the question will be asked, what shall his faith be? We reply; from analogy, it would seem his faith should be in perfect harmony with that of the subject's. He must believe in repentance and faith, as required by scripture, in order to baptism; and baptize the subject, *in faith*, into Jesus Christ according to the faith of the gospel.

"What other degrees of faith may be requisite to a sound theological faith, we pretend not now to say; but to a gospel, valid baptism, we cannot see any thing else necessary, *as to faith*, but an accordance of belief in administrator and subject, and that that be what the gospel requires.

"And in regard to C. W. or any other minister, who may have adopted some articles of faith (say Unitarian,) which dissolves his denominational connexion with the regular Baptists, but yet retains his orderly christian character and his belief in the gospel requirements in order to baptism, and baptizes into the faith of Christ, according to the scripture, we cannot see why his baptisms should not be admitted as valid; because his faith and practice are acknowledged to be good, and he is uncondemned so far as baptism is concerned. And we do not see how unsoundness in articles of faith, which have no regard to the administration of ordinances, can affect the validity of their administration."

Is it consistent, expedient, or proper, to baptize persons when they avow it as their intention to join some other denomination?

"Our opinion upon this subject is that Baptist ministers should forbear. The inconsistency of these persons, of itself, is sufficient to warrant such a course. They would be regularly baptized upon a profession of their faith, and yet retain a connexion with those who, it would seem from their conduct, they think are not baptized! What does it signify to hold right views ourselves, and to practise accordingly, and at the same time connive at error in others by being connected with them in a church capacity? We are decidedly of the opinion, that to baptize, under such circumstances, is not 'consistent, expedient, or proper.'

"It is certainly desirable to commune with those we think are christians; but to do this, we must not compromit truth, or encourage others to hold it in unrighteousness."

The use of the Violin.

(From a Letter to a Friend.)

"You may ask me, if there is any evil in a fiddle or its use? I answer, perhaps no more than there is in an idol, or in meats offered in sacrifice to an idol. Yet it is evil for any man to eat or play with offence. Though YOU may have the knowledge that these things are simple and innocent, yet all good christians have not, and will be grieved with your meat, or playing the fiddle. If, then, you persist, you walk uncharitably towards your weak brethren, and will be condemned by the apostle, Rom. 14 chap., latter part, and 1 Cor. 8 : 9—13. I trust you will digest this matter according to this rule, and act accordingly, as one who must give account.

"But it is not certain that the use of the fiddle is innocent, because things are always estimated according to their accustomed use. The fiddle has, within my knowledge, been mostly used in parties of pleasure, or in dancing assemblies, sumptuous feasts, and balls, &c., and not in the worship of God; so that its use will be associated with these in the mind, and therefore tend to strengthen them. But if the *viol* of scripture is the violin or fiddle of our day, it is never mentioned but in connexion with such things as are an abomination to God!

"There is wo pronounced against those that invented to themselves instruments of music like David—perhaps the fiddle is one! I know of no instrumental worship approved in the New Testament in the church of Christ, and am of opinion it is too doubtful to be patronized. 'He that doubteth is damned if he eat,' &c. I trust you will strive to do good and not evil in all you do—study the apostle's advice, that whether you eat or drink, or whatsoever you do, do all to the glory of God."

Divorce.

Mr. Mercer (contrary to the opinion of many divines,) contended that under the gospel dispensation no act whatever disannuls the marriage contract, so as to allow a remarriage of either of the parties. Matt. 5 : 32, and other parallel passages he considered as simply an exposition of the Jewish law as it was originally given by Moses, but which had become sadly perverted by human traditions. The exception there made in case of adultery, he did not conceive to be incorporated with the gospel law of marriage.

Usury.

This he considered a "vexed question," admitting much to be said on both sides; but as for himself he stated that he had never gained his consent to receive more than lawful interest for money loaned, and he advised all his brethren to pursue the same course. It is to be regretted that on this subject Mr. Mercer did not take a more decided stand. The loaning of money at an exorbitant interest, has been a most serious evil to the country, and it would seem that the christian, who by his profession acknowledges his subjection to "the powers that be," ought not to feel at liberty to violate the law of the state. If the laws regulating this matter are unwise, let them be modified, or repealed; but whilst they remain as they are, let them be honored.

Feet Washing.

"In regard to *washing the saints' feet*," says Mr. Sherwood, "his opinion was that it should be attended whensoever brethren desired to exhibit a token of friendship for one another. This ceremony was attended to once in the meeting-house at Eatonton on Sabbath evening, while he was pastor. It was with great hesitancy that I yielded to his request to wash mine. A few years after, when it was attempted to prove it to be an ordinance, and to be observed in connexion with the Lord's Supper, he ceased the use entirely. He did not regard it as an ordinance, nor to be attended to with the Eucharist. He did not, so far as I could learn, engage in it for some fifteen years prior to his death. He looked upon it as a *social duty* among brethren."

Chastisement of Christian Servants.

It was his opinion that servants in the church ought to be dealt with and excluded before they were chastised by their masters.

Prerequisites to Ordination.

"1. He (a proper candidate for ordination,) must be regenerate and born of God.

"2. He must be of good report, both in and out of the church.

"3. He must be called of God to the work: and,

"4. He must have gifts suitable to the discharge of the duties of the office."

Meaning of Ordination.

"The meaning of ordination is, that the individual ordained is approved as a minister of God, and sent forth, *endued with power from on high*, to preach the gospel and administer its ordinances, wherever he may be called in the providence of God."

The Manner of Ordination.

"The *manner* of ordination will be found in those rites and ceremonies used by the apostles in setting men apart to the gospel ministry—and these appear to be

"1. *Designation.* To ascertain whom God has called and fitted for the work is an important part in 'the manner of ordination.' This lies at the foundation. It is the preservative of a sound and spiritual ministry. * * *

"But it may be asked whose duty is it? It is answered even nature teaches us that the church has the first concern in this important duty. She is the mother. It must be her's to rear her sons in the service of God, according to their several ability. * * * But the work of designation stops not here. Ministers, especially *pas-*

tors, have a very responsible part in this business; they are the watchmen on the walls, have the care of the churches and the ministry both in their hands. Responsible office!

"2. *Examination.* * * * If a man must *desire the office, be apt to teach and blameless*, these things must be inquired into. But by whom shall the examination be conducted? By the church? By no means; (the church is the only proper judge of character;) but by the Presbytery, or session of Elders. * * * And if all (both church and presbytery) are *unanimously* and *comfortably* agreed, (for there must be no schism in this case) that *the thing is of the Lord*, then let the presbytery proceed;

"3. By prayer and fasting (the church uniting in these) with the laying on of the hands of the presbytery, (or of one on the part of the rest) to set him apart to the great work of the ministry.

* * * * *

" From the scriptural account we have of this rite in ordination to church, or ministerial offices, (for it is used in both,) and from the fitness of its meaning to convey the sense of the presbytery in approving and receiving a fellow-brother into the ministry; and from its being the only *outward sign* used in ordinations, recorded in the practice of the apostles, we are decidedly of opinion it should never be wanting in the *manner* of ordination among us."

Ministerial aid in ordination necessary to ministerial fellowship.

In reply to one differing from him in opinion, Mr. Mercer remarks as follows:

" It may be proper to say a little on the necessity of *ministerial aid* in ministerial investiture, in order to ministerial fellowship. This you rightly define to be ' the union and recognition of brethren, who have, in accordance with divine direction, been regularly inducted into the ministerial office.' This is very just. And when evidence of this is ' satisfactorily obtained,' *union, recognition,* and cordial acceptance will be secured. But can mere church competency effect this object? Ministers of different countries can have fellowship, readily and cordially, only as they have confidence in the competency and authority of the body who invested them with the ministerial office. But is the scheme of mere church appointment to that office capable of such confidence? The ministry is to ministers, what the church is to common brethren; and a man might as soon be introduced to the fellowship of the church, without being received by the members of the church, or some other in whom they had full confidence, as any one can be brought into the fellowship of the ministry without being received by the members of the ministry. The capacity of a church to inspire and sustain the necessary confidence to secure ministerial fellowship, will more fully appear by considering what a church may be. It is not fixed, I believe, what number of members may constitute a church. But very few, two or three, a single family, a bare sufficiency to carry on discipline; let us fix at seven. How can this church afford confidence in the *fitness* of her appointments to the end of the world? It cannot reasonably be! But your scheme is less tenable, when it is recollected, that it renders the ministerial office *elective*. Then in that case, not seven, but four against three (and these three may be the strength of the church,) appoints *one of themselves* to the office of gospel minister. Is it possible that such an appointment can give to any one an authoritative claim on all churches and ministers, to their cordial acceptance and brotherly companionship? * * * Besides the door it would throw wide open to *vile* speculation and *base* electioneering in reference to the gospel ministry. 'Men of corrupt minds—of cunning craftiness, who lie in wait to deceive,' and all high-minded, self-complacent, and designing men would find it easy to operate on these small and weak churches, an influence favorable to their base designs. Once establish it as the accredited rule, 'that the church has the *only* and the *sole* authority' to induct into the ministerial office, and that it is elective, and that instant you have opened the floodgates to error, and exposed the church to divisions, feuds, strife and destruction!

The duty of the Churches in relation to the gifts of their members.

(From a Report prepared for the Ga. Association.)

" *First*. Let it be held, in all the churches, as the *sacred* and *unrestrained* right of any male member, of orderly deportment, to exercise himself in the *use* of any gift he may think given him of the Lord, in exhortation or doctrine, for the edification and comfort of his hearers.

" *Secondly*. Let it be regarded as the bounden duty of the churches, to have a godly care over such members, and to judge prudently and faithfully of the usefulness of their exercises. And after a *fair* trial, if any should appear *unprofitable*, to forbear them in love; if any *mischievous*, to stop them; and if any should be found *useful* in any degree, encourage them, and when their profiting is manifest *at home*, commend them to the neighboring churches and ministers.

" *Thirdly*. Let the ministers in the churches, especially the pastors, be careful to notice and encourage such licentiates in the exercise of their gifts, and in connexion with the churches, endeavor to prepare and ripen them for ordination, so that their *profiting* may appear to all, and that they are, in the office of gospel ministers, workmen *not to be ashamed*."

" *Resemblances and Differences between church authority, and that of an Association.*"

"I. RESEMBLANCES.—1. Church authority is competent, *in a judgment of charity*, to receive or refuse any, who apply for membership, according to the requirements of the gospel—so the Association has the right to judge of the soundness of any church, applying for reception, and to receive or refuse her accordingly, in conformity with the bonds of Associational union.

" 2. The church by her authority is bound in duty to watch over and preserve her members in purity of faith and practice according to godliness—so the Association has power to keep a jealous guard over the churches *in union*, to preserve them in *unity and peace*, according to the covenanted rules of agreement.

"3. Church authority is restricted to the members of her own body—so the Association has power over no church, beyond those of her own connexion.

"4. Church authority can do nothing but what is in accordance with the plain dictates of God's word—so an Association is bound to exercise her power by the principles of sacred morality, in violation of no scripture requirement. But—

"II. DIFFERENCES.—1. Church authority is from Christ, as Head and King *alone;* but that of an Association is from the churches *only.*

"2. Church authority extends to every member *individually;* but that of an Association has nothing to do with the government of *individuals, as such,* but regards churches *alone*, according to the articles of union.

"3. Church authority is competent to the examination of refractory members—to deliver them to Satan—to render them as heathen men or publicans; but an Association has no excommunicatory authority—no, not of a church! This belongs to Christ, as Head *exclusively*. See Rev. 2 : 5. 3 : 16. No church, Association, or ecclesiastical body, has any power *to excommunicate, or injure, or unchurch a* church of Christ; or even to dissolve one. This last act can only be done by the mutual consent of the members, by whose will *alone* they were constituted a church.

"4. Church authority extends over ministers. The church has primary and final jurisdiction over them as members. She alone can call them out, and (by the aid of a presbytery) ordain them; and for false doctrines or immoral conduct, stop them from preaching and even excommunicate them; but an Association has no power over a minister to call, ordain, censure, stop, or exclude him, but only through the authority of the church of which he is a member.

"5. Church authority commands her members, and for disobedience disciplines them; but an Association can act only, *as an advisory council to* the churches in cases of difficulty."

Ministerial aid not absolutely necessary at the constitution of a church, or an association.

"We have never seen one syllable on the subject of a presbytery for the constitution of a church or an association. And never till lately knew that it was *sine qua non* to either being received as orderly bodies. We have no objection to ministers attending the constitution of churches and associations, as a matter of expediency; but to make their presence and office *indispensable,* is to set up a regulation nowhere to be found in scripture, and consequently to be prudent above what is written. What constitutes, in our judgment, any number of believers in Christ a church, is their coming together into one body, according to the rules and faith of the gospel. And wheresoever any body of professed christians is found so walking together, they should be acknowledged and received as a true church. And when any number of gospel churches agree to be united into one body, to act more efficiently in the cause of God, they should be received into correspondence unhesitatingly."

CORRECTIONS.

As this volume has been passing through the press, the printer has made a few mistakes, none of them however of much importance. The principal one noticed in the following list (with perhaps one or two others) resulted from the oversight of the *Writer* when correcting his materials for the press.

On page 16, bottom line, for *North Carolina*, read *Wilkes County*.

Page 58, bottom line, for *church*, read *churches*.

Page 101, 4th line from top, for *9th verse*, read *8th verse*.

Page 107, for *S. L. Brooks*, read *I. L. Brookes*.

Page 137, 7th line from top, for *contribute*, read *contributed*.

Page 158, 9th line from bottom, for *identifying himself in*, read *identifying himself with*.

Page 176, 7th line from bottom, for *Medway*, read *Midway*.

Page 241, 2d line from top, for *resolved*, read *revolved*.

Page 257, 13th line from bottom, for *goodly discipline*, read *godly discipline*.

Page 436, the printer by mistake omitted the letter which should designate Appendix C.

Addendum

** Publisher's Note: The following is a circular letter presented by Jesse Mercer to the "Elders and brethren" of the Georgia Baptist Association in 1811 and recorded in <u>A History of the Georgia Baptist Association</u> (Washington, GA: by the association, 1838) pages 196-201.

REASONS WHY PEDOBAPTIST ORDINANCES ARE DISORDERLY AND INVALID

"The Elders and brethren of the Georgia Association, to the brethren they represent: greeting:

Beloved in Christ, - From our earliest connection we have studiously selected for the subjects of our addresses to you, those doctrines and duties which seemed the best suited to confirm and increase your faith in Christ; to edify and comfort your hearts, being knit together in love; and to lead you on to that light and perfection, which would honor and commend the cause in which you have embarked, and reflect the highest praise and glory of God who has called you into his marvelous light. But while you have endeavored to keep yourselves unmixed with, and unspotted from the world *as a chaste virgin to Christ*, you have excited some unpleasantness among the religious denominations around you, because you have not found it consistent to admit *them* and their *administrations* AS ORDERLY AND VALID. We therefore propose as the subject of this letter, *the reasons*, briefly, *which lead us to deem Pedobaptist administrations, though in the proper mode, invalid.* That this subject may be as clear as our epistolary limits will admit, we propose to lay down a few Scriptural propositions, whose legitimate inferences will, we trust, bring into, though a concise, yet sufficiently clear view, the reasons in question.

I. *The* APOSTOLIC CHURCH, *continued through all ages to the end of the world, is the only* TRUE GOSPEL CHURCH.

The truth of this proposition is not only frequently intimated, but strongly affirmed by the prophets. They speak of a glorious state of religious affairs to take place on the coming of the Messiah, which they say, Shall continue or endure, as the sun, or days of heaven, Psalm 89:29, 36, 37 - Shall never be cut off, Isaiah 55:14 and - Shall stand forever, Daniel 2:44. Christ affirms nothing shall prevail against his church, no, not the gates of hell, Matthew 16:18. But John puts this point beyond all contradiction in his prophetic history of the church, in which, though he admits of various outward modification, he maintains an uninterrupted succession from the Apostolic age, till the world shall end.

II. *Of this church,* CHRIST *is the only* HEAD, *and true source of all ecclesiastical authority.*

Although the Scriptures are illumined by this truth yet it may not be impertinent to cite a few passages in point. To me, says Christ, is authority given, John 5:22, 27. And knowing the love of power, and the strong propensity to rule, in the human heart, he frequently and emphatically, declares himself, to his Apostles, to be their only LORD AND MASTER, Matthew 23:8, 10. The Apostles concur in ascribing this honor to him; and transmit it to all after ages of the church, Acts 2:36 - Ephesians 1:22; 5:23 - Colossians 2:10. But the commission of the Apostles, the matter, manner, and majesty of which are enough to make a saint triumph, and angel rejoice, and a devil tremble, caps the whole, Matthew 28:18, 19.

III. *Gospel ministers are servants in the church, are all equal, and have no power to lord it over the heritage of their Lord.*

By the examples of a little child in their midst, and the exercise of dominion over the gentiles by their princes, our Lord teaches humility, and denies to his Apostles the exercise of lordship over his church, Matthew 18:2, 6; 20:25, 26. He calls them brethren, and directs that they should not be called master, but servants, Matthew 22:8, 11. The Acts and Epistles of the Apostles shew their observance of their Lord's commands.

Here we see them as the MESSENGERS AND SERVANTS, of the churches, which proves the power to be in the churches and not in them, Acts 6:5; 15:4, 22 - 2 Corinthians 4:5; 8:23; - Philippians 2:25. Timothy is instructed how to behave himself in the church, which is the *pillar and ground* of truth; but if the power had been constituted in him, the advice should have been given to the church, that she might have known how to behave herself in the presence of her BISHOP, 1 Timothy 3:15. Compare with Matthew 18:17.

IV. *All things are to be done in* FAITH, *according to the gospel pattern.*
Faith is made capital in the Scriptures, and the want of it equals unbelief. The house of Israel is often complained of for the lack of it; the apostles are admonished to have it, upbraided for their unbelief, Deuteronomy 32:22 - Mark 11:22; 16:14. The apostles, and Paul declares without it, it is impossible to please God, and that he that doubts of what he does is damned in doing it because he acts without faith, Romans 4:23 - 1 Corinthians 4:13 - Hebrews 11:6.

From these propositions, thus established, we draw the following inferences, *as clear and certain truths*:

I. That all churches and ministers, who originated since the apostles, and not successively to them, are not in gospel order; and therefore cannot be acknowledged as such.

II. That all, who have been ordained to the work of the ministry without the knowledge and call of the church, by popes, councils, & c., are the creatures of those who constituted them, and not the servants of Christ, or his church, and therefore have no right to administer for them.

III. That those who have set aside the discipline of the gospel, and have given law to, and exercised dominion over the church, are usurpers over the place and office of Christ, are against him; and therefore may not be accepted in their offices.

IV. That they, who administer contrary to their own faith, or the faith of the gospel, cannot administer for God; since without the gospel faith he has nothing to minister; and without their own he accepts no service; therefore the administrations of such are unwarrantable impositions in any way.

Our reasons, therefore for rejecting baptism by immersion when administered by Pedobaptist ministers, are:

I. That they are connected with churches clearly out of the apostolic succession, and therefore clearly out of the apostolic commission.

II. That they have derived their authority, by ordination, from the bishops of Rome, or from individuals, who have taken it on themselves to give it.

III. That they that hold a higher rank in the churches than the apostles did, are not accountable to, and of consequence not triable by the church; but are amenable only to, or among themselves.

IV. That they all, as we think, administer contrary to the pattern of the Gospel, and some, when occasion requires, will act contrary to their own professed faith. Now as we know of none implicated in this case, but are in some or all of the above defects, either of which we deem sufficient to disqualify for meet gospel administration, therefore we hold their administrations invalid.

But if it should be said, that the apostolic succession cannot be ascertained, and then it is proper to act without it; we say, that the loss of the succession can never prove it futile, nor justify anyone out of it. The Pedobaptists, by their own histories, admit they are not of it; *but we do not*, and shall think ourselves entitled to the claim, until the reverse be clearly shewn. *And should any think* authority derived from the MOTHER OF HARLOTS, sufficient to qualify to administer a gospel ordinance, they will be so charitable as not to condemn us for preferring that which is derived from Christ instead. *And should any still more absurdly plead* that ordination, received from an individual, is sufficient; we leave them to shew what is the use of ordination, and why it exists. *If any think an administration will suffice* which has no pattern in the gospel; they will suffer us to act according to the divine order with impunity. *And if it should be said* that faith in the subject is all that is necessary, we beg have to require it where the Scriptures do, and *that is everywhere*. But we must close; we beseech you brethren while you hold fast the form of our profession, be ready to unite with those from whom you differ, as far as the principles of eternal truth will justify. And while you firmly oppose that shadowy union, so often urged, be instant in prayer and exert ourselves to bring about that which is in heart, and after godliness. *Which the Lord hasten in its season.* Amen and Amen.

THE BAPTIST STANDARD BEARER, INC.
A non-profit, tax-exempt corporation
committed to the Publication & Preservation
of The Baptist Heritage.

SAMPLE TITLES FOR PUBLICATIONS AVAILABLE IN OUR VARIOUS SERIES:

THE BAPTIST *COMMENTARY* SERIES
Sample of authors/works in or near republication:
John Gill - *Exposition of the Old & New Testaments (9 & 18 Vol. Sets)*
(Volumes from the 18 vol. set can be purchased individually)

THE BAPTIST *FAITH* SERIES:
Sample of authors/works in or near republication:
Abraham Booth - *The Reign of Grace*
John Fawcett - *Christ Precious to Those That Believe*
John Gill - *A Complete Body of Doctrinal & Practical Divinity (2 Vols.)*

THE BAPTIST *HISTORY* SERIES:
Sample of authors/works in or near republication:
Thomas Armitage - *A History of the Baptists (2 Vols.)*
Isaac Backus - *History of the New England Baptists (2 Vols.)*
William Cathcart - *The Baptist Encyclopaedia (3 Vols.)*
J. M. Cramp - *Baptist History*

THE BAPTIST *DISTINCTIVES* SERIES:
Sample of authors/works in or near republication:
Abraham Booth - *Paedobaptism Examined (3 Vols.)*
Alexander Carson - *Ecclesiastical Polity of the New Testament Churches*
E. C. Dargan - *Ecclesiology: A Study of the Churches*
J. M. Frost - *Pedobaptism: Is It From Heaven?*
R. B. C. Howell - *The Evils of Infant Baptism*

THE *DISSENT & NONCONFORMITY* SERIES:
Sample of authors/works in or near republication:
Champlin Burrage - *The Early English Dissenters (2 Vols.)*
Albert H. Newman - *History of Anti-Pedobaptism*
Walter Wilson - *The History & Antiquities of the Dissenting Churches (4 Vols.)*

For a complete list of current authors/titles, visit our internet site at
www.standardbearer.com or write us at:

The Baptist Standard Bearer, Inc.
No. 1 Iron Oaks Drive • Paris, Arkansas 72855

Telephone: (501) 963-3831   Fax: (501) 963-8083
E-mail: baptist@arkansas.net
Internet: http://www.standardbearer.com

Specialists in Baptist Reprints and Rare Books
Thou hast given a *standard* to them that fear thee; that it may be displayed because of the truth. -- *Psalm 60:4*

www.ingramcontent.com/pod-product-compliance
Lightning Source LLC
Chambersburg PA
CBHW021845300426
44115CB00005B/25